# RUSSIA

# RUSSIA
## WAR, PEACE AND DIPLOMACY

ESSAYS IN HONOUR OF
**JOHN ERICKSON**

EDITED BY
**LJUBICA ERICKSON AND
MARK ERICKSON**

Weidenfeld & Nicolson
LONDON

First published in Great Britain in 2004
by Weidenfeld & Nicolson

The right of Ljubica Erickson and Mark Erickson to be
identified as the editors of this work has been asserted in accordance
with the Copyright, Designs and Patents Act 1988.

A CIP catalogue record for this book
is available from the British Library.

ISBN 0 297 84913 1

Typeset, printed and bound in Great Britain by
Butler and Tanner Ltd, Frome and London

Weidenfeld & Nicolson

The Orion Publishing Group Ltd
Orion House
5 Upper Saint Martin's Lane
London, WC2H 9EA

www.orionbooks.co.uk

# CONTENTS

•

# FOREWORD

Some time in the early 1980s, at a conference with the Soviet Union on arms control, when such meetings had ceased to be grim farces and seemed to be making some progress, I asked a Soviet delegate what proportion of the Soviet budget he believed to be allocated to military affairs. It was of course an ironic question to which I did not expect a credible answer, but the one I received astonished me. 'It's no good asking us,' he replied; 'we don't know anything about it. The only person who does is your Professor Erickson, and we go to him if there is anything we really want to know.'

This may have been an exaggeration, but it was only a slight one. By the time he died John Erickson had built up an expertise on Soviet military history and strategic affairs second to none in the world, an expertise based not on the usual doubtful melange of intelligence 'sources', but on solid research in archives to which he seemed to have unique access. In fact, as he constantly pointed out, much of this material was available, to anyone who knew where to find and had the skill to interpret it. Even more material was forthcoming to someone who, like John, was prepared to deal with the Soviet military on their own terms and treat them as human beings; but there were surprisingly few people in the West who had the capacity, the patience, and not least the courage to do so.

How did John ever attain this eminence? He came from a working-class background, shipbuilders on Tyneside, and saw his future as a naval engineer, but at school he learned Russian, and when he did his national service he was drafted into the Intelligence Corps. Posted to Austria at the end of the war, he rapidly acquired Serbo-Croat among other central European languages, and was attached as an interpreter to the Allied (Soviet and Yugoslav) War Crimes Commission. He was thus already something of an expert on central Europe when he went up to Cambridge in 1949, where he gained a predictable First and remained to do graduate work on central European history. In 1956 he moved to St Antony's College, Oxford, where he laid the foundations of his expertise as a military historian, visiting the Soviet Union and establishing good relations with Soviet military figures who respected his expertise, his fairness, and his sympathy – all characteristics of the path-breaking work, *The Soviet High Command 1918–1941*, that he published in 1962.

The two subsequent volumes of what proved to be a trilogy, *The Road to Stalingrad* (1975) and *The Road to Berlin* (1984), established John as a major historian whose work was indispensable to historians of the Second World War. This might be regarded as sufficient achievement for any ordinary scholar; but John was far from ordinary. His historical work was only part, and perhaps not even the major part, of his lifetime achievement. By the 1960s he was virtually in world demand, especially in the United States, to attend conferences, write articles, give lectures, and act as a consultant on the nature of Soviet military power and the extent of 'the Soviet threat' – invitations that he found difficult to resist. How he managed this, while holding full-time posts, first at St Andrews and then at Manchester Universities, is a mystery. When I first knew him in the mid-sixties he always looked on the verge of collapse; but his appetite for work remained inexhaustible.

New opportunities opened in 1968, when the Ministry of Defence, under Denis Healey's inspired leadership, encouraged and financed a number of universities to establish posts in 'Higher Defence Studies', and the University of Edinburgh had the wisdom to invite John to accept one of them. For the first time he was his own master, and Edinburgh, now coming into its own as a great international city, proved the perfect base for him. The flood of publications did not diminish as he organised courses that attracted first-rate graduate students and senior serving officers whom he expected to work as hard as he did himself. Initially he focused on the broad and then fashionable subject of 'the armed forces and society', forging links not only with other Scottish universities but with American and German institutions as well. But arms control and the Soviet military remained his own major preoccupation. His by now unassailable reputation on both sides of the Iron Curtain enabled him to establish an informal framework for arms-control discussions known as 'The Edinburgh Conversations' attended by senior Soviet and American officials who, if they did not trust one another, certainly trusted him. The Scottish dimension, with its remoteness from London, probably helped a great deal, and John had become a passionate Scot. One of his last achievements was to organise a symposium on 'Scotland and the Russian Navy' that showed the crucial role that Scots had played in the development of that service since its foundation. Had Scotland achieved independence, John would have been a major figure in its defence establishment.

I mentioned earlier how when I first met him John always seemed in the last stages of exhaustion. Later I realised that this was his normal appearance and that it belied an insatiable appetite, and capacity, for work. Deep lines of fatigue and worry were etched into his pale and narrow face, topped as it was by a mass of unruly grey hair in whose depths there usually nestled, as if seeking refuge from an implacable taskmaster, a pair of steel-rimmed spectacles. But it must be said that John had plenty to worry about. Nobody realised better than he the depth of misunderstanding that had developed between the Soviet Union and the West during the Cold War, and how appalling its consequences might be. (His acceptance of the presidency of the UK Association of Civil Defence and Emergency Planning Officers showed that he was prepared not only to foresee but to do something practical about it.) Nobody worked harder than he to avert catastrophe; and nobody deserves more credit for the ultimate dissolution of these misunderstandings that brought the Cold War to an end and enabled the peoples of Russia and their Western neighbours to live in peace. The magnificent archive that he has left to the National Library of Scotland is a fitting memorial.

Sir Michael Howard

# INTRODUCTION

The flag is ablaze, in the midst of the enemy.
And all hasten towards it.
                    Rainer Maria Rilke, 'Cornet'

When we first thought of producing this volume we realised that we faced a daunting prospect. However, it was nothing in comparison with the opposition, discouragement and difficulties that John faced when he decided in the 1950s to research and write about the Soviet military. And since he produced *The Soviet High Command* against all odds we were not going to be deterred. Trying to represent the many facets of John's career and interests would be nigh on impossible. We thus abandoned this approach in favour of asking John's colleagues, students and friends to contribute what *they* considered to be appropriate material for a collection of 'essays in honour'.

The extremely positive and sympathetic responses from the contributors to this volume was hugely encouraging to us. We were greatly heartened by the fact that so many of John's colleagues agreed so readily to participate in this project despite their many other commitments. Our thanks are also due to Weidenfeld & Nicolson, who agreed so promptly to support this project.

John never produced a memoir or an account of his work, other than brief synopses for research funding applications, and we feel the lack of such a source of comprehensive reference quite acutely. In addition to providing us with first-class material for this book, many contributors also offered us some personal glimpses of John, for which we are very grateful and which we value highly. We actually learned some things about John that we didn't know and the reminiscences of his support for his friends, colleagues and students affirmed our decision to produce this volume. Although we knew that John had helped many fellow academics throughout his career, in the course of producing this volume we learned more of the extent and range of this support and the effect that it had upon others.

With such a great variety of essays in terms of themes, periods covered, theories addressed, we hope that this volume will be of interest to many readers engaged in the diverse fields that John drew from and contributed to. Some of the chapters in this book may appear contradictory, but this would be appreciated by John. Disagreement, dissent and debate were a central part of John's style of working: what was paramount was that work was well researched, well argued and well written. The essays contained in this volume all conform to that ideal and as such are a fitting tribute.

Ljubica Erickson                                            Mark Erickson
Edinburgh                                                        Brighton
November 2003

# JOHN ERICKSON AND RUSSO-SCOTTISH CONNECTIONS[1]

John Erickson wrote with a fountain pen in an elegant and persuasive manner. A graphologist might well have said, *Here is a man who knows where he wants to go and how to get there*; and, indeed, this would have been a reasonably accurate interpretation, except that, during the time I got to know him well, he depended greatly for his road map on the other half of the Erickson partnership, Ljubica.

At the end of 1995, John wrote to me suggesting that we might work together to organise a celebration of Scotland and the Russian Fleet, 1696–1996. Since Russo-Scottish connections were a subject close to my heart anyway, the beautifully written letter was more than enough to get me down to Edinburgh for a series of committee meetings under the benign chairmanship of Fred Last at the Royal Society of Edinburgh. As well as being impressed by John's diplomacy in those meetings, I enjoyed tremendously the conversations with him afterwards, often at the Erickson house, sometimes at the Edinburgh Arts Club. Apart from being hospitality itself, he talked in as interesting a manner as I have ever met with, about all kinds of subjects, not least of course the comings and goings of the Cold War, in which he had played such a significant part. Piquant sauce was added to this wonderful fare by the fact that now and again I had no idea what he was on about, especially when the subject was to do with cloak and dagger.

On Russo-Scottish connections, I was on firmer ground, even able to suggest that the official celebrations of the foundation of the Russian navy in 1696 were two years too late. For in 1694 Peter the Great had been involved in naval exercises on the White Sea, with Patrick Gordon of Auchleuchries as rear-admiral. Moreover, there had been some shipbuilding and navigation earlier on the River Don, while those living near the White Sea might have wondered what all the fuss was about since they had been seafarers for centuries. Among other topics discussed by the committee were the Royal Society of Edinburgh's own connections with the theme of the conference. One example was the career of one of its members, Professor John Robison, whose portrait is still to be seen at the Royal Society of Edinburgh. Acting as secretary to Admiral Sir Charles Knowles on a visit to Russia from 1770, Robison was involved in making plans for the improvement of the methods of building, rigging and navigating Russian ships of war, and the reform of the modes of operation of the naval arsenals of the empire. He was also appointed to the mathematical chair attached to the Imperial Sea Cadet Corps of Nobles at Kronstadt, thus following in the footsteps of Henry Farquharson of Marischal College, Aberdeen, who had held a similar position at the beginning of the eighteenth century. But, unlike Farquharson, who remained in Russia until his death, Robison returned to Scotland in 1774 to become Professor of Natural Philosophy at the University of Edinburgh.[2]

John Erickson's own predilection for scientific intricacies and model-making was particularly aroused by a nineteenth-century correspondence between Otto Struve, Director of the Pulkovo Observatory (whose construction had been supervised by Admiral Aleksei Samuilovich Greig, a member of a Russo-Scottish dynasty) and Charles Piazzi Smyth, Astronomer Royal of Scotland, son of a British rear-admiral. For example, on 3 June 1857 Piazzi Smyth wrote to Struve about the latter's 'important discovery of the parallaxes of three more stars' and his own invention of a 'free-revolver stand and artificial horizon'. Prompted by John's enthusiasm, I paid a visit to the Edinburgh Observatory to see more examples of Piazzi Smyth's work, including photographs taken in Moscow, St Petersburg and Novgorod during a visit to Russia in 1859 recorded in his book *Three Cities of Russia* (London, 1862).[3] Among the items in Piazzi Smyth's sketchbook were drawings of Otto Struve, 1850, and of Count V. Krazinskii lecturing in the Elder Street Chapel on Panslavism, 1849. The Count's topic was to be among those addressed by John Erickson more than a hundred years later.

The Conference 'Russian Fleet 300' duly took place in October 1996. It began with a lecture at the National Museum by Dmitry Fedosov, 'Under the Saltire: Scotland and the Russian Fleet', and continued with a symposium entitled 'Scotland and the Russian Fleet, 1696–1996: War, Trade and Industry' at the Royal Society of Edinburgh itself, with illuminating contributions from Tony Cross and Lindsey Hughes among others. The conference was a great success, and followed by a handsome publication.[4]

Much more could be said about the subject of Russo-Scottish connections.[5] These would include the recent activities of the Moscow Caledonian Club and a similar organisation in St Petersburg. Probably, there is a special affinity between the Russians and the Scots, in evidence also in the Edinburgh Conversations which took place throughout the eighties, involving top Soviet and Western officers and defence specialists, notably John Erickson.

In the later 1990s, John gave great support to a number of Russo-Scottish academic meetings that we held in Aberdeen. He participated in most of them, and always gave sound advice. On a number of such occasions, as immigrants from England, we discussed the influence that the Scottish tradition had exerted on us. It is surely not out of place, therefore, to conclude this brief memoir with an apposite quotation from the conclusion to Arthur Herman's recent book *The Scottish Enlightenment: The Scots' Invention of the Modern World* (London, 2003), p. 410:

> As the first modern nation and culture, the Scots have by and large made the world a better place. They taught the world that true liberty requires a sense of personal obligation as well as individual rights. They showed how modern life can be spiritually as well as materially fulfilling. They showed how respect for science and technology can combine with a love for the arts, how private affluence can enhance a sense of civic responsibility; how political and economic democracy can flourish side by side; and how a confidence in the future depends on a reverence for the past. The Scottish mind grasped how, in Hume's words, 'liberty is the perfection of civil society', but 'authority must be acknowledged essential to its very existence'; and how a strong faith in progress also requires a keen appreciation of its limitations.

Much of this paragraph could be adapted to form part of a summation of the life and work of John Erickson, FBA, FRSE, FRSA.

Paul Dukes, FRSE, University of Aberdeen

# I

## *Cock of the East: a Gordon Blade Abroad*

DMITRY FEDOSOV

The pursuits and feats of itinerant Scots all over the world have long been acknowledged and admired, even by their 'auld enemies'. An eighteenth-century Englishman observed that 'they penetrate into every climate: you meet them in all the various departments of travellers, soldiers, merchants, adventurers, domestics. ... If any dangerous and difficult enterprise has been undertaken, any uncommon proofs given of patience or activity, any new countries visited and improved, a Scotchman has borne some share in the performance.'[1] Their military record, in particular, is quite astonishing, and few major land or sea campaigns were enacted in Europe and beyond from the Middle Ages to the present without their contribution.

Trying to do justice to the achievements of a single clan, John Malcolm Bulloch took decades to produce three enormous tomes of his *House of Gordon*. The last of them presents a 'muster roll' of officers of that name in the armies and navies of Britain, Europe and America. Although far from complete, it lists 2116 men on active service from the Crusades to the eve of World War I, some fighting for or in Portugal, Italy, Greece, Palestine and Africa.[2] Inevitably, the vast Russian tsardom and other East European lands, often in need of Western skills, were also an enticing destination.

The figure of Patrick Gordon of Auchleuchries (1635–99), a petty laird's son from Aberdeenshire who rose to become principal advisor to Tsar Peter the Great, is rather familiar to historians.[3] However, his celebrated diary still remains unpublished properly and fully,[4] while many relevant documents are scattered in different archives in Russia, Britain and elsewhere. The present article seeks to highlight some new or little-known facets of Gordon's life and character, especially during his younger years, overshadowed by later exploits.

Even by seventeenth-century standards his career is eventful, including long spells of distinguished service for three great powers, Sweden, Poland-Lithuania and Russia, while the man always deemed himself a subject of Great Britain. Patrick's boyhood memories already speak of 'great troubles'. It was but a few miles from his home that the first

I

blood of British civil wars was shed in May 1639 ('Trot of Turriff'),
which made his father and clansmen take up arms for the king. Too
green to fight and with little to hope for in Scotland as a second son
and a Roman Catholic, Patrick sailed from Aberdeen to Danzig in June
1651, on the brink of Cromwell's triumphant invasion.

It took a while to become a 'son of Mars', and first came two years
at the Jesuit College of Braunsberg (Braniewo) in Eastern Prussia.
Although he never finished the course and dismissed this period of
study in a few terse lines, Patrick seems to have been an able and
diligent scholar. He gradually mastered oral and written Latin, and later
German, Polish (taking lessons even in jail) and Russian. An avid reader
all his life, he knew, among other authors, Livy, Ovid, Walter of
Chatillon, Thomas à Kempis, Ariosto, Caesar Baronius, Cervantes,
Marlowe, Camden and Siegmund von Herberstein.[5] But his spirit could
not 'endure a still and strict way of liveing'[6] and soon yielded to warlike
inclination, so natural for a penniless young Scot. After some travels
Gordon reached Hamburg and in spring of 1655 joined the Duke of
Saxe-Lauenburg's regiment of horse employed by King Charles X of
Sweden, who was about to descend on Poland (the Northern War of
1655–60).

With no experience, privileges or pay, and no German or Swedish to
understand his comrades in arms, the novice had to start from the very
bottom and could only rely on his own mettle. But origin proved a
great advantage, for wherever he went – Baltic ports, Polish prisons,
German taverns, Russian garrisons or London palaces – fellow Scots
were always there.[7] Being obliged to them in many ways, Gordon, for
his part, never failed to lend a hand to a countryman, saving, for instance,
a Corporal Balfour from execution, or securing the advancement of
many others. 'Good Scots hearts and swords' are the main heroes
throughout his journal, and the diarist himself turned out as *bonnie* a
*fechter* as they come. According to the patent sealed by the renowned
commander of the age, Prince Jerzy Lubomirski, Grand Marshal of
Poland, the officer then in charge of his dragoons 'has gained praise
and honour, and was most equal to the name of the Scottish nation,
famed everywhere for military prowess'.[8] Indeed, all his superiors,
whether Swedes, Poles or Russians, were very reluctant to part with
him.

From his maiden campaign in 1655 the young soldier of fortune (as
he styled himself) readily volunteered for reconnaissance missions and
vanguard battles, which cost him several wounds. Gordon's earnest
chronicle testifies to his bravery, composure and resilience in both war
and peace. Such episodes are not exaggerated or embellished – quite
the opposite. Since the diary was 'not intended for publick view', it
made no sense to vaunt or deceive. Reading his accounts of hot and

bloody engagements we often learn of the author's own role at the very
last, almost by chance. We can only guess how he fared in a cavalry
skirmish between the Swedes and Danzigers in January 1657, until an
entry elsewhere reveals that he got a sword slash in the head. The battle
of Chudnov, one of the greatest in the Russo-Polish war, is emotionally
described at length, but only the very last phrase dryly tells us that
Gordon was hit by two musket shots. 'Courage carryeth throw!'[9] was
his motto. Of course, to judge a man solely by his own words can be
misleading. But Gordon's high reputation is well borne out by other
sources and testimonies of those who knew him.[10] The latter, as well
as historians from different countries and ages who dealt with the
subject, are unanimous: here was a true brave, devoid of vanity or
bragging.

The Swedish army, reformed by Gustavus Adolphus and strengthened
by Charles X, was deemed the best in Europe, a model of discipline
and tactical art. Raw recruits were sternly treated, and even for minor
offences Gordon's back quickly felt the impact of a colonel's cane,
lieutenant's small sword and corporal's broadsword. Constant jeers from
his German comrades, 'meere bowres come from the flaile', made his
plight even worse. But Patrick never forgot his noble lineage (Gordons
of Haddo and Ogilvies of Cullen) and managed to assert himself so
that no one could offend him unpunished. A sense of dignity always
remained, which in time made him acquire the best military equipment,
gallant attire and a suite of servants including Polish gentlemen. This
feeling usually led Gordon to join the van for the offensive and to
cover his comrades in retreat; such were his actions during the Polish
pursuit of his small party between Przasnysz and Mława, against the
Russians and Cossacks at Chudnov and Slobodishcha, and against the
Turks and Tartars at Chigirin.

The first officer's rank, that of an ensign under Swedes, took two
and a half years to attain, but talents of a leader became manifest
from early on. Significantly, the Swedish field marshal Robert Douglas
entrusted the recruitment of his 'life company' to none other than
Gordon, who later upheld its interests before King Charles X himself.
Besides, Patrick strove to improve his knowledge of the art of war; he
says that during the siege of Warsaw, in addition to his duties, 'I went
often to the leaguer, especially when I heard of any action or assault to
be, on purpose to inure my self to dangers and better my understanding
in martiall effaires.'[11] Very soon, by the end of the Northern War in
1660, he turned into a seasoned verteran, increasingly valued by the
high command. Having besieged the town of Graudenz, Hetman
Lubomirski asked his advice on the deployment of forces, followed it
and captured the stronghold in just a week. Thus came 'the full trust
of persons of different nations and ranks' and 'respect wherewith

[Gordon's] name was pronounced by warriors of three nations'.[12]

Assiduous in carrying out his orders, Gordon expected the same from his subordinates as soon as he got some. Worthy of note are his instructions to his first company of dragoons, made up of captive Swedes, during a march through Poland: [T]hey should by no meanes offer violence to any person, be content with such entertainment as the countrey people should be able to give them; that they who were in health should take a speciall care of the sick, and both help them forwards and to accommodate them in their quarters ... I promised to take a care for their accommodation in quartering and marching, and see to furnish them with whole and warme cloaths and boots as soone as possible'; which is supplemented with this statement: 'I kept strict discipline, and when complaints were verified by witnesses or otherwise, I punished sever[e]ly and to the satisfaction of the complainers.'[13] Such measures may seem natural and commonplace, but seventeenth-century warfare was rife with abuse, cruelty and extortion, as officers and soldiers treated their own folk little better than the enemy would, while commanders often fleeced their own rank and file. Having long been in a simple trooper's skin, Gordon sincerely cared for his men and did his best to arm, equip and train the units in his charge, from Lubomirski's dragoons to the tsar's Butyrsky regiment. For all that, his strictness and demands were not excessive.

Needless to say, Patrick Gordon was no saint, and not all of his actions merit praise. His code of honour was that of a mercenary gentleman, which had little against horse- and cattle-stealing or pillage of the populace, especially subjects of a hostile crown. 'Sometimes he rather naively confesses to ulterior motives and some leanings for intrigue.'[14] We can also suspect that the diary does not give an exhaustive account of its author's sins. Nevertheless, he admits that 'many things justly deserve a publick judgement and punishment from God Almighty', calls his horse-stealing 'a most hainous crime, punishable by all civill and even martiall law' and makes an excuse that 'one can scarse be a souldier without being an oppressour and committing many crimes and enormityes'.[15] For a long while he could not obtain a penny from the Swedes, and some of the more scrupulous cavaliers in their employ starved to death or went insane. Although Gordon usually seized a good chance to fill his purse, he was neither heartless nor avaricious. The cases mentioned above belong to the early stage of his career. Having become an officer with regular pay, he did not allow such 'shifts' either to himself or his men.

As for changing sides, at that period it was customary, and under certain conditions (expiry of the term set for ransom or exchange of prisoners) perfectly legal. Largely because of his 'youthfull bravery', in just over three years Patrick was captured six times by nearly all sides,

Poles, Brandenburgers, Danzigers and 'Imperialists'! He managed to escape twice, got exchanged once and thrice gained freedom by agreeing to enemy proposals. The various reasons given in the diary, though not always consistent, amount to the conclusion that it made more sense than to face execution or rot in jail. Neither Poles nor Swedes blamed the Scot for his conduct when he returned to their banner, and welcomed him back. In all fairness I have to stress that, on taking a pledge of allegiance to any crown, he served it with loyalty and dedication, often putting his very life at risk. For all his movements to and fro he is not known to have broken an oath.

Other traits can be added to the portrait. Devout in his youth, Gordon grew ever more so; one of his greatest deeds was the foundation in 1684 of the first Roman Catholic church in Muscovy.[16] His 'nature was always averse to intemperancy', and although he could spend a night 'in no Christian exercise',[17] the vices common to his trade and circle were unlike him. An expert duellist and courteous cavalier, he enjoyed a dance with a lady, a glass of good wine, a round at cards or a horse race, but never had a reputation of a rake or a *bretteur*. He also appears to have been good and witty company, well endowed with a sense of humour even in extremity of deadly threat. Closely pursued by a far superior force and about to break through a bog, he encouraged fellow Scots 'to fight at least for a dry place to dy on, that it might not be said wee dyed in a gutter'.[18] But something quite different lay in store.

In 1659, having been captured for the last time, Gordon faced a choice. Jan Sobieski, future king of Poland and liberator of Vienna, promised him a company of dragoons based on rich Sobieski estates. But the prisoner proudly replied that he left home 'to seeke honour, and that by lying upon lands and in quarters nothing of that nature was to be expected'.[19] The Scot was then handed over to Prince Lubomirski, who virtually held sway over the Polish government and armed forces. This magnate too had his initial offer turned down, because Gordon absolutely refused to serve in his former rank of ensign, finally accepting that of a quartermaster of dragoons.

Patrick saw some action against his late employers, the Swedes, but on getting the charge of his first company other matters had to be dealt with. During the march to winter quarters through the whole length of Poland, whose people were ruined and desperate, Gordon's poorly clothed and barely armed men fell victim to disease. The villages assigned for winter were found to be occupied by rival hussars, while local gentry, burgesses and peasants waged a veritable war on Polish units in search of 'transeant free quarters'. The Scots captain[20] had to do his best to survive, and the diary vividly describes his clashes with the *starosta* of Babimost and a nobleman named Krupka Przeclawski as

well as his audacious storming (literally!) of the town of Przemyśl, which
failed to meet his expenses, and subsequent battle with rustics.

The crucial chapter in the Polish part of the saga is the Ukrainian
expedition of 1660, usually called by historians after its focus, the town
of Chudnov. At the time Gordon held a respectable post in charge of
Marshal Lubomirski's own dragoons (a double company of 200 men).
Lubomirski was formally second in command to Great Crown Hetman
Potocki, but owing to the latter's old age and infirmity assumed a
leading role in the events, which brought one of his best officers to the
fore. Gordon's thorough, almost daily account of the campaign generally
agrees with Polish sources and adds a lot to them; we learn, for example,
not only the composition of Lubomirski's corps, but also the strength
of each unit.[21] However, the Scot does not eulogise the winning side,
paying tribute to the swift manoeuvres and tenacious defence of the
Muscovites, who, even on laying down arms, resisted the Tartars with
cudgels and horse bones. He shows the grave difficulties and losses of
the Poles, who panicked on the approach of a pro-Muscovite Cossack
army and had to risk dividing their forces to intercept it. As usual,
victory went to those who made fewer mistakes, and Gordon duly
points out the blunders of Boyar Sheremetev, the Russian commander.
The diarist himself kept his favourite place in the van. Referring to his
part at the battle of Slobodishcha, the Polish historian Romuald
Romański observes: 'Lubomirski vested his trust in that officer, having
twice given him such responsible tasks in one day.'[22] In the decisive
battle near Chudnov on 4 (14) October 1660 Patrick received two
wounds, and during that campaign he lost at least twenty-six of his
company killed and fifty-nine wounded, some fatally, i.e. nearly half the
complement.

Ironically, less than a year after the Polish triumph, Gordon all of a
sudden found himself with the beaten side. Overjoyed by the Stuart
restoration, he with much effort obtained a discharge from Prince
Lubomirski, who held him in high esteem. But it appeared impossible
to find employment at home, while the proposal to raise a regiment of
horse for the German emperor, which he had accepted, was reversed.
Feeling awkward about rejoining the Poles, Patrick finally yielded to the
'great temptations' of the tsar's ambassador Zamiata Leontyev, his
doubts dispelled by Colonel Daniel Crawford, a 'Russian Scot' captured
at Chudnov. In early September 1661 Gordon arrived in Moscow to be
graciously received by Tsar Alexey Mikhailovich, proved his skill in
handling arms and enrolled as major in Crawford's regiment of foot, a
novel branch for the former cavalryman and dragoon. 'Major Patricius'
got the reward usually granted to foreign officers who entered Russian
service,[23] and all seemed to go smoothly.

At this moment, however, the calm, measured tone of the diary explodes into a deadly invective against Muscovy and its people. Denunciations of a similar kind were, of course, widespread among contemporary Western writers, but this passage has so much venom that all German and Russian translators utterly expurgated it from their editions. Here is just the conclusion: Muscovites are 'morose, avaricious, niggard, deceitfull, false, insolent and tirrannous where they have command, and being under command, submissive and even slavish, sloven and base, and yet overweening and valuing themselves above all other nations.'[24] What was it, then, that so infuriated the hardy Scot?

Not only the impossiblity of getting his lawful pay without a bribe for the 'chancellor' (*dyak*), or being paid in copper money instead of silver (by 1663 the rate fell from 4:1 to 15:1), which was bad enough. Gordon suffered the shock of plunging into another world, West to East, Catholicism to Orthodoxy, 'liberal' Poland, where one could freely converse in Latin, to autocratic Russia, which until the conquest of Kiev with its famous college could not boast a high educational institution. The man respectfully treated by the Polish elite now had to sign his petitions to the tsar as *kholop Petrushka* ('Petrie the serf'). The great monarch who Westerned Russia was not yet born, and his father, Tsar Alexey, for all his Western leanings, remained conservative. His tsardom's transition 'from steppe to sea', where Gordon was to play a huge part, had just begun.

Not surprisingly the newcomer, 'almost at wits end with vexation', desired to quit at once, but the authorities made it clear that Polish spies were destined for Siberia. He was so anxious to leave the country that out of 600 ducats brought from Poland the thrifty Scot spent nearly a quarter on 'gifts' to join a Russian mission to Persia, but to no avail. Until his final years Gordon renewed solicitations for dismissal, hoping to return home, but he was only allowed to go once to London (with the tsar's letter to King Charles II in 1666–7) and twice to Scotland (about his private affairs in 1669–70 and 1686).[25]

Although Patrick did not take the field during his first Russian years, they were probably the hardest in his entire life. He fell gravely ill, even to the verge of death, which he explains thus: 'All this tyme I remained hugely discontented with my present condition in this place and considered of all wayes imageinable how to disengage my self of this place and service. But seeing no possibility, I grew very melancolious, which indeed was the occasion of the continuance of my sicknes.'[26] But it did not befit a Scots soldier to succumb to adverse conditions. By and by he learned to accept Muscovite ways if not admire them, and his fluency in Polish certainly helped with the kindred tongue. The diary shows a quick change from new- to old-style calendar, from miles to versts etc., while, contrary to what some historians say, most Russian names are rendered with care and can be easily recognised.

Despite his afflictions Gordon remained his earnest and efficient self, taking 'inexpressible paines and trouble' to drill his regiment. Throughout the seventeenth century the Russian government, well aware of the West's military superiority, adopted Western organisation, hierarchy and tactics, invited hundreds of mercenary officers and craftsmen, imported large quantities of armaments, and sponsored the translation and edition of treatises on warfare. But before Peter the Great's time innovations went slowly and inconsistently, leaving such important branches as artillery, fortification and navy almost unaffected. More traditional arms were also far from ideal: Gordon was not alone in rueing the mass desertions and breaches of discipline, which sometimes led to open mutiny (the 'Copper Riot' and *streltsy* rebellions), or the dubious qualities of hireling officers ('many, if not the most part, were naughty base people, many whereof had never served in any honourable conditon'[27]). The latter reproach could not have been aimed at Gordon himself even by his ill-wishers, for he won honourable ranks in the armies of three different crowns. Before long, regardless of frequent changes of personnel, his regiment proved best in a shooting competition in Tsar Alexey's presence.

Prior to the Russo-Polish truce of 1667, between May and November 1664, Lieutenant Colonel Gordon served as virtual commander of his regiment in the garrison of the strategic border city of Smolensk. In view of his background and mood Russian authorities thought it prudent not to send him to the front, but there is no indication of their mistrust. On the contrary, in February 1665, soon after his marriage to Katherine Bockhoven, the Scot was promoted to colonel. The following year he was dispatched on a delicate mission to London with a letter to King Charles II from the tsar, who wished to maintain neutrality in the struggle between Russia's two principal Western partners, Britain and the United Provinces. Gordon became one of the first foreign subjects to be so honoured, while his status was raised to colonel of cavalry, although his regiment belonged to infantry.[28]

Many years to come were spent in several strongholds and campaigns in southern Russia and Ukraine, at Trubchevsk, Briansk, Novy Oskol, Sevsk and Pereyaslav, often threatened by unruly Cossacks and Tartars. Several volumes of the diary covering this period are lost, and we know much less about it, although Russian sources supply some of the missing links. Perhaps Gordon's finest hour arrived at the second Chigirin expedition of 1678. The bulk of the besieging host of the Turks and allies, about 120,000 men, was the same as at Vienna five years later; so was its command under Grand Vizier Kara Mustafa. The Chigirin garrison had barely a tenth of that number, but managed to hold out under hellish bombardment and fierce assaults for more than a month. A sizeable Russian army stood nearby, doing precious little to help; it turned out that the tsar has issued secret orders to surrender the place, and no one had told the defenders! Gordon acted as chief engineer responsible for all works, and assumed command when the governor fell. On 11 August, blowing up the powder magazine, which destroyed over 4000 of the enemy, he was the last to leave the castle, and miraculously made his way through the Turks, who brandished Christian heads.[29] His conduct earned him the rank of major general and the post of garrison commander in Kiev, heart of Ukraine, where he stayed until 1686.

In the late 1680s and 90s Gordon distinguished himself in the Crimean and Azov campaigns. The conquest of Crimea, which he advocated, took another century to achieve, but the key Turkish fortress of Azov was captured on the second attempt in 1696, largely thanks to Gordon's ingenious 'moveable rampart'. Chigirin was thus avenged. All that time the trusty Scot remained the closest friend and counsellor to Tsar Peter, having a say in his early enterprises and reforms, especially in the military sphere. It was Patrick Gordon's house that Peter went to on his very first visit to the Foreign Quarter on 30 April 1690, after which they rarely parted. Twice, during the troubles of 1689 and 1698,[30] the general took decisive action and secured the throne for the young tsar. When Gordon died on 29 November 1699, Peter closed his eyes and gave him a magnificent state funeral with supreme military honours. The tsar's farewell words were: 'I and my realm have lost a diligent, loyal and brave general. If it were not for Gordon, Moscow would have been in great calamity. I am giving him but a handful of earth, but he has given me a whole expanse of land with Azov.'[31]

Since the late Middle Ages the chief of the Gordons, the Marquis of Huntly, was known as 'Cock of the North' because of his proud dominance of north-eastern Scotland. Patrick Gordon, one of the greatest sons of the clan, accomplished everything he could dream of, becoming the 'patriarch' of Moscow's foreign quarter and the most high-ranking foreigner in the country, full general (the tsar had no field marshal then) and rear admiral for his efforts in the making of the Russian navy. Had he lived a little longer, other honours would have doubtless accrued, as the first and highest Russian order of St Andrew,[32] and the title of count of the Holy Roman Empire, bestowed after his demise on his second son James. Moreover, Patrick established his own sept of Russian Gordons, staunchly loyal to the House of Stuart. As *de facto* Jacobite ambassador to the court of Muscovy Patrick for years prevented Tsars Ivan and Peter from acknowledging William of Orange as king. All this is surely sufficient to style him, with no shade of irony, 'Cock of the East'.

Lastly, I should note that my quest of the life and times of Patrick Gordon was much advanced in 2002 by a Royal Society of

Edinburgh/Caledonian Research Foundation fellowship, for which I was nominated by John Erickson and Paul Dukes. I could not wish for better recommendations, and the best token of gratitude I can offer is the full scholarly edition of Gordon's journal both in Russian and English, which is my ultimate goal.

# 2

## *Jomini versus Clausewitz*

A. N. MERTSALOV

Two names, and their competing ideas, dominated the historiography and theory of war in the nineteenth century, those of Jomini (1779–1869) and Clausewitz (1780–1831). Their influence can be clearly identified throughout the twentieth century and up to the present day. This persistence has been challenged by some authors, who felt that Clausewitz, in particular, was obsolete by the start of the Great War in 1914, although B. H. Liddle Hart's comprehensive work on military strategy makes clear, if critical, mention of his importance. Yet it is notable that Hart does not mention Jomini even though Clausewitz followed in his footsteps,[1] an omission that is characteristic of the relative fortunes of these two military thinkers.

In the USA, Britain and France many recognise the superiority of Jomini, but in Germany and Russia (including the USSR) Clausewitz is regarded as superior, an ironic situation given Jomini's long-term, prominent and intimate involvement with the Russian military. Recently the senior members of the Academy of the General Staff (GS), on the occasion of their 170th anniversary, mistakenly concluded that the two 'most distinguished military theoreticians of the first half of the 19th century, the classics of military science, are studied and referred to at present'.[2] In fact, in Russian and Soviet literature Jomini's name has almost disappeared. How has this situation come about?

Our attention was drawn to Jomini partly under the influence of John Erickson.[3] It was by good fortune that I met that distinguished military thinker and expert in the military history of the USSR at a Moscow conference held on the occasion of the twentieth anniversary of the victory over Nazi Germany. He made a great impression on me. With his total dedication to science, his perception of its role in the modern society, in my opinion he is equal to Ilya Borozdin, a distinguished Russian-Soviet historian, professor of Moscow and Voronezh Universities, my tutor and mentor, and Professor Albert Stachel.[4] My co-author Dr L. A. Mertsalova and I are pleased and honoured that our modest volume on Jomini was received favourably by Ljubica and John Erickson.[5]

John Erickson's analysis of the role of the historian gave him great insight. This allowed him to see, for example, that Soviet historians often do not know of each others' works, and tend to operate in isolation. Similarly, his analysis of the conservative German historian G. A. Jacobsen revealed that he was more interested in publicity than historical science. Thirty years ago I was present on the occasion when Erickson heard Jacobsen gratuitously repeating his own theory about 'preventive war'. Erickson sharply disapproved of the ideas of Jacobsen and his follower V. Rezun (Suvorov), and historians who comply with the methodological precepts of historical analysis would no doubt agree with Erickson. In the Russian Federation, Erickson's books (although still awaiting Russian publication) are held in high esteem, and many historians call *The Road to Berlin* 'fundamental'.[6]

Turning our attention to Jomini, I would like to examine whether he has only historical relevance. I would argue that Jomini's work and ideas are still relevant today, and that his thought is alive and evolving. Jomini's works, and the literature surrounding these written in the nineteenth century, have been added to by a volume of material generated from the application of Jomini's thought during the Second World War. Jomini is frequently associated with Clausewitz, although it is Clausewitz who is more often described as the founder of the science of military theory. The thrust of most commentaries is that it is Clausewitz who is the military 'genius', and Jomini is, if mentioned, assigned a marginal role in the history of military science; however, close analysis of such commentaries is instructive, and allows us to challenge the 'genius' status that has been ascribed to Clausewitz.

Jomini, major in the Swiss army, brigadier general in the Napoleonic army, full general in the Russian army, came to prominence in the first decade of the nineteenth century. In his writings he relied on the works of G. Lloyd, A. Byulov, Archduke Charles and other predecessors and contemporaries, from Sun Tzu to Napoleon. His work produced an interpretation of the military history of the last thousand years, its radical changes during the course of revolutions and wars (most notably, for Jomini, the Napoleonic Wars) and the application of that knowledge to military science. Prior to Jomini, historiography celebrated monarchs and military leaders; his work transformed historiography and made it into a laboratory of theory. Jomini advocated as a main principle of strategy the idea of concentration, namely: decisive superiority on the decisive sector and at the decisive moment. One of his followers explained the mastery of the military leader as: 'having weaker forces than the enemy he has greater strength than the enemy at the point where he is being attacked or he is attacking the enemy'.[7] According to Jomini the task of an army should correspond to its capabilities: it is not the duty of a military commander to fulfil impossible orders by sacrificing his men and incurring massive losses. Some write that Jomini was a 'metaphysician'.[8] We can see a philosophical aspect to Jomini's work – many of Jomini's simple truths are timeless, and does not arithmetic, one of the simpler sciences, have similar truths? – but throughout his writings he encourages a focus on the concrete situation, place and time. Jomini's work is complex and flexible. As an admirer of the direct strike he did not, in principle, reject indirect action, defence or withdrawal. In his doctrine, action and manoeuvrability play a significant part. Jomini also introduced the concept of offensive defence.

He paid special attention to the selection process of the supreme commander, suggesting that, should it be impossible to find a man who meets all the technical requirements necessary for a commander (strong will, high general education, morality, experience of command, theoretical grounding, control of the theatre of war etc.), it was then necessary to appoint a commander of integrity. Sometimes he used the term 'military science' simultaneously with 'military experience', which in our view is debatable usage. His conflation of the two terms implies that we are supposed to combine the two in a figurative sense. Whilst it is true that a military leader needs intuition, we have to question whether this is the same as experience. Equally, we must ask if intuition alone without science is sufficient. Regardless, we can see that Jomini bettered his contemporaries by accurately forecasting events. For example, in a letter to Tsar Nicholas I he foresaw the British landing on the Crimea. It is knowledge that underpins his predictions: knowledge of strategy, of the resources of the countries involved, of the theatre of war and of other factors.

Jomini's writings are not only a celebration of science, but a celebration of humanism. His hope, as a humanist, was that the force confronting the enemy should be reduced to the lowest level possible, that the scale of the troops should be limited, that they should be subject to law, that the strength of armies should be cut, and that the spilling of blood, both of one's own and the enemy's soldiers and civilians, should be guarded against with all means at one's disposal. Recognising the right of people to resist even after the army has been defeated, he condemned the exploitation of enthusiasm that led to casualties. Throughout his career, even though he served monarchs, he remained a republican. Jomini's 'Tsar and God' was science, and this learned man had an exceptional independence of thought. His materialist historiography is free from party, class, caste, nationalist, religious, personal and other biases. Admittedly he made enemies easily, but this is most likely because he was not prepared to abandon his principles rather than being a product of some character flaw or his temperament. To him mental indolence was alien and personal mastery of theory of knowledge and professional honour were a social responsibility.

Many of Jomini's ideas were utilised not just in military spheres. Although Jomini's logistics is the science used by the general staff – and we should note that he called it the science of supreme command – it has a far wider applicability. In our own day, for thousands of educated individuals, logistics is a creative science that directs human, material and financial information sources and constitutes an important part of knowledge, particularly economic knowledge and action.[9]

It is wrong to regard him as a 'Western theoretician who disparaged the Russian military school'.[10] Whilst it is true that Jomini did not seek service in the Russian army, once recruited he was a loyal servant. The account of his entry into the service of the tsar is significant. For some considerable time the agents of Tsar Alexander I tried to recruit him, which resulted in Jomini being threatened by the might of Napoleon. However, during the armistice of 1813, and after the intervention of the malevoent Swiss Marshal L. Berte, Jomini changed sides and joined the allies. In the course of fifty-six years Jomini was adjutant general to three emperors of Russia, his portrait was placed in the Hermitage gallery and his name was entered in the list of the heroes of Russia in the Church of Christ the Saviour. On the orders of the tsar he prepared the plans for the defence of Russia, especially its western borders, analysed the military potential of opponents, and wrote theoretical works, constitutions and manuals. He won supporters in Russia and further abroad; his publications received international acclaim and were studied by specialists and the general public alike.

Jomini did not merely show initiative, he made it an imperative that the officers of the general staff receive instruction and that the advancement of science be implemented in the army. The academy, the most important factor in the creation of the educated officer, was called upon to look at the educational experiences of foreign countries and to surpass these. The founding of the academy caused some controversy and raised tensions between Jomini and the tsar. In the jubilee articles of the academy Jomini is called 'one of the founders', yet it is said that 'the tsar founded' the academy. This discrepancy came about from an order to please the ruling regime, when chiefs of the Russian Academy of the General Staff, together with the restoration of religious prayers in the army, revived the false designation 'Nikolayevskaya', to suggest that Alexander III had backed and promoted the academy. Conflict between the tsar and Jomini that began during the reign of Alexander I regarding the place of science in the education and the details to be included, continued between Jomini and Nicholas I. Tsars were more interested in the drill of the students of the academy, their billeting in the barracks, their supervisors, than in the science and curriculum. But what Jomini advocated, and what was needed, was intelligent, thinking listeners, capable of gaining education and producing research.

The best among them kept in touch with the academy after graduation and they published their works, which would often give a special place to history.

Officially, in 1832 science won. The Constitution of the Academy preserved Jomini's concepts and teachings. But Jomini did not become its director. Instead I. Sukhozanet, an arrogant, autocratic bureaucrat got the post. He had no ability to organise education and even less the scientific teaching.[11] One cannot avoid asking: Did not this appointment determine the policy of the academic training of future cadres for the next 170 years? Did not Sukhozanet become the symbol of military affairs in Russia?

An analytical comparison of the works of Jomini and Clausewitz confirms the superiority of the former. Clausewitz's book *On War* appeared nearly thirty years after Jomini's *Treatise On Grand Military Operations* (1804–10, 5 vols.). Clausewitz not only knew Jomini's work, but also borrowed and paraphrased many of his ideas.[12] Clausewitz arrogantly elevated himself above all his predecessors – 'the throng of theoreticians'[13] – yet he was dissatisfied with the best part of his work and intended to change it completely. After his sudden death his widow decided differently, publishing quickly this hard-to-read book, complete with repetitions, contradictions and obscure passages.

As distinct from Jomini, Clausewitz was taken up with side issues. He had no first-hand knowledge of diplomacy or the strategy of coalitions, nor did he know leaders who had led such endeavours; and, most importantly, he was bound by his predilections. Critics call Clausewitz 'anti Jomini', but it is not just a matter of envy, jealousy and argument with Jomini that we need to note. One cannot understand Clausewitz without Jomini. Clausewitz owed a great deal to his predecessors, but he wished to appear original. He did not recognise the science in military affairs: for him no war could be repeated. As for rules, he regarded them as harmful. In sharp contrast to Jomini he was a monarchist and a militarist. His concept of 'total war' is, quite simply, inhuman. It is said that in the later chapters of *On War* he stopped extolling 'total war'[14], but those ideas permeate the whole book.[15] Svechin called Jomini an 'internationalist' whose ideas were applicable to any army. Clausewitz, on the other hand, was a chauvinist. He reflected the great ambitions of a young but weak state intent on plunder, hence his reliance on the preventive, short war by any means and we must note that that was exactly Hitler's strategy for dealing with large and powerful states. Clausewitz looked down on the French, Russians, Poles and, in his later years, even the Germans, whom he called 'fainthearted animals' who needed a 'whipping' to awaken them. No wonder they called him 'the greatest Barbarian of the 19th Century'.[16]

The unfinished *On War* became like a bible to the military.[17] Prussian and later German militarists needed this transformation in the status of the text, searching as they were for their 'own' thinker, especially after the victory over France in 1871. Clausewitz, who was well suited to the spirit of the German general staff, was developed further by Ludendorff in his *Total War* (1935). A cult of Clausewitz has survived in the new Federal Republic of Germany, where his works are reprinted and authors make obligatory references to his book.[18] Towards the end of the nineteenth century, the pro-German Russian court imposed Clausewitz on Russia. It was an irony of fate that the view in the USSR was that it was Lenin who shaped the attitude towards Clausewitz[19] and that Lenin's dictum that war is a continuation of politics is taken from the work of this anti-humanist anti-revolutionary.[20] Yet although Lenin called Clausewitz 'one of the great military writers', this opinion was formed from a rather superficial reading, an approach that was adopted by the newly in power Soviet dogmatists. From this (or, more often, from the works of Lenin) they prudently take only already mentioned statements and thoughts. But do these snippets truly represent Clausewitz? is it right to apply them to *all* wars? and did he narrow down the meaning of 'war'?

Strong connections were made between Lenin and Clausewitz, with Lenin even being seen as Clausewitz's 'most prominent pupil', and the Lenin–Clausewitz teachings (not just to win, but to destroy the enemy[21]), despite a lack of hard evidence, represented as demonstrating this. Stalin went so far as to try to halt this focus on German militarist ideology, denouncing its proponents in 'The answer to Comrade Razin'.[22] In spite of this, *On War* is still seen by many Russian experts as 'unsurpassed, illustrious, inimitable', the work that has established the foundation for the present theory.[23] However, this is not a view that is universally held by Russian commentators. The Russian *Military-Historical Journal* (*Voenno-istoricheskii Zhurnal*) (nos. 1 and 2, 2003) recently published an article by A. Snesarev.[24] Although in the main it is an apologetic article, Snesarev does offer some objective evaluations of Clausewitz, contradicting the current orthodoxy. For him, Clausewitz the historian is 'too biased and despotic' and he borrowed many of his central ideas.

In the USSR and Russia Clausewitz was reprinted many times, Jomini's *Summary of the Art of War* only once (Moscow 1939); but Jomini's teachings were not totally forgotten. Despite opposition to Jomini's teaching by the revolutionary dogmatism and communist conceit, all of which were sharply denounced by Lenin, officers who joined the RKKA (Workers' and Peasants' Red Army) brought forward his ideas. However, in spite of all the efforts of A. Snesarev, A. Svechin and other progressive theoreticians of the early revolutionary period, during Stalin's autocracy the position of military science was weakened more and more. Svechin, for example, was denounced by 'the learned participants' of one conference, led by M. Tukhachevskii,[25] as 'an agent of imperialism', and this presaged further repression of military thinkers and scientists. From this point onwards, only offensive strategies were considered to be 'revolutionary': defence and, especially, retreat were disparaged. Heroism, self-sacrifice and hatred of the enemy were greatly cultivated and elevated and military science was regarded as 'class orientated and nationalist'. The expulsion from the army of some 40,000 soldiers, and the murder of 30,000 officers,[26] did not just remove real and imagined enemies. It also eradicated revolutionary traditions of the nineteenth and twentieth centuries, established anti-democratic institutions, and introduced barbaric methods of coercion and rules of warfare. Fear and suspicion became the order of the day and the catastrophe of 1941 exacerbated this situation greatly. The threat of Nazism was the overt justification for the brutality. Ineffective 'simple' measures (not a step back, to the last soldier, assaults and counter-strokes without the necessary means, offensive by the weaker against the stronger side, deliberate throwing of human waves against fortifications) all this squeezed out the theory.[27] Stalin's irrational strategy and diplomacy produced a combination of superiority and adventurism.[28] Documents like the directive No. 3 (regarding the counter-stroke of June 1941) are worthy of a madman's pen. Fortunately, during the war some better traditions that had survived managed to surface. The contest was not between 'good generals and bad politicians', but between scientific and non-scientific tendencies. B. Shaposhnikov and A. Vasilevskii exerted useful influence and K. Rokossovskii and N. Kuznetsov were very active in vindicating the principles of the scientific approach to Stalin and his emissaries (G. Zhukov, L. Beriya, L. Mekhlis).[29] Professional dignity was preserved among some young military leaders. Officers commanding the front troops, relying on official declarations of principles, restrained the arbitrariness and wanton consequences of some decisions coming from the Kremlin. In time, this led to a series of operations in 1944–5 adopting military science for their execution. Even the ministers' newspaper, *Krasnaya Zvezda*, sometimes writes about the 'superiority' of Vasilevskii and Rokossovskii over Zhukov.[30] These marshals, following the recommendations of Jomini and other classical military thinkers, both advanced and retreated in battles.[31] But on the whole classical military thinkers were ignored, especially their precepts concerning the necessary characteristics for military leaders. Command and ability, military experience and knowledge of theory went their separate ways. The result was this protracted war, a victory gained through the maiming and killing of tens of thousands, a cost that we will probably never be able to quantify exactly. The attempts of the

Russian General G. Krivosheev to do so mention only the losses of those who were registered by the army. Such figures are of little value. They omit all the other victims and losses: on the battlefields, in the rear from hunger, in the gas chambers. Ultimately, blame for all of these casualties should be shared between political and military leaders. It was, after all, the latter who allowed the interference of political leaders in military affairs.[32]

After the Great Patriotic War the legacy of classical military thinkers was undervalued and underutilised in the USSR and subsequently the Russian Federation. An analysis of the General Staff Academy in these years reveals that any attempt to develop military theory on the basis of military history and the lessons we can take from military history has been rejected. Poor-quality ministers closed military-historical faculties, and the Russian Academy of the General Staff, formerly a centre of military theory, ceased to carry out historical and military studies. Instead, the study of war was delegated to departments of the general staff and the Central Committee of the Communist Party, parts of the Academy of Sciences of the USSR, and the Ministry of Defence's own Institute of Military History, the self-styled Academy of Military Science. The majority of this institution's employees were erstwhile officers, political workers, translators; and most were ignorant of historiography: the founder was a chemist, and his successor was a philosopher. For decades the institution collected data, discovered new themes to investigate, altered its interpretation of events a number of times and ruthlessly exposed dissenters. This has not gone unnoticed: both I. Rodionov and M. Gareev have pointed out that bias and tendentiousness have been rife.[33] In recent years a new cult has been created, that of the 'First Marshal' (i.e. Zhukov) and this has set back the central problem of studying and managing war by ten years. The cult presents Zhukov as being separate from the Stalinist system, despite the weight of evidence that shows him to have been fiercely controlled by Stalin. By any standard, not just Jomini's, we would see that Zhukov was no military leader.[34]

Lessons from the Second World War are studied superficially. In the later editions of their *Vtoraya Mirovaya Voina: Itogi i Uroki* the authors altered their work to talk of the 'new theory of victory', the 'price of victory and the price of war', military danger and military threat and noted that 'the lessons of the war and the victory must be seen as binding and must be remembered'. With their conflation and blurring of 'defence of the motherland' and 'defence of the country', it is unlikely such lessons will be learned.[35] The authors are silent where the most topical issues are concerned. What are these issues? The inability to wage a war and the defects of management are compensated for by the old Soviet rhetoric of 'the highest effectiveness',[36] yet what is at stake is the most stupendous and exceptional exhaustion of the nation, both physical and spiritual:[37] no nation has had to withstand a constant mobilisation for a whole century.

At the end of the eighties and the beginning of the nineties bureaucrats from the Central Committee of the Communist Party of the Soviet Union brought about an unprecedented military-political imbalance. The inevitably disastrous consequences of their actions that will follow are difficult to predict. But Jomini has warned us of their danger. The necessity for the reform of the army, obvious since 1945, is now palpable, although all we hear is: 'We do not have the money.' Such reforms should be on the basis of Jomini's precepts: democracy, law, morality and science. Yet there is one further point that we should add for today's circumstances: the restoration of the dignity of the army, especially their right not to carry out unlawful orders.[38]

# 3

## 'Catastrophes to come...':
## Russian and Soviet Visions of
## Future War, 1866 to the Present

CHRISTOPHER BELLAMY

Shadowy and symbolic these battles might have been, but as
if in some giant mystic projection they showed, albeit dimly,
the shape of catastrophes to come.

John Erickson, *The Road to Stalingrad*[1]

Russian and Soviet writers on war, whether professional soldiers or
men of letters, have produced more than their fair share of 'giant,
mystic projections' of the character of future war – *budushchaya voyna* –
in the last century and a half. It was during the nineteenth century that
a vision of a future technologically and socially different from the past
and present became essential for military planning.[2] In addition to
objective, professional studies of the character of future war, some
writers were further inspired. Take, for example, a poem called 'The
Western Front', by the Russian poet Valeriy Bryusov, who worked as a
war correspondent during World War I. All his service was on the
Eastern Front, but his picture of the far-distant western front, penned
on 30 November 1914, is fascinating:

> From the rock-solid Alps to the Pas-de-Calais,
> Across the terrain snakes a strange kind of highway:
> Absolutely no colour, lifeless and dense,
> A narrow strip slicing its way across France.
> Everything's dead here: no houses, no bushes:
> Here there are two, maybe three, wooden crosses:
> There, the remains of what once was a building,
> And corpses, more corpses – bodies, not moving!
>
> From the rock-solid Alps to the Pas-de-Calais,
> Across the terrain snakes a strange kind of highway:
> To right and to left – for mile upon mile –
> Rough-hewn walls and trenches the landscape defile.
> And from deep down inside them, by night and by day,

The dull peal of gunfire rumbles away.
And in time with the thunder, synchronised tight,
That strange pinkish glow, those white flashes of light.[3]

Bryusov's image of a ribbon of barren wasteland stretching from the immobile Alps to the sea, a strip of hell, recalls many of the descriptions from later in the war. A Frenchman at Verdun similarly described 'a sinister brown belt, a strip of murdered nature. It seemed to belong to another world. Every sign of humanity had been swept away.'[4] But Bryusov was not writing in 1916. The poem, dated 30 November, was published in mid-December 1914. At that time, this vision of a 'strip of murdered nature', booming and flickering like a giant electrified model or a modern computer graphic, perhaps in a documentary on the Discovery Channel, was more a prediction of the future than a description of the present.[5]

Such an expansive vision of the character of future war is not the exclusive preserve of novelists and poets. In the 1890s, Ivan Bloch (as the Warsaw banker is usually known in the West – Bliokh, in Russian) (1836–1901), foretold 'a great war of entrenchments ... the duration of battle, which may be prolonged for several days, and which ... may yield no decisive results'.[6] In 1939, with equal prescience, V. A. Melikov foretold 'the gigantic scale of modern war (*sovremennaya voyna*) in which the most powerful armed coalitions with millions of people and many thousands of armoured vehicles will participate, which may be brought to a victorious conclusion only by the skilful employment of three types of armed forces acting on land, in the air [note order!], and at sea'.[7] Future war will be Combined – multinational – it will be Joint – tri-service. It was above Melikov's pay-grade, although he well knew it, that it would also be Integrated – inter-agency. Armed forces, diplomats, security services, industry, crossword-puzzle competition winners, broadcasting corporations ... Stalin and Lavrenty Beria and a man they had erased the previous year, Major General Aleksandr Svechin,[8] knew that, too, and Winston Churchill certainly did.[9]

In 1970, Colonel A. A. Sidorenko described a vision of the possible nuclear battlefield, with forces fighting 'under conditions involving the presence of vast zones of contamination, destruction, fires and floods'.[10] Cheerful stuff. But then, the Russians are famous for that. Just read Dostoyevskiy.

All these visions appear almost biblical in their apocalyptic scope, but they were also spot-on as predictions of the character of future war. Sidorenko's prognosis, it must be added, has, thankfully, remained untested. Clearly the Russians are not just a nation of 'incorrigible dreamers', as the retired former major general Sir Alfred Knox (1870–1964) famously commented after the 1935 London showing of a film of the first large-scale trials of paratroops in the western Soviet Union.[11]

Some other Western analysts have noted the scope, sweep and long historical perspective of Russian treatments of future war. Raymond Garthoff, introducing his 1959 translation of General G. I. Pokrovskiy's prescient works on science and technology in contemporary war, warned the reader not to be surprised when Pokrovskiy began by detailing the Carthaginians' technological superiority over the Romans.[12] General Kuropatkin, Russian war minister from 1900 to 1904 presented the tsar with a prescient analysis of the Russian Empire's optimal strategy for the twentieth century. He used as his database a study of all the wars fought by Russia during the previous two centuries (1700 to 1900). The expansiveness and coherence of the report was not lost on the British translator. 'The forethought and care with which the possible price of Empire in the twentieth century was worked out by the Russian War Ministry is enlightening, for who has estimated the possible cost in blood and treasure of the expansion or maintenance of the British Empire during the next hundred years?'[13] Who, indeed? A hundred years on, the fates of the Russian and British Empires make an interesting comparison.

## The Concept of 'Future War'

Russian examination of *budushchaya voyna* has a distinguished pedigree. One of the first references to a technologically different Russian future, however, appears not in Russian, but in French. The renowned military thinker, Swiss General Antoine-Henri de Jomini (1779–1869) had dedicated his *Précis de l'Art de la Guerre* to the Russian tsar and played a major role in the creation of the Russian General Staff Academy. In September 1866 he wrote to the reforming Russian War Minister Dmitry Miliyutin (1816–1912) about the changes that railways would bring about in future wars: *'J'ai reçu ... la letter que Votre Excellence a bien voulu m'addresser en réponse à celle que je lui avais ecrité au sujet des changements que les Chemins de fer opéreront sur les future guerres et Surtout dans les guerres défensives.'*[14] Jomini stressed the importance of distinguishing between railways which were advantageous for commerce and international relations and 'strategic railways of principally military value'.

Although the higher Russian aristocracy were fluent in French, professional military debate was conducted in Russian.[15] The first use of the terms *budushchaya voyna* – '(a) future war' – and *sovremennaya voyna* – 'modern' or 'contemporary war(fare)' – in their modern sense encountered by the author occurs in an article published in *Voyenny Sbornik* in September 1877.[16] The article, by one 'N.Z.', whom the author has, unfortunately, been unable to track down, is titled 'The Tasks of

Cavalry in Contemporary Wars'. But just seven lines down 'N.Z.' starts talking about 'future wars'.[17] The terms *budushchaya* and *sovremennaya voyna* are often encountered as virtual synonyms from this time on, until at least the 1980s. The term *budushchaya voyna* appears to refer to a particular war in the future, as an occurrence or a political event, and Bloch was clearly using it as such in the title of his 1898 book. *Sovremennaya voyna* can be translated as modern war*fare*: the art of war in its present state and as likely to be applied in (a) future war. To Russians, *budushchaya voyna* certainly has the flavour of our own 'World War III', and that was how one former officer in the Soviet Main Intelligence Directorate (GRU) translated it when the author sprang it on him.'[18] Furthermore, the term seems to have fallen out of favour in the 1980s, in part because it contains a suggestion of inevitability.[19]

Recent military encyclopedias[20] have not included specific entries entitled *budushchaya voyna* but the *Soviet Military Encyclopedia* of 1933 does: 'Views on the character of future war form a most important part of the Military Doctrine ... of one state or another and exercise a significant influence on its practical preparations for war.'[21] The statement that 'future war' is 'a most important part of Military Doctrine'[22] is revealing. The terms 'Military Doctrine', 'Military Art' and 'Military Science' all have precise and defined meanings. These related concepts are shown in figure 1.

The overall study of war during the Soviet period and since was Military Science, a phrase that embraces pretty much everything within

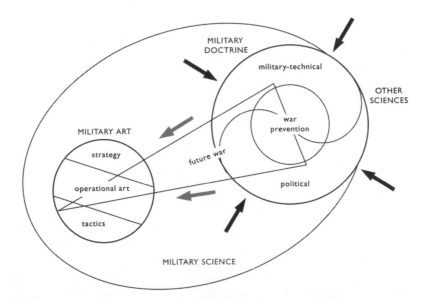

Figure 1. Relationship of Military Science, Doctrine and Art, the political and military-technical aspects of Doctrine, and the character of future war.

our own fields of 'war', 'peace', 'strategic' and 'security studies'.[23] Debate is permitted within Military Science, which also draws conclusions from other sciences. But eventually, as the eminent military historian and analyst of the late Soviet period, Lieutenant General Makhmut Gareyev explained, 'common sense dictates that we need certain common points of view'.[24] Otherwise we would go on arguing for ever. Therefore the swell of opinion that has been burgeoning in the military-scientific community reaches a tidal intensity, and becomes dominant theory and practice in the (military)-scientific community. The wording is intentional, because it reflects perfectly the late Thomas F. Kuhn's theory of Scientific Revolutions.[25] Old assumptions are found wanting, are challenged, and eventually the weight of new evidence supplants the old theory and practice to create a new paradigm. In Kuhn's thesis, a paradigm is a whole body or package of assumptions, procedures and methodologies that are institutionalised practice within the scientific community. Similarly, military-scientific 'revolutions' – or, as they are now called, 'transformations', because no one with a proper job has time to waste arguing whether what is happening in the real world is a revolution or an evolution – occur.[26]

'Military Doctrine', in the Russian definition, is therefore the current paradigm in Military Science – no more, no less.

The relevant 1977 volume of the *Soviet Military Encyclopedia* defined Military Doctrine as 'the state-accepted system of views on the aims and character of a possible war accepted at a given time'.[27] Five years later, Marshal Nikolay Ogarkov reinforced the definition as 'the system of views on the essence, aims and character of a possible future war adopted in a given country for a given (specific) time'.[28] This form of words was reported verbatim in the 1983 and 1986 editions of the *Military-Encyclopedic Dictionary*.[29] The stress on 'for a given (specific) time' is important, because it braces the student for periodic doctrinal change – in other words, for paradigm shift.

However, by this time debate was widespread on whether Doctrine should be redefined as a 'system of basic views on the *prevention* of war'.[30] Given the unwinnability of a major, nuclear war, such a change in definition was timely and not just for reasons of 'political correctness'. The final change to the Soviet definition came in January 1988, when the leader in the authoritative journal *Military Thought*, still then restricted to 'Generals and Admirals of the Soviet armed Forces', redefined Doctrine as 'a system of officially accepted, fundamental views on the *prevention* of war...'[31]

After the dissolution of the Soviet Union, Doctrine was again redefined, though not fundamentally. The latest definition is in the 2002 Russian *Military-Historical Dictionary. Doktrina voyennaya* – Military Doctrine – is 'a system of state-accepted official views, for a given time, on the use of military power for political aims, on the character of military tasks and means of resolving them, on the basic direction of military development'.[32]

Military Doctrine – the state-accepted system of views on the character of future war (until 1988) or then, on the prevention of war and now, on the use of military power for political aims – then drives Military Art. That means preparation for and conduct of military operations. It also drives the development and design of equipment. It is probable that the Soviet emphasis on tanks and armoured vehicles in the post-World War II period was driven not so much by the importance of armoured operations in that war but by the fact the best place to be on a nuclear battlefield was in an armoured vehicle. Thus the revised paradigm (from 1962) that the next war would be a nuclear-rocket war influenced the design of generations of equipment.

Such a system has great strength but also a cardinal weakness. What happens when your vision of a 'future war' does not match the war that actually happens? This brings us to the key hiatus in the vast body of Russian and Soviet literature about 'future war'.

### 'We don't do "small wars".'

The instinctive Russian tendency to translate *budushchaya voyna* as 'World War III', noted above, is revealing. Throughout the last 140 years, Russian and Soviet writing on future war has focused almost exclusively on the next big war. There has been very little writing about what Charles Callwell called, in his 1896 classic, 'small wars' – what later became 'low-intensity operations' (a phrase this author dislikes, but which is widely understood) and now 'asymmetric conflict'.[33] When 'local wars', such as the 1967 and 1973 wars in the Middle East, are studied, it is still principally because of their relevance and lessons for the big one.[34] A military system designed from the 'top down' – in which the conceptual component drives the development of the moral (training, discipline and morale) and the physical (numbers, weapons and equipment) – is ill-suited to respond in the face of unexpected circumstances. For the Russians, this happened both in Afghanistan in the 1980s and in Chechnya in the 1990s.

It is not as if the Russians are short of examples of asymmetric conflict within the area of their own empire or just outside it. The Russians acquired extensive experience of warfare against 'partisan groups', including one of the greatest guerrilla commanders of all time, Shamil, in the Caucasus in the mid-nineteenth century. Callwell himself draws heavily on the Russian experience in central Asia, where some of their most famous and flamboyant commanders operated, including

Mikhail Skobelev (1843–82).[35] As for what they would encounter in
Afghanistan in 1980, they only had to read Kipling. In the 1920s, the
Soviets conducted wide-ranging operations against 'bandits' in Asiatic
Russia, including the Basmachis from 1917 to 1931.[36] And during and
after World War II there were extensive Soviet partisan and anti-
partisan operations throughout eastern Europe, notably in Ukraine and
the Baltic States. Forces of the NKVD, later the MGB, waged anti-
partisan campaigns in Lithuania until 1953 and in Latvia and Estonia
until 1956. The last Estonian 'Forest Brother' to die fighting was shot
by KGB troops in 1974.[37]

There are, however, understandable reasons for the lack of treatment
of future asymmetric operations in the Russian and Soviet military
literature.

The first is the conviction, also shared by the Russians' fellow Euro-
Asiatic imperial army, the British, that if you can handle the big one,
the small ones will take care of themselves. In current jargon, 'You can
trade down but you can't trade up.' The big war, even if it is the
most unlikely, still requires the greatest investment in peacetime and
commitment to the highest levels in technology, so that is the one that
receives most attention.

The second reason, as already indicated, is simply institutional. The
Russian and Soviet armed forces' role has been to defend that mighty
land against foreign attack. Dealing with internal security problems is
not their job – in fact, to fire on Russians is actually illegal, as one
Russian general famously said in Chechnya early in 1995. As noted
above, it was the NKVD-MGB-KGB's job to engage anti-Soviet
partisans in the Baltic States, and dealing with internal security is now
the job of the Interior Ministry, which has entire divisions of armed
troops, as well as *Spetsnaz* forces like those seen in the Moscow Theatre
siege in October 2002. If we seek visions of future 'low-intensity
operations' and internal security problems, we would not find them in
the Russian military press, but in the journals and archives of the
NKVD, KGB and the interior forces (VV) of the Ministry of Internal
Affairs (MVD). Unlike the Soviet armed forces' journals, these did not
become openly available on subscription until late 1989.[38] In 1990 the
author interviewed General Vitaly Shabanov, then Soviet Deputy Minister for Armaments. What about 'low-intensity operations? Did he
understand the term? '*Operatsii nizkoy intensivnosti*', he replied, 'of course
I understand the term. But who would start a "low-intensity" war
against us?'[39] It was a fair point. But within five years Chechen rebels
had done just that, although it did not feel very 'low-intensity' when
you were there.[40]

After the end of the Soviet Union, and more particularly after the
first Chechen war, from 1994, there has been a shift in emphasis

towards Interior Ministry and specialist anti-terrorist (*Spetsnaz*) forces. This is a reflection of changed security priorities, which are obvious enough and are enunciated in the latest Russian *National Security Concept* (2000)[41] and *Military Doctrine* (2000).[42] Counter-insurgency and anti-terrorist operations, by their nature, are comparatively small-scale, secretive and do not readily lend themselves to imaginative and expansive visions of the future in the same way as large-scale armed conflict, to which we now return.

## Armies of Millions – the Road to World War I

From the first use of the terms 'future' and 'contemporary war' in their recognisably modern context in 1877, Russian military writers expended barrels of ink analysing its future nature. Indeed, the most famous, and in many respects most accurate, prediction of the character of World War I in European literature was produced by the Russian Empire. Ivan Bloch's study *Future War...* was published in Russian in 1898 and in French, German and Polish, the following year. The sixth volume, *General Conclusions*, was also published in English in 1899. It was the culmination of nearly a decade of research, funded and led by the prominent Warsaw banker (Poland was then part of the Russian Empire). Bloch certainly did not write the whole six volumes himself.[43]

The mammoth study has been the subject of many misunderstandings. The futurist I. F. Clarke described Bloch as 'an amateur' and said, '[N]obody will ever know what the Russian generals made of the book.'[44] We know exactly what the chief of staff of the Warsaw Military District, General A. K. Puzyrevskiy and the notorious advocate of the bayonet General V. I. Dragomirov thought of it, because they reviewed it not only for Russian military audiences but also in daily newspapers.[45] General A. N. Kuropatkin, the war minister from 1900, headed a committee that recommended all Russian officers should read it, and reviewers noted its popularity among Russian officers, 'in spite of its enormous size'.[46] The Bloch study drew heavily on professional military literature from the 1890s and his conclusions on the character of a future great war mirrored those sources. The spade would become as important to the soldier as his rifle, for example – a phrase taken straight from an article by a French officer.[47] The last imperial Russian *Military Encyclopedia* confirmed that Bloch had also obtained advice from the Russian and foreign General Staffs.[48]

The reviewers respected Bloch's handling of the technical matter and his *kartina boya* – 'picture of the battle' – proved very accurate apart from one key omission. Artillerymen were busily discussing the transition from direct to indirect fire, which the Bloch study does not mention, but which gave World War I its distinctive nature.[49] Bloch's main error, however, was in the very areas where a civilian might be expected to have an advantage: the political and economic consequences of this prolonged, positional, attritional war. The Bloch study predicted that Russia's agricultural population and economy would sustain the privations of war longer than the wimpish, decadent and over-sophisticated Westerners of the UK, France and Germany The study was wrong there, but Bloch's team may have imbibed that error from other 'experts' as well.[50]

A number of talented Russian military staff officers had been working on the development of a unified military doctrine before World War I started, in August 1914. 'Future war', the latest Russian military-encyclopedic dictionary summarises, 'was envisaged as an all-European, coalition war with multi-millioned armies'.[51] The Russian ruling elite seemed to disregard the opinion of a large body of its own and foreign professional soldiers and analysts, including General N. P. Mikhnevich (1849–1927), chief of the imperial Russian general staff from 1911 to 1917, and the renowned military theorist Lieutenant Colonel A. A. Neznamov, and hoped that the impending war would be short (less than a year). However, in 1912 the burgeoning discussions about a unified military doctrine were terminated by Tsar Nicholas II, who apparently regarded such questions as his own exclusive prerogative (much as Stalin regarded 'Strategy' in the 1930s to 50s).[52] There is, indeed, a high degree of continuity between the late imperial period and the Soviet. Mikhnevich and Neznamov carried on working for Russia, and then for Soviet Russia. As an instructor at the General Staff Academy, Neznamov had also taught Boris Shaposhnikov, who later, in 1941, became Chief of the Soviet general staff.

Mikhnevich's *Principles of Strategy* (1913)[53] and Neznamov's *War Plan* (1913)[54] remained key texts into the Soviet period. Furthermore, while the first volume of Neznamov's *Modern Warfare, the Action of the Field Army* appeared in 1912,[55] the second, on *The War Plan, the Fortress and Military Training of the Army*, did not come out until 1921.[56] As if to underline the strong continuity, the title page of the copy of the latter that the author received on inter-library loan from the Lenin State Library bore the stamp of the Library of the Imperial Russian General Staff, complete with double-headed eagle, evidently applied conscientiously at least four years after the 1917 Russian revolutions! Although that seemed noteworthy at the time, the reverse process, which took place from the end of 1991, suggests it was not so strange. After all, the Russian Federation carried on using its USSR rubber stamps and visa forms, and St Petersburg street signs still said 'Leningrad' for years after 1992.

The dominant question from the 1890s was: What would war with multi-million-strong armies be like? The Russsian debate foreshadowed what happened over the ensuing forty years. Some, like Captain E. A. Martynov in 1894, argued that mass armies would be impossibly cumbersome to manoeuvre, 'riveted to railway lines', and that this would bring about a decline in military art.[57] Others, like A. Petrov, responded saying the way ahead lay with smaller but better-quality armies, arguing that this was the trend in industry and that multi-million armies would be neither feasible nor necessary.[58] H. G. Wells put the same argument in Britain in *War and Common Sense* (1913) and *The War that will End War* [some hope!] (1914).[59] Martynov responded robustly saying that big blunt instruments would win over stilettos. States, he said, were not interested 'in the *purity of strategic art* but in military *success*', and that a return to small, professional armies was *'completely impossible'*.[60]

General Mikhnevich, showing the classic qualities that would get him and scores of other generals to become chiefs of general staffs around the world, compromised. Responding to another article by Petrov in 1898, he agreed that battles would be extended in time and space, lasting two to three days, and moving these gigantic armies would be difficult. However, with a good railway network it might be possible to shift a 'significant mass' of forces to a sector of the front and thus achieve a super-Napoleonic concentration of force. A battle employing Napoleonic principles, but on a vastly greater scale. 'New, powerful factors – electricity and steam, which have increased the modern army to colossal dimensions, can increase the power of the commander correspondingly.'[61]

These arguments have crystallised in the light of the past century and have stunning relevance today. Martynov's view of the deadening effect of massive armies colliding like rams, of the constricting dependence on railways and the immobility of vast armies once they left their railheads, of logistics dominating strategy and some equally wooden generalship, was certainly reflected in much of the character of World War I. Petrov's view, that smaller, higher quality armies would evolve, corresponding to the evolution of industry, became popular among military thinkers in the 1920s and 30s. In World War II, as Mikhnevich predicted, 'multi-millioned armies' reacquired mobility, though through the internal combustion engine rather than electricity or steam. They were able to concentrate, in millions, in secret, and then launch swift strokes, as the Red Army demonstrated so spectacularly on the Eastern Front; and by the 1990s and 2000s Petrov's vision had finally come to pass. Relatively small, very high-quality forces dismantled Iraq's army in 1991, and in 2003 its remnants simply evaporated as a single US division drove straight for Baghdad. In the New World Order Russia no longer needs or wants massive conscript forces, and the creation of a compact, high-quality professional military and security force is the military priority of the day. The Russians of around a hundred years ago, it seems, had got their visions of future war about right.

## 'A war of engines and reserves'[62] – the Road to World War II

World War I showed clearly that industrial mobilisation was the key to victory – or at least, survival – in any future great war. Soviet preparations for total war began in earnest in 1925.[63] The Soviet government and general staff rejected the sometimes persuasive arguments for a small, high-quality army and embarked instead on the creation of forces that were, as the talented Soviet military thinker Vladimir Triandafillov (1894–1931) put it, 'of high quality *and* in sufficient numbers'.[64] The Soviet Union had a star-studded (in many senses) cast of thinkers about future war. Triandafillov's untimely death in an air crash in 1931 robbed them of one, and many others, led by the flamboyant and intriguing former Imperial Guard officer Mikhail Tukhachevskiy,[65] were liquidated from 1937, including Tukhachevskiy's *bête noir*, Aleksandr Svechin (1878–1938), the author of the magnum opus *Strategy*, the blueprint for the 1941–5 Great Patriotic War.[66] But in spite of the self-destructive madness of the regime, the vision and planning for future war survived and was vindicated.

The small, elite armies advocated by Western commentators including John F. C. Fuller in the UK and Charles de Gaulle in France, were obviously an ideological red rag to the Soviet bull. Tukhachevskiy railed at Fuller in his introduction to the 1931 Soviet translation of Fuller's 1923 book *The Reformation of War*.[67] His colleague, R. Eydeman, also writing in 1931, put it passionately:

> At the basis of this theory lies 'massophobia' – fear of the growth of revolutionary fighting, a recognition of the fact that a nation-state, having created mass armies, will be torn apart by class contradictions. The theory of little fascistized [*sic*] armies cannot be regarded as a product of the present-day development of military technology, as a *new word* in military art, but as a product of the *dead end* in which the capitalist world has put itself. In a future war the side that comes out on top will be the side that disposes of masses – masses at the front and masses in the rear...[68]

The strength of feeling apparent here probably contributed to Russian resistance to the idea of small, professional armed forces as late as the 1990s. However, Eydeman was clearly wrong about the '*dead end*' that capitalism was facing, so it is probably time for the Russians to ditch his views on small professional armed forces as well.

Looking first at the front in future war, it was obvious that any major war would change its character as it went. As Tukhachevskiy succinctly observed:

> To answer the question what character will *any* future war (*vsya budushchaya voyna*) have is impossible, since as a result of its development any war will change its form, its character, and one may not foresee these in advance. For example, in the period of large manoeuvre battles in 1914 and even in 1915, nobody could say what form attack and defence would finally assume by 1918.[69]

Clearly, it is common sense to pay particular attention to the 'opening period' of any future war because you do not know how it will develop. That might be one justification for the apparent failure of US planners to anticipate what happened in Iraq after they arrived in Baghdad in 2003. However, this author believes that the 'security gap' which opened up between 'war fighting' and 'peace building' could and should have been anticipated and planned for.

On 16 July 1930 Tukhachevskiy delivered a seminal paper to the Communist Academy (Komakad). Although he attacked Svechin, he had actually lifted many of Svechin's ideas. He dismissed the idea of 'little wars' as he and his colleagues had dismissed the idea of 'little armies':

> The scale of a future war will be grandiose ... in a future war the mobilisation of industry will, first of all, take place in a much shorter time than before and, secondly, in this short time industry will produce much more military hardware than in the past war ... The future (*gryadushchaya*) world imperialist war will not only be a mechanised war, during which huge material resources will be used up, but, together with this, it will be a war which will embrace multi-million-strong masses and the majority of the population of the combatant nations. The frontiers between the front and the rear will be erased more and more.'[70]

Svechin had already concluded that future wars were unlikely to be concluded by a single, decisive battlefield victory. Not that one should not aim for decisive victories, but that many of them might be required. That is what he meant by a strategy of 'exhaustion' (*izmor*).[71] Long wars put more stress on the internal workings of the state. War was not, as some had regarded it, 'medicine for a state's internal illness, but a serious examination of the health of its internal politics'.[72] The 'rear' was as important as the 'front':

The Department of Internal Affairs must have its own mobilisation plan, which must take into account the steps necessary to maintain firm order in the national territory during the period when huge masses are torn away from their work in the country and proceed to collection points to flesh out the armies, and the population of the towns doubles to meet the requirements of war industry. The crisis ... will be compounded by enemy propaganda, sharpened by the activities of enemies of the existing system, by the hopes which individual national and class groups will have as the ruling class grows weary under the impositions of war. It is essential to think through the measures necessary to maintain order along lines of com-munications most thoroughly, to take into account all dubious [pol-itically unreliable or disaffected] elements, desertion, enemy intelligence and propaganda, measures for censorship, and so on. And also, if necessary, to substitute special formations made up of reliable elements for military units leaving for the front, or to strengthen the police. ... Aviation, the radio, the need for an unbroken flow of huge masses of troops to the front, supplying them with munitions, home leave from the active army which was previously unknown [it still was, largely, in the Red Army 1941–5]. All these factors now merge the front and the rear.[73]

It was emphatically the blueprint for the Soviet conduct of the Great Patriotic War. The urban populations swelled by the demands of war industry and refugees were exemplified by Leningrad. The special detachments comprising 'reliable elements' were the 'destroyer bat-talions' that, for example, ruthlessly stopped people fleeing Moscow in the near-panic of October 1941. Once again, the Russians had got their vision of future war and catastrophes to come about right.

## Flights of Fancy

So far we have picked a few ripe cherries from the basket of Russian and Soviet Military Science which flavoured the state-accepted system of views on future war – Military Doctrine. However, creative literature – exemplified by the Bryusov poem – also reflects current science and, conversely, sometimes produces visions which scientists subconsciously translate into futures. The 'non-state actor': a billionaire private individual with resources, determination, expertise and cunning that can challenge superpowers, was familiar to fans of James Bond long before anyone had heard of Osama bin-Laden.

As noted above, the term 'future war' has first been identified in its current sense in Russian in 1877. That, and the following year, was also the time when a world war between Russia and the UK looked about as likely as at any time before or since. While the Congress of Berlin was trying to make peace, the Russians deployed twenty-two cruisers worldwide to be in positions to attack British commerce if negotiations broke down.[74] Such a scenario provided the context for two fictional Russian 'future war' books published in 1887 and 1889. The latter, *The Fatal War of 18??*[75] was authored by Vice Admiral A. K. Belomor and it hardly seems improbable that the former, *The Cruiser 'Russkaya Nadezhda' ['Russian Hope']*, by one 'A.K.' was by the same.[76] *The Fatal War* was also translated, ominously, into German.[77]

The *Russian Hope*, or *Russkaya Nadezhda*, as we shall call her, since neither the British nor the Russians translate the names of ships, is dispatched from Kronstadt before the outbreak of war with the UK, which starts in central Asia. The captain has sealed orders to be opened when he reaches 44° N, 31° E. The cruiser itself is described but it is 'far inferior to the one predicted in *Morskoy Sbornik*' (the Russian *Naval Review*). The Russians proceed to sink large amounts of British trade, though with scrupulous regard for International Law. Most intriguing is the capture of the *City of Birmingham*, which is carrying fifty collapsible torpedo boats that the dastardly British plan to carry overland from the Persian Gulf to the Caspian Sea. They then plan to launch them to wreak havoc on the flank of Russian forces in central Asia. One can only admire 'A.K.'s ingenuity, which may have exceeded that of the British themselves. The Russians win the war, as the attacks on the nerve system of the British Empire have a disproportionate effect. Ireland and most of India rise in revolt. This is what we now call 'effects-based warfare'. Australia expresses displeasure at the UK's inability to protect it. The Russian army then attacks from central Asia and reaches the Indus and the Russian navy sets fire to Bombay harbour.[78]

*The Fatal War of 18??* (1889) is a more minute and considered scenario than the *Russkaya Nadezhda*. It provides startling predictions of the real Great War of a quarter of a century later. The Germans invade France and reach the environs of Paris, just as they did in 1914. They then lay their 'heavy hand' on Belgium and the Netherlands. Finally, Germany starts threatening the UK at sea. Belomor then makes the same error as Bloch: Russia, with its 120 million people, is not seriously threatened, behind her 'unassailable frontiers'; the Abyssinians attack the Suez Canal and sever the UK's communications with India. The 'new naval power' – Germany – requires colonies overseas. 'But what colonies could be more useful, more accessible, more desirable, than Britain's?'[79] Belomor also used the important analogy of a *guerre de course* at sea and partisan operations on land. The book is a striking analogy with what really happened – or might have happened – in 1914.[80]

The way creative fiction can capture contemporary styles of warfare is evident from *The Fatal Eggs*, written by the literary heavyweight Mikhail Bulgakov in 1924 and set in the close future of 1928.[81] The Red Army moves through Moscow en route to battle with mutant reptiles:

> Now and then, interrupting the columns of horsemen with their uncovered faces, came strange mounted figures in strange hooded helmets, with hoses flung over their shoulders and cylinders fastened to straps across their backs. Behind them crept huge tank trucks, with longer sleeves and hoses, like fire engines, and heavy pavement-crushing caterpillar tanks, hermetically sealed and their narrow firing slits gleaming. Also interrupting the mounted columns were cars which rolled along solidly encased in grey armour with the same kind of tubes protruding and with white skulls painted on their sides inscribed 'gas' and 'goodchem'.[82]

Bulgakov had clearly assimilated the gist of current predictions of what contemporary warfare would be like. All he had to do, after all, was watch the annual parade in Red Square. Cavalry was still enormously prevalent, but mixed in with armour, as official reports and plans for mobilisation bear witness.[83] And so, too, were preparations for chemical warfare. The story is illuminating in many ways. Lenses for the ray which caused the eggs to mutate and produce the monster snakes were imported from Germany and special glass from Königsberg, reflecting Russian respect for German engineering and dependence on German craftsmanship and technical know-how at this time. It also contains an apocalyptic prophecy. Just as the reptiles have all but surrounded Moscow, they are killed by the sudden onset of the Russian winter. Watch out, Germans, in 1941.

Shortly afterwards another literary heavyweight, Aleksey Tolstoy, produced what became a Russian science-fiction classic, *Engineer Garin's Hyperboloid* (Death-Ray).[84] The precise date of the first version is elusive, but most sources agree it was written in 1926–7. The fictional inventor works in Petrograd, which was renamed Leningrad in 1924, suggesting the story was written shortly after that time. 'In this monstrous and titanic decade', wrote Tolstoy, 'the amazing minds of scientists gleamed here and there like torches.'[85] Tolstoy accurately described the structure and potential power of the atom: 'The principle by which an atom can be forcibly disintegrated ought to be very simple ... we are getting very close to the heart of the atom, to its nucleus. In that nucleus lies the whole secret of power over matter. The future of mankind depends on whether or not we can master the atomic nucleus, a tiny fragment of material energy one hundred billionth of a centimetre in size.'[86]

It seems that by the mid-1920s Tolstoy was pretty clued up about nuclear physics. Using heated carbon as a compact source of radiant energy and two hyperbolic mirrors, one made of a fictitious material called shamonite, Garin was able to construct a device essentially the same as a laser. It could produce a ray powerful enough to cut through a railway bridge in a few seconds.[87] 'Do you realise what possibilities this offers? There is nothing in the whole world that can stand up against the power ray... Buildings, fortresses, dreadnoughts, airships, rocks, the earth's crust ... my ray will pierce, and cut through and destroy everything.'[88]

Garin's ambition as a non-state actor leads him into conflict with the United States, which sends the US navy to attack his private island refuge in a dénouement which would become a cliché of James Bond:

> A dull, expanding sound came from the sea. Like a bubble bursting in the sky... Rolling adjusted the pince-nez on his perspiring nose and looked towards the squadron. There floated three mushrooms of the yellowish-white smoke. To the left of them, ragged clouds welled up, turned blood-red and grew into a fourth mushroom. The fourth peal of thunder rolled towards the island ... he stood there ... and watched the mushrooms grow on the horizon as, one after the other, the eight warships of the American squadron were blown into the air.[89]

So, in about 1926–7, we have an accurate forecast, emanating from the scientific community in Petrograd/Leningrad, of non-state actors, of the principles of nuclear fission and of Directed Energy Weapons. A 'nation of incorrigible dreamers', as Knox said in 1935? The world needs a few dreamers. And this time, again, another Russian seems to have got his distant vision of future war ... about right.

A few years back the author attended a seminar with Russian delegates at the University of Birmingham's retreat in the former Cadbury family mansion at Wast Hills, south of that city. A visiting Russian general, declaiming on the subjects that Russian generals do, dismissed an improbable or fantastic suggestion (the author forgets exactly what) as 'Giperboloid inzhenera Garina...' That was a tough one for the official translator... But now you know.

## Revolutions in Military Affairs: Missile, Nuclear and Digital

In April 1944 the Soviet young people's magazine *Youth Technology* featured an article 'The employment of long-range rockets' by Major General G. Pokrovskiy. It was illustrated with a striking graphic showing

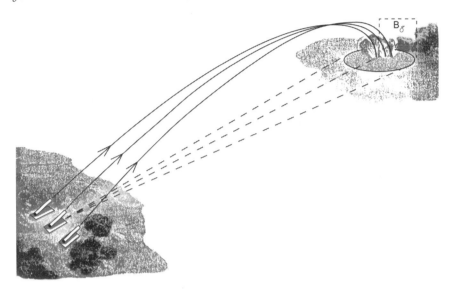

Figure 2. 'The Employment of Long-Range Rockets', *Tekhnika Molodezhi* April 1944.

a battery of such rockets fired from Transporter-Erector-Launchers at a distant, area target (see figure 2).[90] They were not very accurate, he said, and their main area of employment would therefore be *'mass destruction* (massovoye porazheniye) of comparatively large areas'.[91] Not until 8 September that year would the first ballistic missile used in war, a German V2, fall unexpectedly on Chiswick. So before the German secret weapons programme was revealed, the Soviets had anticipated the development of such weapons and also the concept of Weapons of Mass Destruction, the Russian term that has now become common parlance in English.

Soviet commentators immediately realised the effect nuclear weapons would have on international security.[92] Like their Western colleagues, they were initially sceptical about the effect of the small nuclear weapons dropped on Japan, as the Soviet scientist Peter Kapitsa (1894–1984) wrote to Molotov in December 1945 (the letter was not released until 1990):

> The effectiveness of atomic energy against military targets, as used in Japan in the form of bombs, has not been proved. This is not only because its effect is not proportionate to the cost, as technology will soon overcome this problem, but mainly because ... in a nuclear burst, thanks to its small mass, only a part of its huge energy goes into the shock wave, which therefore does not have the expected destructive power ... if the Japanese had not lived in 'paper houses', and had they not been taken by surprise then casualties would have been considerably smaller.[93]

Kapitsa went on to plead that nuclear energy was 'irretrievably and barbarously wasted' by military use and should be used for peaceful purposes. It was the appearance of thermonuclear weapons with yields up to a thousand times greater, plus intercontinental ballistic missiles to deliver them, that brought about the Revolution in Military Affairs, (*Revolyutsiya v voyennom dele*), another term which has come to English from Russian. A different kind of 'future war' meant a change in Doctrine. Svechin's *Strategy*, the study of protracted, total war, which had been the only textbook on the subject since 1926, was replaced in 1962 by Sokolovskiy's *Military Strategy*.[94] That dealt with nuclear rocket war which, by definition, was absolute, rather than total. In nuclear rocket war, it seems most of the population was written off and the 'opening period of the war', which could be won or lost in seconds, acquired even greater significance.

By the 1970s the next Revolution in Military Affairs (RMA) – or paradigm shift – was clearly under way. Many of its components dated back to the 1960s: navigation and communication satellites, tactical computers, the first precision-guided bombs (from 1972). What brought them all together was the microchip, permitting cheap and widespread use of information technology, miniaturisation, and automated command-and-control. The US Assault Breaker concept was mirrored in Soviet Reconnaissance-Fire and Reconnaissance-Strike complexes. As this new RMA gathered pace, the Soviet system was in deep trouble. Realising that nuclear war was unwinnable, and could hardly be a rational tool of politics, the Soviet general staff sought to devise a means of defeating Nato rapidly before the ponderous alliance decision-making machinery could authorise the use of nuclear weapons. This led to the Soviet Operational Manoeuvre Group concept from the late 1970s, based on long Russian and Soviet experience of deep raiding and forward detachments, which jostled with the US concepts of AirLand battle and Follow-On Forces Attack (FOFA) in the early 1980s. To cap it all, there was the US Strategic Defense Initiative (SDI), or 'Star Wars' of 1983, mirrored by Soviet interest in Directed Energy Weapons and 'weapons employing new physical principles' – a challenge which, in spite of its immense inventiveness, the Soviet Union was in no economic position to meet.

During the 1970s and 80s Soviet military literature showed an enormous interest in automated command-and-control and real-time reconnaissance and target acquisition, showing that they were aware of the character of the burgeoning transformation towards the digitised battlefield.[95] But although the Soviets clearly understood the coming digital revolution, they could not keep pace. The 1991 Gulf War provided a real example of the interaction between automated command and control systems, intelligence, target acquisition and surveillance systems, and precision guided munitions. At that point, the Soviet Union broke up. The successor states, especially Russia, could not expect to keep up in these areas – not for a while, anyway.

In 1995 General Makhmut Gareyev, one of Russia's top military writers, produced a book very much in the old Russian future-war tradition *If there is War Tomorrow?*[96] It addressed the changed world order, and the sources of new threats, particularly caused by environmental and demographic factors, and the shift from east–west confrontation to north–south.[97] It analysed the 1991 Gulf War as the archetypal high-technology war, while also addressing the role of armed forces in 'local wars' and peace-support operation. It defines Military Doctrine as 'a system of officially accepted basic views on the prevention of war, military organisation, the preparation of the Armed Forces for the defence of the country, methods of preparing for and conducting armed struggle to deflect large-scale aggression, in local wars and armed conflicts'.[98]

Russian views on global and national security in the new strategic environment are now set out in three principal documents: the National Security Concept, a revised version of which was approved on 10 January 2000, replacing that of 1997; the Foreign Policy Concept, a revised version of which was approved on 28 June 2000, replacing that of 1993; and the Military Doctrine, approved on 21 April 2000, replacing the provisional Military Doctrine of 1993.[99]

The National Security Concept reflects Russian concern about Nato enlargement and the 1999 war on Serbia–Montenegro. It dwells on the 'increased level and scope of military threats' to Russia and the 'grave threats' posed by organised crime and terrorism. It also recognises that the main threat to Russian security is economic, demographic and environmental, which is probably right. The Military Doctrine addresses the nature and causes of modern wars, external and internal threats to Russia, the organisation and funding of the Russian military and the principles governing Russia's use of force. Because of the weakness of Russia's conventional forces, it lowers the threshold for first use of nuclear weapons, of which Russia still has plenty. It calls on the Russian armed forces to be ready to deal with internal unrest and secession – not traditionally their job, as noted above – and to challenge US domination of the international system.

## Conclusion

Throughout the past 140 years, Russian and Soviet writers have produced striking visions of future war, and in many cases they were spot-on. World War I, World War II, the modern return to small, high-quality elite forces, nuclear and Directed Energy weapons, the current transformation using integrated intelligence, surveillance, target acquisition and reconnaissance systems, information and command-and-control ... Most of the time, they got it right. The adoption of Russian military terms by the West and of classic Russian styles of war – the insertion of the 1st British Armoured Division as an OMG in the 1991 Gulf War, the utterly audacious advance of the 3rd Infantry Division (Mechanised) straight for Baghdad in the late 2003 war, for example – shows that where the Russians themselves cannot exploit their insights, other people do.

At the time of writing, in 2003, Russia does not face a large-scale conventional military threat. Its problems are economic, demographic, environmental, and a serious but not massive threat from terrorists. Russia cannot hope to challenge the global dominance of the United States, although, perhaps in combination with a united Europe, it may one day help do so.

Even so, the Russians can still spring imaginative surprises in the military and security sector. It is widely believed that the Russians killed Chechen rebel leader Dzhokhar Dudayev by targeting a missile on the emissions from his mobile phone, which has a certain Russianness about it. So did the use of a new and initially mysterious but very effective knock-out gas by Interior Ministry *Spetsnaz* troops to terminate the October 2002 Moscow Nord-Est Theatre siege. A slight overdose, admittedly. The old Russian combination: brute force *and* genius.

When examining military transformations, as the author prefers to call Revolutions (or Evolutions...) in Military Affairs, there is a useful diagram. It plots the time that a group of systems or type of technology has been around (the 'x' axis) against its remaining potential utility (the 'y' axis). 'Heavy metal' systems, like tanks and artillery, lie to the top right – they have been evolving for a long time, and would seem to have little scope for further evolution. Back down the curve are information systems, which still have a long way to go. And down towards the point of origin, to the bottom left, lie new sciences and technologies: biotechnology, genetics, parapsychology and reflexive control – areas whose potential is still largely untapped. A nation wishing to catch up in the sphere of military and security science and technology should concentrate on these, to by-pass arsenals which, sure enough, will someday become outdated encumbrances. Perhaps it is not surprising that while Russia's still massive armed forces moulder, research and development proceed, sparks of innovation, even genius, like the 'torches' in *Engineer Garin's Hyperboloid*. After all, the Russian *Artillery Journal* might seem a bizarre source for the following thought: 'The questions of the day are only resolved correctly when those deciding them look into the distant future. In fact, the prime movers in developing the whole affair are not those who think as their contemporaries think, but those who think as mankind will think, half a century hence.'[100]

People like John Erickson.

# 4

## Russia, Germany and Anglo-Japanese Intelligence Collaboration, 1898–1906

### JOHN W. M. CHAPMAN

In the summer of 2000 the Kyodo News Agency in London filed a story which indicated that the Admiralty had supplied the Japanese navy with translations of directives of May 1904 sent by the Russian Navy Ministry at St Petersburg to the command of the Black Sea Fleet at Sevastopol. The suggestion was that these directives had somehow been intercepted by the British and that British intelligence assistance had contributed to a Japanese victory in the Russo-Japanese War.[1] When consulted, the late John Erickson found the suggestion difficult to accept because of the fact that by this time a secure courier arrangement had already been put in place between St Petersburg and the command centres of the three principal Russian fleets and also that, while urgent use of the telegraph connection between St Petersburg and Port Arthur would have been justified, this was hardly the case so far as the line from St Petersburg to Odessa and Sevastopol was concerned. The fact that the text of two directives of 4 and 6 May 1904 took the form of translations from Russian into English suggested a British source of origin and further investigation of the information in the Japanese diplomatic and military archives seemed merited.[2]

As it turned out, English-language summaries of the directives were found in both British and Japanese archives, but these were the only examples discovered, which would tend to suggest that a one-off interception was achieved and pointed to the absence of evidence supporting any sustained interception of telegraphs or submarine cables.[3] These English-language summaries were of diplomatic telegrams sent to Tokyo on 6 June 1904 and copied – without prior authorisation from the Japanese Foreign Ministry – to the British ambassador in Vienna by Japanese Minister Makino there. A photographic copy of the original Russian directives was also located and this confirmed the source as human and not electronic intelligence.[4] The Foreign Office relayed the parallel telegram from Vienna to the Admiralty's Naval Intelligence Department (NID), where the material was likely to have been discussed by the Japanese naval attaché in London, Captain Kaburagi, with

Captain Stuart Nicholson, the Assistant Director (ADNI).[5] There is no indication, however, that copies of the original directives were shared with the Admiralty and internal evidence in the Japanese archives confirms that the photographs were supplied by a Polish agent named Miiecyzslaw Woroniecki, who sold them to the Japanese legation in Vienna, having first failed to interest the Japanese naval attaché in Berlin, Captain Takigawa, in them.[6] This investigation consequently verified John Erickson's contentions in full on these factual points.

The writer of a brief history of British signals intelligence claimed in 1998 that there was no evidence, in the archives of GCHQ or in the public records, of pre-1914 British interception and decryption of foreign signals but conceded 'possible minor exceptions'.[7] One of the exceptions he cites was concerned with the Admiralty's interest in wireless telegraphy and the control of ships at sea and goes on to say: 'There is a story which I have not yet traced, of British interception of Russian naval traffic which was given to the Japanese round the time of the Russo-Japanese naval conflict of 1905.' New evidence, mainly in Foreign Office and MI5 files, has since been lodged at Kew, however, which underpins materials in Admiralty, War Office and private papers and confirms the perception that both Britain and Japan engaged in a very extensive collection of military and naval intelligence about Russia for some years before January 1902, as well as in the subsequent course of the Anglo-Japanese Alliance. From at least 1894 there was a widespread perception in Britain about Japan that 'the organization and efficiency of her Secret Service are perfect'.[8]

## The International Cable System

Russia enjoyed the benefit of considerably greater communications security in that the telegraph and cable connections with the Far East were controlled almost wholly by the Great Northern Telegraph Co. based in Denmark, which linked Libau on the Baltic with Vladivostock and Nagasaki from 1872 and connected Nagasaki with Shanghai and Hong Kong via Amoy in 1873. Great Northern secured a monopoly of Japan's international communications with a thirty-year agreement beginning in 1882, but it became a significant obstruction to Japanese efforts to extend its links with Korea because the Great Northern was effectively highly dependent on the goodwill of the Russian authorities. Japanese diplomats remained highly dependent on Great Northern for the most direct communications with Europe until the late 1890s following the victory in the Sino-Japanese War, when a Japanese-owned and -controlled line was erected via Formosa to Foochow, where it linked up with the British-owned Eastern Extension line, which was extended northwards from Hong Kong via Shanghai and Chefoo to Wei-hai-wei after the latter was leased to Britain by China in 1898. Japan subsequently had a choice of lines to Europe that was spelled out in Japanese diplomatic telegrams: 'VN' indicated via Great Northern and 'VE' indicated via Eastern. This meant that the Japanese authorities could largely evade Russian monitoring of the bulk of their communications with Europe, but in peacetime could relay information via Russia which could be intended to mislead or distract Russian censors.

In the event of war, however, the Japanese government became wholly dependent on British goodwill, and efforts were made in the negotiation of the military and naval agreements attached to the Anglo-Japanese Alliance to obtain promises from Britain that it would use its good offices to ensure that Eastern would accord to Japan the same rights as enjoyed by British official telegrams and to make lengths of submarine cable available to Japan in the event of war. The first of these accords could be met to a very high degree, but in the second case a problem arose in that Eastern and Great Northern operated cartel agreements in the Far East which made it necessary for Eastern to reveal to Great Northern any sales of submarine cable, especially to Japan, because both had been actively co-operating together to freeze Japan out of cable business in the China market for many years previously. Since any such cable in the Far East would normally be laid by a cable ship belonging to Great Northern, the Japanese government was not prepared to do any deals with Eastern, even though the Admiralty, which enjoyed good working relations with Eastern in other areas of the world, endeavoured to obtain the co-operation of Eastern Extension. It was later revealed, following the end of the Russo-Japanese War, that some leakages had occurred on Eastern lines at Hong Kong, and this may well have been linked to the fact that both companies pooled personnel and facilities.

In southern Europe and Asia, too, Eastern had emerged as the dominant overseas cable company and the purchase by Eastern of the Black Sea Telegraph Co. in 1873 and their acquisition of a thirty-year lease from the Ottoman government provided Eastern with control over the line from Constantinople to Odessa. In 1900, officers of the British Mediterranean Fleet made contact with Eastern's manager at its Syra relay station in the Aegean, W. H. Cottrell, to co-operate with the Royal Navy and Sir John Fisher at Malta reinforced this link with personal conversations with Sir John Wolfe-Barry, Eastern's chairman, in 1902.[9] Cottrell had indicated that no fewer than 2500 messages were being handled by the Syra station every day and it was agreed with him that he should notify Malta direct by cable should he come across 'suspicious' signals being sent by the representatives of powers hostile to Britain in order to cover the possibility that British bases in the

Mediterranean might be subject to a surprise attack while the bulk of British forces were tied down in South Africa. Fisher subsequently praised Cottrell's ability to identify and make sense of French activities in the eastern Mediterranean, but clearly the line to Odessa also carried Russian traffic at the same time as Russian traffic from southern Africa was being closely monitored by Indian army censors at Aden and relayed to Bombay and Simla for scrutiny by Indian police and general staff officers. French traffic was of direct interest to the War Office, which received large amounts of Boer traffic with Europe, which was being decrypted by a special unit headed by Major Anderson, and information about the Cottrell–Fisher exchanges was passed on to the Foreign and War Offices in the course of 1901 by Selborne in response to a request by Fisher to have Cottrell rewarded from the Secret Service budget in view of his considerable importance as a source of covert information.

### British Assessment of the Russian Threat

The Director of Military Intelligence (DMI), Sir John Ardagh, was particularly experienced in Balkan issues and had himself visited the Crimea in 1894, when he had come to the conclusion that the Russians could very well seize the Bosphorus by *coup de main* before any of the major powers could do anything to stop them. Ardagh was the military expert assigned to the First Hague Conference in 1899, while Sir John Fisher represented the Admiralty. Both viewed Russia with deep suspicion and accepted the view that the Russians were liable to act like unpredictable adventurers. The War Office view was, however, that it would be unwise to attempt a landing at the Straits and Goschen, the First Lord of the Admiralty, went along with the advisability of a naval ambush of Russian forces in the Aegean. Fisher conducted his annual manoeuvres on the premise that the sultan could be expected to accept a Russian bribe to permit passage of the Straits and was unprepared to act against Russia with the sort of resistance organised by Japan in the Far East. Ardagh sympathised with Fisher's position, but did not go so far as Fisher in expecting surprise Russian expeditions against Egypt, a French surprise attack on Malta or close Franco-Russian operational co-operation in the Mediterranean, perceptions viewed by Salisbury as 'hallucinations' and by Lansdowne as pursuit of 'mares' tails'.[10]

Fisher clung for some time to the preferability of a return to a Disraelian policy where Turkey might permit the Royal Navy to confront the Russians in the Black Sea and cited General Kuropatkin, the Russian war minister, in claiming that Russia was most vulnerable in the Levant. However, in addition to the long-held fears of a Russian threat from

Central Asia to India, concern about Russian expansionism in China and Korea had been mounting since 1895, when the DNI, Admiral Beaumont, had confessed that he was unable to judge why the Russians had heavily reinforced their Pacific Fleet and no heed was paid to warnings of the need to increase Britain's military capabilities in the Far East until it was too late to counteract the surprise adhesion of Germany to the Franco-Russian alliance in the form of the Triple Intervention against Japan.[11]

British policymakers were taken by surprise in 1895 and by the consequences of the Triple Intervention, including the German seizure of Kiaochow Bay and the Russian acquisition of Port Arthur from the Chinese in 1898. Britain was subsequently also taken by surprise by the Boers in October 1899 and Fisher was determined that steps should be taken by the Mediterranean Fleet to prevent French and Russian attacks while British forces were tied down in South Africa. Lord Selborne (First Lord of the Admiralty) was convinced by Fisher's arguments during a visit in April 1901 to Malta, where Fisher had also convinced the governor of the need to intercept the mail of the Russian consul and was finding it hard to convince the Foreign Office of inadequate British communications security and of the inadequacy of the political information forthcoming from British diplomatic representatives. Fisher built up his own sources of intelligence and sought to integrate the methods of communication by wireless with those of cable and consular reporting 'from Brest to Perim' and to make active preparations for involvement in war.[12]

He had already praised Japanese preparations for the threat of Russian attack through the use of torpedo weapons. While Controller at the Admiralty (Third Sea Lord) in 1894–5 during the Sino-Japanese War, Fisher had taken careful note of the tactics of the Japanese Combined Fleet in the sea battle off Wei-hai-wei, after which the Japanese commander had permitted the British China Fleet to send down divers to examine the sunken Chinese warships. The Admiralty was advised to take note of holes of some twenty feet punched by Japanese torpedo boats in the hulls of the Chinese vessels and urged to give the commanding officers of British torpedo boats far more practice in firing torpedoes at targets than in the past. Fisher pressed hard for the Mediterranean Fleet to be reinforced with torpedo-boat destroyers on the ground that the lessons derived from manoeuvres were that enemy battleships could be ambushed by torpedo boats at their anchorages and sunk as a result of the greatly increased accuracy and offensive capabilities of torpedo weapons. In defensive terms, too, British battle fleets could no longer afford not to be accompanied by a destroyer screen to fend off such attacks successfully.[13]

The Admiralty was aware of the first efforts by the Japanese government to equip its fleet with battleships because orders for the construction of six battleships had been placed with British yards. Japanese naval engineering, construction and seagoing officers had been admitted to training establishments such as the Greenwich Naval College for decades and the Japanese navy's own establishments and warships had been very closely modelled on British practice, with the assistance of able officers, such as Admirals Douglas and Wilson. Although at first the British China Fleet had been sceptical and suspicious about the Japanese military intentions toward China, sympathy towards Japan was expressed openly by Admiral Fremantle in the summer of 1895, when it became clear what action the Russian Pacific Fleet under Admiral Tyrtov planned to undertake against a Japanese fleet which did not then possess a single warship in excess of 5000 tons. The Admiralty belatedly instructed Admiral Buller to compile intelligence reports about Russian defences at Vladivostock and Petropavlovsk in the autumn of 1895 and passed these on to the War Office, which had assembled a detailed database on the Russian army and employed a considerable number of consuls and agents on the collection of data about Russian military preparations and movements.[14]

A network of military agents in southern Russia was centred on the British consulate at Batum in the Caucasus and supported by individuals recruited by the Indian army, but reinforced at times of perceived crisis by military officers sent as travelling observers to specific locations of interest. In 1900 General Ardagh's deputy was sent to Berlin to organise a parallel network of agents who would report to London principally all Russian military movements on the eastern frontier. The War Office had been seconding a military attaché to the British embassy at St Petersburg for some time as a major supplier of 'legal' data, and support was forthcoming from both British and Indian armies for the acquisition of Russian language skills as a matter of course.[15] In 1902 proposals were submitted by the Indian army's intelligence unit at Tientsin for closer co-operation among the various British agencies in China about Russia and this was extended to co-operation between the Japanese army's intelligence personnel in the area following secret proposals by General Fukushima to General Nicholson (DMI) and to the viceroy and the C.-in-C. in India, Lord Kitchener. The Indian army, which enjoyed fewer restrictions on the collection of intelligence in peacetime, consequently served as the key link between the British and Japanese secret services.[16]

The British Consul-General at Odessa was in regular contact with the vice-consul at Sevastopol: both were individuals with naval training who had instructions to report on developments in the Black Sea Fleet. However, as a result of the evolution of the NID, permanent naval attachés were not assigned to such capitals as St Petersburg or Tokyo before 1902. The naval attaché at St Petersburg in 1901–2, Captain Charles Ottley, had initially been appointed to Washington in 1900, but had been moved on to Tokyo, where he found that there was a serious lack of recording of naval developments in Japan that had resulted in part from the secretiveness of the Japanese authorities and in part from the difficulties of the language. The minister, Sir Ernest Satow, had given strong support for Ottley to be permitted to remain in Tokyo for at least a year and his numerous, detailed reports provided a far more up-to-date picture of developments with the arrival of numerous larger warships mostly constructed in Britain and other foreign yards. But in the autumn of 1901 Ottley was transferred to St Petersburg, much to the annoyance of Sir Claude MacDonald, who found that he could only respond to technical queries about the Japanese navy posed by Admiral Sir Cyprian Bridge on his annual visit to Japanese ports at the end of 1901 with the China Squadron with the assistance of the US naval attaché, who happened to be a personal friend.[17]

On arriving in Russia, Ottley (as well as his colleague in Paris) had been asked directly by Selborne for the most accurate and up-to-date information on Russian and French naval construction early in September 1901.[18] These enquiries appear to have been undertaken without reference to Admiral Custance (DNI), but followed on from Selborne's presentation of his secret memorandum to the Cabinet on the naval balance of power in the Far East in which the alliance with Japan was proposed and spelled out the projections for future construction.[19] Ottley's papers on Russia, produced in typewritten form and accompanied by photographs, pointed out the length of time taken to produce battleships in Russia and observed that 'the Black Sea Fleet did not impress me favourably'. At Yalta, he had a meeting with the Grand Duke Alexander Michaelovitch who was reported to wield greater influence than his C.-in-C. These enquiries were followed by Admiralty attempts to identify the manpower employed by the Russian navy and to examine its budget. Sir Thomas Sanderson reported secretly to Lord Selborne on 24 April 1902 that the Foreign Office had admired 'the very ingenious process' by which the Admiralty had ascertained the manpower costs, but that it remained difficult to obtain accurate estimates of construction costs in view of the fact that the Russian government had a tendency to allocate funds in an *ad hoc* fashion not determined by any previously allocated heads of expenditure. Sanderson reported that the British embassy and foreign naval attachés believed it to be correct that

on receipt of the news of the Anglo-Japanese Agreement, a Board of 8 officers, under the presidency of the Grand Duke Alexander Michaelovitch, was ordered to consider the steps to be taken to increase the Russian Naval Forces, that it was decided that the annual sum of £3,600,000, allocated to shipbuilding under the 1898–1904 scheme, should be raised to £5,000,000 annually, and that it was further resolved that 4 Battleships (each of 15,000 tons) and 2 first-class cruisers should be commenced as soon as possible either in Russian Yards or abroad.[20]

Sanderson had been aware of the problems of keeping communications with the embassy and consulates in Russia secure at least since 1898, when the best available British cipher had been inadvertently compromised.[21] Admiral Fisher had been instrumental in pressing for the replacement of the Army & Navy cipher with the Boats Signal Book in 1895 and made haste in 1899 to make sure that communications between Malta and London would be rerouted without touching French territory. The first recorded British interception of Russian naval signals was off the Egyptian coast in 1901 and this had been extended to the Far East by 1903. Fisher was informed by the journalist Arnold White, in the spring of 1901, that the system used by British consuls, Cipher K, had been sold to a hostile power by a vice-consul who had been put on trial. The new system, however, was one that the Foreign Office was not happy for its consular officers to employ as its use tended merely to alert the counter-intelligence agencies abroad and encourage them to take steps to bring pressure to bear on consuls, many of whom did not enjoy diplomatic immunity.

## US Perceptions

The British consul-general at Odessa, former naval commander Charles S. Smith, for example, was allegedly always complaining to his colleagues about *Okhrana* harassment according to his US colleague, Thomas Heenan, who wrote home disbelievingly on 24 July 1903 after Smith's residence had been burgled:

> My colleague is bitterly anti-Russian and believes himself to be constantly under police or secret service supervision. It appears to be part of the stock-in-trade of British Consular Officers to convince their Foreign Office that they are watched day and night by spies. This condition of affairs would be amusing were it not for the gravity of the situation which men thus prejudiced may be able to produce. It is to be hoped that the British Foreign Office is better informed than its representatives abroad.[22]

Although Heenan produced a number of detailed and interesting reports on a number of local issues, he was clearly unaware of the high-level exchanges taking place between President Theodore Roosevelt and the first secretary of the British embassy at St Petersburg, Cecil Spring-Rice, who had been his best man during a much earlier posting to Washington.[23]

US foreign policy at this period was heavily restricted by Congressional obstruction of presidential initiatives, but there is no doubt that Secretary Hay from 1899 and Roosevelt, first as McKinley's vice-president and then as his successor in office from September 1901, shared British and Japanese hostility towards Russian expansionism in the Far East so long as it was handled in the public context as multilateral support for the 'Open Door' in China. Spring-Rice was a radical antagonist towards both Russian and German autocracies, though Roosevelt tended far more towards opposition to the tsarist autocracy and was somewhat sceptical of the depth of Anglo-German antagonism. Roosevelt was one of the few foreign heads of government made privy to the text of the Anglo-Japanese Alliance and himself subsequently stated that he had read the text before ratification and approved in particular the role of Japan in Korea in much the same light as he regarded the societies of Central and South America as beneficiaries of enlightened American culture.

From the vantage point of the mission in St Petersburg, Spring-Rice could readily confirm the oppressive nature of the *Okhrana* and recorded the steadily mounting efforts of the *Okhrana* to penetrate the mission, especially after the withdrawal of the Japanese legation at the outbreak of war in February 1904. British ambassadors, especially Sir Charles Hardinge, were convinced of the likelihood of Russian penetration of British cipher communications and argued the need for a personal cipher for secret communications with London, but the line taken by Sir Thomas Sanderson was that no cipher 'can be considered absolutely impregnable' and urged Hardinge to resort only to messengers should there be any information he felt it necessary to withhold from his hosts.[24] Consequently, every effort was made to convince the Russian government of Britain's desire to remain neutral in the Russo-Japanese confrontation and to take every precaution to avoid any semblance of interference in Russia's internal affairs, such as the Japanese secret campaign to promote revolution and rebellion during the conflict. Spring-Rice, however, feared that such was the corrupt nature of the regime that, even if the *Okhrana*'s efforts to penetrate the mission's security should fail, their bitter opposition to Britain (and also, he averred, the USA) was such that they were liable to invent communications in order to poison the tsar's mind against Britain.[25]

Roosevelt instructed Harry White in the London embassy to confer as closely as possible with the Foreign Office and his ambassador at

St Petersburg, George Meyer, to contact Spring-Rice and withhold no confidences from him following the dispatch of Spring-Rice to Washington in January 1905, on the instructions of the Foreign Office, to persuade Roosevelt to act as mediator in the Russo-Japanese War once Port Arthur had been captured. With the departure of the Japanese mission from St Petersburg, every effort had been made on the Russian side to target the US and Swedish missions, as well as the British, as the degree of sympathy the three countries were believed to maintain towards Japan made their communications the most desirable to penetrate.

Even before the outbreak of war, the Japanese mission at St Petersburg had identified Britain as the principal likely provider of intelligence about Russia. Minister Kurino was particularly concerned about the security of Japanese communications through Russia and shared with Sanderson the perception that that security was best preserved by means of diplomatic couriers accompanying the movement of written dispatches into and out of Russian territory and that a joint system should be established with the Japanese army and navy. Kurino also identified Sweden as the location most promising after Britain in Europe for the collection of intelligence about Russia and supported the move by his military attaché, Colonel Akashi, to be appointed simultaneously to Stockholm and for members of the mission at St Petersburg to move from there to Sweden at the outbreak of war.[26]

## Japan, Germany and Russia

Akashi had previously been Japanese military attaché in France, which until 1871 had been the prime source of technology and tactical ideas for the emerging Japanese army. But with France's defeat in the Franco-Prussian War, the German army and its general staff was rapidly adopted as the standard to which the Japanese army should aspire in future. By 1900, the training manuals and methods of the German army reigned supreme within the Japanese officer corps and a system for the secondment of the most ambitious officers to the Prussian army ensured that the prime foreign language of the bulk of the officer corps was German. Other officers continued to learn French, but by the time of the Anglo-Japanese Alliance in 1902, it was observed that it was extremely rare for influential Japanese army officers to have a good command of English. A British military attaché had been seconded from China to General Ôyama's headquarters to observe the fighting between Japan and China, but his successor was of the opinion that, even by employing an interpreter, as often as not more time was spent in correcting previous mistaken observations. One of the few exceptions was Major General Fukushima, who had a good knowledge of Russian, German and English, collaborated closely with British-Indian troops during the Boxer Uprising in 1900–1901 and, as chief of the Intelligence Division of the Japanese general staff, represented the army in London and Simla in negotiations with the British and Indian armies about the military implementation of the Anglo-Japanese Alliance.

The Japanese army's admiration for Germany ensured a degree of support in 1901 for a triple alliance of Japan with Britain and Germany against Russia and France, but the inclusion of Germany was fatally undermined by the kaiser's support for the Triple Intervention of 1895 and by repeated evidence – reinforced by British criticisms – of the support that continued to be given by the kaiser to the tsar from 1898 onward. Mistrust of Germany was particularly marked within the British naval officer corps, as can be observed in the views of Custance (DNI) and Lord Selborne, but was fully endorsed within the Foreign Office and supported by the Salisbury Cabinet in the course of 1901.[27] The response of the Germans, as well as the Russians, to the news of the Anglo-Japanese Alliance was closely followed and the press reaction to the kaiser meeting the tsar at Bjørkø on 6 August 1902 that 'we do not doubt that personal intercourse between the sovereigns and their statesmen will tend to fortify and increase friendly neighbouring relations between Germany and Russia' was duly noted in Tokyo.[28] The Japanese perception that they were distasteful so far as Wilhelm was concerned was confirmed in December 1902, when they were informed that no further secondments of Japanese officers to the Prussian army would be entertained. It later transpired that this had been a personal decision on the part of Wilhelm himself (which lasted until November 1906) and the Japanese army desperately tried to mitigate the blow by trying to switch secondments from the Prussian to the Bavarian army. That the move was a deliberate slight was amply verified by Colonel Akashi on the basis of a conversation he had in St Petersburg with the officer on the German general staff in charge of the Japan desk. This officer told Akashi that he had had occasion to have a personal discussion with the kaiser during an informal garden walk and revealed: 'I am surprised to know that the German Emperor has anti-Japanese feeling in a great degree. The Japanese, being the ally of England, communicate to English what they learn in Germany and give all economic profits to England. The German Emperor does not like friendly relations between Japan and England.'[29]

Although the kaiser proposed early in the war humanitarian aid to Japanese troops wounded in Manchuria by offering them the use of German military hospitals in the Far East, in fact he further alienated the Japanese army by publicly sending good wishes to the troops of the Russian regiments of which he was colonel-in-chief. Baron Suematsu, who had been given a roving commission as a Japanese propagandist in Europe, reported home in July 1904 about the German stance: 'Official quarters display much flatteries to Russia but they also have some sort of lurking satisfaction in seeing her neighbour weakened.[30] Minister Hayashi in London had already pointed out on 11 July 1904 reports of Russian efforts to raise finance on German markets and of Russian hopes for German benevolent neutrality in return for commercial concessions. These trends appeared increasingly fully confirmed by events at sea, when auxiliary cruisers of the Russian Volunteer Fleet were shown to have demonstrated preferential treatment to German as opposed to British vessels intercepted in the Red Sea and the Indian Ocean and attributed this to the exercise of influence from above 'in order to smooth the way and facilitate speedy conclusion of Russo-German commercial negotiations which are now pending…'[31] As early as April 1904, Minister Inoue had drawn Tokyo's attention to the fact that Germany was engaged in selling considerable numbers of mail steamers to Russia and as events progressed this assistance was increasingly linked to German support for the provision of coal and supplies to enable the Baltic Fleet to sail to the Far East. Being neutral, German shipping lines could charter colliers from British firms and effectively frustrate support expressed by Admiral Fisher, among others, for prosecutions under the Foreign Enlistment Act of 1870 of firms engaged in the supply of Welsh coal for warlike purposes.

### Britain, Russia and Germany

In London, the idea that the Russians would be able to assemble and transfer the Baltic Fleet to the Far East even with support from French overseas territorial waters was regarded as fanciful in the light of Russian reliance on other countries for such services in the past. In the event, such services were principally provided under contracts with the main German shipping lines, which had gained considerable experience as the suppliers of materials to the German naval units based at Kiaochow in northern China since 1898 and contributed to the gathering of intelligence for the *Marine-Etappendienst*.[32] This was confirmed in December 1904 by Japanese Consul-General Iwasaki in Sydney, who followed up reports in the Australian press to locate the French Lieutenant Colonel Baron de Hardenflycht, then on his way to the Far East, and discovered that the two German firms had contracts covering the areas east and west of Singapore. The latter was reported to have chartered forty-two colliers and planned to refuel the Baltic Fleet in the open sea in the Marshall Islands.[33]

Japanese advances in the course of the war generally had the effect of making the German side try to hedge its bets. The seizure of Port Arthur was followed by a move on the part of the kaiser to confer a decoration on General Nogi and at a diplomatic reception he told Minister Inoue that he hoped this 'had produced a favourable impression in Japan and stated that he was much interested in our military operation and that German army had learned many things from the doings of our army.'[34]

Other evidence, however, suggested that the surrender of Port Arthur was viewed in Berlin with anxiety in respect of its effects on 'the Russian people and whether it would affect the internal situation'[35] and that financial and bureaucratic circles were of the view that 'the eventual victory of Japan over Russia would lead to Japan extending her activity and sphere of influence in China, consequences of which would be detrimental to the interests of Germany in the Far East, and her position at Kiao-chow would be threatened'.[36] Following the Japanese victory at Tsushima, Minister Inoue reported a conversation with the emperor when he had offered his congratulations on the victory and claimed that he had won a bet that he had had with his sceptical senior naval officers that Admiral Togo would be sure to defeat Admiral Rozhestvenski. The event coincided with a visit to Berlin of Prince and Princess Arisugawa, who attended a military review in the company of Japanese army officers on 31 May 1905 and were again greeted with the ovations of the crowd 'vociferously' calling out 'Banzai Japan'. This was also spoken of by the emperor and Inoue's report ended with the acid comment that this 'was a sign that the people in Berlin whom the emperor sometimes found rather difficult to manage are also delighted·to welcome Their Imperial Highnesses'.[37]

On the British side, the press viewed the problem of the interception and sinking of German and British neutral vessels by Russian auxiliary cruisers in the summer of 1904 as a test of German behaviour. The suppression of any strong German protests against Russia was compared with the agitation against the boarding of the steamer *Bundesrath* during the Boer War and the Russian decision to continue with the dispatch of the Baltic Fleet to the Far East despite the fall of Port Arthur was seen at the Admiralty as evidence of German influence over the Tsar.[38] Prince Louis of Battenberg (DNI), reviewing the international situation in November 1904, urged on Fisher, now First Sea Lord, the desirability of more frequent joint manoeuvres between the Channel and Home Fleets in the North Sea and Scandinavian waters rather than between the Channel and Mediterranean Fleets as in the past 'given that the threat from Kiel is greater than from Toulon'.[39]

King Edward VII in conversation with the US diplomat in London, Harry White, had argued that 'England was our real friend and that Germany was only a make-believe friend' in April 1905 when the initial crisis over Morocco began to emerge; but, even though the depth of Anglo-German antipathy had been underscored by Cecil Spring-Rice, Roosevelt found it hard to take the kaiser seriously and also made light of his subsequent statement that he believed that Britain planned to attack Germany.[40] The truth was that Admiral Fisher had pressed Lord Lansdowne to make it possible for the German demand for a port on the Atlantic coast of Morocco to be treated as a *casus belli* and to let the French government know that the Royal Navy and the French navy were to be considered united against the German challenge and that 'we could have the German Fleet, the Kiel Canal and Schleswig-Holstein within a fortnight'.[41] In response, an urgent consultation took place between Lansdowne and Balfour, who advised against such precipitate action, while agreeing with Fisher that 'the Germans are behaving abominably, and we must do what we can to prevent them squeezing any illegitimate advantage out of the situation they have endeavoured to create'.[42]

## Conclusion

The crisis over Morocco did not come to a head until after the end of the Russo-Japanese War, but between March and September 1905 when President Roosevelt acted as mediator between the two sides, the long-standing British policy of preparation for war in Europe predicated on a Franco-Russian threat was replaced by the drawing up of a new policy directive explicitly naming Germany as the future principal threat to British national security in discussions between Sir Thomas Sanderson and Colonel Francis Davies, head of the section in the DMO in the War Office dealing with issues of secret intelligence. The DMO, General Grierson, appointed by Esher and Fisher, had acted promptly in March 1905 by ordering a reconnaisance of the border area between Germany, France and Belgium and initiating closer relations with the French Ministry of War a year before the opening of the Algeciras Conference. However, the background against which Britain's 'continental commitment' was set lay squarely in the interpretation of the behaviour of Germany during the Russo-Japanese War. The 'perfect' quality of the Japanese intelligence services perceived in Britain and their conclusion that Russia's real ally was Germany and not France was fully endorsed in the course of 1905 when the Foreign Office issued its memorandum on 'Secret Service Arrangements in the Event of War with Germany', which remained in force until August 1914.[43]

The text of this memorandum has been withheld, together with the archives of the Secret Intelligence Service (MI6), and this almost certainly is the principal reason why no historian of British signals intelligence prior to 1914 can avoid denying the existence of publicly available evidence on the subject. Extant evidence, however, demonstrates that the War Office made elaborate preparations for the censorship of the British cable system from the 1890s and similar preparations were established by the Admiralty for the surveillance and control of wireless activities after 1900. The actual introduction of cable censorship was legally admissible in wartime from 1899 to 1902, but under Indian law peacetime censorship was admissible and widely practised in areas such as Malaya and China by units of the Indian army in close collaboration with the Japanese army. This device permitted the War Office to receive information from India without any breach of British legal restrictions in force from 1844. Similarly, naval stations overseas operated under colonial conditions in most cases but no controls existed over the operation of wireless telegraphy beyond British territorial waters with the result that signals intelligence activity functioned largely unfettered if not entirely systematically from 1899 to 1914. British policymakers, in alliance with Japan, employed these means of monitoring Russian policy in such a way that they avoided embroilment in conflict with Russia in order to avoid at all costs in Europe an international structure in which Germany would dictate the rules of the game.

# 5

## Britain and Russia, 1914–1917

HEW STRACHAN

'I think this is a good opportunity to let you know what I think of the whole question of Russia and ourselves,' H. A. Gwynne, editor of the *Morning Post*, wrote to his Petrograd correspondent, Victor Marsden, on 1 December 1914. The letter that followed touched on all the key issues in the Anglo-Russian relationship in the First World War. First, was the war the opportunity to convert an *ad hoc* alliance with Russia into a long-term relationship? Or was Russia, not Germany, Britain's real long-term enemy? Its ambitions in regard to the Ottoman Empire, and across Asia Minor and Central Asia, had caused anxiety in some government departments until the very eve of the war. But even if those aims were extensive and possibly aggressive, were they truly threatening? Where did tsarist Russia stand on the social Darwinist spectrum so popular in the vocabulary of 1914? Was it a coming power, about to reap the benefits of its latent potential and its enormous natural resources, or was it a decaying one, about to implode in revolution? If the latter, British long-term fears of Russia would be resolved at a stroke, but in the short term both powers, locked in mutual dependence by a major war, would confront possible defeat and even collapse.

Gwynne and Marsden were newspapermen. They wanted to know what British public opinion thought of its improbable ally. Gwynne declared that 'there was an enormous feeling of gratitude towards Russia for her chivalrous intervention in east Prussia in the early days of the war when she was not altogether ready and when she suffered in order to help us in the west'. Was he right? Did he believe what he said, or was he trying to put Marsden at his ease? After all, it was Marsden, not Gwynne, who had to sit in Petrograd and deal with Russian criticisms of Britain.[1]

In 1907 Britain and Russia had come to an understanding which had overthrown most observers' expectations of the international order. The aim of the entente from Britain's point of view was regional stability in Asia. In 1904–5 the army General Staff in India reckoned it needed to be reinforced by 100,000 men if it was to counter the threat posed by the Russians to the north-west frontier of India.[2] The agreement of

1907 was the eventual solution to that fear, but for the Indian army it created a new problem. If the greatest external threat to India had been removed, it was in danger of becoming redundant. What was it for? Douglas Haig, when he became chief of the general staff in India in 1909, answered that question by beginning to prepare it for war in Europe. In doing so he was reflecting the aspirations of some Conservatives, who had interpreted the Anglo-Russian entente not simply as a device to stop Britain worrying about Asia but also as a means to get it to focus on the more pressing developments created by the challenge of Germany. For them the 1907 agreement was not the solution to a set of Asiatic problems but the final building block in the forging of an alliance for intervention in a European conflict.

This may have made sense in London. However, it did not do so in Delhi. Lord Hardinge, the viceroy, told Haig to abandon plans for shipping an Indian Expeditionary Force to Europe and to concentrate on his real job, the defence of India. This meant not its protection against an outside danger, but the maintenance of its internal order. The army's mutiny in 1857 exercised a long reach, its horrors still etched in the consciousness of old India hands at the beginning of the new century. Moreover, the dangers of religious fundamentalism in clashes between Muslims and Hindus, and the possibility of terrorism on the part of nationalists, gave long-standing fears new resonances. Overt mention of the Russian threat was dropped after 1907, but the requirement to send 100,000 troops to reinforce India was not. More men than would be needed for internal policing, they were evidence that subliminally British India had not forgotten its old fear of its new ally. According to the increases approved in 1913–14, the Russian army would muster 2,245,000 men by 1917, and even then it would have conscripted only 25 per cent of its available manpower. These figures terrified the Germans, but they did not necessarily reassure all Britons: the Russian army still had Asiatic responsibilities as well as European.[3]

Moreover, with the outbreak of war in 1914, the prime minister, Asquith, appointed Lord Kitchener to be secretary of state for war. Kitchener had served as commander-in-chief in India between 1902 and 1909. His infamous run-in with the then-viceroy, Lord Curzon, in which he had set out to consolidate authority in his own office to the detriment of that of his political superior, had possessed a strategic rationale.[4] Kitchener's energies were devoted to readying the army in India to meet the Russians. The outlook which he brought to the War Office was imperial, not European, and the strategy which he then enunciated for the conduct of the war was shaped by his ambitions for Britain's post-war position. The fighting on the continent of Europe should be left to Britain's two allies but longest imperial rivals, France and Russia. They would exhaust their armies in battles with Germany, enabling Britain to step in with decisive effect in 1917. With the war won, essentially on Britain's terms, Britain would be able to launch itself into a post-war world in which the threat not only of Germany but also of France and Russia had been removed.[5]

The view that Russia remained a long-term threat was not confined to the army. It was to be found in the navy as well. Arthur Marder's interpretation of the Dreadnought revolution and the work of Sir John Fisher, the First Sea Lord between 1905 and 1909, conforms with the argument that Britain's overriding concern in the decade before the First World War was to concentrate against Germany. Accordingly, the Anglo-Russian entente enabled the Royal Navy to leave far-eastern waters and bring its major units back to the North Sea. But two lines of qualification have to be entered. First, the battlecruiser, not the battleship, was Fisher's key design. Fisher told Winston Churchill when he became First Lord of the Admiralty, 'Sea fighting is pure common sense. The first of all necessities is SPEED, so as to be able to fight *When* you like *Where* you like and *How* you like.'[6] Fisher therefore wanted a ship whose primary defence was not its armour but its ability to manoeuvre. Its offensive capabilities would be comparable with those of the battleship; the first battlecruisers had 12-inch guns, and in 1912 Fisher was telling Churchill that they should mount 15-inch guns and be capable of 30 knots. Designed to engage their enemy at ranges of 20,000 yards, and to do so on constantly changing courses as they did so, these were vessels best suited to combat in the world's oceans, not in the more confined seas between Britain and Europe. The crushing defeat inflicted on Graf von Spee's East Asiatic Squadron in the South Atlantic at the battle of the Falkland Islands on 8 December 1914 was the vindication of Fisher's designs. But Spee's ships were the only major German units on the world's oceans. The logical opponent of the battlecruiser was not Germany in the North Sea, but any power that threatened Britain's imperial and commercial position throughout the world.

Secondly, therefore, Britain did not abandon its global maritime role in 1905. At the 1909 Imperial Conference, Fisher told the representatives of the Dominions that he planned to create fleet units to police the world's oceans, using the battlecruisers that he hoped they would contribute as the fleets' building blocks. The long-term oceanic threats to Britain were France and Russia, not Germany.[7] True, the Russo-Japanese War had wiped out Russia as a naval power in the immediate sense: its Baltic Fleet had been destroyed at the battle of Tsushima in 1905, and neither its replacement nor the Black Sea Fleet had a single Dreadnought ready for service in 1914. But between 1905 and 1913 Russian naval spending rose 178.4 per cent, outstripping that of

Germany.[8] The Admiralty's approach to war aims during the war showed how lively its global concerns remained: it wanted the Atlantic port of Duala in the German Cameroons, and from the dismemberment of the Ottoman Empire it hoped to secure both Lemnos as a base in the eastern Mediterranean and Mesopotamia as a source of oil for its latest Dreadnoughts.

The long-term anxieties of the armed forces were reflected – albeit, of course, for different reasons – in the attitudes of the British political left. The Anglo-Russian entente appalled the Labour Party, whose members saw an authoritarian and autocratic regime as an inappropriate partner for a liberal and constitutional state. 'The Russian government is the open enemy of every liberty we boast of,' George Bernard Shaw would fulminate in 'Common sense about the war', first published in the *New Statesman* on 14 November 1914. 'Charles I's unsuccessful attempt to arrest five members of the House of Commons for disagreeing with him is ancient history here; it occurred 272 years ago; but the Tsar's successful attempt to arrest thirty members of the Duma and to punish them as dangerous criminals is a fact of today.'[9]

The leverage of radical voices within Asquith's Cabinet was increased after the election of 1910, which left the government, Liberal with a capital 'L' as well as with a small one, dependent on Labour votes. 'Little Englanders', lingering vestiges of a Gladstonian inheritance, were sufficiently powerful for the more strategically minded members of the cabinet to gang warily in July 1914. Sir Edward Grey, Lord Haldane and Asquith himself may have been persuaded that foreign policy was about the realities of power, not ideals, but they still had to convince the rest of their party.

The Foreign Office found itself at the heart of this dilemma, having to mediate between internal pressures and the external dangers in whose context an alliance with Russia made strategic sense. It believed that Russia possessed enormous latent potential. That was not an unusual estimate before 1914. It underpinned Germany's fear of Russia, and it was justified by the phenomenal growth of the Russian economy between the 1905 revolution and the outbreak of the war. Sir Arthur Nicolson, who had been ambassador in Russia, embodied this view. When he became permanent under-secretary at the Foreign Office in 1910, it was installed at the heart of policymaking. 'She has enormously improved [on her position in 1909] and strengthened her army,' Nicolson said of Russia in January 1913, 'and finances are in a stable and very flourishing condition.' Three months later he told his successor in St Petersburg (as it still was), Sir George Buchanan, that Russia was 'the most powerful factor in Europe' and told him always to be friendly to it (or her, as he would have said).[10]

What followed from this was that in the Foreign Office's eyes Russia was an emergent power in the social Darwinist world order, not a degenerating one. The aftermath of the 1905 revolution, with the establishment of the Duma and the dynamism of the Zemstvos at the local level, provided direct evidence of its capacity to adapt and to liberalise, in spite of tsarism. British policy had a clear and viable line to follow, to support the liberals within Russia. Fortunately one of these was deemed to be the foreign minister, Sergei Dmitrievich Sazonov. He had served in Paris, Washington and London: 'He has an English manner,' Stephen Graham was to write after interviewing him in 1915, 'an English way of living, and evidently has a strong personal liking for English things and English ways.'[11]

The personnel responsible for relations between Britain and France immediately before the war were still in place in July 1914, and – broadly speaking – remained so until 1917. Continuity therefore spanned the crisis. But at the same time the war threw up new issues and new bodies to deal with them – principally in the fields of munitions, finance and propaganda. The major challenge which the diplomats confronted was the perception of Britain within Russia. In Russia's eyes Britain's response in the July crisis had been slow and grudging. On 24 July 1914 the Council of Ministers authorised the mobilisation of four military districts. Russia was thus the first power to militarise the crisis; Britain was the last. Sazonov had good reason to feel let down. He had persuaded the council to discount the fears of conservatives, who feared that war would lead to revolution, and to follow the course favoured by the liberal imperialists, arguing that, if hostilities did break out, they would unite the nation, not divide it. In seeing Austria-Hungary as the stalking horse for Germany, he was following a line no different from Sir Edward Grey's.

When Britain did finally commit itself to the entente, it then sent a tiny army to France. Until 1916 it refused to sanction what to Europeans seemed to be the logical corollary of a major land war, the introduction of conscription. Instead it argued that its role in the conflict was to be the arsenal and financier of the alliance. Reginald McKenna, who succeeded Lloyd George as Chancellor of the Exchequer in May 1915, believed that Britain could not commit its manpower twice over. It had to keep skilled workers in factories, not just to sustain its own war production but also to ensure that Britain did not lose its export markets. His justification was not the needs of post-war recovery – that if Britain ceased to export during the war it would not be able to refill its order books after it was over. Instead it was contingent on the exchange rate. If Britain exported goods during the war, the sterling–dollar exchange would remain steady and so London would be in a position to buy more goods from neutral states, and particularly from the United States, for its allies as well as for itself. Russia's response was forthright: in that case, it demanded, let us see your munitions and your cash. The arguments over economic co-operation became the nub of the Anglo-Russian relationship in the First World War.[12]

The co-ordination of strategy in a narrowly military sense proved far less fraught. For a long time the debate between the so-called 'westerners' and 'easterners' dominated British histories of the war. According to this caricature, the westerners were soldiers, or 'brass-hats' in the terminology of the memoirs, and were bent on committing all Britain's resources to the fighting in France and Belgium. The easterners were politicians, or 'frocks', who wanted to avoid sending British soldiers to the trenches of the western front, and preferred to seek alternative theatres in which to operate, especially in the Ottoman empire. This is a travesty of the truth, derived from the polemics of the post-war memoirs. No politician imagined that Britain could walk away from the western front; the debate revolved around relative priorities, not absolutes. Moreover, the generals were not all westerners.

For officers who had been to the Staff College at Camberley, the strategic position in Europe was comprehensible in terms that accorded with the principles enunciated by the dominant military theorist of the nineteenth century, Antoine-Henri Jomini. Jomini, who had incidentally closed his varied and international career in Russia, described Napoleonic warfare in terms of interior and exterior lines. An army on interior lines could put itself in a central position between two opponents, defeating one before turning to face the other. Although the enemy forces had the opportunity to envelop and encircle the army in a central position, the distance between them militated against success. In 1914–18, Germany enjoyed the advantage of the central position. It could move men and equipment to its various fronts, not only east and west but also in due course to Italy, the Balkans and Turkey, using interior lines. The entente was operating on exterior lines, and therefore its problem was that of concentrating its efforts in time and space. To do that it had to attack the Central Powers simultaneously on all their fronts from divergent directions. Then it would reap the benefit of exterior lines, and the resources of Germany and its allies would be dissipated, pulled hither and yon, and not concentrated. This in essence was the entente strategy embraced in December 1915 for 1916, and again in December 1916 for 1917. In this sense British generals were passionate easterners: they wanted an active Russian front.

In particular, this view of the war was to be found located at the War Office in London. Its spokesmen were, first, Kitchener himself, and then, as his star waned, Sir William Robertson. Robertson, who became chief of the imperial general staff in December 1915 and dominated British strategic counsels until he was manoeuvred out of office by Lloyd George in February 1918, was fed information by his director of military intelligence, George Macdonogh. Macdonogh's agents, operating in and out of Belgium, tracked railway movements across Europe as German divisions were shuttled between the western and eastern fronts. Robertson therefore had a reasonably firm grasp of how operations on one front shaped the overall German order of battle. British general headquarters in France, which had its own intelligence organisation, tended to a more parochial perspective. It saw the enemy to its immediate front, and was sensitive to the needs of its French ally to its right. The result was that soldiers in London developed different perspectives on the war from those entertained by the commanders in France. Kitchener and Sir John French were at loggerheads within a month of the war's declaration. In the winter of 1914–15, the secretary of state for war was looking to other theatres for British troops and favouring a defensive posture in the west: the main battle against the Germans would be waged in the east by the Russian 'steamroller'. The heavy and sustained defeats inflicted on Russia by the Germans and Austro-Hungarians in the summer of 1915 forced him to moderate his position. Over the course of that winter, Robertson was more aligned with Haig in favouring a commitment to the western front, but within a year his broader perspective became evident. He recognised the interactive nature of all the fronts and resisted the pressure to over-anticipate Germany's defeat. By 1917 their relationship was cooling, and Haig did not intervene on his colleague's behalf when the prime minister moved against him.

The tensions which the balance between the western and other fronts generated for the British generals ultimately allowed the politicians to divide and rule them. But the frictions between the generals were not generated primarily by manpower. There was no question of sending British troops to Russia. All sides agreed that what Russia possessed in abundance was men. In 1914 Russia had the biggest army in Europe but mobilised only 25 per cent of its men of military age; Germany conscripted 56 per cent and France 87 per cent. By 1917 Russia had raised the massive total of 15 million soldiers, but that still constituted only 39 per cent of its eligible population. Britain, despite its failure to conscript until 1916, put 49 per cent of its men aged fifteen to forty-nine into uniform.[13] The demand that Russia's allies made of it was that it raise yet more men. It replied that it could not because it had not got the equipment for them. Stories of soldiers going into action in 1915 without rifles and being instructed to pick up those they could find on the battlefield were anecdotal corroboration of a statistical truth. In 1914 Russia's maximum annual production of rifles was 700,000, but it needed 2.4 million. In 1915 production only rose to 865,000 rifles, and in 1916 1.3 million.[14] Units were trained with one rifle for every five men, and in the winter of 1915–16 companies were re-formed after the great retreat with two platoons armed and one not. Problems with heavy artillery and shell supply were comparable.

So Russia's answer to Britain was that, if the entente wanted a mass army fit to undertake offensive operations on the eastern front, it would have to provide the weapons to enable it to do so. But in 1914–15 Britain did not have an indigenous arms industry large enough to meet this demand. It could not meet its own needs. By 21 October 1914 orders were out for 781,000 rifles and recruits were training with broomsticks. In the opening year of the war, industry had simultaneously to convert from its patterns of pre-war production, adapting plant from the manufacture of peace goods to war goods, and at the same time to increase output. By and large Britain had completed this process in regard to rifles by mid-1915, but it had not done so for shells and heavy artillery until well into 1916. Accepting Russian orders would therefore only increase the burdens on its order books, and reduce the rate at which it could equip its own New Armies.[15]

Britain had a further concern. Even if it fulfilled all Russia's orders, could it be sure that they would find their way to the front? Russia was virtually blockaded. The Central Powers had closed the overland routes. The North Sea was the no-man's-land of the maritime war, and the Baltic was dominated, as was no other water in the world, by the German navy. To the south, the Dardanelles and the entry to the Black Sea were closed even before the Ottoman Empire's entry to the war at the beginning of November 1914. The routes which remained all presented difficulties. Vladivostok, on the Pacific coast, was not only a long way from Europe and even from the eastern seaboard of America; it was also almost 6000 kilometres from the Russian front. Archangel was closer to both, but it was on the White Sea and only open half the year. Murmansk was nearer to Britain and relatively ice-free, but, like Archangel, its rail links to the interior were poor.

The shipping problem was therefore linked to a railway problem. In 1914 Russia's internal transport network was still inadequate given the size of the country. The attention to rearmament after 1908–9 resulted in munitions production receiving precedence. The rates of additions to both track and rolling stock declined. When the war broke out, Russia had to decide whether new railway construction should go into linking Murmansk to the interior, or into spanning the distance between the resources of the Donets basin and the manufacturing centre of Petrograd. If the latter had priority, Russia might manufacture more munitions on its own account and therefore be less dependent on imports through Murmansk. Moreover, that logic concluded with the argument that Britain should ship rolling stock, not munitions. But the case against went further than the fact that it was a long-term approach to solving the conundrums of the Russian war economy. Britain suspected that Russia was using its wartime needs to secure investment in its post-war infrastructure, not its ability to wage the First World War. If Russia was genuinely a greater threat to the British Empire than was Germany, this made little sense.

One way of obviating these problems was to encourage Russia to place its orders for munitions in the United States, not in Britain. But American liberals were as reluctant as British to deal directly with a regime that they regarded as politically abhorrent. Conveniently, idealism marched in step with financial self-interest. Russia lacked the international credit to fund orders; only London, the world's money market, as well as shipping and insurance capital, could guarantee Russia's overseas purchasing. Thus the conundrums of the Anglo-Russian wartime relationship came full circle. How could Britain support Russia's war effort without damaging its own? In 1915 McKenna was preoccupied with maintaining the dollar–sterling exchange. Standing at par, $4.86 to the pound, in December 1914, it fell to $4.77 by June 1915 and $4.64 by mid-August. American goods were costing more. The value of the pound could only be weakened yet further if sterling was used to sustain the convertibility of the rouble. By April 1917 the rouble had fallen 43.9 per cent against the dollar. By then 58 per cent of all the allies' borrowing, both that contracted between the belligerent powers themselves and that between them and the United States, was generated by the needs of Russia.[16] Through the Commission Internationale de Ravitaillement, established to co-ordinate allied purchasing in August 1914, Russia was able to buy United States products under Anglo-French auspices, and pay for it with debt that it contracted in London and Paris, not in New York. American exports to Russia rose from a value of $32 million in 1913 to $640 million in 1916. Over 70 per cent of the United States funds lent to the two west European allies in the period of American neutrality were actually destined for Russian use.[17]

The fact that these exports to Russia were from the United States and not Britain did not diminish the underlying nature of British worries. American exports could be used just as well as British to improve Russia's civil infrastructure; American goods could also languish in Archangel and Murmansk, unable to get to the front; and American munitions that equipped the Russian army might instead have gone to the British and French armies. The tensions were real, not imagined, because the United States, like the United Kingdom, was in no position to become a really effective arms supplier until 1916. Its arms industry, just like that of the belligerents, had to increase its capacity from the expectations set by a pattern of peacetime orders. Of 1.8 million rifles ordered by Russia from Westinghouse, only 216,000 had been delivered by February 1917. Winchester had fulfilled orders for 27,000 out of 300,000, and Remington 180,000 out of 1.5 million.[18]

Munitions supply was therefore a key lever in the origins, organisation and direction of allied strategy. In February 1915 the finance ministers of Britain, France and Russia met at Boulogne at the behest of David Lloyd George, then still Chancellor of the Exchequer. Lloyd George saw funding the war as a means to an end. Money was required to buy munitions; the allocation of what was acquired would determine strategy. He wanted to arm Russia so that Russia could aid Serbia, and thus the Balkan front could be kept active. In June 1915 Lloyd George took the next step in his own personal journey along that spectrum, when he assumed responsibility for the newly created ministry of munitions. Here he applied what he took to be good French practice in munitions production, striking up a warm relationship with his French equivalent, Albert Thomas. But Thomas took a different view of strategy. He argued that the French army was readier to act than the Russian, and that therefore France, not Russia, should be the beneficiary of any surplus British munitions production. In November 1915 the munitions ministers of all four allies (Italy was now included) met in London, ostensibly to pool resources. Thomas proposed a resolution that the allies establish a central munitions office. Although it came to naught, the idea was approved. For Lloyd George the purpose of the centralisation of munitions was the centralisation of strategic direction. But for most of his colleagues the aim was economic, not military. They wanted to curb Russia's independent purchasing, which persisted despite the Commission Internationale de Ravitaillement, and which drove up prices and threatened exchange rates. Russia for its part was happy to support the centralisation of munitions as it reckoned it would benefit. At the November conference it asked for 1,400 4.8-inch howitzers, 250 8-inch siege howitzers, ninety 6-inch howitzers and fifty-four 12-inch howitzers. Britain did not have heavy artillery in this sort of quantity and what it did have it wanted for its own army on the western front: the battle of the Somme was predicated on massive numbers of heavy guns distributed over a broad front, and its failure was due in large part to the fact that that condition was not met. The British Expeditionary Force was ready to release to the Russians only its surplus 18-pounder field guns. Lloyd George offered 300 4.5-inch field howitzers, a suggestion that appalled Sir William Robertson, who knew by January 1916 that the army in France had received only fifty-one of the 100 heavy howitzers it had been promised.[19] Kitchener was on his way to Russia to sort out this problem when H.M.S. *Hampshire* was sunk on 5 June 1916, and he was drowned.

Between 1914 and 1916 Britain could not meet the expectations foisted on it by Russia, particularly in relation to munitions supply. And yet it needed Russia to carry on fighting in order to implement its strategy for the conduct of the war. This was a matter not just of an active eastern front to draw the Germans away from the west, but also of victories sufficiently convincing to persuade the neutral Balkan powers that they should throw in their lot with the entente. Success in the Caucasus would also help the allies, the British in particular, as it would draw the Turks from their other theatres of war in the Middle East and Central Asia. In September 1914 the three entente powers had agreed that none of them should make a separate peace with Germany. But Britain remained worried lest Russia should opt to do so. Moreover the fear was well founded, in so far as it reflected the preferred policy of Erich von Falkenhayn, Germany's chief of the general staff until the end of August 1916. London had two principal methods which it could use to forestall any such inclination.

The first was military action. In 1915 British strategy was thrice shaped by the needs of Russia. On 2 January 1915, as Enver Pasha led the 3rd Ottoman army in a daring thrust into the Caucasus mountains culminating in the battle of Sarikamish, the Russians demanded that Britain support them in their battle with Turkey. The request was answered at Gallipoli, a blow aimed ultimately at Constantinople itself. In the event Russia saved itself in the Caucasus, and by April 1915 defence had turned to attack. Russian success fed fanciful notions that the allies might converge on Baghdad, the British coming from the south by way of the Persian Gulf and the Russians from the north through Azerbaijan. The lack of progress at Gallipoli increased the pressure for victory in Mesopotamia, but the campaign there ended in surrender at Kut. By the summer of 1915 hopes of reciprocal action by Russia were evaporating, as the Germans and Austro-Hungarians overran Galicia, Poland and Belorussia. In August Kitchener was persuaded that his original preference for limited action only in the west was no longer sustainable and that the Russian 'steamroller' would itself need bailing out. In October the British supported the French offensive in Champagne with their own attack at Loos.[20]

The second method was war aims. The great powers did not go to war in July 1914 to pursue a policy of annexationism and territorial imperialism. But once they were at war they used war aims to regulate the relationships between themselves and to woo fresh allies. In this respect Turkey's entry to the war on the side of the Central Powers was a considerable boon. It enabled the British government to propose gains for Russia at the expense of the Ottoman Empire in exchange for fighting Germany and Austria-Hungary. On 14 November 1914 Sir Edward Grey offered Russia control of both the Dardanelle straits and Constantinople, a policy confirmed in March 1915.[21] Throughout the nineteenth century British foreign policy in the eastern Mediterranean had been predicated on the need to prevent the Russians securing unfettered access to its waters. In 1854 it had even gone to war in pursuit of that policy, and its strategic imperatives had drawn it first to confront and then to conciliate its other long-standing rival, France. The *volte face* represented by the straits agreement was the product of both long-term and short-term considerations.

It was a clear indication that the Foreign Office saw the 1907 entente as more than just an expedient. If Russia was to be accorded permanent access to the eastern Mediterranean, and therefore the opportunity to threaten British interests in Egypt, the Suez canal and the route to India, Anglo-Russian relations had to be put on a secure footing. 'The Russian *aide-mémoire*', the prime minister assured the British war council when it discussed the straits agreement on 10 March 1915, 'referred to a *final* settlement, and not to an interim arrangement.'[22] The corollary of Britain's acceptance that Russia controlled the straits was that Russia recognised Britain's primacy in southern Persia. It was here that Anglo-Russian relations had been nearest to breaking point in 1914. Essentially the security of India and its western approaches was now located in the Gulf and not in the Mediterranean. In this sense the straits agreement was a codicil to the pre-war agreements with France as well as Russia – a package designed to put imperial defence on a footing that squared the principal dangers from Europe. But it required the desperate and immediate circumstances of the winter of 1914–15 to wring it out of Britain. By putting Russia into Constantinople, Britain hoped to convince Bulgaria to join the entente and so to provide Serbia with the direct military support that none of Britain, France or Russia could deliver. Secondly, Grey recognised full well that gaining the straits would prove immensely popular in Russia. It would vindicate Sazonov and so boost the liberals.

The British Foreign Office aspired to liberalise Russia. It did not wish to do so for abstract reasons – or out of idealism. Sir Edward Grey had not so internalized the logic of capitalism to believe that his department was bound to advocate political and individual freedoms. Its and his behaviour was entirely pragmatic: they believed that by liberalising Russia would be better able to fight the war. Liberalism would work in two directions. First, the British – like many Russians – associated those in Russia who were inclined to support Germany with conservatism: Boris Vladimirovich Stürmer, appointed prime minister in January 1916 at the tsarina's behest, was believed to be a case in point. The conservatives favoured a separate peace, but that was a policy stripped of its appeal when the alternative included the guarantee that Russia would get both Constantinople and the straits. Secondly the liberals seemed to possess the potential to unite the country for the better prosecution of the war. They could work with the Unions of the Zemstvos and Towns, as well as with the business interests of the War Industries Committee. A freer society would permit its talent to rise to positions where the country as well as the individual would benefit. Russia would therefore maximise its own economic potential and so be less reliant on arms imports from Britain and the United States.

The dilemma which Britain's ambassador, Sir George Buchanan, and others in the Foreign Office increasingly recognised was that liberalisation in time of war might actually weaken the government, not reinforce it. Buchanan held up the coalition government formed by Asquith in May 1915 as a model for Russian emulation, but it was one thing for a constitutional government to suspend parliamentary practices on a temporary basis in time of war, another for an autocracy to travel in the opposite direction. Moreover, Buchanan's pleas were addressed to the tsar himself, and the effect may have weakened British influence rather than strengthened it. The tsar, although unfailingly polite, resented being told how to run his own country by a foreigner. In September 1915 he took the supreme command into his own hands, and was thereafter located at Stavka, the army's field headquarters, and not in Petrograd, where Buchanan was based. Meetings between the two became infrequent. Thereafter the two rarely met. The liberals themselves dealt directly with other Britons, like the intelligence chief, Sir Samuel Hoare, and the consul-general in Moscow, Robert Bruce Lockhart. By early 1917 Buchanan was under no illusions as to the probability of a coup: 'The only moot point', he later recalled, 'was whether it would come from above or below.'[23]

When the revolution did break out in March (or February in the Russian calendar), the British had little choice but to share the hopes of the Russian generals and of the War Industries Committee, that the tsar's abdication and the creation of a constituent assembly would enable Russia the better to fight the war. It was not a vision in which many in London believed. Lloyd George, now prime minister, feared: 'Russia is not sufficiently advanced for a republic.'[24]

The British sense of Russia's underlying strength was not located in the cities or their bourgeoisie, but in the land and its peasantry. One of the most popular novels of the war, even among British soldiers on the western front, was Hugh Walpole's *The Dark Forest*, published in 1916 and set in a Russian hospital unit on the Galician front during the 'great retreat' in 1915.[25] Walpole's hero is a somewhat dysfunctional English volunteer, Trenchard, who becomes engaged to a Russian nurse. She then breaks off the engagement, falls for a Russian and is killed in action. Trenchard too dies, but the narrator of the novel is able to quote from his diary:

The magnificence of the Russian soldier is surely beyond all praise. I wonder whether people in France and England realise that for the last three months here he has been fighting with one bullet as against ten. He stands in his trench practically unarmed against an enemy whose resources seem endless – but nothing can turn him back. Whatever advances the Germans may make I see Russia returning again and again. I do from the bottom of my soul, and, what is of more importance, from the sober witness of my eyes, here believe that nothing can stop the impetus born of her new spirit. This war is the beginning of a world history for her.[26]

Walpole worked on British propaganda in Russia.[27] He, like Stephen Graham and others who wrote about Russia for British readers during the war, made a hero of the Russian peasant. For all Walpole's evocation of the future, the qualities that he highlighted were not modern but traditional: the peasant was devout, loyal, childlike. In elevating him, British writers evaded the implicit tensions of the Anglo-Russian relationship. They deflected the British left from its worries about consorting with an autocracy, and they found Russia's strengths in areas that said nothing about the imperatives of social Darwinism. What the peasant was doing was defending his patrimony rather than advancing the claims of a coming great power. Within the context of the alliance, they avoided giving offence to either the tsar or his opponents. 'England and Russia! to their strong and confident union I thought I would give every drop of my blood, every beat of my heart,' Walpole had Trenchard write.[28] But that union as Walpole expressed it was essentially a holding operation, a set of circumstances where the options were limited, and which left Britain exposed when revolution changed the rules.

# 6

## Military Policy, International Relations and Soviet Security after October 1917

### ROBERT SERVICE

Among the tendencies in the historiography of the Soviet state in the decade after the October revolution were two which continue to affect the treatment of general topics to this day. The first was an emphasis on the naivety of the Bolshevik leadership at the moment it seized power in Petrograd. Sometimes acknowledgement was made that Lenin, Trotski and a few others had a 'realistic' view on some important matters; but most scholars chose to stress the lack of mental preparedness for the enormous tasks in hand to establish the new revolutionary order. The second tendency was less obvious but none the less influential. This was the growing wish of historians to compartmentalise aspects of the Soviet experience. 'Internal' policies became separated from 'external ones' – and indeed it became the conventional wisdom that, as Stalin and Bukharin strengthened their grip on power during the New Economic Policy, the objectives of internal economic development took overwhelming precedence over foreign-policy considerations. Moreover, much writing about the internal situation of the USSR was devoid of attention to not only foreign policy but even contemporary military and security questions.

It was one of the great merits of John Erickson's *The Soviet High Command* that he exposed the weakness of such an approach in the light of the documentary evidence. Cutting against the grain, he insisted that internal and external policies were constantly linked by a dynamic interaction in the interwar period. His main theme was the construction and development of the high command of the armed forces. But in treating this, he succeeded in showing that even in the 1920s, when Stalin was reputed to be barely interested in international relations (and to make blunders on the few occasions when he indeed became interested), the attentiveness of the Soviet political and military leadership to European questions was deep and persistent. Another point made by Erickson was that the engagements with these questions required an emphasis on 'professionalism' in the functioning of the state institutions, especially the Red Army. The conventional image of Soviet officials as mere automatons or ignoramuses was sturdily rejected. But at the same time Erickson did not overlook the impact of ideology; and the interplay of doctrine and changing circumstances was given due consideration in a work that retains its importance four decades after its first publication.[1]

The European project had lain at the centre of Bolshevism from its beginnings. 'Europe' supplied guiding principles for leading Bolsheviks to elaborate their assumptions, doctrines and policies. The Great War and the February 1917 revolution in Russia served to increase the significance of Europe for the Bolshevik leadership, and strategies for the inauguration of socialism continued to be premised upon 'Europe' not only after the 1918 treaty of Brest-Litovsk but also after the defeat of the Red Army in the Soviet–Polish War of 1920.

Europe's importance in Bolshevik thought and practice has never been a secret. Yet it has also been underrated. Among the reasons for this is that most early treatments of Bolshevism were directed at the Russian *narodnik* ideas in its composition, ideas that are usually interpreted as uniquely Russian and irredeemably hostile to the European versions of socialism. Not every treatment takes this approach. Indeed some emphasise that Bolshevism started as an essentially anti-*narodnik*, Marxist and – by extension – European set of doctrines; but even these treatments tend to postulate a steady dilution of the non-Russian ingredients in Bolshevism over the years. Revulsion at the German Social-Democratic Party's vote in favour of war credits in 1914 is sometimes taken as a cardinal moment for the Bolshevik leaders to turn their back on Europeanism. Still more crucial in other accounts were the setbacks of early Bolshevik foreign policy, especially the signature of the treaty of Brest-Litovsk in 1918. From this standpoint the Soviet invasion of Poland in summer 1920 seemed a temporary aberration, and the longer-term tendency in the orientation of the Bolshevik political leaders was towards the strategy formulated by Stalin: 'socialism in a single country'.

Such treatments of Bolshevism seriously crudify and downgrade the European dimension. Consequently they distort the history of Bolshevik revolutionary strategy before October 1917 and of Soviet foreign, security and military policy thereafter. They also over-pragmatise the internal discussions of the Soviet regime. Ideology, even if not entirely overlooked, is relegated to the background, and this has led to misconceptions about the foundations of the Bolshevik revolutionary project. Nor is ideology the sole casualty of such an approach. Another is the developing nexus of considerations about the USSR's lasting interests in relation to Europe. This nexus was informed by ideology but was also affected by historical experience of conditions in the countries to the west. Between pragmatism and ideology there lay complex interrelationships.

The Bolshevik project, as far back as Lenin's *What Is To Be Done?* in 1902, had been aimed at promoting Marxism in Europe as well as in Russia. Such was the legacy of Marx and Engels, who, as they considered the possibilities of socialism in Russia, retained an expectation of general revolutionary transformation in Europe. Lenin and his fellow Bolsheviks did not question the expectation; on the contrary, they loyally propagated it. Marxists in general took it for granted that countries with a higher level of industrial, educational and administrative performance would inaugurate the socialist order. Doctrinally and politically they associated themselves with fellow Marxists abroad, and their admiration for the German theoretician Karl Kautsky was second only to their feelings for Marx and Engels. Before the Great War they contributed to debates on the political and economic questions exercising the leaderships of socialist parties. They sent their representatives to congresses of the Second Socialist International and Lenin and other factional representatives served on the International Socialist Bureau through to 1914. Thus they endeavoured to contribute to a 'transition' to socialism in Europe.

For the Bolsheviks, the greatest thrust of this effort would be generated not in Russia but in 'Europe'. In Europe, they thought, there existed abundant preconditions for socialist revolution: advanced technology, popular literacy, mass organisation and mature capitalism. There was occasional recognition that not all the most 'modern' states were European. The economic progress made by the USA and Japan were acknowledged. Lenin even suggested that Marxists should hope for a Japanese victory in the Russo-Japanese War in 1904–1905 inasmuch as Japanese capitalism was more 'progressive' than its Russian adversary.² Yet strikingly more attention was given to European capitalism than to capitalism anywhere else. The Bolsheviks – like the Mensheviks – were revolutionary Eurocentricists. For them, what happened in Europe would have a uniquely colossal impact on global politics.

This is not all. When the leading Bolshevik theorists talked and wrote about Europe, they did not refer undifferentiatedly to all European countries. 'Europe' was for them a term describing primarily those countries they regarded as economically, politically and culturally more advanced than Russia. They hardly ever referred to Greece, Portugal and Spain – and did not visit them even for holidays. The exception to the pattern was Italy, where several Bolsheviks sometimes sojourned when the novelist Maxim Gorki opened his villa to them on Capri; but no Bolshevik published a substantial critique of contemporary Italy. To be sure, they had things to say about Austria (but not Hungary), England (but not Scotland or Wales and precious little about Ireland) and France. Yet the country that fascinated them above all others was Germany. In many ways, indeed, 'Europe' was their unconscious metaphor for Germany. They admired German technological brilliance, German administrative efficiency, German cultural and educational excellence; and this strongly positive feeling was reinforced by the fact that Marx, Engels, Kautsky and the SPD were German. Bolshevik theorists did not state all this in so many words. To have done so would have invited charges of vicarious nationalism. But the Germanophilia of Bolshevism was none the weaker for its being obliquely expressed.

This is baffling in a superficial sense. If they were entranced with Germany, why did the *émigré* Bolshevik leaders not choose to live there? For the great cities of the Bolshevik emigration were not Berlin, Stuttgart or – except briefly – Munich but Geneva and Paris. The problem for the Bolsheviks was partly a local political one. The official authorities in Germany, especially the police, were a little too eager to pry into the affairs of the Bolsheviks for any of them to feel very comfortable there. This was the reason why *Iskra* was transferred from Munich to London in 1902. In any case, residence in London, Paris and Geneva did not preclude Bolshevik leaders in emigration from keeping in close touch with German Marxism: the libraries in these three capitals were well stocked with German political literature and the international postal services in western and central Europe were quick and reliable.

The fascination with Germany was anyway not the product of the *émigré* experience but had preceded that experience by many years. An admiration for the path taken by Germany had been one of the primary motives inducing Bolsheviks in their youth to turn towards Marxism. Always, Russia was judged by the German yardstick and found wanting. Always, Russian socialist theorists were assessed as inferior to Marx, Engels and Kautsky.[3] This attitude had been common among the Russian Marxists in the 1880s and 1890s, who headed the Bolshevik faction in the years before and after the Great War. The attitude was so firmly in place that it resisted erosion by lengthy residence in Germany. For Bolsheviks, on emigrating from Russia, tended to live in what virtually were Russian cantonments; they were not noted for their openness to close collaboration with the societies in which they came to reside. In Geneva, Paris and London they tried to keep together in the little districts where the libraries were nearby and where they could also set up newspapers, offices and occasionally even cafeterias. Their wish for solidarity among Bolshevik emigrants was stronger than their keenness to explore the host country.

Consequently Bolshevik attitudes to Germany were not based on sustained direct scrutiny of Germany, its socialists and its working class.

This was evident in diverse ways. The most obvious was displayed by Lenin in his attitude to Kautsky. Repeatedly Lenin was alerted to aspects of Kautsky's thought at variance with Bolshevik ideas – and the alarms were raised by Rosa Luxemburg and other persons acquainted with both men.[4] But until the outbreak of the Great War, Lenin was deaf to Luxemburg's words of admonition. Furthermore, there was a growing number of books before the war on the rather un-internationalist features of the policies and membership of the German Social-Democratic Party (SPD). Some writers who later became Bolsheviks (such as Karl Radek) contributed to this literature.[5] Bolsheviks before 1914, however, did not. The general Bolshevik approach to German socialism was resoundingly positive.

Things changed in 1914. From then it became *de rigueur* for Bolsheviks to condemn the SPD as well as those elements on its edge, such as Kautsky's Independents, who refused to condemn the SPD's support for the German war effort in completely unambiguous terms. The Bolsheviks sought other political allies in Europe even though Lenin was not pleased even with the fellow European far-left socialists who attended the Zimmerwald and Kienthal conferences.

While re-aligning themselves politically, Bolsheviks were not claiming to offer a new vision. They saw themselves as campaigning for the achievement of the old European socialist vision and the charge laid by Lenin and his associates was that the Second International had been betrayed by the SPD whereas Bolshevism had stayed loyal. Bolshevik writers attempted to explain why this had happened. Zinoviev picked up the theme already developed by Radek: namely that German industrial expansion led to the emergence of a 'labour aristocracy' – and a party officialdom that was linked to it – with a material interest in supporting the national objectives set by the German imperial government.[6] A theoretical exploration of the framework of 'imperialism as the highest stage of capitalism' was undertaken by Lenin.[7] And from this period of reconsideration came the project of Lenin and Nikolai Bukharin to reformulate their concepts of the kind of socialist state to be established after any socialist seizure of power. Such concepts informed the revolutionary strategy and policies pursued by the Bolsheviks between the February and October revolutions of 1917.[8]

Yet the focus of Bolshevik intentions was held on Europe and on Germany's significance in Europe. There was obviously no answer to the problem of 'imperialism' without an all-European political reconstruction. Debate was engaged about slogans. Lenin went out on a limb – to the horror of his dwindling band of followers – by advocating the need for a 'European Civil War'.[9] Less notoriously Lenin and Bukharin declared themselves in favour of a United States of

Europe as the alternative to the existing inter-capitalist rivalries across the continent.[10] Yet even about this there was much disquiet among Bolsheviks. Rosa Luxemburg had put it about that if the politics of Europe remained the priority for Marxists, the result would be the neglect of the colonial countries in Africa and Asia. She warned that a United States of Europe might become a supra-imperialist power in its own right.[11] Lenin was sufficiently intimidated by this argument and quietly abandoned the slogan. (No doubt the fact that his rival Lev Trotski supported the slogan was another reason why he changed his stance.)

Nonetheless the debate was started from the premise that Germany needed to have a socialist revolution. From 1914 the Bolsheviks maintained that all the advanced industrial countries were 'ripe' for revolution, and in 1917 this was a prominent clause in the Bolshevik political credo. By then it constituted a point of division between most Bolsheviks and most Mensheviks. Bolsheviks claimed that the industrial strikes and the mutinies in Europe signalled the general revolutionary explosiveness. Mensheviks counter-claimed that such phenomena were not proof of a European revolution in the making; their argument instead was that the predominant mood of discontented workers, soldiers and sailors was one of war-weariness.[12]

So the Bolsheviks justified their seizure of power in Petrograd as being part of an all-European project. Bolshevism in Lenin's lifetime contended that a Russian socialist revolution could not permanently or fully succeed unless followed by revolutions in other capitalist countries. This was why controversy occurred in the mid-1920s when Stalin suggested that socialism could be completely constructed in 'a single country'. A second fundamental element of Bolshevik thought before 1917 was equally important initially after the October revolution. This was the notion that if the Bolsheviks could make a revolution in Russia, it would be easier by far for German far-left socialists to make one in Germany. As yet there was no talk about Russia as being the 'weak link' in the European chain of imperialism. Lenin rationalised his optimism by reference to the food shortages that were beginning to affect the major cities of Germany;[13] and he continued to believe that the German working class was more 'cultured' than the Russian. If the revolution was smooth in Russia, supposedly it would be smoother still in Germany. Mensheviks castigated this analysis as irresponsibly casual, but most Bolsheviks were unpersuadable. Only a few of them, notably Kamenev, Zinoviev and Stalin in 1917–18, felt uneasy.

Thus a European revolutionary policy centred on Germany was maintained by the Bolshevik Party. The party leaders felt they had grounds for sustained optimism. Revolutions, they suggested, could be made by 'the masses' so long as at least a handful of determined, insightful revolutionaries were present. The SPD's grip on the sympathies of German workers could be broken, and abruptly broken at that. It would not matter that few left-wing socialists in Germany were unconditionally hostile to the German war effort. After all, there had not been many Bolsheviks in operation before 1917, and yet the Bolshevik Party had led a socialist seizure of power. Bolsheviks pinned their hopes on Karl Liebknecht becoming the German Lenin.

At the same time an increasingly explicit Russian flavouring was being inserted into the pot. Russians were providing the party-political model to German socialism. But they did this on the assumption that the rest could be left to the German socialists. After seizing power, they would issue decrees in favour of a new international politics without secret diplomacy; their prognosis was that news of the Bolshevik-led socialist government in Russia would immediately provoke revolutionary discontent elsewhere. If this did not happen, the Bolsheviks would make it happen by employing peace negotiations with the Central Powers as an instrument of publicity; and if all else failed, a revolutionary war would have to carry the socialist revolution across Europe. There was no specification as to military method, but the Bolsheviks did not anticipate that it would involve a static, drawn-out conflict like the 'imperialist war' currently raging. The emphasis would be on the political component of warfare. It was postulated that European capitalism would not need to be brought down by armies alone. Europe was deemed to be 'pregnant', 'ripe', 'seething' with revolution.

The willingness of the Central Powers to carry out their threat to invade Russia was a terrible setback, and the treaty of Brest-Litovsk was signed in March 1918. Conventionally the treaty is regarded as a rupture with the approach to international relations undertaken by Sovnarkom. At the level of policy it obviously was. There was a virtual alliance of the Soviet and German governments in spring and summer 1918, to the point that Lenin was willing to use German military power to defend against a British expeditionary force in northern Russia. The alliance, moreover, was not one of equal partners. When Count von Mirbach was assassinated in July 1918, Sovnarkom had to prostrate itself politically before the German authorities. Fear of a German invasion remained acute until the Allies on the western front in the First World War started to put decisive pressure on the Germans in August 1918.

But while policy changed, attitudes and assumptions did not. The Bolsheviks continued to rest their hopes on revolution in Europe, especially in Germany itself. Soviet agrarian, military and foreign policy was premised on the need to prepare Russia to give assistance to a socialist regime in Berlin. The requisition squads sent out to the countryside in summer 1918 were building up food supplies not only for the hungry cities of Russia but also for potential dispatch to Germany when the expected revolution took place there.[14] Furthermore, the huge expansion of conscription to the Red Army was carried out largely so that, when the time came, decisive military aid might be proffered.[15] Thus the Bolshevik Party leadership quietly used the cover of the Brest-Litovsk treaty to continue the approach in international relations in the October 1917 revolution. The policy of a tacit alliance with the kaiser's Germany was tactical and provisional. How could it have been otherwise? Lenin, the campaigner for the Soviet regime's acceptance of the separate peace, was not so foolish as to believe that Wilhelm II would leave him in power if imperial Germany were to win the war in the west. On both sides, the tacit alliance was but a distasteful expedient.

The German military collapse on the western front in November 1918 seemed at last to afford Lenin his pan-European opportunity. Diplomatic support was offered to Berlin from Moscow.[16] Efforts were also put in hand to organise a founding conference of a Third International with the purpose of promoting revolution across Europe. Soviet regimes were established in Estonia, Latvia, Lithuania and Belorussia to spread the revolutionary frontiers westwards; and although this was done with 'native' Bolshevik forces, crucial military assistance was also forthcoming from Moscow.

Revolutionary socialism, however, quickly suffered defeat. The Spartakist rising under Karl Liebknecht, Rosa Luxemburg and Leo Jogiches was crushed and the three leaders were brutally killed. Although Soviet republics were created in Bavaria and Hungary, they were liquidated by counter-revolutionary forces. Sovnarkom in Moscow did what it could to maintain them in power.[17] But Soviet assistance could not at that time be very substantial since Kolchak and Denikin had yet to be defeated. If the Russian theatre of the civil war in the former Russian Empire had been brought more quickly to its final act, there might have been a different outcome in central Europe. The Red Army would have been dispatched to the rescue of Béla Kun in Hungary. Perhaps the result would have been the same as in Poland in summer 1920 and the Reds would have been defeated in central Europe. But the point here is that the Soviet government was still committed to its supreme priority of facilitating revolution in Europe. The hope of hopes was for that revolution to take place in Germany. But it was assumed that revolution practically anywhere was a worthwhile cause to fight for and that 'European socialist revolution' would eventually ensue.

Thus the Bolshevik central leadership continued to look for signs that such a revolution was 'ripening'. In 1919–20 there were evident possibilities that the Czech Republic and northern Italy might become Soviet-style states. There was even a suggestion that revolution was on the boil in Britain. At the First Congress of the Communist International it was announced that factory workers in the Midlands had formed a Birmingham Soviet. Revolution was expected by Bolsheviks in the United Kingdom.[18] It is possible that Lenin knew that this information was of dubious credibility and that he was using it as a means of putting political pressure on Hugo Eberlein and German delegates at the congress; but the general sentiment about the imminence of European socialist revolution was sincere.

This was the sentiment impelling Lenin in summer 1920 to get the Politburo to order the Red Army, which had been embroiled in border conflicts with Poland since 1918, to chase Piłsudski back to Warsaw, sovietise Poland and move into Germany. Poland would be the bridge to the European socialist revolution. The result was a disaster for the Red Army, and an alteration was hurriedly made to both immediate policy and medium-term assumptions. In the foreseeable future, Lenin asserted, there should be no attempt to export revolution on the point of a bayonet. This was an important turn in Bolshevik policy. Whereas Lenin had gone on preparing for revolutionary war in Europe for the duration of the treaty of Brest-Litovsk, he proceeded in 1921 to cut back the size of the Red Army. The reversal of policy lasted several years. The Anglo-Soviet treaty of March 1921 strengthened this trend whereby the Soviet government aimed to avoid giving offence to one of the continent's two great powers of the period, and this involved a suspension of revolutionary activity in regions where Britain's vital interests were at stake.

Yet the change of policy was not a definitive rupture. The disarray in the Politburo was such that the newly created German Communist Party, prodded by Béla Kun, attempted a rising in Berlin in March 1921. Almost certainly Zinoviev was also involved in instigating the action:[19] the need to spread the revolution westwards was being felt even by a Bolshevik Politburo member who was in close support of Lenin's New Economic Policy. Unfortunately for Kun and Zinoviev, the March action was botched. Lenin was infuriated that the whole business, which could have undone every diplomatic gain he had made with Poland and Britain in recent months, had been undertaken behind his back.

Immediately he argued that the Bolshevik party should accept that Soviet strategy abroad had to be much more restricted, and at the Tenth Party Conference in May 1921 he denounced foreign adventurism of the type favoured by Kun. It is usually supposed that his intervention did the trick. But events were not so straightforward as this; for when Lenin lay mortally ill in November 1923, another attempt at revolution in Berlin was ordered from the Comintern headquarters in Russia. Yet again the initiative lay with Zinoviev,[20] and again the result was fiasco. Only then was the endeavour to manufacture European socialist revolution from Moscow laid to rest for some years as active state policy. Even then, however, the basic assumptions about the needs of the revolution in Russia did not change altogether. When Stalin delivered his lectures on the feasibility of 'socialism in a single country', his words were criticised by the party's left wing and did not become official policy for the duration of the New Economic Policy. It remained a Bolshevik axiom that the Russian socialist revolution could not come to maturity unless counterparted by revolutions abroad, especially in Germany.

Yet it would be wrong to give the impression that Bolshevik foreign policy underwent no change; in fact there were discontinuities of massive importance. The Brest-Litovsk treaty was a massive early precedent in 1918. Soviet overtures to the Allies took place in the following year, and diplomatic negotiations with Sweden and other Scandinavian countries were undertaken as a means of breaking up the 'capitalist encirclement' of Russia. Even while the Red Army was invading Poland, Lev Kamenev was on a mission to Britain in pursuit of a diplomatic *rapprochement*.[21] In March 1921 an Anglo-Soviet trade treaty was signed. In some accounts these events have been seen as a conscious attempt by Lenin steadily to give increasing weight to 'pragmatic' factors in Soviet foreign policy. A more appropriate interpretation would be that Lenin was attempting to gain clever, temporary advantage from his manoeuvres while still being focused on the main prize: the sovietisation of Germany. Thus the balance of the ingredients remained tipped in favour of the foreign-policy objectives set by the party when it seized power in 1917.

Here it becomes obvious that adjectives such as 'ideological' and 'pragmatic' are inadequate when treated as mutually exclusive. Viewed from the Bolshevik standpoint on the October revolution and the civil war, the need to promote revolution abroad and thereby (anticipatedly) relieve the threat of external military intervention did not stem exclusively from ideological prejudices; it came, too, from a pragmatic acknowledgement that the Soviet state would be a potential prey for the European great powers until fraternal republics could be established elsewhere. Sooner or later the Bolsheviks had to acquire friends in power to the west if they wished to feel more secure.

Despite the interpenetration of adjectives, though, ideological compromises undeniably took place from the treaty of Brest-Litovsk onwards. Indeed even the Decree on Peace on 26 October contained a dilution of previous Bolshevik language. From Brest-Litovsk through to the Anglo-Soviet trade treaty and the treaty of Rapallo there were turnabouts that no Bolshevik before the October revolution had predicted. The significance of these compromises was not unambiguous. The Bolshevik central leadership, while using the various international treaties as a means of shielding the Soviet state from a crusade by the great powers, saw them also as an unplanned means of pursuing the previous goal of modernising society. Bolshevism had always had the objective of transforming Russia's economy and culture; and although the priority for Sovnarkom was to do this mainly by means of domestic resources, there remained a strong assumption that foreign assistance was also required. Assistance was sought, above all, from Germany. In this fashion the German orientation survived the attrition of the specifically Marxist ingredient from Bolshevik foreign-policy planning.

Throughout the months between the Brest-Litovsk treaty and the Armistice on the western front Lenin insisted that the Soviet government and Bolshevik party should seek and seal an economic deal with German industrial capitalism.[22] His reasoning was that German capital and expertise offered a quick route to Russia's regeneration. In making this remarkable – and until recently overlooked – argument he was urging Bolsheviks to accept that since they were currently incapable of sparking off a socialist revolution in Germany and securing a fraternal exchange of Russian grain for German machinery, then the machinery had to be obtained from a non-socialist German source: German capitalism. This was not a controversial policy in the upper levels of the government even though Sovnarkom had passed it, and the policy fell into abeyance because the kaiser abdicated in November 1918 and for a while the prospects of a German socialist revolution again seemed bright. But it is a sign that the German preoccupation with Bolshevism was strong enough, especially in Lenin's case, to be sustained even without its socialist ingredient.

This preoccupation recurred also in a political guise. When the Red Army stormed into Poland in summer 1920, Lenin foresaw that his forces would be too weak to instigate a socialist revolution in Germany without armed support from non-socialists as well as far-left socialists. He urged German communists to make overtures to the German far right.[23] The proposal was that a war of national liberation should be undertaken by this unlikely alliance with the purpose of smashing the treaty of Versailles. Lenin had no illusion about the longevity of the alliance if its members were to succeed in freeing Germany from control by France and the United Kingdom; but he had faith that the communists would proceed in turn to crush the far right in any conflict.[24] The result would be the creation of a union of Soviet republics across eastern and central Europe. Once Germany was 'sovietised', the rest of the European countries would tumble into line. The principal question that would then arise would be how to integrate Germany into the union. For

Lenin, the question was no problem. Germany, like Russia, would be a constituent republic of the union; this had been his expectation since the beginning of the Great War and remained so.

Lenin's discussant was Stalin, who had always given a less optimistic prognosis of a German socialist revolution. But this was not what divided them in their confidential debate in summer 1920. Against Lenin, Stalin judged that Germany – even a German Soviet republic – would feel uncomfortable in a union founded by Russia and extended into Germany. He therefore proposed that revolutionary Germany should stay separate from Russia. So, too, should Poland.[25] Essentially Stalin had concluded that national traditions could not lightly be flouted and that not all European countries could be treated like Ukraine in its relations with the RSFSR (Russian Soviet Federal Socialist Republic). Lenin and Stalin nonetheless agreed that the German question had somehow or other to be solved and that this was crucial for the furtherance of European socialist revolution.

Lenin resumed his preoccupation of 1918 even before the Red Army's defeat before Warsaw: namely, the attraction of foreign capitalism into the Soviet republics. As before, his assumption was that advanced capitalist techniques and culture as well as industrial capital itself were vital for the country's regeneration. The scale of his fascination with Europe, especially Germany, was highly controversial among Bolsheviks and therefore deliberately veiled somewhat from the general public. It was urgent, he asserted, to get the Nobel Company back into the oil industry in the south of the country. The fact that Azerbaijan had practically no advanced industry apart from the petrochemical plants of Baku and that the return of the Nobels would amount virtually to a re-imposition of capitalism on Azerbaijan's entire economy did not concern him. The goal was economic regeneration, and he was willing to incur the rage of Bolshevik critics working in Azerbaijan from Anastas Mikoyan downwards if this was what it was going to take.[26] Nor should it be forgotten that this scheme, which was in fact still-born, was conceived not in the course of the New Economic Policy but while War Communism was still in operation. The economic Europeanisation of Russia remained a major state priority – and on this Lenin had the rest of the Politburo with him.

The extent to which he was willing to go was truly remarkable. He seriously proposed inviting German businesses to tender for contracts to take over large farms in the River Don area.[27] Rapid agricultural reconstruction, he thought, would occur only if he could secure European participation. That such a project would prove dangerously obnoxious to the peasants of the region to whom he had promised the freedom to arrange agrarian affairs as they liked in his October 1917 Land Decree did not bother him. Nor did he worry that he might undermine any affections for him among the non-Russian groups in the area. The Soviet state, he stressed, lacked the material and cultural resources to accomplish things fast enough on her own. And so German private farmer-entrepreneurs were the sole way to achieve this aim.

He also sent People's Commissar for External Affairs Georgi Chicherin to Italy in 1922 in quest of a separate diplomatic deal with Germany. The Soviet authorities had no particular confidence in a multilateral settlement of the painful questions of Europe, and their hope was that the comparative economic stabilisation would not long endure. Germany, Lenin declared, had been reduced to colonial status and the treaty of Versailles could not last. In the interim it was sensible for Soviet Russia to seek common cause with Germany by signing the Rapallo treaty to induce closer commercial relations between the two countries. Moves were set up, too, to enable the Wehrmacht to hold exercises and test military equipment secretly on Soviet soil on the calculation that the Red Army could benefit from the collaboration.[28] Other Western countries were important for the Politburo before and after Lenin's death. The United Kingdom in particular was a country not to be recklessly annoyed; and closer relations with Mussolini's Italy, too, were warmly fostered. Yet the Soviet–German relationship was cardinal and served practical strategic interests of a political, economic and military nature.

To be sure, there had been a Russifying trend in Bolshevik doctrines and policies in the years after the October 1917 revolution. Increasing pride was expressed in the Russian revolutionary experiment. Russian workers had done things attempted unsuccessfully by German workers. Russian Marxists had made a revolution whereas their German comrades had not. Russia, unlike Germany, had not been conquered.

Yet Germany remained at the core of Bolshevism; and it is this aspect of Bolshevik attitudes and behaviour that needs to be highlighted. For Lenin in 1914, the defeat of tsarism had been a thousand times more to be welcomed than the defeat of kaiserism. Germany was regarded – even the kaiser's Germany in the Great War – as being essentially a cultured country. There was also among Bolsheviks a considerable admiration for the state's ability to co-ordinate the economy. The features of the German wartime administration commended themselves at least to Lenin as the basis for the kind of 'state capitalism' that he wanted to introduce, albeit in the service of a regime whose ultimate objective was the introduction of socialism, when he and his party seized power in October 1917.[29] There was much about central Europe that Lenin never ceased to admire. Famously in *The State and Revolution* he adduced the Swiss postal services as an organisational model for the construction of a socialist order.[30] By this he was referring to the *kul 'turnost'* of administrative reliability, of registration and supervision (*uchët i kontrol'*), of well-expedited management. And he never failed to identify this with his image of European achievements.

This fateful identification had been born of the selective image held by the leading early Bolsheviks about socialism in Germany and about the economy and culture from which this socialism had arisen. It survived even the self-criticism offered by the SPD's internal critics; and the Great War, too, failed to shatter the powerful image and paradigm of German socialism from Bolshevism. The commitment to material, cultural and even – to a certain extent – political transfer of German resources to Russia endured long after the confidence in the rapid arrival of the European socialist revolution had faded.

It would be wrong to suggest that the Bolsheviks stayed exclusively fixated by their European orientation. Undoubtedly they hoped to raise the peoples of the colonial countries against the great powers, and the Congress of Peoples of the East in 1920 was the embodiment of this. As the problems with the promotion of revolution in Europe deepened, both Lenin and Trotski in the mid-1920s looked for national-liberation movements especially in Asia to start the break-up of European imperialism. China became a preoccupation at the end of the decade. Furthermore, the importance of America started to impose itself upon the Bolshevik mind. Jenö Varga produced an influential economic analysis of the results of the Great War, and the industrial achievements of 'Fordism' in the USA began to be appreciated. So, too, did the ideas of the time-and-motion specialist F. W. Taylor. The shift away from Eurocentric communism was under way and was strengthened in the 1930s, and by the end of the 1940s the USA had taken Europe's place in Soviet communist attitudes – and Germany had become a defeated and divided former power. Although the Bolsheviks had always paid attention to the world outside Europe before the Great War, after 1917 they increased the account they took of it.

Yet the preoccupation with Europe persisted in the first decade of 'Soviet power'. Europeanism was accompanied by Americanism and even by Orientalism, but Europe in the image of Germany retained its superior fascination. Doing something about Europe remained the primary object of Soviet foreign policy.

Consequently the Bolshevik central leadership looked at Germany and went on hoping. They felt that even though the street politics of 1919 had faded, the severity of the treaty of Versailles would continue to agitate Germans and limit economic regeneration. They delightedly concluded that the peace imposed by the Allies would do their revolutionary work for them. Stalin had constantly had his doubts about the immediate prospects of German socialist revolution, and expressed them in Central Committee discussions in 1917–18. But even he, according to at least some sources, assumed that Versailles would facilitate communist politics. Reportedly this is what he said to German communist leaders who questioned his instruction to them in 1932 to regard the social-democrats rather than the Nazis as their main adversary. Stalin's reply was that it would little matter if the Nazis came to power. The Nazis were enemies of Versailles and would destabilise European politics – and in the not-so-long run the Comintern would benefit. The European socialist revolution would eventually become reality.[31]

Here the old Bolshevik conception of Germany was being exhibited. The USSR had lived with Italian fascism and come to an accommodation commercially and diplomatically. Why could it not do the same if Hitler survived in power? Moreover, was not Germany with its advanced industry, its science and technology and its educational system a 'cultured' country? It is common to blame Stalin for his selective vision, for his blunders and for his unsophisticated handling of European affairs in the 1930s. Yet as in so many other ways, he was following the precepts of his teacher. Many factors explain the path to the Second World War. One that has been neglected is the Bolshevik tradition in ideology and practical security planning, a tradition that fitted a very particular pair of distorting spectacles on the nose of the party leadership. The frequent consequence was that Europe, especially Germany, had been seen imperfectly.

It would be unconvincing to highlight the theme of Germany in Europe to the exclusion of everything else in the history of the first years of the USSR. The Soviet communist revolution's vicissitudes involved a lot more than just the ideological hangover from the pre-1914 Bolshevism or the strategic calculations of 1917–18. The effects of the Great War and the civil war; the economic ruination; the administrative and social dislocation; the establishment of a one-party, one-ideology state; the existence of the USSR as a solitary communist state; the internal organisation of the party; the peculiar national, religious and cultural legacy of the Russian Empire – and indeed the turbulent and unpredictable flow of events from 1917: all these had a huge effect upon Bolshevik politics. But so, too, did that pre-war ideology and those post-October doctrines. Ideas, once a prominent topic for research, have widely lost their interest in recent years. This is a pity. Indubitably ideology has to be analysed with caution, and the unscrambling has to involve not only textual excerpts but also attitudes and assumptions. The European theme in Bolshevik ideas repays attention: its hold on the imagination of the party leadership conditioned the way that the Bolsheviks formulated their intentions in world affairs in the 1920s – and they could not get Germany out of their head.

Unfortunately for the USSR their objective of exploiting the perceived superiority of the German partner proved illusory. In 1941 Hitler ordered Operation Barbarossa and the Wehrmacht exploited its Soviet conquests with ruthless efficiency. Only in 1945 were the roles reversed. But by then not even Stalin saw his German policy as the main key to the USSR's survival as a world power. The world was turning on an axis of the USSR and the USA.

# 7

## *Turkey in the Russian Mirror*

NORMAN STONE

In 1957, talking to the Central Committee, Khrushchev had an outburst against Stalin's foreign policies. He had even managed to make an enemy of Turkey – Turkey, he said, where, in the 1930s, there had been a square in Izmir named after Voroshilov.[1] Relations between republican Turkey and the Soviet Union had been close, and sometimes very close indeed, the word 'comrade' (*yoldas*) being much used. They existed on various levels. The two sides had been in alliance during the Turkish War of Independence. They had come in contact in the Caucasus in 1919, and although communications between Ankara and Moscow, at the time, could take three months, they seem to have understood each other very well. In Kars museum, the train used by General Kazim Karabekir is preserved, and has proletarian slogans plastered on it, in an illiterate combination of Russian and Turkish. Lenin had worked out that 'anti-imperialism' would make for alliance between the Russian working class and people who, though 'bourgeois', nevertheless also suffered from Western capitalists' doings, and he thought Turkey could be useful as far as other Muslim countries were concerned. Bolshevik gold and weaponry contributed a great deal to the Turkish nationalists' success against the French in 1920 (in Cilicia) and, later on, a bargain was struck. The nationalists in effect renounced any plans for 'Greater Turkey', and the Bolsheviks retroceded once-Turkish territory in eastern Anatolia. The nationalists at the time referred to themselves as revolutionaries, and called ministers 'commissars'.[2] There was even 'revolutionary porcelain', as in Russia, and an Ataturk statue is as ubiquitous in Turkey as a Lenin one in Russia.

To some extent they had the same aim: 'Progress'. Ataturk's wife, Latife, had corresponded with the sister of Lunacharsky, commissar for education: progressive ladies together, thinking how you made peasants literate if they spoke a Turkic language that until then had only been written in a very unsuitable Arabic script.[3] In fact, the first instance this writer has ever seen of Latinised Turkish is a dedication of a photograph of Ataturk to the then Soviet diplomatic representative Aralov, in Ankara in 1924 (it is on display in the Russian embassy). There were

Soviet presentations of armaments, at knock-down prices, and in the early 1930s Soviet experts helped set up a textile factory at Kayseri, with a gold loan of 8,000,000 roubles. The oddest outcome of this period of close collaboration was the exile of Trotsky on an island of the Sea of Marmara for four years after his expulsion from the Soviet Union in February 1929. Stalin, then, could not have killed Trotsky, as would no doubt have happened later on; he could not keep him in the USSR with the great travails of collectivisation and the Five Year Plan coming up; very few foreign governments would have taken Trotsky (who found refuge in Mexico only by a fluke of fate). Comparative isolation on Buyuk Ada (Prinkipo, in Greek) was the answer. We do not know the Turkish side of the story. We do, however, know from the Soviet archives that Trotsky's correspondence landed on Stalin's desk, and this can only have been by arrangement with Turkish Intelligence.[4] After 1945 Stalin upset all this, said Khrushchev – demanding a base at the Dardanelles, and a return of the districts of north-eastern Turkey that Lenin had renounced. Stalin had also occupied (mainly Azeri) northern Iran until 1946. Turkey took Marshall aid, and joined NATO. American missiles were stationed there.

Khrushchev was right to object. True, Turkey and Russia had historically been enemies, but there was a great deal in common, and there was much room for co-operation, to which this essay will be devoted. Its title has a certain resonance. In 1970, Alexander Gerschenkron published a set of lectures, *Europe in the Russian Mirror*, that he had given at Cambridge.[5] He said (not, at that time and place, fashionably) that tsarist Russia had followed a continental European method of industrialisation, not a British one; that Germany, with protection and even a degree of state planning, had been the model, and that it had, by 1914, been quite successful. At the time, the dominant opinion in Cambridge was not on his side: Maurice Dobb was not long dead, and E. H. Carr was present – the fourth of Gerschenkron's lectures attacked him. Nowadays, it is Carr, with his Stalinism, who is out of favour and few people would nowadays bother to question the idea that tsarist Russia in 1914 had a go-ahead economy. Still, something clearly went off the European track: what? And there is a Eurasian parallel, or tangent, to Russian history that might, with profit, be considered. For it is not just *Europe in the Russian Mirror*. There is an interesting set of lectures to be done on *Europe in the Turkish Mirror* – the way in which European lessons were used in the country which has, it is this essay's intention to show, many unfamiliar parallels with Russia. After 1922, Kemal Ataturk and his associates started a concentrated process of Westernisation, doing in a generation what the Russians had in effect been doing for two and a half centuries, perhaps even more, if you consider that when Ivan the Terrible took Kazan from the Tatars in 1552 he used Italian gunnery experts.

For a long time, no comparison between Russia and Turkey would
have been thought at all interesting (though Marx learned Turkish, and
was learning Russian when he died in 1883.[6] Russian nationalists defined
themselves by the war on Turkey and took their model as Germany.
Turks also regarded Russia as the great enemy to the north, and millions
of refugees poured into Anatolia from the Balkans, the Caucasus, the
Crimea, as the Russians advanced.[7] In the later nineteenth century,
Sultan Abdul Hamit II was driven towards some sort of official
nationalism in reaction to this, though in an empire made up of so
many different elements, the best he could do was to make it Islamic
(certainly not Turkish nationalist) in character. Over the past two or
three generations, with Turkey as part of NATO, the Soviet Union
counted as the great enemy, and there is still considerable sympathy for
Muslim breakaway elements.[8] The comparison of Russia and Turkey
may therefore seem to both sides an unfruitful proposition.

This essay will argue differently: that Turkey and Russia have far
more in common than either might recognise. There is some novelty
involved, which affects the sources: there are books which, in various
languages, consider 'the Eastern Question', but there is nothing comparable with the longer-term studies of relations between, say, Great
Britain and Germany and much of this present picture has to be
assembled from various, often apparently quite unrelated, places. At any
rate, one obstacle to comparison has been overcome. Turkey since 1923
has made much economic progress, and, despite alarms, continues to
do so. Back in 1923 Ataturk made a famous speech in Izmir, saying
that economic liberation must mean learning from the West – fair
enough, when you remember that, back then, it was advisable to use
an Armenian carpenter, because Turks often did not know how to
prevent wood from warping and tables wobbling. Nowadays, Turkey
wins prizes for aircraft, has a foreign trade two-thirds of Russia's,
and, with great regional variations, has an overall standard of living
some way ahead of Russia's, the average age on death of a male
being not far from seventy. However, this essay is not meant to
deal with topicalities – oil and gas, the strategic position, trade,
disagreements over this or that nationality issue in the Caucasus or
eastern Anatolia. We should look beyond them, and consider what
John Erickson called the great winds of history going over the Caucasus
between the two countries. In fact, as Russia redefines herself in
national terms, she might look at Turkey with some interest, for here
is a prime example of a nation that made itself out of the ruins of an
empire.

Times have changed, and there has been a considerable volume of
co-operation: trade and investment. It remains true that translations of

Russian theatre and literature are prominent in Turkey's cultural life;[9] but study of Russian became identified with the left, and it is only latterly that an effort can seriously be made to launch Russian studies in a properly academic spirit.[10] For some reason, Turkish businessmen seem to have thrived in Russia, not even losing significantly in the crash of 1998. Mayor Luzhkov says that he likes dealing with Turkish construction companies – they built the headquarters of Gazprom and reconstructed the White House itself after 1993 – because, unlike Americans, they do not appear with platoons of lawyers. The business mentality seems to appeal. Why? It is here that we might consider the larger picture and here, as the determinant of character, that history matters.

There are some interesting parallels, worth exploring in detail. Both countries lie at a tangent to the Latin West, and 'Westernisation' is *the* great theme in both. Peter the Great and Kemal Ataturk, two centuries apart, are the outstanding figures, Ataturk nowadays with a symbolical importance transcending Turkey's boundaries (why did Turkey succeed, and Iran fail?).[11] Westernisation implies an inferiority complex: a country incapable of producing its own formula, and having to remake itself in depth, Germans well to the fore (Peter the Great's Academy of Sciences, under Leibniz, used their language, and when Ataturk refounded Istanbul University in 1932, he recruited Germans, headed by Einstein).[12] Here, there is especial tension concerning religion, deprived of anything beyond a state-dictated public role. Peter got rid of the patriarch, substituting, in effect, himself. Ataturk dethroned the Ottoman caliph, and though (contrary to legend) he did not knock down mosques or denounce Islam in public, there was no doubt that he regarded it as an obstacle to Progress (and is recorded, at least in private, as complaining that the sayings of a Beduin should dictate even the most minute doings of people a millennium and a half later).[13] The challenge to popular ways was vast, and it required harshness, or at any rate authoritarian methods of enlightenment. It also provoked a reaction, in that people on the religious side, Orthodox or Muslim, claimed that the harshness was unnecessary, that society was producing its own pressures for progress, that 'the predecessors of Peter the Great' were worthy of attention, that Turkish modernisation was proceeding well before 1914, with the 'Union and Progress' (*Ittihad ve Terakki*) nationalists who took over from Abdul Hamit II in 1908–9. 'Politics, Economics, Islam – choose two,' says a young Turkish historian of Central Asia, H. A. Karasar, but you could have much the same argument over Orthodoxy. Why was there no equivalent of Catholic-dominated *Solidarnosc* in the Soviet Union? This is not an up-to-date, modern argument at all: it really goes back to the eleventh century, when the differences between Latin and Orthodox became unbridgeable. In the Fourth Crusade, when, in 1204, the Venetians and their Germanic mercenaries sacked Constantinople, the Byzantines wondered why these savages were so proficient when it came to technology. The Venetians could build siege towers wrapped in leather, soaked with some mysterious chemical that resisted Greek Fire, an inextinguishable compound that had saved Constantinople several times in the past because it burned the besiegers' ships.[14] Byzantium never really recovered, though its soul went marching on in Muscovy. For well over a century now, good Muslims have been asking themselves why the secular West is so far ahead in technology: an early Turkish nationalist, the administrator-poet Ziya Pasha, wrote:

> *Diyar-i kufru gezdim beldeler kasaneler*
> *Dolastim mulki Islami butun viraneler gordum*

(roughly 'As I go around, I see that Christianity is palaces and Islam equals ruins'). Is there something in the past, nevertheless, to restore religious confidence in this respect?[15]

The troubles of identity in each country have resulted in a curious parallel debate – in Russia, as to the Tatar past, in Turkey, as to the Byzantine. Of course, each in a sense defined itself by the long battle against the religious or ethnic opponent, Mongol and Islamic, Greek and Christian. The debates are related, because it is legitimate to put Turkey into the central Asian and Tatar context[16] and it is also legitimate to put Russia into the Orthodox, Byzantine one. But we can examine this rather more closely. Be it said, incidentally, that there is nothing unusual or unhealthy about these debates. One or two generations ago it was quite standard in England for historians to be asking whether the country was at bottom Anglo-Saxon, i.e. parliamentarian, and what the role of the Normans had really been.[17] Such debates can become very complicated, and push historians into a prodigious amount of difficult work – examining, for instance, old legal documents – not necessarily a national-neurotic business at all, though when religion enters the picture battles may result.

What Russia owed to the Vikings – *iz Varyag v Greki* – is by now quite an old question. A Dane around 1240 referred to Rus as *Svethia Magna*: what should be read into such things?[18] But there is a more important dimension than this. It is not one altogether familiar or welcome in Russia, but it is there just the same, and all too visible even if you just take a bus to the Golden Circle towns east and north-east of Moscow – Suzdal, Rostov, Pereslavl Zalesski. By a river with a Finnic or Turkic name – Nerli – there are villages with obviously Turkic names – Bakshevo, Abashevo, Berendeyevo (from 'Pecheneg'). What should be read into this? There is, first of all, the Turkic or Tatar character of the Russian past. It is a contentious subject, the general theme of *yevraziystvo*, which emerged towards the end of the nineteenth century, perhaps essentially as a Nietzschean and anti-Christian cause. Most observers noted, somewhere along the line, that there were Tatars in Russia and the problem of their integration is also noted by the more sharp-sighted. L. N. Gumilev's *Tysyacheletiye vokrug Kaspiya* and his work on the 'ancient Turks' – *Drevniye Tyurki* – became a famous text for Russians examining their relationship with central Asia and the Caspian, but there is much else. Much of the old Russian nobility, for instance, was of Tatar origin – Muravyov from Murat, Yusupov from Yusuf, Saburov from *sabir*, 'patient', Dostoyevsky from *dost*, 'friend', or Godunov, of which the origin may even be obscene (the family name was changed to 'Zernov'). For that matter, Gumilev's mother was the poetess Akhmatova – 'Ahmet', though in her case a *nom de plume*. The great Prince Igor himself was three-quarters Polovtsian (Kipchak) and spoke a Turkic mother-tongue.[19] Russian nationalists of anti-Western stamp of course played up this element of their past: why was Russia the only Slav country that had 'succeeded'? Some said Germans, Vikings – at any rate, the West. N. M. Karamzin himself said, 'Moscow owes its greatness to the khans,' and Vernadsky noted that Muscovy's state centralisation came through 'Mongol principles of administration'.[20] In modern times, the Tatar dimension of Russian history went underground. Vasily III had married the converted heir of the Kazan khanate, Kagan Kul, to his sister, and nearly made him his own heir; Ivan the Terrible descended through his mother from Genghiz Khan. It was Peter the Great who stamped hard on the Tatar side. Catherine the Great greatly relaxed the pressure, and gave the Muslim clergy privileges similar to those of the Orthodox; in return, Tatar cavalry became an essential part of the tsarist army, and in 1905 received a telegram of thanks from Nicholas II for putting down revolutionary troubles in Odessa. By then, Tatars were counting among those backward peoples that Engels had claimed long before (with the South Slavs in 1848) would always fight on the reactionary side and would, in the longer term, just vanish. Stalin deported the Crimean Tatars, and they were allowed back only with long delays – longer than in the case of other deported peoples. In the last decade or so of the Soviet Union, an interest in proper Tatar history revived. At any rate, the most go-ahead representative of the Tatars, Ismail Gaspirali, had at one time been able to claim that Russia offered the greatest hope – 'the Russian Muslims will be more civilised than any other Muslim nation' – and that Russia would be 'one of the greatest Muslim states in the world'.[21] In the present-day context, this is not altogether pipe-dreaming.

By marriage, the two daughters of Kagan Kul entered the Mstislavsky and Shuisky families (which thus descend from Genghiz Khan). Their aunt, Zoe – Tsaritsa Sophia – Paleologus had come from Byzantium, via Rome, where the Muscovite marriage was arranged. She had two Paleologus first cousins, nephews of the last emperor, Constantine XI, who had been killed in the fall of Constantinople in 1453. The boys were brought up by Mehmet II. They became respectively admiral of the Ottoman fleet, and *Beylerbeyi* of Rumelia; a curious book, Theodore Spandounes's *On the Origin of the Ottoman Emperors*,[22] related the connections that existed in his time – the mid-sixteenth century – between Ottoman Konstantiniye (its proper name, 'Istanbul', came much later) and Italy. Half of the Byzantine aristocracy had converted – not just in 1453, but long before. Descendants of Genghiz Khan sat in Moscow; but the early Ottomans descended from the Comnenoi, and Mehmet II – after all, ruler of an empire that was more than half Christian – described himself as Roman emperor. Why, in the seventeenth century, the empire adopted a stricter Islam is a good question, and so is the relationship between this and the decline that set in just as Russia was rising as a European power.

What did the Ottomans owe to Byzantium? Russia – 'the Third Rome' – of course obviously owed a great deal, and the late Dmitry Obolensky's *Byzantine Commonwealth* bears rereading for Turkish historians. No doubt romantic pan-Slavism made too much of the Byzantine theme – the idea of Muscovy as Third Rome has been rightly sneered at as an early instance of Russian megalomania, given that the Third Rome in Filotey's time was mainly given over to forest, snow, wolves and bears – but there is an obvious connection just the same.[23] An original of Our Lady of Vladimir can be found in the depths of Cappadocia, in central Anatolia, at the Tokali church in Goreme, dating back to the middle of the eleventh century. At any rate, arguing that Russia had Byzantine origins at least got writers off the Germanic hook, with all its implications of cultural inferiority. Meyendorff asserts that 'Byzantine medieval civilisation was part of the very texture of Russian life', and even claims that the Byzantine influence made Moscow, rather than Vilna or Tver, the centre of a new Russia. Zoe Paleologus came at the end of a long process – a counterpart, no doubt, to the thesis that Germanic Vikings were needed to make anything of Slavs.

But there is an interesting Turkish parallel. It goes back to an old book, H. A. Gibbons's *Foundation of the Ottoman Empire* (Oxford, 1916). There were, in history, several Turkish or Turkic empires, the 'empires of the steppe', Grousset's *l'empire du levant*.[24] There were three such empires after the sixth century on the Chinese borders; to the Chinese, 'Turks' – it is the first reference to them, historically – were *T'u Chueh* and the Uyghurs of Sinkiang are the remnant, today. But these were nomadic empires, their capitals in elaborate tent cities, their badge the horsetail, their inspiration the sky and the colour blue (*gok*). Such empires were dependent upon pasture, and otherwise lasted for three or four generations: once settled, the nomads take on the colouring of the locals, such that China, India, Persia had Turkic (or Mongol) dynasties and aristocracies that retained of the Turkic past little more than some symbols and some words (Urdu reflects the Turkish word for 'army', *ordu*, which also appears as (Golden) 'Horde'). But the Ottoman Empire was different: it lasted for about seven centuries or perhaps even longer, if you count the Seljuks, who took most of Anatolia in the twelfth century, as proto-Ottoman. Why? Gibbons said that the Turks had taken over the imperial machinery of Byzantium and made it work, for the first time since the Venetians had sacked Constantinople in the Fourth Crusade, in 1204. Other writers have followed in his traces and gone further – for instance, a Greek historian, Dimitri Kitzikis. It emerges that the very word *efendi*, the best-known honorific in the Middle East, is a corruption of *authentes* – 'sovereign' – with which title Mehmet the Conqueror addressed the patriarch when giving him a charter of privileges that made him one of the greatest landowners of the empire.

We should add, in fairness, that Gibbons, Kitzikis and others of their inclination have been quite seriously challenged, whether by Paul Wittek on the grounds that the Ottomans represented a sort of Holy War against the Infidel – 'the *gazi* thesis' – or by M. Fuat Koprulu, who stressed the Turkic, or tribal side and believed that the borrowings were Persian, not Byzantine. It is a complicated matter, the sources of which are exceedingly difficult. The latest survey, in itself a remarkably authoritative and original work, is by Heath Lowry.[25] He sees the early Ottoman centuries as a Turkish–Greek enterprise, a 'predatory confederacy' on the Bithynian border of Byzantium. Osman was simply elected chief by three main colleagues, his equals, who were Christian. He exposes the scholarship of Wittek, and people who copied his sources uncritically, as shoddy – woefully incomplete readings of written sources, wilful misunderstandings of inscriptions in Arabic. Of course, later on, the idea of the *gazi*, of Holy War, became part of the dynastic mystique, but that is an anachronism. Lowry does not go as far as Kitzikis, who claims that the early Ottoman centuries marked 'a Greek–Turkish condominium', but he argues along such lines (and does so with mastery of sources in obsolete versions of far-flung languages). It is at the least a necessary correction to the equivalent pan-Slav opinion, that Orthodoxy, the essence of Byzantium, was the 'Holy of Holies' for the Greeks and South Slavs and 'saved them from dissolution in the Turkish flood', in Meyendorff's words.

Vryonis[26] remarks that 'the similarities between the Ottoman and Byzantine Empires are so numerous that the drawing of parallels is an old game in which practically all Byzantinists and Ottomanists have indulged'. The Ottomans presided over 'a Byzantine–Balkan base with a veneer of the Turkish language and the Islamic religion'. Perhaps symbolically, the huge gun that brought about the decisive breach in the Walls of Constantinople in 1453 was built by an Hungarian, Urban;[27] and a senior Byzantine, the *Megadux* Lukas Notaras, exasperated by the Latins, famously exclaimed, 'Better the Sultan's turban than the Cardinal's Hat.' Almost the first thing the Conqueror did was to meet the Byzantine patriarch, Gennadios, and come to terms: the Orthodox Church became the greatest landowner in the empire, and its dignitaries had ranks equivalent to the very highest Ottoman ones (the badge of this – the characteristic of an imperial regime that never forgot its nomadic origins – was the horse-tail). Pashas and patriarchs had a right to three of them, on their coaches. This business is not as happy as all that: as Steven Runciman[28] shows, deprived of central authority, the 'Great Church' became demoralised and corrupt, and only four patriarchs, from 1453 until 1918, died in office, in their beds. Of its performance, we may remember Gibbon's lines: 'The subjects of the Byzantine Empire present a dead uniformity of abject vices, which are neither softened by the weakness of humanity nor animated by the vigour of memorable crimes.' But in many ways, the early Ottoman Empire was a revived Byzantium:[29] Constantinople, for instance, which was a huge terrain of ruin in the early fifteenth century, with a population of 50,000, was made to flourish again because the sultans repopulated it (partly with Armenians, whose patriarchate was transferred there).

It is even possible to argue that some Ottoman institutions were taken straight from Byzantium, along with a considerable number of the Byzantines involved – the Byzantine taxes, says Halil Inalcik, were just lumped over, the *zeugarion* becoming the Turks' *çift resmi*. There is at least an argument that the feudal arrangements were the same – the *pronoia* linked cavalry with land-holding, exactly as did the Ottoman *timar* and the standard land measurement was the same, *donum* and *stremma*, or roughly 1000 square metres. The problem was that the *timar* represented only a temporary grant: over time, it did become hereditary, but heritable property was insecure, in Turkey as in Russia under the *pomestye* system. At any rate, we are a long way from Western feudalism, with its corpus of law and obligations; in fact, until the disintegration of the Ottoman Empire in the eighteenth century (in Gilles Vainstein's felicitous phrase,[30] '*du voleur héroïque au gendarme pilleur*') the Orthodox population sided with Turks against Venetians (as in Cyprus and Crete, though not apparently in Rhodes). Venetian and Frankish feudalism offered a species of serfdom antipathetic to the Orthodox locals. At any rate, with the feudalism in both empires, creation of a hereditary, substantial aristocracy became problematical, though in the Ottoman case matters were worse. It would in fact be interesting to explore the effects in both empires of the basic instability of property in land – an

instability that of course set strict limits to the development of capitalism.[31] It was mainly left to minorities and foreigners, in both cases,
and the Byzantines had already been in effect taken over by Venetians
and Genoese in the last century or two of their existence as an empire.
At any rate, we might explore what, through Byzantium, Russia and the
Ottomans had in common.

One obvious final point is that Turks learned from Russians, because
a considerable part of the population of western Anatolia arrived, at
varying stages in the later nineteenth century, as refugees. In republican
Turkey, they or their children made up half of the urban population.
Vast numbers of them came from Russia – the Crimea or the Caucasus,
as it fell under Russian rule. The Crimean Tatars especially had had a
relatively strong state tradition and they learned from Russia to such an
extent that their role in the Turkish higher education system was
remarkable. In fact Crimean Tatars were the spearhead of 'modernisation' for the Muslims of Russia in general in the late nineteenth
century.[32] The influence of Russia upon Turkey through the tsarist
education system deserves some stress. Intelligent Ottomans knew that
they had something to learn from Russia, however much they also
feared her. There is an interesting literature as to the efforts of Crimean
Tatars to standardise a Turkic language for Russia, and on the efforts
of such scholars later on to promote higher education in republican
Turkey. The makers of Turkish nationalism really learned much of their
trade from the Russians. The final point of comparison is in the role
of foreigners. There was of course a large time gap in the Westernisation
and it was also quite different in nature, but it meant using Westerners
just the same: the past of both countries had not encouraged private
property and 'capitalism', the bureaucracy was sometimes hostile and/or
corrupt, Westerners were needed. Peter the Great attempted to alter
the very character of his people – away from Muscovy, towards a
northern European model, complete with its own new capital, laws,
nobility, navy, flag (the Dutch colours) and army (the ranks of which
had German names, down to *Yefreyter* for 'corporal'). There was a small
invasion of foreigners, usually northern Protestants, and then Peter
aimed to capture the Baltic littoral, especially Riga, where the Hanseatic
inheritance gave him commercial and technical skills of which Russians
were mainly incapable. Even as late as 1914, half of the army commanders had German names; very few of the suppliers of the war effort
had native Russian names (and the greatest, Putilov, was not a success).
Russia had generations in which to acquire Western characteristics, and
intermarriage between Orthodox and Protestant no doubt helped. But
in any event, the Russian Empire, until the end, had a *soslovny* and pre-
national character – the dynasty largely Germanic, and Protestant models
often used (as with 'Defender of the Faith' – *khranitel' dogmatov*); the

nobility came from anywhere and everywhere. Ordinary Russians could
well feel that they were impoverished by their own alleged imperial
state: they could be serfs of Tatar noblemen, but the process did not
work the other way around, since Catherine the Great (like Ivan the
Terrible before her) knew that Muslims would not be enserfed.[33] In the
pre-war Duma there were complaints of *oskudenie tsentra*, the sapping of
the centre; Russian peasants were less well-off than Polish or Baltic
ones, when it came to emancipation, and N. E. Markov complained
that, just as Alexander I was granting the Finns a constitution, his own
subjects were 'still slaves, sold in bazaars'. '*Rus* was the victim of *Rossiya*,'
is a well-established line. Geoffrey Hosking rightly says that 'a fractured
and underdeveloped nationood has been [the Russians'] principal historical burden'.[34] The same could be said, and still more so, for Turkish
nationalism.

It greatly mattered, in both countries, that 'capitalism' was heavily
foreign. There have been many studies of the role of foreigners in
Russia, from the students of Orthodoxy through Catherine the Great's
Scotsmen to the 'Pioneers for Profit' who arrived on the wave of
foreign investment before 1914. In the time of the First Five Year Plan,
there were thousands of American engineers.[35] There has also been a
large Western presence in the Westernization of Turkey, but we do not
seem to have been as well served as regards studies of foreigners' role
in the Ottoman Empire and modern Turkey as in the Russian case.
The German refugees of the thirties have received attention in Germany
(and elsewhere) but not in Turkey, where their doings, though legendary,
have never been studied by a native scholar. Any educated foreigner
arriving was very interested in the country, and there are some classic
memoirs.[36] Quite a number – probably, more than might be thought –
stayed and 'went native', but we have not been at all well served as
regards the literature on this. The only book that this writer knows in
this respect is rather remarkable just the same, Mahmut Celik's *Bogazdaki
asireti* ('Bosphorus Tribe'), which takes the descendants of five central
European Ottoman grandees and shows how, in the republic period,
their descendants supplied Ataturk's envoy to Moscow, Ali Fuat
Cebesoy, main national poet, Nazim Hikmet, the 'Leyla Hanim' who
introduced piano teaching, and a number of other prominent people,
from two secretaries of the Communist Party to the upper-class
'masher' – an Edwardian term – whose photograph, in evening dress,
is still used on bottles of the best raki, Kulup (the man spent a lifetime
doing nothing in Izmir). When Nazim Hikmet had gone too far,
encouraging a naval mutiny in the middle of the 1930s, a cousin in the
Ministry of the Interior sent a car for him and warned him that it would
end in prison – a warning ignored. Even his eventual escape to exile in
Rumania seems to have been arranged because another cousin was in

charge of the fleet in the Sea of Marmara, though this is not clear. One way and another, not altogether popular people in central Anatolia. But it was not just the foreigners.[37] There was also a problem, which grew with the *Tanzimat* changes after 1839, of Christian minorities, who moved some way ahead of most of the Anatolian Muslims. In 1911, for instance, of 654 wholesale concerns in Istanbul, 528 were Greek; and after the opening up of Asia Minor there was considerable imbalance in education, overall – in 1861, the non-Muslims had 571 primary and ninety-four secondary schools, with 140,000 pupils, a number somewhat ahead of that for the more numerous Muslim children, who, in any case, had to spend an inordinate amount of time learning (and not understanding) Arabic for religious purposes.[38] The foreigners tended to deal with the Christians – Greek or Armenian – and they prospered. You can still see the results in Cappadocia, or 'Karamania', where the Orthodox (and Turkish-speaking) population put up prosperous and well-built towns, almost of Mediterranean style, in Sinasos (today's Mustafapasa) or Gelveri (the locals still prefer that name to the official 'Guzelyurt'). In that region, relations between Christians and Muslims were by all accounts good, but in 1923–4, with the population exchange, the Christians were forced to leave for Greece.

Turkish nationalism only really developed very late in the day. The process of Westernisation got under way as a conscious strategy only in the later eighteenth century (when the Ottomans began to appreciate the significance of 'Mad Peter' – as they called him – and his doings). Before then, there had been considerable religious obstruction: – even, in 1734, when a school of mathematics was set up, on a Frenchman's advice, to help with gunnery, the clergy objected, in the name of theodicy – unsuitable probing of God's secrets – and when, in 1759, a Vezier re-opened the school (*Hendeshane*) he had to do so semi-clandestinely. Bernard Lewis's classic book on the Ottoman learning process, though forty years old, remains the best overall account.[39] Matters started with a desire to imitate military success; there are artillery schools; then there is understanding that the problem runs deeper, that mathematicians, foundrymen, repairers etc. are needed; then money, and more money; then the *Tanzimat-i hayriye* ('beneficent re-orderings') of 1839 and the *Hatt-i serif* of 1856, with free trade and, later, a constitution to make the empire appear modern, treating all its subjects even-handedly. In the 1860s, the Ottoman Empire therefore saw something of the same progressive formula applied as did Russia under Alexander II or for that matter in the Austrian empire, with the Schmerling *Reichsverfassung* of 1861.[40] However, there was an immediate problem, in that the empire was becoming more, not less, Muslim. In the eighteenth century, it had had to take in Muslim refugees from the lost parts of the Balkans (and Hungary); in 1783, when it finally lost the Crimea, the sultan insisted upon continuing to protect the Muslims, now ruled by Russia, and he declared himself caliph of all Islam – not a claim made before. In the later nineteenth century, under Abdul Hamit II, Islam, rather than any sort of Turkish nationalism, was meant to offer the unifying principle, and he constructed the Hejaz railway, to promote the *Hac*, when it would no doubt have been more sensible to use the same resources for the Taurus mountain tunnels and the line to Baghdad.[41]

At the time, the very word 'Turkey' was only used by foreigners – the original was medieval-Italian (*Turchia* – the republic took over the name) and 'Turk' for the Ottomans had connotations of rustic buffoonery. There was an Arabic pun, *etrak-bi-itrak* ('stupid Turk') often used in mid-nineteenth-century court circles, the *Enderun-i humayun*, which itself consisted of Christians or Albanians. They had what amounted to a private language, with what amounted to its own script, impenetrable to ordinary Anatolians, and several modern expressions simply had no equivalent. 'Civil liberty', for instance, could only be *ruhsat-i-seriyye* ('permission of religious law') – Arabic – and 'nationalism' itself was impossible to convey. The original Turkish nationalists were simply men who could see that language was being made available to peasants in the Balkans and could not see why the same should not apply in Anatolia. Even Greek, after all, had to be updated, and modern words invented (thus *taxidiotico grafio* means 'travel agency'; there are many such) and with other Balkan languages the invention amounted almost to an Esperanto. Although a certain sneering has sometimes resulted in Anglo-Saxon circles that have never experienced the problem, the process did at least make the language more comprehensible to ordinary people. Namik Kemal, born in Tekirdag on the Marmara coast in 1840, at the time a largely Greek place (Rodosto), has a claim to be the first writer using Turkish rather than Arabo-Persian. Eventually, as happened in the Habsburg Empire, the process of linguistic revival turned political, and by 1889, no doubt using the cheap travel arrangements prevailing in France to mark the anniversary of the revolution, Ali Riza, a follower of Auguste Comte, established an association among the Ottoman exiles, the *Jeunes Turcs*,[42] who produced a 'Committee for Union and Progress', probably through a masonic connection, in the mid-1890s. There follows a period in which the historiographical problems are remarkably parallel to those of late-tsarist Russia: what appear to be groupuscules in exile, quarrelling among themselves, sometimes in exile or prison, only important for the future that they, with almost microscopic hindsight, represent. Not long before the meeting in Brussels in 1903 that established Bolshevism, there was a meeting in Paris of some forty men (they had women sympathisers) to discuss unification of the Young Turk programme: it divided.[43] Islam and its attitude to women?

Arabs? Armenians? The Turkish nationalist programme that involved invocations of 'Great Turan', i.e. Central Asia? Which ally and model in the West, France or Germany or England? What sort of constitution? The exiled Ottoman Prince Sabahattin, a liberal publicist, familiar with the Khedive's court in Cairo, such as Ali Kemal[44] Bey, and army officers such as (the later) Enver Pasha were not likely to be united on anything except the overthrow of Abdul Hamit II. At the time, the ideologist of Turkish nationalism was Ziya Gokalp (1875–1924), himself of Kurdish origin, who had studied the new sociology, and thought that the nation-state would be the building block of progress. Durkheim, who gave a sociological underpinning to collectivism, and not, of course, Marx, was the inspiration.

These two exile conferences, a few miles and a few months apart in timing, produced, in 1922, an alliance over half of Eurasia. The Bolsheviks succeeded in Russia, with a civil war that ended in 1921, when peace treaties were arranged with Poland. In a very tangled period between 1908 and 1913, Abdul Hamit was overthrown, 'Union and Progress' took power through a military coup, and by 1914 represented the moving wheel of the Ottoman machinery. It set in train the beginnings of the Ataturkist reforms, or, at any rate, there is controversy as to how far it did so (women's education and language reform, for instance). By 1914 the Triple Entente was clearly set on dividing the Ottoman Empire, and when the archduke was assassinated a treaty was awaiting ratification, for the autonomy of Armenians in eastern Anatolia. Enver Pasha in collusion with the Germans provoked a war and the deportation of Armenians.[45] That war cost Turkey one quarter of her population, and also threw up all of the problems discussed by the forty Young Turks present in 1902 at the Paris conference. Defeat was followed by invasion by predatory foreign powers, and in 1921 the Greeks had almost reached Ankara.[46] Turkey would have been divided; the sultan might have kept some central latter-day emirate based on Ankara or Kayseri, but even then, not, because both towns contained substantial Armenian populations (Ankara at that time contained a higher proportion of Armenians than many other towns in Turkey). The fight-back of the Turkish nationalists at that time is still, for a neutral observer, remarkable. One of the most remarkable aspects was that they understood what they might expect from Moscow, and Moscow understood what might be expected from them. Nationalist envoys went to Moscow, and Chicherin appreciated their importance. The communications took two or three months, and even the business of physical travel, in winter across the Black Sea and a Ukraine where travellers were stopped by Nestor Makhno's men, was difficult. How *did* an upper-class Ottoman like Bekr Sami immediately understand, in those circumstances, a Radek or a Zinoviev?[47] At any rate, it worked.

The Bolsheviks of 1920 had an extraordinary understanding as to how central Asia, the Turkic world of 'Great Turan', should be handled. They played a very weird chess. Enver Pasha, on behalf of General von Seeckt (late chief of staff of Falkenhayn's *Heeresgruppe Yildirim* in Palestine) accompanied Klara Zetkin, Communist deputy of the *Reichstag* down Tverskaya in Moscow. To counter Enver, the Bolsheviks used the Ankara nationalists, and did a bargain: Turkey would renounce the Caucasus and Central Asia.[48] A thousand kilograms of gold, and thousands of rifles, reached Ankara, and that defeated the French in Cilicia. Then the French came to terms; and in 1921 the nationalists were strong enough to defeat the Anglo-Greek attack on the River Sakarya in September.

Istanbul itself was liberated in November 1922. The last sultan, forty-first child of his father, by the fifth wife, tottered off, with a certain sad symbolism, in a fake ambulance to a British ship and exile.[49] A Turkish republic was proclaimed in 1923, and its chief figure, Kemal Ataturk, entered the world pantheon: anyone interested in what can now be seen as one of the most important themes, ever, in history, the modernisation of Islam, would appreciate the importance both of Ataturk himself and of Turkey in general. Turks themselves think only of their relationship with the West – latterly, particularly, Europe or America. Might it be put to them that the real question is the comparison with Russia. Turkey has caught up. Ziya Gokalp, John Stuart Mill and – where is our Russian? – were right. The building block of progress is the nation-state, but *how* one sympathises with the empires.

# 8

## The Ideology and Realities of Soviet Women's Tractor Driving in the 1930s

MARY BUCKLEY

John Erickson's work was thoroughly steeped in Soviet primary sources, including extensive archival documents. Although best known for his work on the Red Army and on the Great Patriotic War, and renowned as a military historian first and foremost, John was highly sensitive to the relevance of society to polity and not one to produce ungendered history. His writings on women in the Red Army best attest to this.[1]

My contribution to this commemorative volume analyses the aims, hurdles and consequences of attempts to draw rural women into tractor driving. This is not a topic that John examined, but one that in some respects shows similar patterns to his study of women's roles at the front from 1941 to 1945. Women's enthusiasm and commitment to the war effort and to tractor driving, both 'heroic' achievements, were nonetheless mocked and ridiculed by many a general and farm leader as not women's work. Whilst thousands of women were not deterred by this lack of encouragement, it had complex repercussions for daily life in the army and on the farm and affected recruitment, training, teamwork and interpersonal relations.

Scrutiny of Soviet primary sources reveals a predictably contradictory story. On the one hand, it was highly likely that women would be officially encouraged into tractor driving since Marxist–Leninist ideology championed equality of the sexes and leaders were calling for women to enter the labour force at a time of industrialisation 'from above' and forced collectivisation. Moreover, Machine Tractor Stations (MTS) were being set up to service collective farms and there was an increase in the production of tractors and combines for both the MTS and for state farms. On the other hand, however, social attitudes resisted some of the necessary prerequisites for drawing women into tractor driving.

Firstly, many men and women mocked the idea that women could apply themselves to tractor driving, or become sufficiently skilled. Secondly, not all training courses willingly took women. Thirdly, once women were skilled, they were not automatically assigned work on tractors, but sidelined into other jobs or most reluctantly taken into brigades with men, where expectations of them were low. They worked best, it seemed, in women-only brigades, which were formed mainly after 1936.

Overall, results were mixed. Despite huge cultural, attitudinal and institutional barriers, thousands of women did successfully end up driving tractors and combines and also participated in socialist competitions with other brigades. But the numbers trained fell short of planned targets, the Komsomol did not always take the campaigns seriously and women endured discrimination on the job and verbal abuse on the farm, both at home and at work.

### Machines, Ideology and Images

The increased production of tractors and combines was part of the First and Second Five Year Plans. More technology for the countryside was designed to increase productivity and to boost harvests. The number of tractors increased hugely on the MTS from 7100 in 1930 to 356,800 in 1937. Similarly, the supply of combine harvesters rose from 10,400 in 1933 to 96,300 in 1937.[2] State farms had their own tractors and these went up from 9700 in 1929 to 85,000 in 1938.[3] A growing number of machines, then, needed to be driven by ideologically equal men and women. Moreover, they presented an opportunity to women who wanted to drive them. Peasants who cared for their machines, worked efficiently and exceeded targets merited the title 'shock worker', or 'Stakhanovite' for even greater output.[4]

Ideological lines of the 1930s claimed that women were 'a great force' and moved forward 'shoulder to shoulder' and 'side by side' with men.[5] Allegedly only Soviet socialism offered thousands of women opportunities unknown in the capitalist states or in the dark tsarist past. *Baba*, therefore, was destined to drive a tractor or combine. This message was reinforced by movies such as *Traktoristy* (*The Tractor Drivers*) and *Kubanskie Kazaki* (*Cossacks of the Kuban*), both of which portayed successful female tractor brigades. Mar'iana Bazhan in *Traktoristy* is a smiling brigade leader whose women's team works enthusiastically, efficiently and frequently outperforms the men's brigade. Dynamic scenes show her women's brigade speedily combing the fields, with sun umbrellas to shield them, conveying both the importance of new technology for Soviet agriculture and the capability of women at the wheel. Powerful images in *Kubanskie Kazaki* of tractors and combines racing across the fields to stirring music as corn blows dramatically in the wind and red flags flap on combines and trucks also gives the didactic message that technology conquers nature to humankind's advantage. Tractors and combines were symbols of progress and of the onward march to communism.[6]

The front covers of women's magazines such as *Krest'ianka* and *Kolkhoznitsa* also carried pictures of smiling and capable female tractor drivers. Celebrating International Women's Day on 8 March 1935, *Kolkhoznitsa*'s front cover showed three women and one man on a tractor. A woman grips the wheel, steering with confidence and seriousness, her eyes on the path ahead. The suggestion is that she has no problem controlling her machine. Another woman holds a banner showing Lenin and Stalin. The message here is that these great leaders supported sexual equality. The remaining man and woman hold a banner extolling the collective farms and the cultured and prosperous life resulting from them. With women outnumbering men, there is no doubt that woman's place is legitimately on the tractor.[7] A year later in April, *Krest'ianka*'s front page showed a very calm and serious Pasha Kovardak on her tractor, soon to be a winner in the 1936 socialist competition among women's tractor brigades. Her eyes look directly at the reader, implying a straightforward and efficient person. The tread of a huge tyre between the reader and Pasha indicates that she has trained to control a machine of some size and power and is now triumphant.[8] The smiling Stakhanovite Liuba Mamrukova is celebrated on *Krest'ianka*'s front page in 1937, here with a large steering wheel between the reader and herself. The rest of the machine is largely unseen, but there is a trail of ploughed field behind her. This shows a happy peasant, confident to manage a sturdy machine and to bring positive results to the fields.[9] With Stakhanovite numbers falling on some farms, this picture also encouraged women to attain Stakhanovite results. In 1939, *Krest'ianka* portrayed a woman and a man on threshing machines at harvest time. The woman is in front and much larger. Not only does this suggest female adeptness, but also that women could easily take over men's work should war extend to the USSR.[10] Each image needs to be set in historical context to grasp its full meaning.

Photographs and images adorned inside pages too. The consistent themes were female skill and success. *Krest'ianka*, for example, in 1938 carried a picture of Praskov'ia (Pasha) Angelina's women's brigade. Pasha is giving instructions and pointing, suggesting that she is an effective leader, in command. Two women on one machine are listening attentively to her, while four others are attending to another machine to keep it in good order.[11] The general message is that women can lead, work well together as a team, and keep their machines in good running order. Neglect and indifference have no place here.

Poems and songs also lauded female tractor drivers, showing their affection for the machine, the happiness, glory and exalted emotions that it brought and the dreams it fulfilled. *Krest'ianka* printed a 'Female Tractor Drivers' Song' which included such lines as: 'You tractor, my tractor, "Stalinets" my glorious one,' and 'You and I make up happy songs for our own *krai*, we multiply happiness.'[12] In short, the tractor was a fond friend and tractor driving was an elevating part of the utopian project to build communism.

Despite these bold socialist realist images, it was economic necessity and pragmatism as well as ideology that required that women drive tractors. Propaganda extolled the importance of women's contribution and delivered the message that work emancipated women. Likewise, those who wished to emphasise the importance of equality of the sexes could cite the existence of female tractor drivers as shining testimony.

### Attracting and Training Women

Although the campaigns to entice women onto tractors and combines were characteristic of the 1930s, among the first Soviet women to receive training were Mariia Soboleva and Lidiia Artemova in the late 1920s.[13] The most famous female tractor driver, however, was the aforementioned Pasha Angelina, who also took lessons in 1929 and formed her women's brigade in 1933. Pasha Angelina became a Soviet icon – a capable, smiling woman who overcame all opposition to her tractor driving from her father, brother, friends and other peasants. Against huge social pressure not to become a tractor driver, she insisted upon her chosen path. With Stalin and other leaders present, it was Pasha's rallying speeches at conferences of shock workers and Stakhanovites, such as the Second All-Union Congress of Kolkhoz Shock Workers in February 1935 and the Conference of Advanced Agricultural Workers in December 1935, which inspired other women, such as Dar'ia Garmash and Pasha Ledovskaia, to follow her example.[14] In December 1935 Pasha promised Stalin she would organise ten women's tractor brigades in Staro-Beshevskii district and also work up to 1600 hectares on her tractor.[15]

Pasha enjoyed the regime's approval and official promotion into celebrity status. She was also co-opted onto political structures, becoming a party member, a member of the Supreme Soviet, and also a delegate to the eighteenth, nineteenth, twentieth and twenty-first Party Congresses in 1939, 1952, 1956 and 1959.[16] It was therefore fitting that Pasha Angelina, in 1936, should instigate the first socialist competition of women tractor drivers, to be repeated by competitions in subsequent years. Owing to an increased number of women tractor drivers, totalling 545 brigades, 1937 brought the All-Union Conference of Women Tractor Drivers and Brigade Leaders.[17] As her fame increased, allegedly on one day alone, in 1937, Pasha received 300 letters and 120 telegrams of support.[18]

By 1939 the threat of war led to renewed emphasis on the need to draw more women into tractor driving. Throughout the 1930s, the official Soviet line was that thousands of women were successfully drawn into mechanised labour, an indication of the progressive nature of the Soviet state. The general message in 1936 was: 'With every day the ranks of female tractor drivers multiply.'[19] And, indeed, this was intended. Komsomol archives hold plans of the number of female tractor and combine drivers to be trained in given years, as well as plans for training women to become car mechanics, tractor and combine mechanics and car drivers. Specified targets for each of these skills were part of 'The plan for preparing skilled cadres for agriculture from female youth in 1936–37'.[20] For instance, in 1936–7, in Moscow oblast, 3000 women were meant to train on simple tractors, 120 on the more complicated ChTz tractor and 320 on combines. In Azovo-Chernomore *krai* the corresponding figures were 1250, 180 and 1520.[21]

Such targets were devised to help correct previous indifference to training girls and young women in skilled work. The report noted that the Secretariat of the Central Committee of the Komsomol was dissatisfied with the selection process of girls into mechanised work. In Dnepropetrovsk oblast, out of 1769 chosen for the school of combine drivers, just 150 were women. In Saratov *krai*, out of forty-five trainee mechanics, only three were women. The secretariat ordered all Komsomol *obkomy* and *kraikomy* to implement the People's Commissariat of Agriculture's (*Narodnyi kommissariat zemledeliia* or Narkomzem) plan to train female cadres.[22]

A *prikaz* (order) issued by Narkomzem in April 1936 had noted that 'the drawing in of women into study is weakly conducted'.[23] In Kalinin oblast, out of 6441 studying the tractor, only 528 were women. In Leningrad oblast, the same pattern showed 5419 on courses, of whom 544 were women. In the whole of Belorussia, 6865 were training, of whom 564 were women. The trend across the USSR was for women to be in a minority. Narkomzem concluded that 'formal attitudes' to implementing former decisions of the party and government prevailed.[24] Narkomzem ordered that courses for women be organised.

A separate report written in November 1935 on Azovo-Chernomore commented that girls who were tractor and combine drivers or mechanics suffered 'rude uncomradely' treatment. Conditions were described as 'extraordinarily inadequate'.[25] The report castigated the 'inadmissible inactivity' on the part of all local organisations and the apparat of the Komsomol in the field of educating rural youth. In short, decisions of the Central Committee of the Komsomol were not being put into practice. Moreover, district and town party organisations 'were not hurrying' to act and clearly 'did not value the political importance of this question'.[26] Training women to become tractor drivers was not high on all local political agendas. Specific targets were therefore needed, but not necessarily met.

Despite the allegedly 'huge demand' among young women to take to the tractor, they were not always included on courses. A Komsomol report written in 1937 concluded that women's tractor brigades were not valued in Ukraine. On one course which was training forty tractor drivers, not one was a woman. Moreover, 'political education with them was badly organised'.[27] Another report on Ordzhonikidze *krai* noted that whereas across forty-two MTS there had been thirty-two women's brigades, by the end of 1937 the figure had actually fallen to fifteen. Women worked on the worst tractors, which were not permanently allocated to them, and they were always the last to receive fuel. For these reasons women's brigades were not stable in composition.[28] Although not stated in these terms, women were discriminated against in the supply of good tractors and fuel. Disgruntled, many quit tractor driving rather than endure work in unfavourable conditions.

Women's own accounts echoed these charges. A common response was that tractor driving was a man's job. Pasha Angelina, Pasha Kovardak, Dar'ia Garmash and A. K. Kofanova all experienced this reaction. Kovardak told readers of *Traktorist-Kombainer* that she had been laughed at and told that it was not women's business to sit at the wheel.[29] Combine driver, A. F. Kofanova, was similarly asked: 'Can a woman come to grips with such a machine? This business is not for a woman's mind.'[30] When she first drove her combine into the fields, she felt she could have achieved more if only there had been spare parts.[31] This was a problem that beset men and women. Some women, however, felt that it affected them more. *Krest'ianka* published letters claiming that women were given spare parts last and an old plough 'on the assumption that woman won't understand anything.'[32]

Another common problem was the reluctance of male brigade leaders to have women on their teams. Even Pasha Angelina, once trained and having worked 'excellently', was suddenly taken off the tractor and told to go and work in the storehouse instead. Many of her complaints went unheeded and she was told to stop making a fuss, until finally the *politotdel* (political department) on the MTS defended her and she returned to tractor driving.[33]

Pasha Kubrakova's brigade leader believed that 'a young woman pulls the brigade back, ruins the machine and uses too much fuel'.[34] Even when Kubrakova worked better than others the brigade leader reproached her for 'galloping across hectares, but not ploughing'. Apparently, 'unjust reproaches, caustic remarks and ridicule' were common.[35] In this case, speed and hectares covered could have been at the expense of work quality, a common problem with norm busting. Sources do not clarify whether this was the case, or not.

Praskov'ia Ledovskaia similarly narrated how she had been given 'an old machine'. The situation on the MTS was that 'they paid us little attention: girls, what do you do with them?!'[36] The refrain always ran as follows: 'We do not take women in our brigades. First, they don't have enough experience working on tractors; second, it happens that we have to help them all the time, tearing ourselves away from work. It is calmer without them.'[37] A letter from Uzbekistan noted that women in a brigade were asked to participate by bringing tea and oil, but not by driving a tractor. Slowly they would be eased out of the brigade altogether.[38] It is perhaps little wonder that women preferred to work in all-women brigades. When she organised a Stakhanovite brigade with other women, Ledovskaia commented that she was overjoyed that it would be 'such a friendly brigade'.[39]

Personal life was affected too, since parents, siblings, boyfriends and husbands often objected. Pasha Angelina's father forbade her to train and her brother persistently tried to dissuade her.[40] Khanat Fidarova's mother despaired: 'Don't go and work on a tractor, Khanat! Who will marry you?'[41] Dar'ia Garmash's boyfriend announced that she should give up tractor driving since his future wife could not do a man's job.[42] Faced with his ultimatum, Dar'ia chose the tractor. Marfa Kozh-emiakina's husband similarly exclaimed, 'My wife must not be a tractor driver! What sort of woman are you if you smell of kerosene!'[43] Criticisms also came from peasants in the village. Pasha Angelina told stories of old women spitting at her, of women blocking the path of her women's team to keep the tractors out of the fields to prevent them from spoiling the crops, and of an attack on her person that nearly killed her and led to a spell in hospital.[44]

A range of forms of opposition to women becoming tractor drivers therefore existed. It extended from dissuasion, forbidding and mockery of women's abilities to refusal to take women on courses, reluctance to include them in brigades with men and general doubt about their prowess in the fields. Occasionally there were physical attacks on them, which were often due to their 'Stakhanovite' status rather than to the fact that they drove tractors.[45] This was because peasants did not wish to see work norms raised, since it called for more exertion on their part.

## Socialist Competition

After forming her own women's tractor brigade in 1933 and then promising Stalin in 1935 that she would organise ten more women's brigades in her district, Pasha Angelina inspired other Soviet women both to take up tractor driving and to form women's brigades.[46] It logically followed that it was Pasha who called upon women's brigades to engage in socialist competition amongst themselves. These competitions were integral to the Stalinist drive for increased productivity and took place in both industry and in agriculture. In the countryside, the general pattern was for one farm or district to challenge another, itself pledging to attain a certain output. The challenger sought to meet or outstrip its own pledge and the challenged aimed to beat the challenger. One aim of socialist competitions from late 1935 on was to produce Stakhanovites.

In the case of the women's competition, Pasha called for it in order to meet Stalin's goal of producing 7–8 million poods of grain.[47] It was organised under the auspices of the Komsomol and Narkomzem. A meeting of the bureau of the Central Committee of the Komsomol in April 1936 discussed both the women's tractor competition and also the training of women in mechanised work.[48] Archives show that, to be considered a winner, a brigade had to merit no less than 'good' for its work throughout the whole of 1936, increase the output of every tractor in the brigade by at least 20 per cent, lower the cost price of work not less than 20 per cent, complete all the required work in the fields in a specified time period and take proper technical care of the tractors.[49] It was reported a year later that 1220 women's brigades had participated, involving over 10,000 drivers.[50] Official reporting of female tractor drivers' response to the 1936 socialist competition declared it to be one of 'great enthusiasm'.[51]

The campaign was used to champion women tractor drivers and to advertise their achievements. Participants gathered in Moscow in February 1937 to celebrate the results. Headlines such as 'Forward to new victories' revealed that among the best performers were the brigades of Pasha Ledovskaia, M. Timasheva, A. Lapteva, Pasha Angelina, M. Kosiuchenko and Khanat Fidarova. Ledovskaia's brigade, for example, on average worked 2.058 hectares.[52] The rural paper, *Krest'ianksia gazeta* gave two days' coverage to the event, printing detailed results of the competition and also interviews with the winners. The general message here concerning the secret of success from a winner was: 'We looked after our machines with love, carefully organised technical care and, most important, worked honestly.'[53] This was consistent with official stress throughout the 1930s on the need to know machines well, to care for them rather than neglect and abuse them, and to plan and organise one's work.

On the ground, however, the picture was not so rosy. Lack of enthusiasm in the Komsomol for the 1936 socialist competition among the women's tractor brigade was evident. Komsomol activists were meant to take an interest and to encourage the women, not least because the Komsomol was one of the organisations responsible for spearheading the campaign. Internal Komsomol reports reveal that in Kiev oblast 'absolutely nobody studied the work of the women's tractor brigades, of female tractor drivers or of female combine drivers'.[54] The Komsomol did not know which MTS had female brigades or how many. On the Khartsyzsk MTS in Donets oblast, for example, 'political study was poorly organised' and on the Chstiakovsk MTS 'for the entire year not one female tractor driver was admitted to the Komsomol, although there were forms for this, but nobody worked on this question'.[55] The archival report on women's tractor competitions in Donets and Kiev oblasts concluded that neither Narkomzem in Ukraine nor the Ukrainian Central Committee of the Komsomol applied themselves to the question of women's tractor brigades.[56] So both the republican people's commissariat and youth group of the party were under fire for not taking the women's competition seriously.

Calls for women to participate in socialist competitions nonetheless continued throughout the 1930s. In late March and early April 1937, archives show that the Komsomol discussed the matter and issued another *postanovlenie*.[57] In May, *Krest'ianskaia gazeta* reported that the Central Committee of the Komsomol and Narkomzem confirmed that there would be another socialist competition in 1937 among women's brigades.[58] In 1938 *Krest'ianka* lauded the 1937 competition for bringing 'a new wave of productive and politically active women tractor drivers'. Fifty-one brigades on average worked more than one thousand hectares, with the highest reaching 2145 hectares. Not in the lead, but still among the high achievers, Pasha Angelina's brigade averaged 1714 hectares.[59] The involvement of girls as trailerhands, as well as women, was stressed as 'one of the greatest results of the competition'.[60]

After the successes, however, came the criticisms. *Krest'ianka* castigated that in some oblasts leaders did not understand the meaning of competition and did not help the competitors.[61] On some MTS, moreover, brigades were given unrepaired tractors, combines and trailers. Spare parts and fuel were also withheld. The women's brigades thus found it hard to meet their targets and some brigades were even disbanded.[62] Several letters of complaint from women described these problems on their farms, which *Krest'ianka* put down to 'enemies of the people, Trotskyists, Bukharinites, bourgeois nationalists, spies and divertionists'.[63] Taking place during the Great Purges of 1936–8, the women's tractor competitions could not escape these politically correct accusations. Documents in the Komsomol archive discussing preparations for spring sowing also included remarks on the lack of support in land departments for training women on tractors and combines. Sometimes where a circle of women on an MTS had been formed, indifference from the director of the MTS meant that it disbanded.[64]

These enemies, however, according to official lines, had not succeeded in breaking the Stakhanovite movement among women's tractor brigades. Yet again, a socialist competition had meant that 'the number of women's brigades has significantly risen'.[65] In 1937, for instance, the number of women's brigades had increased in Voronezh oblast from twenty-three to 200, in Iaroslav from thirty-two to 179, in the Bashkir Autonomous republic (ASSR) from twenty-six to ninety-five and in the Tatar ASSR from eight to seventy-five. After praising these figures, *Krest'ianka* noted that the women had pledged to attain even higher output in 1938. The magazine insisted that Narkomzem through its local land departments and farm leaders should help the women to engage in socialist competition and also to become Stakhanovites. Young mothers, it stressed, needed special help.[66] A spate of letters of complaint from nursing mothers was printed in 1938, noting the dust and filth of their working conditions, the hazards associated with taking a baby into the fields, and the great distance from home, making it difficult to return there during the day for feeding. Others moaned about the design of the tractor and how uncomfortable it was to sit on.[67]

In 1938, Pasha Angelina and Nataliia Radchenko called out to women with the famous slogan: 'A hundred thousand women friends – to the tractor!' Apparently, 200,000 responded.[68] The district committee of the party and the local soviet in their own district of Staro-Beshevo pledged immediately to train twenty more women, aiming to bring the district total in 1939 to ninety. The party in Monastyrshchenksii district in Vinnitsa oblast committed itself to train sixty women.[69] In December 1938 the Moscow committee of the Komsomol organised an oblast conference of women tractor and combine drivers to discuss the slogan. Some who attended made promises to increase the number of women on training courses to 50 per cent.[70]

Throughout 1939 this call reappeared in the press, journals and magazines. Pasha Angelina, Pasha Kovardak and other tractor drivers now at the Timiriazevskii Agricultural Academy appealed to members of the Komsomol and to youth generally as 'patriots' to learn how to drive the tractor. The Third Five Year Plan outlined in 1939 at the Eighteenth Party Congress specified that a further 1500 machine tractor stations would be set up. Famous women tractor drivers argued in *Traktorist-Kombainer*: 'The number of women tractor drivers now on the MTS and on state farms is quite inadequate. Already far from everywhere are there permanent women's tractor brigades.'[71] Reasoning that the country had 6000 MTS already, they stressed

that if each one trained twenty more women, then a figure over
100,000 would be attained. They also emphasised that, through
training women, 'we help to strengthen the defence might of our
socialist motherland'. Moreover, when 'our husbands and brothers
exchange the tractor for the tank, we shall strengthen our socialist
motherland, working in the socialist fields'.[72]

Although Pasha Angelina, with other women, was yet again the
'instigator' of these calls, the one-party state used them as mouthpieces.
The Central Committee of the Komsomol, Narkomzem and the People's
Commissariat of State Farms (Narodnyi Kommissariat Sovkhozov, or
Narkomsovkhozov) issued a postanovlenie 'On the training of 100,000 women
tractor drivers without time out of production'.[73] It claimed to implement
Pasha's call and also to facilitate the goals of the Eighteenth Party
Congress. The postanovlenie stated that the Komsomol at republic, oblast
and krai levels would be instructed to organise a 'mass movement' to
accomplish this task, as would the land departments and directors of
the MTS and state farms. The postanovlenie also recommended socialist
competitions take place throughout the country and made Komsomol'skaia
pravda, Sotsialisticheskoe zemledelie and Sovkhoznaia gazeta, as well as local
newspapers, responsible for their coverage. The importance of the work
was heavily emphasised and all the institutions involved were told to
give the women 'maximum attention and comradely care'. A special
commission was set up to examine the results of the campaign, which
was to run up to 15 December 1939.[74] The document was signed by
N. Mikhailov as Secretary of the Central Committee of the Komsomol
and People's Commissars Benediktov and Lobanov. The women's call
was splashed over the newspapers making headlines in Pravda on 1
April 1939.

In response, keen districts made pledges to train certain numbers
of women, as had Staro-Beshevo and other districts earlier. For
example, the Riazhskii MTS in Riazhskii raion of Riazan oblast
committed itself to training no fewer than twenty women.[75] Other
districts publicly castigated themselves for not responding quickly
enough. One MTS in June 1939 admitted it should have trained
women for the spring sowing, but had not taken the opportunity.
This was a 'big mistake' and now thirty-five women would be trained
by autumn. The MTS took self-criticism further, rebuking itself for
not having yet produced one female tractor brigade leader.[76] Obviously
by June, the party was exerting pressure on those MTS which had
been inactive – hence the self-castigation in line with official priorities.
On an altogether different note, particularly keen women declared
that they were not only training to work on tractors, but, in the
event of war, were prepared to progress to the tank, not leaving
defence to men alone.[77]

Official responses also came from Komsomol central committees at republican and oblast levels. The Komsomol and Narkomzem in the republic of Kirgizia, for example, pledged to train 1000 women tractor drivers. Together with the People's Commissariat of State Farms, these two organisations in Uzbekistan committed themselves to producing thirty women for every MTS. The Stalingrad Komsomol *obkom* expressed readiness to instruct 5000 women. The Saratov *obkom* of the Komsomol together with the oblast land department declared it would teach 3000 women. The Komsomol at district level also made numerous pledges.[78]

The calls, then, for 100,000 women tractor drivers were official, loud and repeated, coming from 'above' and 'below'. But how successful were they? As late as June 1939, the magazine *Krest'ianka* lamented that 'leaders of certain MTS and state farms apparently have still not recognised the great state significance of this business'.[79] With the gloom of war on the horizon, *Krest'ianka* criticised several regions and districts for not fulfilling their obligations. Across fifteen districts in Saratov oblast where 1500 girls had expressed an interest in tractor driving, only 285 had received any instruction. On the 'Peremoga Zhovtnia' collective farm in Kazatinskii district of Vinnitsa oblast, ten girls wanted to drive tractors, but the leaders of the MTS could not organise lessons. *Krest'ianka* went on to list other MTS where this was happening. Pledges had indeed been made, but 'up until now, these remain unrealised'. Still another problem was that on MTS and state farms where lessons were offered, study was 'unplanned, irregular and sometimes organised only around theory'.[80]

Archives confirm this lack of enthusiasm. In early October 1939 a meeting of the bureau of the Central Committee of the Komsomol took Voronezh oblast to task for 'unsatisfactory' performance. The oblast had pledged to train 4000 women, but just 2415 were on courses and only 210 had completed them. Seven districts in the oblast had organised nothing. The local Komsomol and local land departments were blamed for not creating the necessary conditions for training. A *postanovlenie* castigated Voronezh for its 'irresponsible attitude towards fulfilling its obligations' in this matter. The Central Committee instructed the Komsomol *obkom* to take advantage of autumn field work to train women and to organise ten to fifteen seminars on theory to be run by the MTS and state farms.[81] It added that socialist competitions among women tractor drivers should be covered in *Molodoi Kommunar*, which should pass on the 'best experience' to readers and also 'conduct a decisive struggle against unvalued women's work on tractors'.[82] A more detailed report on Voronezh observed that where training did take place it was often 'irregular' and broke down altogether when those leading it failed to turn up. Some women were not given any theoretical training, there were not enough books for them and anyway the semi-literate struggled with these.[83]

Kalinin oblast also came under fire in December 1939 from the Bureau of the Central Committee of the Komsomol for not meeting its pledge to train 2500 women in that year. A *postanovlenie* was issued criticising the oblast for its 'irresponsible attititude' and for not valuing the political and economic significance of the women's tractor movement. Kalinin oblast was instructed to ensure that 1000 women undergoing training were able to complete it by January 1940. The Central Committee also recommended that the *obkom* of the Kalinin Komsomol select 2740 women for courses.[84] It added the warning: 'If in the near future, the situation is not corrected, then more strict measures will be taken.'[85]

Other documents lambasted Narkomzem. The general conclusion was: 'Many land organs write bureaucratic directives' but in reality 'irresponsibly lead the training of women tractor drivers'. In short, they said one thing and did another. The Iaroslav oblast land department, together with the *obkom* of the Komsomol, had declared it would train 1500 women. The land department actually failed to collect any statistics on this, but those gathered by the Komsomol showed that only 974 women were on courses. It was also evident that the land department was not leading this.[86]

Nonetheless, the Iaroslav land department did send directives to all MTS to say that most of them had not yet agreed to participate in competitions and that they should also organise courses for women. When no replies followed, the oblast sent telegrams calling for 'decisive measures' to overcome 'unsatisfactory' work in the training of women.[87] Only three MTS bothered to reply to the telegram and not always positively. The Boshchazhnikovskaia MTS simply informed that women were not trained there, and the oblast land department did nothing to correct this. Moreover, similar situations could be found in a series of other regions and territories, including Tambov, Voronezh, Cheliabinsk and Krasnoiarsk.[88] What was described as boorish behaviour towards women tractor drivers plagued these regions. For example, on an MTS in Irkutsk oblast the best female tractor driver, also a candidate for the Agricultural Exhibition, was taken off her job just because she noted that a radiator needed repairing.[89] Women who were overly enthusiastic were sometimes removed to make life calmer rather than permitted to persist with their complaints.

Certain regional and district committees of the Komsomol also exhibited a gap between words and deeds. Archival documents accused the Komsomol committees of 'ceremony and noise'.[90] They were loud about what they would do, but then failed to deliver. In Petrovskii district of Iaroslav, for example, eighty women wanted to train. Brigade leaders declared they could handle seventy. The *raikom* of the Komsomol decided on fifty. In the end, only seventeen were trained. Quite who these women were or how they were getting on was unknown to comrade Kolinnikov, the secretary of the Komsomol district committee.[91] Even worse was the case of the Komsomol in Tambov. In four districts work with women had stopped. A total of 100 women had been on courses, but now there was no one at all. Secretaries in Komsomol district committees were reported to have no idea what was happening.[92]

Throughout the decade, then, documents show that the Komsomol scolded its workers for not sufficiently encouraging women to drive tractors and for not vigilantly checking the adequate provision of training to meet demand. Local party organisations, too, were criticised as indifferent to the question, slow to act and unaware of developments that were taking place. The press and magazines took Narkomzem to task for its failures. This, however, was consistent with official charges that on broader questions Narkomzem's local organs 'ha[d] not learned how to solve quickly questions which arise' and did not implement party and government decisions.[93] Documents in the party archive castigated the commissariat for its failures and also for its cumbersome structures and mismanagement.[94]

## Conclusion

A report from the Komsomol to Andrei Andreev in the secretariat of the party informed that in September 1939 there were 483,500 tractor drivers in the USSR and 153,300 combine drivers. Of these, 40,000 and 6000 respectively were women. Secretary Gromov of the Komsomol Central Committee commented that this was 'very few'.[95] Another report of 1940 observed that incomplete data suggested that although 90,000 women had been trained to drive tractors, only 50,984 were employed to do so.[96] Another source suggests that, by June 1940, 64,000 women worked as tractor drivers.[97]

There was indeed official commitment to increasing the number of women tractor drivers. A report sent from the Komsomol on 23 February 1940 to Andreev and to Georgii Malenkov in the seretariat of the party informed that on 15 February 1940, 44,000 women were newly qualified tractor drivers and 90,000 were still on courses.[98] It also indicated that the republic of Kirgizia and Stalinskii *obkom* had surpassed their pledges. The former had planned to train 820 women, but in fact put 1324 through courses; the latter had promised to produce 500 female drivers, but had delivered 1664. Other republics, including Armenia, Georgia and Azerbaijan had fulfilled their plans, whereas five republics, six *krai* and forty-six oblasts had failed to do so.[99] Thus the degree of achievement varied across and within republics. In addition, special mention was made of the inattention shown by land departments in Kalinin, Voronezh and Kuibyshev oblasts, despite warnings.[100] The report recommended to the party that women be trained with a break from work, rather than on top of their jobs.[101] It also noted that, once women had been trained, their placement in tractor and combine brigades 'goes very slowly'. Only 5000 of the recently trained had, in fact, been allocated work. The finger again pointed at local land organs for not organising 'this business'.[102] A *svodka* (summary) also detailed by republic, *krai* and oblast the disappointing statistical gap between the number trained and the number actually working on a tractor.[103]

The effort to encourage women into tractor driving, planned from above, was indeed to some extent successful in numerical terms, even if numbers in some areas fell short of plans and notwithstanding the fact that by mid-1940, women constituted a tiny minority among tractor and combine drivers – just 8 per cent.[104] Moreover, this was achieved in a traditional culture with relatively rigid notions of appropriate male and female work. All the time, Marxist ideology spurred the effort on in the name of equality and heroic icons like Pasha Angelina and Pasha Kovardak made rousing speeches to inspire more women to train for the 'home front'.

Throughout, however, many Komsomol reports castigated lax Machine Tractor Stations and state farms for their disinterest in training women. There was not a groundswell of enthusiasm to give women instruction. When women were taught, they also had to endure mockery from male tractor drivers and strained personal relations with family, friends and fellow peasants. While not all male peasants or relatives objected to women's presence on tractors or combines, a sufficient number did to merit regular comment on the topic in newspaper and magazine articles and in memoirs. *Baba*, then, did get on her tractor, but managing to do this, and to stay on it, was far from the smooth process portrayed by socialist realist images. Only when the grim and serious pressures of war demanded it, did the percentage of women on courses escalate from 8.5 to 51 per cent.[105] And women's tractor competitions also persisted during the war.[106]

Painful necessity, then, rather than ideology, spurred women's eventual advancement on the tractor, a 'success' which predictably waned when war ended.[107] Like millions of women in different political systems across the world who were mobilised and lauded in the war effort, the female tractor driver was less welcome after the Great Patriotic War than during it. But the Stalinist utopian dreams of the 1930s also made her more welcome on a tractor or combine in that decade than in the 1950s and after. The heroic visions of change, dreams of monumental possibilities, spectacular advances and whirlwind progress – all characteristic of the grand experiments and exhortations of 'high Stalinism' – made her presence politically appropriate, legitimate and grand. Traditional culture may have been allergic to this development, but it was nonetheless badgered to accommodate it.

# 9

## The German Military's Image of Russia

### JÜRGEN FÖRSTER

The Russo-German war was, for Germany, Russia and Europe, the most important event of the Second World War. Its political repercussions can still be felt today, over sixty years after 22 June 1941. The spectrum of interpretations on the nature of the Russo-German war ranges from a preventive campaign on the part of Germany to a war of *Weltanschauungen*, from an unavoidable showdown between national socialism and Bolshevism to a fascist attack on the first socialist state, from a notion of an offensive against London via Moscow to that of a European crusade against Bolshevism. Moreover, the Cold War between the two victorious blocs after 1945, which lasted more than forty years, prevented old stereotypes of the enemy from being removed. A *historical* knowledge of the past is required if the general understanding of the two dictators' policies between 1939 and 1941 is finally to be put on a solid footing. There is no question of attributing Hitler's misdeeds to Stalin, or counterbalancing Nazi crimes with Soviet ones. It is also unhistorical to draw conclusions about an aggressive Soviet foreign policy simply on the grounds of Stalin's domestic brutality. However, any new knowledge meets tough resistance from both tradition and misconceptions. The latter are the hardest to eradicate.

The history of Nazi–Soviet relations seems to be to a high degree one of mutual misjudgement. In regard to the respective enemy's objectives, strategy and military strength, the climax of self-deception was reached in 1941. While Stalin did not believe the available information about an imminent German attack and avoided provoking Hitler, the latter was convinced of an easy victory over the Soviet Union.[1] Without doubt, Hitler was the central figure in 1940–41. He had dominated German policy since 1933 and was by now master of western and central Europe. Hitler's *Mein Kampf* and *Zweites Buch* give an important insight into his rigidly held political principles, his *Weltanschauung*, his sense of his own unique mission to lead Germany from its existing misery to greatness, his vision of a racially pure *Volksgemeinschaft* (national community), and his long-term aims. Hitler's all-embracing obsession with the 'Jewish question' was inextricably interwoven with the evils of Soviet Bolshevism and the benefits of German *Lebensraum* (living space). Once the link between the enemy images of Bolshevism and Semitism was made, war against Russia would be a fight to the death between two competing ideologies and would at the same time deliver national socialist Germany its salvation by providing necessary living space. A forcible expansion at the expense of the Soviet Union seemed to Hitler so promising because 'Jewish Bolshevism', together with 'Slav racial instincts', had exterminated the last remnants of the former leading Germanic elements in Russia. But the presumed rule of the Jews was racially diagnosed as a source of weakness, since they lacked the ability for organisation. That was why Hitler believed that the 'empire in the east [was] ripe for collapse. And the end of Jewish rule in Russia [would] also be the end of Russia as a state'.[2] This set of beliefs should not be underrated, as they were articles of faith and an estimation of the enemy at the same time. These basic tenets gave Hitler the strength of will and sense of knowing his own destiny. His authority among his followers derived in no small measure from the certainty in his own conviction and the fact that his programme slotted into the continuity of German history.

The long-standing German image of Russia (*Rußlandbild*), dating back to the Crimean War, had at least two mutually contradictory aspects. On the one hand, the nightmarish vision of a growing empire whose political drive westwards (*Drang nach Westen*) would overpower all peoples like a steamroller (*Dampfwalze*). On the other hand, Russia was viewed as a colossus of clay without a head, politically unstable, filled with discontented minorities, and ineffectively ruled. It posed no real obstacle to German expansionist aspirations and could be toppled with one good blow.[3] This dualistic, ambiguous image acquired new, glaring colours after the Bolshevik takeover in Russia and the socialist uprisings in Germany after her collapse in November 1918. As early as the summer of 1918, Karl von Bothmer, the Supreme Army Command's plenipotentiary in Moscow, associated the Bolsheviks with a 'gang of Jews' and wished to see a 'few hundred of those louts hanging on the Kremlin wall'.[4] In particular, the councils of soldiers, 'the darling children of Bolshevik-inspired revolution', were seen as the originators of the disintegration of the German fighting forces, undermining their discipline. The Jews especially were regarded as the 'principal exponents of Bolshevik propaganda'.[5] Many a soldier of the *Reichswehr* found 'domestic and foreign Bolshevism' particularly troubling, not only for himself, but also for the German bourgeois national state and Western culture in general.[6] In July 1926 a navy officer and former Free Corps leader also saw the danger of the Bolshevisation of Europe and stressed that Soviet Russia was the greatest enemy of Germany.[7] In assessing the stability of Stalin's regime or the quality and morale of the Red Army, many a German deluded himself about the racial weaknesses of Russia and came to snap judgements based on ideological preconceptions or ethnic stereotypes. In the fall of 1932, Ewald Banse published his 'thoughts on a national military doctrine'.[8] Anything but a nonentity, Banse was professor at the Technical University of Braunschweig and a prominent member of the National Association for Military Sciences. This organisation, secretly sponsored by the *Reichswehr*, campaigned against pacifism and for a renaissance of German militarism. Convinced that one day, 'in horror of Anglo-Saxon mechanisation and Russian extermination', the world would cry for the 'intellectual world domination' of the German people, Banse analysed Russia's national character knowing that he was quantifying the unquantifiable. Describing the true Russian (*Großrussen*), he differentiates two categories: the giant amorphous mass of ordinary people and the very small group of diverse, mostly Nordic, leadership. The first type was characterised by a snub nose, short legs, fair hair and blue eyes, as well as a contradictory character, due to its Mongolian traits. Dull indifference can suddenly change into violence, incurable apathy into boundless fantasy, vague feelings of inferiority into ludicrous superiority. The Russian mass was incapable of any progressive development or initiative of its own, but in the hands of energetic leaders it could be used to accomplish greater tasks. The true Russian people never knew what they wanted. They fluctuated between deed and dream, remorsefully kissing their icons of saints, and then drank themselves into oblivion. The second type, the leading stratum, was characterised by its international, east-Jewish, Tartarian, Caucasian peculiarities. Leadership and people were not connected by mutual sympathy; the former did not arise out of the latter. Instead, the leadership and the people were like oil and water. What bound them together was the knout. Banse's image of the Russian soldier reflects, of course, these ethnic stereotypes. Looking back on the tsarist army in the First World War, the *mushik* is described as having accepted military discipline uncomprehendingly but willingly, being used to force by his nature. Utterly fearless, he went into battle in waves. Knowing the enemy's superiority in command, training and arms technology, the Russian soldier was brave and clumsy, servile and expecting of his fate. The only self-critical remark comes at the end when Banse admits that the victories that the quantitatively inferior German troops gained in the First World War had, to a high degree, been due to Russian weaknesses.[9] Nine years earlier, Maxim Gorki had visited Germany. Curing his tuberculosis in Bad Saarow near Berlin in the summer of 1923, the Russian writer found the Germans 'strange, very strange people.

Their cultural poverty and rudeness is striking. The political situation is unbelievably hard for them, and their patience is most amazing. And I always thought that no people are more patient than the Russian.'[10]

At the time that Banse's stereotyped image of Russia and its soldiers was published, the *Reichswehr* was still secretly co-operating with the Red Army. Through this, the German military not only gained first-hand insight into the state of Soviet armaments, but made many personal contacts, some of which became close. While almost all German judgements on the Red Army and its gradual development were positive, those on its role in state and society, on the influence of the Communist Party, and on Soviet military leaders and commissars were less unified. Majors General Werner von Blomberg and Hilmar von Mittelberger as well as the diplomats Fritz von Twardowski and Herbert von Dirksen, for instance, held the opinion that Russian nationalism was the main driving force within the Soviet army. Lieutenant Colonel Hermann Geyer, on the other hand, stressed the internationalist character of Soviet ideology, and Major General Hans Halm, visiting the Twenty-Fourth Division in the summer of 1930, an intensive phase of collectivisation in the Ukraine, viewed the troops as nothing but a communist cell. Most German officers favourably noted the 'healthy militarism' in the Soviet Union and its value as an ally.[11] Evaluations of individual Soviet commanders show signs of racism, when Kliment Voroshilov's anti-Semitism, Lev Snitman's 'Jewish slyness' or Leonid Vajner's 'Jewish blood' are mentioned.[12]

On 30 January 1933 Hitler came to power in Germany. He immediately informed his military advisers about his short- and long-term aims. First, Hitler wanted to cast off the chains of Versailles, fight communism and pacifism, and establish an authoritarian rule. Secondly, the military build-up was to be used to conquer living space in the east. Justifications for Germany's expansion and the radical nature and the threat of Jewish Bolshevism became a common pattern of Nazi propaganda. When we analyse, in very general terms, the violence of anti-Soviet images in Nazi propaganda, five phases can be discerned: 1933–5 (moderate), 1935–9 (heated), 1939–41 (cool), 1941–3 (climax of aggressiveness), and 1943–5 (increasingly defensive). Hitler's coup of signing a ten-year non-aggression pact with Poland on 26 January 1934 troubled the Soviet Union as much as the ongoing persecution of communists in Germany. This occasion also marked the formal end of both the *Reichswehr*'s military co-operation with the Red Army, which had rested on the common anti-Polish denominator, and the German military's first-class insight into the state of Soviet armaments and military development. From then on, with direct intelligence gathering becoming nearly impossible, the Wehrmacht had little in the way of hard facts. Where those were lacking, education, training, experience, instinct and intelligent guesswork prevailed over information. Speculations about Stalin's murderous purge within the Red Army, and older assumptions about Russia, had to bridge the growing gaps in the German military's knowledge of Soviet society, economy and armed forces. It is true to say that the problem with German intelligence in respect to the Soviet Union was not structural but attitudinal. Bias and prejudice, and an unwillingness to use intelligence itself, served to hamper German understanding of the Soviet Union.

The first military manual on the Red Army under the new German regime was published in November 1933. It was an un-ideological, matter-of-fact compilation. The section on the soldier's political instruction, for example, reflected more Blomberg's interpretation than Halm's contrasting view. Section V of the manual clearly evaluated the work of the commissars and *politruks* as fostering national thinking, not as 'politicisation' as such. It came to the conclusion that the Red Army was an important fighting machine, despite all its deficiencies and weaknesses. Quantitative strength would increase its importance. Its fighting quality would, however, be highly dependent on the Soviet Union's further structural and economic development which, in the early 1930s, was still in its infancy.[13] The Franco-Soviet pact of May 1935, followed by a similar Soviet–Czech alliance, revived Germany's old anxiety of being encircled. The accompanying battle of words and ink heated the ideological temperature between national socialist Germany and the Soviet Union. A mostly factual report on the Red Army's corps of commissioned and non-commissioned officers that coincided with the signing of the Franco-Soviet pact, included a highly ideological paragraph. Admitting certain increases in levels of education, Colonel Carl-Heinrich von Stülpnagel went on to say: 'The only tradition which has been valid since tsarist times lies in the Russian ethnic character. It is the tendency to pattern, accepting another's will, and connected with this trait, shyness of personal responsibility and initiative. These characteristics, seemingly inextricably intertwined within a Russian, dominate education and training up to today. Its unmilitary and damaging influences will, however, not be felt before going to war.' While noting quantitative and qualitative developments of the political work towards communist ideology, the head of T3 revealed himself as an anti-Semite. Criticising the ever-present distrust within the ranks, Stülpnagel held the attitude and activities of junior politicians, i.e. the commissars, 'mostly of Jewish race', responsible for it.[14] The ideological heat of German military propaganda against the Red Army peaked for the first time in November 1935 when a psychological laboratory of the Reich war ministry submitted a study on the many nationalities in the Soviet Union and the opportunity for their propagandistic exploitation. It included pamphlets drafted in Russian. They had been prepared by a Russian fascist party residing in Harbin (Manchukuo) that stood for a Russia belonging to Russians only. The 'Gentlemen commissars and party functionaries' were not merely defamed as 'mostly filthy Jews', but the 'brother soldiers' of the Red Army were also encouraged to rise against the Jewish-Communist regime and kill the Jewish political commissars.[15] Two years later, analysing the Red Army's doctrine of 1936, army intelligence prepared an un-ideological memorandum. Sülpnagel's successor, Kurt von Tippelskirch, even admitted that it represented signs of eliminating 'the Russian's basic evil', the lack of decisiveness, and praised the manual as often reading like a German one.[16]

In September 1939, when Wehrmacht and Red Army met on friendly terms in divided and occupied Poland, both sides had the rare opportunity of confirming or correcting their respective suppositions. In regard to the tactical capabilities of the Red Army, as well as the appearance and manner of Soviet troops, the Germans felt their former judgements confirmed. The Red Army was seen as a quantitatively huge war instrument, with modern doctrine, tanks and weapons. Yet its organisation was incomplete and the division in the command structure between commander and commissars a factor of weakness. There were no reports on the Soviet artillery. The assessment of Soviet officers and commissars in general was not so unified, but highly ambivalent. The German judgements oscillated between 'intelligent, astute, self-confident, mediocre, cumbersome, sly, obsequious, disciplined, fresh, casual, wily, ruthless, arrogant, uncultured, polite, dishonest, unkempt, inept etc.'. While the German officers were glad to register signs of friendliness and comradeship due to the official 'German–Russian alliance', at common meals they also noticed that their counterparts merely covered up their 'Asiatic manners'. In regard to the troops, the Wehrmacht's supposition was confirmed. 'The Soviet Russian soldier, like the former Russian one, is good-natured, willing, undemanding, and has stamina.'[17] Such frank and critical judgements were confined to the military as, becoming public, they might damage the 'new orientation of German foreign policy in the sense of a German–Russian friendship'.[18] Colonel General Ludwig Beck, the former chief of the army general staff, was an adherent of the more traditional image of the enemy. On 20 November 1939 he spoke of Germany's victory over Poland as being halved by the 'Russian colossus having been set into motion' westwards by the German political leadership.[19] This judgement was in line with his successor's views. General Franz Halder was ordered to prepare a study of 'Security in the east against Russia while the war in the west continues'. Taking captured Polish documents as welcome sources about the dispositions of Soviet formations in eastern Poland, it was concluded that a Soviet attack was not impending and only probable in the event of a German defeat in the west.[20]

Interestingly enough, the Red Army's invasions into Finland, the Baltic States and Bessarabia (1939–40) were closely followed and strengthened the prevailing German military's view that the Red Army was not capable of large-scale operations. Its greatest weaknesses were thought to be stereotyped tactics and a lack of initiative as well as a lack of a trained middle-ranking and senior officer class. The Red Army's more successful performance against Japan in Manchuria (1939) was not taken into account, just like General Köstring's earlier warning that the Red Army would remain a considerable factor in war despite its obvious loss in operational ability through the purges.[21] Overlooked too was an earlier positive report by the army's assistant chief of staff for operations on the Soviet tank force fighting in Spain.[22] Noting the tenacious Finnish resistance against superior Soviet strength, the assistant chief of staff for intelligence was sure on 19 December 1939 that the Red Army's weight of numbers would not be a determining factor when pitted against a large, modern army, i.e. the Wehrmacht.[23]

The attitudinal biases of German intelligence did not greatly impair its tactical usefulness after 22 June 1941. It was Germany's *under*-estimation of the Soviet Union and the *over*estimation of her own capabilities on the strategic level that mattered most. Major General Erich Marcks, who prepared the first operational plan in August 1940, went as far as openly to regret the fact that the Russians would not do the Germans the favour of attacking first, because defence was more suited to the Red Army's character.[24] Yet any major Soviet operation west of the large forest zone and the wide rivers would have been welcomed as a good turn.[25] Colonel Eberhard Kinzel, head of army intelligence on the Soviet Union, supported this view. Though the Red Army's 'regulations and megalomania demand [tactical] attack', it would not even dare to launch a limited campaign against the vital Rumanian oil fields, since 'fear of the German army paralyses [the Red Army's] resolution'.[26] The former Austro-Hungarian officer, Major General Edmund Glaise von Horstenau, was convinced that he could reach the Ural Mountains if he had fair weather and three German panzer corps at his command.[27] When presented with the army's draft plan of operation on 5 December 1940, Hitler stated:

The Russian is inferior. The army is without leadership. It is more than doubtful whether the correct findings of the [Soviet] military leadership that have been noted occasionally in recent times will have been properly evaluated [by the lower echelons]. The internal restructuring of the Russian army will not be better in the spring. [At that time] we will have a perceptibly better position in leadership,

matériel, troops, while the Russians will be at an unmistakably low
point. Once the Russians army is beaten, then disaster cannot be
forestalled.[28]

Four weeks later, Hitler wavered between his old prejudices and newer
facts. Addressing the Wehrmacht leaders at his private home in the
Alps above Berchtesgaden, the Supreme C.-in-C. assessed the Soviet
Union as a 'colossus of clay without a head'. At the same time, Hitler
spoke of Stalin as a clever politician and of the Red Army as undergoing
a reform. He even warned the generals and admirals that the 'Russian
must not be underestimated.'[29]

The most wide-ranging assessment from Foreign Armies East was
issued on 15 January 1941.[30] The study 'The wartime armed forces of the
USSR', which had a circulation of 2000 copies, presented information
gathered in the course of 1940 as well as incorporating older prejudices.
Although army intelligence admitted that its sources were extremely
limited, it nevertheless proceeded to draw broad conclusions about the
Soviet order of battle, doctrine, capabilities and intentions. The study
concluded that the strength of the Red Army rested upon its size and
the quantity of its weapons. The Soviet armed forces were undergoing
a thorough reform and were on the road to becoming as modern as
the Wehrmacht. The mechanised forces were the elite of the army, it
continued, but, technically, the known Soviet tanks and armoured
vehicles were either outdated or developments of foreign models.
Because of the simplicity, stoicism, toughness and bravery of the
ordinary Russian soldier, singular achievements in defence could be
expected: 'The ability to hold out, even in defeat and under heavy
pressure, is particularly in line with the Russian character.' Furthermore,
German intelligence admitted that the Russians had improved culturally.
The so-called *mushik* of 1914 no longer existed. The individual soldier's
cognitive and technical abilities had grown. Still, Foreign Armies East
believed that the Red Army's weaknesses would more than cancel out
its strengths. Soviet training and doctrine were not yet up to German
standards and would not allow the leadership to carry out modern
mobile operations. Soviet officers were clumsy, unwilling to make
decisions or accept responsibility, and too methodical. This study was
followed by a leaflet on the 'peculiarities of Russian warfare'. In contrast
to his performance in the Finnish Winter War, the Soviet soldier would
be inspired by the idea of defending his proletarian fatherland. 'The
Russian [...] usually allows himself to be killed at the spot where his
leader has placed him.'[31] By the end of March 1941 Hitler had partly
corrected his contemptuous judgement of Germany's 'mortal enemy'
in the east. He now regarded the Red Army as a 'tenacious adversary'
with a strong air force and strong tank force, but without leadership,

and he still had no doubts about crushing the Soviet Union within months.[32]

These assumptions of Hitler and his military advisors are one side of the coin, the other being the *Rußlandbild* of the recipients of the information coming from above. They, too, viewed the Soviet Union not merely as a normal state with whose forces a clash of arms had to be considered for reasons of power politics or the assertion of territorial claims. Before Hitler had addressed the Wehrmacht leaders at the Reich chancellery on 30 March 1941, the C.-in-C. of the army, Field Marshal Walther von Brauchitsch, told his commanders that the German troops must be clear that the struggle against the Soviet Union 'will be carried out from race to race, and proceed with necessary severity'.[33] One of those troop commanders, having been present both at Zossen and the Reich chancellery, instructed his divisional commanders:

We are separated from Russia, ideologically and racially, by a deep abyss. Russia is, if only by the mass of her territory, an Asian state [...] The Führer does not wish to palm off responsibility for Germany's existence on to a later generation; he has decided to force the dispute with Russia before the year is out. If Germany wishes to live in peace for generations, safe from the threatening danger in the east, this cannot be a case of pushing Russia back a little — or even hundreds of kilometres — but the aim must be to annihilate European Russia, to dissolve the Russian state in Europe.

The political commissars and the GPU people, Colonel General Georg von Küchler continued on 25 April 1941, are 'criminals. They are the people who enslave the population [...] They are to be put before a court martial and sentenced on the strength of the inhabitants' testimony. There is also the point that these measures should drive a wedge between the political leadership and the probably quite decent Russian soldier. [...] These measures will save us German blood and we shall make headway faster.'[34] Another, equally characteristic example of the optimistic assessment of German and Soviet capabilities on the eve of Barbarossa is that of the chief of staff of the Fourteenth Army, Major General Günther Blumentritt. On 18 April 1941 he stated:

Maybe the Russians really intend to stand and fight the Germans between the western border and the Dnieper, a move that would be desirable [...] Even the Imperial Army was no match for the German command, and the Russian commanders today are at an even greater disadvantage. The shortcomings of the middle ranks are even greater [...] The effects of the German weapons, whose prestige has increased with the campaign against Yugoslavia, will soon be felt! There will be fourteen days of heavy fighting. Hopefully, by then we shall have made it.[35]

In regard to the strength of Communism within the Red Army, Blumentritt looked back to the First World War. Then he had outlined in a memorandum: 'On warfare and the inner value of the Russian opponent, the dull mass had had two kind of "ideas": the tsar and God. Today, there is neither. Bolshevism has taken their place. I consider that as a weakness since I never believe that this idea means anything to the bulk of the Russian people. That is why I do not believe that this people will be carried away by Bolshevism. They will soon be indifferent and fatalistic.'[36] In replying to Benito Mussolini, Hitler claimed that Stalin had transformed Bolshevism into 'a Russian-national state ideology and economic idea'.[37]

In June–July 1941, just before and after the first shot was fired on the eastern front, the German troops were literally bombarded with political and moral justifications for fighting the Soviet Union. Nazi ideology dominated over political objectives, long-held negative stereo-types were dug up. Distorted enemy images, supposed vital needs of the German people and alleged military necessities gave Wehrmacht and SS something like a clear conscience to apply unlawful methods. The Wehrmacht's own deliberate linkage of military needs with ideo-logical aims, of punitive with preventive measures against all real or alleged resisters, paved the way for soldiers to join the SS in striking a fatal blow against those they identified with the phantom of Jewish Bolshevism. The Wehrmacht's tendency to suspect barbarity and treach-ery of the enemy coincided with its own attitude to dehumanise Soviet soldiers, especially Asiatic, communist and Jewish ones. Unlike the German soldier, the Soviet soldier was portrayed as lacking humanity. Soviet atrocities in turn fanned the fires of a war without mercy. Ordinary men performed extraordinary tasks. The murder of political prisoners or the mutilation of captive German soldiers seemed to confirm what the Wehrmacht rank and file had been told about the 'barbaric Asiatic fighting' methods of the Red Army under the influence of hate-filled Jewish-Bolshevik commissars.[38] The main theme of Wehrmacht propaganda, directed against the Red Army and the popu-lation in the east or channelled to the troops, was that Germany's enemies were not the 'nations of the Soviet Union, but exclusively the Jewish-Bolshevik Soviet government with its functionaries and the Communist Party', which was 'working for world revolution'. The Wehrmacht was entering the country as a liberator and would 'save' the population 'from the tyranny of the Soviets'.[39] Along with the Soviet leadership, the commissar was 'enemy Number One'. He was the 'centre-piece' of both the German leaflet propaganda against the Red

Army, developing the foundations laid in 1935 by the psychological laboratory in the Reich War Ministry, and the internal information that was to facilitate the Wehrmacht's implementation of the unlawful commissar decree. The first June issue of the official 'Information for the troops' (*Mitteilungen für die Truppe*) carried the hate propaganda to a new height:

> Anyone who has ever looked into the face of a Red commissar knows what Bolsheviks are. There is no need here for theoretical reflections. It would be an insult to animals if one were to call the features of these, largely Jewish, tormentors of people beasts. They are the embodiment of the infernal, of personified insane hatred of everything that is noble humanity. In the shape of these commissars we witness the revolt of the subhuman against the noble blood. The masses whom they are driving to their deaths with every means of icy terror and lunatic incitement would have brought about an end of all meaningful life, had the incursion not been prevented at the last moment.[40]

Adolf Hitler was depicted as the 'instrument of providence' for the salvation of Europe. This was potent imagery and rhetoric, ambiguous, yet uncompromising and reflected in soldiers' letters. Addressing his father, who had already fought in the First World War, a tank soldier wrote on 4 August 1941:

> The pitiful hordes on the other side are nothing but felons who are driven by alcohol and the [commissars'] threat of pistols at their heads [...] They are nothing but a bunch of assholes! [...] Having encountered these Bolshevik hordes and having seen how they live has made a lasting impression on me. Everyone, even the last doubter, knows today, that the battle against these sub-humans, who've been whipped into frenzy by the Jews, was not only necessary but came in the nick of time. Our Führer has saved Europe from certain chaos.[41]

On 22 June 1941, neither Hitler nor his military had doubted that they had enough time and means to destroy the Soviet forces, thereby also striking a decisive blow against Britain. The huge successes of the early days confirmed these expectations. German military confidence and self-esteem rose to unprecedented heights. After only two weeks, the army's chief of general staff regarded the campaign as won.[42] Yet four weeks later it became apparent that Operation Barbarossa had failed.[43] The 'Russian colossus' had been underestimated in terms of its military and economic strength, its ability to organise an effective defence, as well as of the power of its idea, Bolshevism.[44] The time factor now favoured the Red Army and the 'vastness of the Russian space' provided the Wehrmacht with problems which became ever more difficult to solve as German attacking strength declined. Situation reports and ethnic stereotypes had to be amended to conform with realities. Foreign Armies East assessment of the Red Army, re-issued in 1200 copies in December 1941, shows that realism was still out of sight and prejudices prevailed.[45] Even the unexpected Soviet winter offensive did not shatter the Wehrmacht's belief in its military and racial superiority over the Red Army. Thus the illusion of victory persisted though the soldiers knew that they had to fight a longer war against a fierce and stubborn foe. The German leadership skills, 'harder will', and proven resilience of the soldiers, it was considered, were more important than other factors: enormous losses in matériel and personnel, terrain, and climate. But the misperception of 1942 was different from that of 1940–41. Since Hitler and the German military establishment refused to think of any other way out of the war, they felt compelled to believe in victory in 1942 although the planned decisive offensive was to commence in only one sector of the eastern front.[46]

Even after the second onslaught in the east had failed, the German leadership was not willing to shut its eyes and await catastrophe. It demanded that the troops fight the coming defensive battles in the proud knowledge of former victories, strong confidence in their own ability, and the uncompromising will to crush the enemy again. Yet there were signs of repainting the Wehrmacht's image of Russia. On 25 November 1942, Colonel Reinhard Gehlen, head of Foreign Armies East, wrote:

> The Russian is different from us. He feels, where we think – without being more stupid. He lets things take their course, where we organise. He endures where we rebel. He still has reserves where we think he is broken, and he judges differently from us. We see from the standpoint of community, he personally. If the Russian feels he is well ruled, not downgraded to an inferior people, and the leadership is partly in Russian hands, his ambition will essentially be satisfied. His drive to the Dardanelles was always less important than ours eastwards. Thus, his nationalism is different from ours, but it exists and leads to clear demands. If they are met, then he follows the one that granted them, willingly and reliably. If he has any doubts, then he becomes, slowly but surely, a dangerous instrument in the hands of the opponent, due to Russian tenacity and fearlessness in the face of death. Of his accepted leadership, the Russian demands justice, organisational talents, understanding, and welfare. If those demands are met, he grants his leadership severity and harshness, makes great sacrifices and achieves outstanding results, willingly and indefatigably.[47]

Captain Wilfred Strik-Strikfeldt and the popular writer Edwin Erich Dwinger argued along similar lines.[48] The oscillation between ideology and pragmatism can clearly be seen in the letters of a critical general staff officer at the front: 'That's really something: that the "beasts" we fought up to now are, after being taken prisoner, honourably recruited as service personnel (*Hilfswillige, Hiwis*) and living with us in our community. It is advisable not to think too deeply about those things.'[49]

Russia remained an enigma to the very end, just as the traditional image of the 'ugly' Russian persisted.[50] As I stated at the beginning, the Cold War between the two victorious blocs after 1945 prevented old stereotypes of the enemy from being removed. When West Germany's contribution to the European Defence Community was discussed in parliament in 1952, Lieutenant General (ret.) Adolf Heusinger, the former chief of army operations and now military advisor of Chancellor Konrad Adenauer, told the members of the relevant committee:

> We have always experienced, and we will do so again if it comes to it, that in mobile operations we are absolutely superior to the Russian. The moment the Russian is hindered to follow his concept, he becomes clumsy and ponderous [...] The only soldier who knows the Russian is the German [...] The advantage the West gets of twelve German divisions, from the nation that fought the Russian for many years, this advantage in mobility of European defence must not be underestimated [...] I personally have – I must frankly say – such an unshakeable confidence in German men (*den deutschen Menschen*) and German qualities that I believe we can hope that the new troops will gain the same degree of steadfastness and tenacity to fight the Russian which the old troops had had.[51]

There it was again, the old image of German superiority.

# 10

## Celluloid Soldiers
## Cinematic Images of
## the Wehrmacht

OMER BARTOV

# I

The German Wehrmacht is popularly best known for its introduction of the concept and practice of *Blitzkrieg*. This type of modern warfare, whose roots can be traced back to World War I, changed the realities of the battlefield in the middle of the twentieth century and facilitated Nazi Germany's extraordinary military victories in the first two years of the war. What is often less well appreciated is that *Blitzkrieg* did not only consist of a combination of mobile armoured units, close air support, and tactics of penetration and envelopment, but also of creating a certain image of the attacking forces that made them appear to their foes as practically invincible. Indeed, *Blitzkrieg* called for shocking the enemy both physically and psychologically. Such psychological preparation could come in the form of screaming dive-bombers and endless columns of rapidly advancing tanks; it could also be created by means of a sophisticated use of the modern media, among which film was the most effective and by far the most popular.

In a series of documentaries produced in Nazi Germany during World War II, the Wehrmacht was depicted as the best military machine ever fielded.[1] Its complete superiority over its enemies was not merely material or tactical, but also related to the innate quality of its men and to the urgency and rightness of its cause. Thus the excellence of German war machines, the daring of Wehrmacht tactical innovations, the physical prowess and high morale of the soldiers, and the pressing necessity of the Third Reich's policies of expansion and occupation, were seamlessly linked to each other in screen images and spoken texts intended to intimidate future enemies just as much as to encourage the population at home. To be sure, soon thereafter Germany's opponents learned how to use its *Blitzkrieg* tactics against it and ultimately crushed the Reich by employing superior numbers of men and machines; they also learned how to make increasingly effective use of the media, and most especially of film documentaries and features, in order to provide a very different image both of the enemy and of their own armies. By the time the Wehrmacht finally capitulated, all that remained of its former image of material and moral superiority was the films made during the Third Reich's heyday.

Yet this was not where the story ended. As I have written elsewhere, the notion of *Blitzkrieg* as a swift, clean, and exhilarating war never disappeared, and was employed both as an image and as a reality on several occasions since 1945.[2] Among the most important cases one can mention the Arab–Israeli Six Day War of 1967 and, most recently, the American conquest of Iraq in spring 2003. Thus, while the Wehrmacht was defeated, the concept and image of *Blitzkrieg* retained its popularity. Moreover, while Nazi Germany came to be seen as the embodiment of evil in the twentieth century, the German army successfully resisted being implicated in Hitler's crimes for many decades after the fall of the Third Reich. Hence both the tactical aspect of Nazi Germany's war (during its days of lightning victories) and the image of its soldiers as not only untainted by any crimes but in fact as morally superior was maintained long after the fighting ended.

Indeed, to some extent this image was reworked and improved in the post-war period, not least with the help of German (as well as some foreign) filmmakers. As indicated by the debate over the exhibition 'War of Extermination: Crimes of the Wehrmacht, 1941–44', which roamed Germany and Austria in the second half of the 1990s, there were still powerful reserves of apologetics regarding the German army's 'decency' and 'honour' despite an impressive list of scholarly works that had, by then, conclusively shown how deeply the military was implicated in war crimes and genocide.[3] There is little doubt that one major source for the preservation and reformulation of the Wehrmacht's 'clean' image was popular feature films, in which a certain type of the 'good' soldier was created and developed. Interestingly, while this celluloid soldier was intended to protect the good name of the Wehrmacht long after its physical and institutional demise, it also came to reflect certain needs and opinions in post-war West Germany. These included a powerful anti-war and anti-militaristic sentiment, abhorrence of Nazism, sympathy for its (German) victims and the 'little man' manipulated by the wheels of fortune and the powers that be, and admiration for those who stood up against evil. How such sentiments could be reconciled with cinematic representations that were largely defensive of Hitler's army is a question well worth investigating.[4]

In what follows I briefly analyse several German feature films that have been particularly instrumental in creating this celluloid image of the Wehrmacht. I show that while this image is simplistic, indeed almost cartoon like, it has simultaneously fulfilled a complex set of demands in German post-war society. By way of conclusion I discuss two recent

German documentaries that have tried to provide a more nuanced and critical view of the Wehrmacht. This provides an opportunity to gauge the extent to which the German public's own views of the Wehrmacht have evolved over time.

## II

Helmut Käutner's *The Devil's General* (1954) is a cinematic dramatisation of Carl Zuckmayer's play of 1946.[5] The story is loosely based on the life of Ernst Udet, World War I flying ace and later inspector-general of the Luftwaffe, who was pressured into committing suicide in November 1941 both because of the deficiencies of German aircraft performance and because of his criticism of the Nazi regime.[6] Yet General Harras (Curt Juergens), Udet's cinematic persona, goes somewhat further than the historical character. Initially Harras appears as a frivolous womaniser and drinker who may be willing to poke fun at the regime but is too dedicated to his profession and too cynical a character to actually make a stand against Hitler. Yet as the film develops Harras comes under the suspicion that he is producing intentionally flawed aircraft. It thus appears that beneath his veneer of lighthearted irony Harras may be concealing a determined resister to the Nazis. Indeed, when he realises that there is no way out, Harras climbs into one of his own sabotaged aircraft and crashes right after take-off.

Whereas Udet was accused of having erred by insisting on the production of medium bombers and fighter planes rather than the kind of heavy bombers that were eventually produced in vast numbers by Germany's foes, Harras, his cinematic double, is therefore consciously sabotaging Hitler's war effort. This is never clearly spelled out in the film, however, since German viewers in the 1950s might have found it rather distasteful that a German general, even if only in the movies, was deliberately causing the death of combat pilots by producing badly designed machines. Harras thus enjoys a rather ambivalent role: he is resisting an evil regime, and indeed pays for his courage with his own life; but he does so without any clear evidence of the price such resistance may cost others. The entire story has some echoes of Arthur Miller's play, *All My Sons* (1947), about a corrupt defence contractor whose faulty airplane parts cause the death of his son and other fliers during World War II, only that in *The Devil's General* Harras turns out to be a hero rather than a crook.[7]

This film is still somewhat in the traditional mode of contrasting a high-ranking traditional Wehrmacht officer, an elegant, handsome, courageous, and skilful representative of the old military elite, with the corrupt, power-hungry, opportunistic, crass, and fanatical servants of the Nazi regime. To be sure, Harras is torn between his patriotism, soldierly loyalty and professional dedication, on the one hand, and his realisation that he is serving the devil, on the other. But he ultimately makes the right choice and, despite all the historical evidence to the contrary, is thus seen as representative of the upright officer corps as a whole and as having protected the Wehrmacht's shield of honour by his sacrifice. The culprits, those who dragged Germany in the mud, caused its destruction and also wreaked destruction on (rarely seen) others, are Hitler and his cronies, the SS, Gestapo, and a few corrupt but unrepresentative officers.

By identifying with Harras's plight and admiring his lightly worn valour, never overplayed and always accompanied by the right measure of irony, flirting and social grace even as he mocks the obviously low-class Nazis, German middle-glass audiences could also reinterpret their own wartime experience in a similarly self-forgiving manner. The old elites had behaved correctly, even if initially they might have been fooled by the Nazi rabble. And the viewers, who had followed these elites, could not be blamed for having done so, for they had merely emulated the example of such upright men as Harras – even if in reality for every Harras there were a thousand officers who led their men to kill and to die for Hitler.

*The Devil's General* is very much in the mode of memoirs by real-life generals such as Heinz Guderian and Erich von Manstein, who claimed (quite falsely) to have either opposed or not to have known about Hitler's policies of mass murder and genocide and to have been entirely unblemished as professional soldiers.[8] Indeed, this was the general tenor of representation of the senior officers and traditional elites in the conservative 1950s in the Federal Republic.[9] It took until the later 1960s and 1970s for the younger generation to rebel against this view of Nazism as having been a takeover by foreign and underworld elements that shoved aside the good old upper class of upright officers, decent civil servants, and exemplary clergy and enforced a rule of moral depravity on the Germans. Such interpretations naturally enough served to justify the return of the old elites in the name of reinforcing the social and moral order. They also neatly concealed the vast extent of crucial collaboration with Hitler's regime by the old officer corps, the bureaucracy, and the churches, without which the Nazis could have made very little headway domestically and practically none in terms of waging a war of conquest and expansion. Parallel to this conservative view of the past, however, a new mode of representation of war and soldiers began emerging both in prose fiction and in cinema.

# III

If General Harras is troubled by the 'abominations' (*Scheusslichkeiten*) of the regime, it is never quite clear whether these refer to the corruption of the Reich, the mismanagement of the war, the oppression of the Germans, or the mass murder of the Jews. Harras, of course, both is complicit with the regime – in that he runs its military aircraft production – and is risking his neck by saving some Jews. As Himmler complained in his infamous Posen speech of October 1943, although everyone knew that the Jews had to be done away with, once the extermination process got into gear every German came up with his one 'decent' Jew who had to be spared.[10] But while this statement merely reflected Himmler's obsession with creating a *'judenrein'* universe, after the war numerous 'decent' Germans did indeed claim – rarely with any evidence – that they had saved at least one Jew, no matter how much Jewish blood they might have otherwise had on their hands. Similarly, Guderian averred in his memoirs that he had never passed on the criminal sections of the 'Barbarossa Decree' for the invasion of the Soviet Union to his troops; but the files of his formations belie his assertion. Manstein, for his part, claimed that he even contemplated joining the resistance (he never did); in fact, he issued a particularly vicious anti-Jewish order to his troops in Ukraine as early as November 1941.[11]

The image of the heroic, correct, and decent general was tarnished in Germany even before the war ended. After all, for the regular front-line soldier, the generals had become implicated in the regime's failures and crimes: not so much those committed against the political and 'biological' enemies of Nazism, but rather the destruction of Germany and the annihilation of its armies. For more committed soldiers, the July 1944 putsch attempt against Hitler was seen as evidence that the senior Wehrmacht leadership was infected with treason and defeatism. All of this led to the emergence of a new type of heroic soldier, one that was destined to a very long life indeed, both because he served the purpose of saving German masculinity and honour without implicating them in Nazi crimes, and because he provided a link with post-war sentiments not only in Germany but also in many other countries in the West.[12]

In order for this type of heroic German soldier to be acceptable in the Federal Republic, however, he had to be insulated from the reality of sentiments and prejudices that pervaded Nazi Germany. Thus any anti-Semitic and anti-Slav views had to be suppressed, although anti-communism was not only acceptable but even a crucial link between the German past and present and between the new Germany and its

Western allies. Further, this refashioned hero had to figure as a victim rather than an instrument of Hitler's rule, and as a helpless pawn rather than a willing actor in the military machine into which he had been pressed. Obviously, such heroes could not have any knowledge of, and certainly were allowed no complicity in, the crimes carried out 'behind the back' of the fighting troops. While the new hero was patriotic, he was no nationalist; he was ready to sacrifice himself any time, but only for his comrades, not for such abstractions as *Volk* and *Führer*. Unlike the square-jawed poster boy of the SS, this new hero was emotionally sensitive (he often played the piano), but never fanatical. Attractive and sexually potent, this type might encounter both German and occasionally also 'exotic' Slavic women but he never abused his power even when (as was expected) he was betrayed by female spies and partisans or merely by unfaithful women at home.

In short, the heroic German soldier at the sharp end of war was created both as an ideal male and as the precise opposite of everything that would have made him into one of the Third Reich's real tools of expansion and destruction. Yet this heroic figure retained a measure of authenticity because he did reflect the qualities increasingly heralded by the Wehrmacht itself in the latter phases of the war: rugged, cool and efficient determination, and impatience with empty rhetoric, barracks discipline and safely installed staff officers and propagandists. Conversely, these celluloid heroes were deprived of the driving ideological motiv-ation, the fierce loyalty to the Führer, the intense ruthlessness vis-à-vis all those perceived as the Reich's enemies, and the general brutality and nihilism that increasingly characterised the real soldiers of the Wehr-macht. It was this combination of truth and lies that made the appearance of the cinematic soldier on German screens in the 1950s and beyond especially welcome, providing as it did a kind of antidote to the 'typical' Nazi criminal one occasionally encountered in the courtroom but never associated with the proud soldiers of yesteryear.

The films that created this type were also often based on prose fiction.[13] Their popularity demonstrated that they quite accurately antici-pated the sensibilities of the public in 1950s Germany. That they set the tone for war movies in the next few decades showed that these sensibilities, however much they changed from one generation to another, retained certain fixed elements as far as the German public's perception of the war was concerned. Moreover, since several of these films also gained foreign attention and popularity, it appears that the German view of World War II, and Western perceptions of war in general, began to converge – even though their points of departure and implications were quite different. Indeed, the European and American celluloid soldier of the late twentieth and early twenty-first centuries seems by and large to have the same characteristics no matter what language he speaks, and appears to be fighting the same battle against the same enemies no matter which war is actually being depicted in the movie.

One of the most popular films of the early post-war period was Paul (Ostermayr) May's three-part production *08/15* (1954–5), based on Hans Hellmut Kirst's best-selling trilogy of the same name.[14] Somewhat reminiscent of Erich Maria Remarque's *All Quiet on the Western Front* in structure and atmosphere, this novel and film tell the story of Private, later Sergeant and finally Lieutenant Asch (Joachim Fuchsberger) from his time in a stereotypically stupid, abusive, and humiliating boot camp on the eve of World War II all the way to service on the Russian front and the final collapse and occupation of Germany. Described as 'an anti-war satire of epic proportions', the film is notable for several central features. First, its main character, Asch, is indeed a sensitive, piano-playing, good-hearted, and courageous young man. Second, the army is largely divided between such types as Asch along with older, no-nonsense, more senior combat officers, on the one hand, and brutal, heavy-drinking, cowardly, and corrupt NCOs and officers both at the barracks and at the front, on the other hand. Third, the war is stupid, nobody knows why it is being fought, and while the good soldiers fight it well they are doomed to victimhood because of their military and (rarely mentioned) political leadership. Fourth, the soldiers on both sides of the front, as well as the populations of Germany and occupied Russia, are all in the same soup, even though their task is to kill each other. Fifth, neither ideology nor war crimes are ever mentioned, so that this film (and many others) could just as well be about World War I. The fact that Germany went out to a war of extermination in the east and that it was simultaneously carrying out the genocide of the Jews simply does not appear in the film. Finally, the collapse of the Third Reich and its occupation (in the film's case) by the Americans is seen in rather ambivalent terms. Happy to be rid of the (hardly ever mentioned) Nazis, the good German soldiers are obviously superior to their gum-chewing, dumb-looking American occupiers. Disturbingly, the most intelligent among the Americans is an officer with distinct Jewish features who speaks perfect German and is obviously a refugee who came back with the US army. The manner in which this Jew is portrayed (no other Jews appear during the approximately 300 minutes of this trilogy) makes it clear that the price Germany paid for its defeat was the return of such unsavoury characters thankfully flushed out by the Nazis only a few years earlier.

Behind the film's cinematic rhetoric is a simple and easily digestible argument that clearly spoke to German audiences at the time. The war was unleashed by a stupid political leadership supported only by similarly stupid and cowardly NCOs and officers. It was fought bravely by the best of Germany's youth, who lost because they were led by idiots and confronted insurmountable odds. The survivors of the war will build a better Germany, having got rid of the regime that betrayed them and of the occupiers who know nothing about Germany. Victimised both by its own leaders and by its enemies, Germany will nevertheless make it because young brave men such as Asch will lead it into a better future.

Other films made in the 1950s followed a similar pattern. Geza von Radvanyi's popular *Der Arzt von Stalingrad* (*The Doctor from Stalingrad*, 1958), based on Heinz Günther Konsalik's 1956 bestseller of the same name, tells the story of German prisoners of war captured in Stalingrad and doomed to a wretched existence in a Siberian camp for many years after the end of World War II.[15] The hero, Doctor Fritz Böhler (O. E. Hasse, who also plays in *08/15*), is both an expert surgeon and the heart and soul of the camp, encouraging the prisoners to wait patiently for their (obviously much deserved) liberation. This older, experienced man, who had also experienced World War I, is juxtaposed with the younger and more impetuous Doctor Sellnow (Walter Reyer), who has an affair with the tough, beautiful, and passionate Russian Captain Alexandra Kasalniskaya (Eva Bartok). Thanks to his professional skills, Böhler manages to arrange for the liberation of the prisoners. But when Kasalniskaya's lover, camp commandant Piotr Markov (Hannes Messemer) discovers her kissing Sellnow he shoots the German and imprisons the female Russian officer for supposedly fraternising with the enemy.

As has been noted by Robert Moeller, this film, though made by a Hungarian émigré, fully rehabilitates the German man and soldier as honest, brave, tough, skilful and masculine. The older Böhler's charisma wins over not only the Germans but also their captors, and his professional skills as a surgeon surpass anything one can find in the Soviet Union. While conscious that the Germans deserve some sort of punishment (even if their crimes are never clearly spelled out) he is also naturally convinced that they should be given back their freedom. The younger Sellnow belies all anxieties about the decline of German masculinity: he wins over the tough Russian beauty who clearly prefers him to the mutilated camp commandant despite the risks involved. It is possible, as the film seems to hint, that the Germans had not fought the right war, but it is much clearer that they have become victims of crimes they had not committed and that their victimisers are both at least as bad as the worst Germans (of whom we have no examples in the film) and are definitely their inferiors culturally, professionally, and racially (as exemplified by the Mongols who play the Soviet troops). Clearly the racist sentiments that lurked very close to the surface among German audiences in the 1950s were confirmed by this contrast between a rehabilitated Germany and a threatening East still populated by remnants of 'subhumans' taken directly from Nazi propaganda.[16]

The biggest box-office hit of this period, however, was Frank Wisbar's *Hunde, wollt ihr ewig leben? (Dogs, do you want to live for ever?)* (1959). Though Wismar left Germany in 1938 and returned from the United States only in 1955, his film captured better than any other the German attitudes of the time – and many years later – towards the war. Indeed, Wismar created a cast of soldier heroes and villains that both reflected and created the acceptable image of German martial qualities and masculinity. What is remarkable about this film is that in many ways it can be seen as the essential link between the self-representation of German soldiers in the last years of the war, the image of the celluloid German hero of the 1950s, and the recreation of that image in full Technicolor and Dolby sound since the 1980s. What we have here is Wehrmacht soldiers who are always unvanquished even though they lose the battle and the war; men who are untainted by any allegiance to a criminal regime precisely because they start off as its tools and end up as its victims; Germans whose best qualities of loyalty, dedication, and willingness to sacrifice have been abused and exploited, yet whose innate moral superiority nevertheless shines though. Stark battle scenes interspersed with documentary material, confrontations with a few and obviously despicable Nazi officers, deep despair in the face of certain defeat yet almost inhuman resilience – all of these manage to turn the reality of the battle of Stalingrad on its head. In 1943 Josef Goebbels succeeded in turning the catastrophic destruction of the Sixth Army into a rallying cry for total war rather than conceding that it was the beginning of the end of Nazi Germany. Sixteen years later *Hunde* transformed an event in which Soviet armour put an end to fantasies of German superiority into the birthplace of post-war German manhood. From the site that saw hundreds of thousands die for a criminal regime sprang forth the legend of a victimised, betrayed and for that very reason cleansed and heroic German soldier.

# IV

The battle of Stalingrad has fascinated numerous military historians, writers, and filmmakers. It was the turning point of the war, the beginning of the relentless Soviet march westward that ended in Berlin, and one of the most destructive battles ever fought. In the 1970s the German filmmaker Alexander Kluge became obsessed with this battle of vast losses and endless sacrifice.[17] And yet, in some ways, very little has changed in the representation of Stalingrad and the meanings given to it. Because it was so filled with despair, death, and devastation, the battle has been seen (along with, most recently, the strategic bombing of Germany) as an instance of undeniable German victimhood. In *Hunde*, we do not hear about the trail of death left by the Sixth Army as it traversed Ukraine, murdering thousands upon thousands of Soviet citizens, mostly Jews, as well as facilitating the organisation of the Holocaust in these areas by Himmler's *Einsatzgruppen*.[18] Nor are we told what precisely these brave German soldiers were doing in Stalingrad in the first place, wasting their undeniable courage in fighting and dying for Hitler rather than turning against him or refusing to go where they had no business being. In this sense we can say that the post-war celluloid soldier was born in West German cinema from the mass graves of his victims: it is not only that this hero was necessary to save German masculinity, honour, and hope in the future following the defeats, humiliations, and self-inflicted catastrophe of Nazism; he was also necessary so as to cover up that other soldier, the man who, multiplied by tens upon tens of thousands, participated, willingly or not, in the destruction of European Jewry and many other alleged biological and political enemies of Nazism.

That this was the case in a film made in 1959, only a few years after the last German POWs returned from the Soviet Union, when the Cold War was at its height, and while West Germany was still in the hold of the conservative elites that took over the country ten years earlier, is perhaps understandable. But when comparing *Hunde* to what can only be seen as its weaker remake, Joseph Wilsmaier's *Stalingrad* (1993), one is stunned by the extent to which precisely these same themes can be identified there. Here again we have desperate soldiers, mostly decent men who only want to survive the hell of battle; a sadistic Nazi officer who ultimately gets what he deserves; and a particularly heroic lieutenant who not only goes against the Nazis and protects his men but also saves a Russian woman raped by some of the less worthy elements of the Wehrmacht. Once more, the central figures in the film are its heroic victims, the simple men and tough officers of the German army. The battle is fought in a political and historical void: where they came from, what they would have done had they won, who they were fighting for and who they killed on the way to their own mass grave we can only guess. They are, it seems, the victims of war like all others. War is hell, as the saying goes, and in this hell, these particular victims conduct themselves with great honour and dignity. We can only salute them as they march to captivity.

*Stalingrad* was, however, not as successful as Wolfgang Petersen's film *Das Boot* (1985), which may have served it as a model along with *Hunde*. Petersen uses the ideal setting for the kind of cinematic rhetoric I have outlined. Here we have a submarine crew, locked inside the steel hull of its boat under the water and therefore totally insulated from the politics and crimes of the war. In the silence of the ocean and within the narrow confines of an airless and crowded space everything depends on skill, courage, good nerves and co-operation. This is the perfect arena for heroes, men who can exercise charisma in time of crisis and gain the unending trust and loyalty of their crew without any reference to ideological convictions, historical context, or future goals.

One of the most popular war movies ever made, *Das Boot* has precisely the same ingredients as many of the previous films I have mentioned: it masquerades as an anti-war film even as it celebrates the manly qualities that are best manifested at time of war and crisis; it makes its audience believe that they are expressing their abhorrence of war even as they go to watch it in their multitudes precisely because they too are complicit in the kind of exhilaration that so many men feel at the sight of death and destruction. In a sense, there is no difference between this film and, for instance, such more recent war movies as *Black Hawk Down* (2001), even though the latter does not even bother to offer any anti-war perspectives. They both relish situations of extremity and peril, and glorify male camaraderie and loyalty. They claim to be independent of any politics and ideology even as they become complicit in them by the very fact that they present the tools of these policies as having nothing to do with them. And they both attract young male audiences who, while they may avoid actually killing and dying in battle, get a great thrill out of seeing this happen on the big screen.

In this sense, we can say that the circle has been closed, and the celluloid soldiers of German post-war cinema have joined the ranks of Hollywood's cinematic heroes, from John Wayne and Gary Cooper to Tom Hanks and Mel Gibson, those reluctant American supermen who defy authority, fight only for their men, and win their country freedom and glory. But because Germany's heroes of World War II were also its tools of genocide, the normalisation of these celluloid soldiers is hardly an uncontested process. Indeed, some recent films have tried to confront this dilemma from an entirely different perspective. By way of conclusion, I briefly examine two of the more important (though far less popular) movies in this genre.

Harriet Eder and Thomas Kufus's *Mein Krieg* (*My Private War*) (1991) is an extraordinary documentary on the manner in which German soldiers experienced World War II. The film presents this view through showing the amateur films taken during the war by six Wehrmacht soldiers and interviewing them in between screenings of this footage. Now elderly men, the veterans reminisce, sentimentally recall their lost youth, fallen friends, and, increasingly, come to talk about the nature of the war they fought and how they have subsequently learned to think about it. Most of them are apologetic about their own experience as well as about their comrades and, indeed, the entire war. One of them is more than defensive, indeed, is outright aggressive in his rhetoric about the rightness of their cause. Another is bitter and critical; he recalls the humiliation of training (remindful of *08/15*) the brutality of the fighting, and hints at much greater atrocities he has observed. For a brief moment, one of these amateur films captures the sight of a mass grave. It is clear that a murder of innocents has taken place. But both the veterans and the filmmakers (who do the interviewing) shrink away from further inquiry.

By the end of the film, we realise that the men who have taken these pictures know more than they are willing to talk about or even remember. We know that, like all older people, they are nostalgic about the good old days of physical health and great hopes. The celluloid soldiers we glimpse in their homemade movies are not victims: they are young, healthy, often quite cheerful and proud, as they march into a future that ended up devouring many of them and many more of their victims. Of their victims we see and hear little. If they filmed them (which as we know many soldiers actually did), we are not shown these pictures.[19]

*Mein Krieg* gives a very different twist to the cinematic image of the German soldier in World War II, and shows the trajectory of that image from youthful ebullience to old age. But with one exception, old age is not more contemplative, although it is definitely nostalgic. Have these veterans learned something from the past? It seems that they kept their worst memories of it locked in the same closets that contained their amateur films for decades. Did they talk about their experiences with their children and grandchildren? It appears that for the most part, they did not.

Ruth Beckermann's *Jenseits des Krieges* (distributed in the US as *East of War* in 1996) takes a much more critical and confrontational view of Germany's war and its soldiers. This is largely because the film was shot in 1995 when the exhibition 'War of Extermination: Crimes of the Wehrmacht 1941–1944' was shown in Vienna. Hence this is a cinematic record of the reactions of visitors to an exhibition whose impact was due to the hundreds of photographs, often taken by soldiers, of atrocities committed by the Wehrmacht and other German and non-German agencies in Serbia and the Soviet Union. Here we finally encounter both the reality of the war and the reality of reaction to its truth rather than to its neatly packaged fictions. Ironically, the exhibition itself was charged in 1999 with having manipulated photographic images and, under severe attack from German right-wing and revisionist elements, was forced to close pending an investigation by a commission of experts. Eventually, it was found that from well over a thousand photos, less than ten had been mislabelled, and the commission pointed out that the main assertion of the exhibition, by now well documented by historians, that the Wehrmacht was indeed complicit in a war of extermination, was correct. Since then the exhibition has been reorganised and has reopened.[20]

Yet during the exhibition's visit to Vienna emotions ran high. Quite apart from younger revisionists, deniers, and defenders of the honour of the Wehrmacht, elderly veterans often felt humiliated, degraded, and maligned by photos that clearly showed the brutality of the Wehrmacht (which of course included also Austrian soldiers since the Anschluss of 1938). Nevertheless, reactions were far from uniform. Beckermann's camera captures discussions between veterans who keep denying their army's involvement in crimes and others who express what can only be described as relief that finally the taboo has been lifted. Other arguments are between veterans and members of younger generations, some of whom are children and grandchildren of these or other old soldiers. We also meet people who had fled the Nazis in 1938 and have since come back. Each of the visitors is trying to articulate his or her view about the past in a manner that must somehow both relate to the atrocities on the wall and to these onlookers' own perceptions of that past – indeed, in the case of veterans, to their memory of their own role in it.

It is between such films as *Stalingrad* and *Jenseits des Krieges* that Germany's celluloid soldiers exist. Today, it is no longer possible to claim that the Wehrmacht's troops had nothing to do with the crimes of the regime but were merely Hitler's victims, just as Austria can no longer claim to have been Hitler's first victim rather than his first collaborator. But of course it is also not enough to say that the Wehrmacht was made up of criminals. There is a certain truth in those films that depict young German men as being caught between their patriotism, loyalty and comradeship, on the one hand, and a stupid, unnecessary war that killed so many of them, on the other. The dashed hopes and dreams of these young men were real enough, as were their courage and self-sacrifice. But we have not yet seen a single German (or, for that matter, non-German) film that has been able to confront the dilemma of the far more unique and specific conundrum of the German soldier in Hitler's service. For soldiers have often been sacrificed in war by cynical generals and politicians, and their best hopes and dreams have been abused for the purpose of aggrandising this or that regime. But in World War II, German soldiers were used not merely as cannon fodder, but also as tools of mass murder and genocide. This reality has still not found its cinematic expression, just as it still lacks any expression in prose fiction.

Shortly after the end of World War II, Heinrich Böll, one of post-war Germany's greatest authors, wrote about the experience of a young soldier sent to die on the eastern front.[21] By then Böll, who later became the moral compass of German intellectuals, knew full well of the genocidal policies of the regime. Having himself served six years in the Wehrmacht, he must have also seen a great many atrocities, even if one would like to think that he did not participate in any. Yet in his stories the only victims were men such as himself. More than fifty years later, another former Wehrmacht soldier, Günter Grass, wrote a novel that was welcomed by critics as the first confrontation with German victimhood, depicting as it did the sinking of a ship carrying German refugees escaping the advancing Red Army in 1945. The idea that Germans had not been able to deal with their own victimhood and mourning, and that Grass, as well as such authors as the late W. G. Sebald and historians such as Jörg Friedrich were the first to confront this issue is, of course, nonsense.[22]

Where German prose fiction and cinema have been unable to make any progress is in two entirely different areas. First, with very few exceptions, of which Sebald is in fact the most remarkable example, they have not been able to empathise with the fate of Germany's victims.[23] Second, and most pertinent to this essay, they have failed in showing the reality of the war and the manner in which it was experienced by the Wehrmacht's soldiers. For the reality of these men, and what made them so different from their celluloid images, was that they were not simply the victims of war and of a murderous regime: they were victims of their faith in that regime and of their attempt to carry out its policies; and in doing so, they became deeply complicit in its crimes. This is a film that is still waiting to be made.

# 11

## *The Devil his Due*
## *American Views of the Soviet Union*
## *Before and After Barbarossa*

ROGER BEAUMONT

After Operation Barbarossa, Hitler's invasion of Russia on 22 June 1941, tensions between the United States and the USSR seemed to ease substantially. Despite many swerves and tumbles in Soviet–American relations throughout the 1930s, admiration for the Red Army and sympathy for the plight of Russia became primary themes in American popular culture from 1941 to 1945. Those sentiments, however, were not by any means universal, nor did they radically affect the attitudes of officials in either nation, including those in the world of security and covert activities. The overall dynamic looked roughly similar to the events that followed the diplomatic recognition of the USSR by the administration of President Franklin D. Roosevelt in 1933. On the one hand, the pseudo-alliance of Britain, the USSR, and the US in the last two-thirds of World War II led many Americans to expect improved relations between the two, while on the other, many remained fearful that it would lead to increased Red subversion and agitation. Throughout the thirties the rhetoric and deeds of the Comintern – the Communist International – and communists throughout the world, which contrasted with Stalin's call for 'socialism in one country', raised concern in many quarters. Some senior American officials, for example, became furious when US delegates were asked to attend the Seventh Comintern Conference after the Soviets promised that diplomatic links would not increase such activities.

Many tensions spiked and ebbed throughout the decade as American communism metamorphosed through such guises as the Popular Front, and 100 per cent up-to-date Americanism while CPUS sought to forge a spirit of common cause with leftists, pacifists and supporters of loyalist Spain.[1] Throughout that turmoil, American journalists usually attributed the meandering of Soviet policy to one of three basic motives: national security, expansion and Russian territoriality,[2] templates which remained in use throughout World War II, although they were used more gently for the most part.

144

From the mid-1930s to the outbreak of World War II, there had been a fugue of bright spots – Russia's joining the League of Nations, aiding republican Spain, and urging Britain and France to join in opposing Hitler under the slogan 'collective security', and the geniality of Maxim Litvinov, Soviet ambassador in Washington – interthreaded with dark episodes like the purges and rigged trials in Moscow, NKVD heavy-handedness in Spain, and the Red Army's pitched battles with Japan. American policy also wavered, however. As isolationism rose to a peak, Congress passed Neutrality Acts, while taking tentative steps toward rearmament under the rubrics of a 'two-ocean navy' and 'hemispheric defense'. As US–Soviet debt resolution talks dragged on throughout the mid- and late thirties amid calls for breaking off diplomatic relations with Russia, the Red-hunters of the House of Representatives' Special Committee on Un-American Activities – better known as the Dies Committee – became increasingly popular, while fascistoid paramilitary 'Shirt' organisations appeared across the country.

There were other lines of cleavage as well. At the same time that US navy officials were blocking Soviet purchases of American equipment, American 'hard core' communists and 'fellow travellers' as well, openly admired the Soviets' ruthless pursuit of lofty goals by heavy-handed means.[3] Edmund Wilson, for example, described 'the Russian Communist leaders' as 'men of superior brain who have triumphed over the ignorance, the stupidity and the short-sighted selfishness of the mass' and 'imposed on them better methods and ideas than they could have arrived at by themselves'.[4] Later in the decade, a journalist deemed Stalin 'the best defender the world has against the criminality of another war which would sweep away the last remnants of our seemingly doomed civilization'.[5]

Although many Americans feared a major surge on the left during the Great Depression, those factions grew only slightly, peaking in the mid-thirties with less than a million votes for the Socialist Party in the 1936 presidential election, then shrank as Stalin's brutalities became more visible, and the Soviet premier sought accommodation with Hitler. Against that backdrop, President Roosevelt's fiercest critics falsely accused him of plotting to communise America, although the Democratic Party did encompass left-wing elements, and drew support from others, including communists. FDR steered wide of that issue, but was brought to bay in early February 1940 when elements of the American Youth Congress opposed US aid to Finland, then under Soviet attack. The president told students assembled on the White House lawn that he, like many liberals, had initially expected much from the USSR, that while dismayed by excesses over time, he had expected improvement, hoping that Russia would 'not interfere with the integrity of its neighbors'. Now, he saw that 'hope ... shattered' in that 'the Soviet Union ... run by a dictatorship ... as absolute as any other dictatorship in the world' and 'allied ... with another dictatorship', had 'invaded a neighbor ... a small nation that seeks only to live at peace and in a democracy'.[6]

Roosevelt's confession reflected the plight of many of the British and American liberals sentimentally attracted to Soviet Russia, like playwright Robert Sherwood, who lamented: 'Like many another who hopes that he is a Liberal, I had great faith in the Soviet Union as a force for world peace' and 'the mightiest opponent of Fascism'. Encouraged by Soviets assisting the republic in Spain, and China, he hoped the Nazi–Soviet Pact reflected Stalin 'playing his own shrewd game'. But Finland brought down 'the last scales of illusion ... The Soviet government was playing the old inhuman game of power politics with the same Machiavellian cynicism which has been Fascism's deadliest weapon against the gullible democracy.'[7] Indeed, from 1937 onward, American communists and fellow-travellers were falling out of the movement with each swerve in Stalinist foreign policy, most dramatically when the Nazi–Soviet pact was revealed in August 1939. Further party defections followed Stalin's invasion of Finland, and occupation of eastern Poland, Bessarabia and the Baltic States, in a spiral of disillusion that led veteran 'progressive' journalist Louis Fischer to describe 'Black Moscow's deadening atmosphere of dread'.[8] While he accepted Stalinist claims that a small 'military-fascist organization' sought 'a pact with the Nazis', and a network of Trotskyite subversives had tried to sell Russia out to foreign interests, Fischer saw the purges as a decapitation of the Red Army.[9] Refusing to write dispatches about the trials, he called them 'a perpetual funeral' and described the rampant fear, distrust, and hypocrisy.[10]

As the 'party line' in the arts and popular culture in the US also shifted course in the 1930s, the strong leftist influences in Hollywood found it difficult to bring their sentiments to bear directly. Few filmmakers tried to portray life in the USSR or even allude to it, aside from satirical light fare like *Ninotchka* and *Comrade X*. *Last Train from Madrid* (1937) left the Spanish Civil War wholly out of focus, and *Blockade* (1938), while slightly less vague, portrayed the war in Spain as a fight for democracy, ignoring political specifics like Franco or Mussolini. Nevertheless, even mentioning the subject raised hackles in some quarters, and *Blockade* was boycotted and picketed by rightists in several American cities.[11]

Between World War II's onset in Europe in September 1939 and the Nazi invasion of Russia in June 1941, British and American leftists found themselves more firmly wedged in a proverbial cleft stick. As Stalin became Hitler's virtual ally logistically, thousands abandoned

communism, but some stalwarts held the line, defending the Nazi–
Soviet pact as Stalinist *realpolitik*, ignoring or excusing the *City of Flint*
affair,[12] castigating British and French imperialism, and deeming the
Soviet–Japanese neutrality pact of April 1941 a shrewd stroke of Russian
diplomacy. Despite widespread revulsion toward Russia's attack on
Finland in late 1939,[13] Stalinists continued to assail the Allies with
propaganda and strikes and/or sabotage at firms making war goods for
Britain and France.[14] As leading American security officials came to fear
communists more than Axis spies, in late 1941, FBI director J. Edgar
Hoover labelled the latter 'agents of a foreign power', while bluntly
noting calls for sabotage at a 'Communist meeting' and 'more subtle
methods' of subversion by 'Communists'.[15] It was an interlude which
many on the left found discomfiting, and left well out of focus later.[16]
The fuller extent of Soviet espionage activities in the United States in
the thirties and during World War II remained out of view until after
the Cold War.[17]

Gallup public opinion polls conducted in the US at the time indicated,
even though most Americans hoped to stay out of World War II until
the Japanese attack on Pearl Harbor in December 1941, that an
overwhelming majority favoured an Allied victory, even after France
fell, and Britain and Russia became the main adversaries of the Axis
powers:[18]

'Which side would you like to see win?' (per cent)

|            | 24 June 1941 | 9 September 1941 |
|------------|:------------:|:----------------:|
| *Russia*     | 73           | 70               |
| *Germany*    | 4            | 4                |
| *Neither*    | 18           | 19               |
| *No opinions*| 5            | 7                |

'Who will win – Germany or Russia?'

|            |    |    |
|------------|:--:|:--:|
| *Germany*    | 48 | 20 |
| *Russia*     | 22 | 41 |
| *Stalemate*  | 9  | 9  |
| *Undecided*  | 21 | 30 |

'Will Germany defeat Russia in the next six months or Russia fight
on longer?'

|            |    |
|------------|:--:|
| *Germany*    | 13 |
| *Russia*     | 60 |
| *Don't know* | 27 |

As Americans on the far left threw the helm over immediately after

Barbarossa, strikes against factories producing war goods for Britain ceased,[19] no-strike pledges were signed, communists ceased demanding Federal racial-equality action, and urged production speed-ups. Barbarossa ended their brief rapport with the America First movement, many of whose members, like Senator Harry Truman, preferred to stand back and let Russia and Germany slug it out. While the left's *volte face* highlighted links between Moscow and American communism, that issue was overshadowed in late autumn 1941 by the titanic battles in the east as the Red Army held on far longer than most observers expected – German, Soviet, British or American.[20] During that hard winter, undertones of admiration and respect began to flavour media accounts of the eastern front in the United States. Observers initially expected the Wehrmacht to finish off the Red Army quickly, with guesses running from ten days to three months.[21] But throughout 1942 the Russians endured, and in early 1943, after the Soviet triumph at Stalingrad, Joseph E. Davies, US ambassador to the USSR in the late thirties, and famously sympathetic to Stalin's regime, summed up the situation in a tone similar to most American media at the time: '[A]gain the Red Army' has carried 'the brunt of the war with Germany', suffering 'immeasurably heavier losses than the other United Nations during the summer campaigns of 1942' as it 'inflicted heavier losses on the Germans' upsetting 'Hitler's schedule for two years running and making mincemeat of his prophecies and promises. Last year's miracle of Moscow was repeated this year at Stalingrad.'[22]

Depicting the Soviets as valiant and generically populist allies, however, was not universally popular in the United States.[23] A fog bank of political vagueness still hung over Hollywood, leading critics to assail the political sterility of the film based on Ernest Hemingway's novel *For Whom the Bell Tolls* (1943), and ridicule *Mission to Moscow* (1943), based on Davies' book, for white-washing Stalinism. Movies of Russia at war like *The North Star*, *Song of Russia*, and *Days of Glory* were also flayed, but more for flawed artistry than for political sterility or distortion.

Censorship and self-censorship were far more intense in the USSR, where foreign journalists were rigorously censored before and after Barbarossa.[24] Under the successive Soviet regimes, some foreign correspondents were favoured more than others, and returned the favour, like John Reed. Several who worked in Russia in the twenties and thirties, like Eugene Lyons, and William Henry Chamberlin, returned home to castigate Stalinism, but more recent returnees were more restrained. For example, after his 1941 visit, Chicago newspaper editor Ralph Ingersoll grappled with such diverse Soviet inconsistencies[25] as pervasive poverty that made him 'almost constantly depressed',[26] drab design and art,[27] and hyper-secrecy.[28] Puzzling over the fate of 'kulaks ... the most famous of the disenfranchised' who had 'wholly disappeared, I do not know where,'[29] and the 'maze of special privilege' surrounding the party elite, Ingersoll found 'no racial discrimination', nor 'Negro problem' since 'tolerance' was 'a prime virtue of the Soviet Union', along with a 'real, solid and lasting elimination of anti-Semitism in a land in which it was a vicious tradition ... one of the new state's major achievements'.[30] Ingersoll asserted: '...many innocent men were shot in the purges ... but so were the Pétains and Lavals', echoing both apologist and Soviet views that 'many, many innocent people ... had been punished. Everyone now agrees it was carried too far. But how else can you get rid of traitors?'[31] He saw it as part of a great balance sheet on which 'Scores of millions were set free for hundreds of thousands whose opportunities were curtailed,' and supported the claims of a 'military observer ... that the morale of the Army' was 'improved by the purges, not damaged' and that 'The history of the war has shown ... the Red Army was purged of ... Fifth Columnists.'[32]

While Ingersoll warned against jumping 'to conclusions about the significance of things like the NKVD and purges in other peoples' lives', *Collier*'s correspondent Alice-Leone Moats, after returning to the US, wrote of Soviet state terror, millions of political prisoners, the pervasive fear of secret police, and massacres.[33] (Even Ambassador Davies deemed the 'NKVD ... unbelievably efficient and ruthless' with 'an army of its own numbering about two million men'.)[34] Moats, however, also admired the Soviets' ability 'to keep secret ... how efficient they could be in an emergency'. In contrast with ordinary snarling of 'the simplest transaction with bureaucracy, red tape, and procrastination', she saw the emergency decrees as proof of 'how fast the Soviet authorities could move in a crisis. It was really extraordinary how within a few hours Russia was on a full wartime basis.'[35]

CBS radio correspondent Larry Leseuer, after working in Russia following Barbarossa, predicted Russia would 'be both a great European and great Eastern power', not 'a democracy of the American type', but one with 'no private ownership of the means of production'.[36] Defending Stalin's seizure of the Baltic States,[37] he attributed Western underestimates of Soviet endurance to a 'false comparison with ... America one hundred years ago, or with Czarist Russia' and belief that 'the purges ... had reduced the Russian staff to the impotence of party "hacks"'. Anticipating Russia's collapse was due to 'lack of understanding of the remarkably efficient methods of the Communist zealots in organizing the civilian population for total war', and discounting 'the incredible sacrifices the Russians would endure', Leseuer extolled 'the effectiveness of the massive logic of the complete materialists who run Russia...', 'who believe ... men can make "history" suit their purposes

... the pick of the people in the Soviet Union, the brightest and most intelligent men, whose talents would earn them good livings in America or England'.[38] A popular illustrated history, *War in Our Time*, was also well laced with Sovietophilia,[39] but such lyrical enthusiasm had little influence on US public opinion. Pollsters found Americans respecting Russian stamina, but disinclined to 'believe their Allies in this war are angels. Most notably ... the Soviet Union; many are the protests against an "alliance with Communism."'[40] Many continued to hope that Russia would soon engage Japan in battle.[41]

Sympathy for Soviet ideology and controversial Stalinist manoeuvres and excesses led many writers to warp and expunge history.[42] Some described the Nazi–Soviet pact as the product of British diplomatic blundering,[43] others as Stalin's way of buying time while preparing for the Nazi onslaught.[44] In his bestseller *Total Peace*, Ely Culbertson, a famous bridge expert turned internationalist pundit, attributed 'ruthless' Stalinist diplomacy to Soviet recognition of 'power politics and the struggle for survival among states'. Culbertson attributed 'much that is of a tyrannical, ruthless and dictatorial nature in the Russia of today' to 'the continuous threat of capitalist aggression from outside, and ideological threats from within...'[45] More startling to a much broader public was an effusively pro-Soviet issue of Republican Henry Luce's *Life* magazine in which Ambassador Davies described Russia's leaders as 'Men of Good Will ... straightforward and direct' favouring 'religious freedom' and opposing 'world revolution'.[46] In a similar vein, an anonymous article in that magazine proclaimed Lenin 'perhaps the greatest man of modern times ... a normal, well-balanced man ... dedicated to rescuing 140,000,000 from a brutal and incompetent tyranny' who 'made the revolution make sense and saved it from much of the folly of the French Revolution. It is impossible to imagine what the history of Russia and the world would have been had he not lived.'[47] A piece dealing with the late thirties' purges described 'a final synthesis' of Trotskyite animus toward 'the Stalinist regime' and Hitler's determination to 'expand eastward at the expense of the USSR', which produced an 'efficient organization to develop conspiratorial action, sabotage and especially within the USSR and to conduct propaganda abroad'.[48] Another deemed 'Red leaders ... tough, loyal, capable administrators ... [and] extremely efficient', who 'did not achieve high office because of their personalities, their looks, their voices, their families or their education' (a blatant bank-shot at Roosevelt) but 'fought to the upper crust because they were able to prove themselves tough, intelligent executives, loyal to the USSR'.[49] (Frequently quoted from that *Life* issue was a definition of 'the United NKVD' as 'a national police similar to the FBI'.)[50]

Strong sympathy for Soviet policies and actions also flavoured some officials' pronouncements, like Assistant Secretary of State Sumner Welles' description of 'collectivizing the farms' as 'a bitter process' which 'wealthy peasantry resisted with all its strength and the contest with the "kulaks" … became a veritable civil war.' In that 'struggle … considered a glory by the Russian' although 'many critics have deplored its cost and suffering … "Kulaks" … nearly wrecked the Soviet economy' by slaughtering 'far too many animals', resulting in 'famine … in certain areas'. Welles suggested that 'World-wide scepticism' towards the 1937 purge trials was refuted when 'examples of traitors in other lands like Quisling' made 'these charges seem less melodramatic and far-fetched than they did in 1935–37'.[51] The US army 'Why We Fight' indoctrination film *The Battle of Russia* explained 'away the Russo-German Pact and the seizure of Finland [*sic*] as defensive moves',[52] voicing a respect for Soviet arms echoed by US army chief of staff, General of the Army George C. Marshall in his final war report: 'Even with two-thirds of the German Army engaged by Russia, it took every man the Nation saw fit to mobilize to do our part of the job in Europe and at the same time to keep the Japanese enemy under control in the Pacific. What would have been the result if the Red Army had been defeated and the British Isles invaded we can only guess. The possibility is rather terrifying.'[53] Secretary of War Henry L. Stimson agreed, describing the Soviets 'in their own strange way' as 'magnificent allies. They fought as they had promised, and they made no separate peace.'[54]

Another popular theme in the American media during World War II was looking for similarities between Americans and Russians.[55] Some of the parallels that were drawn were fanciful, but occasionally there was some substance to such exercises. Many Americans had worked as labourers, technicians and engineers in Russia between the World Wars, and some had become Soviet citizens. Beyond that was the American tinge to Soviet industrial expansion stemming from the fascination of many Bolsheviks, including Lenin, with US industrial techniques.[56] But some of the comparisons were very strained, e.g., 'The Russian synthesis of super-modern American engineering and the ancient tradition of cavalry armies expressed itself to some extent in cavalry divisions comprising mechanized groups',[57] and an assertion that 'the only country in the world where one could conceive of the publishing of a magazine like *Fortune*, outside of the United States, is Soviet Russia.'[58]

On the farthest fringe of the left, Edgar Snow identified a set of American–Russian commonalities: a preference for the direct approach in discussion; a tendency to exaggerate and brag; enthusiasm for heroic engineering and constructions; and a 'generosity of spirit' without 'meanness and pettiness of the sort you find in some Europeans'. But even the arch-conservative Eddie Rickenbacker, champion racing driver, World War I ace and airline executive, proclaimed: 'The Russians are our kind of people ... more like Americans than any other people in Europe.'[59] At the same time, Trotsky was often roughly handled for working 'with the Nazis for the overthrow of the Soviets' when he was 'assassinated by one of his own followers',[60] as were the *kulaks*, described in a military history of Russia as 'almost the major part' of the 'peasant masses who fought collectivization', and 'the main military manpower base' whose plight led Army leaders to form a 'military conspiracy' with Trotskyites and those seeking preventive war against Japan. Finally, 'when it became clear to everybody that the march of history had put the opposition in the wrong, the regime poised for a crushing blow ... [and] destroyed the conspirators' including 'Tukhachevsky at its head'.[61]

On balance, neither extreme adulation nor condemnation of the Soviets was popular in the US. Behind the glowing images of comrades-in-arms, fists remained tight and eyes narrow in some circles. In describing Soviet official hostility, John R. Deane, a senior US representative in Moscow during the war, observed: 'Despite innumerable opportunities for cooperative action' that would have been 'mutually beneficial ... no action was initiated by the Soviet Union ... to facilitate the task of the western allies.'[62] Out of public view, Russian–American diplomatic and economic relations were often tortuous and frustrating. Some tensions were rooted in the Bolshevik era, others stemmed from the 1939–41 interlude,[63] and others arose from the Soviets' tough negotiating style. Beyond displaying substantial legal prowess, the Russians had a trump card to play: the fact that the Red Army was fighting the bulk of the Wehrmacht, a reality well-recognised in the West, especially in 1941–2, as the battered USSR held the metaphorical bridge while the Western allies strove to get their war machines under way.[64] At that point, media across the political spectrum in Britain and the US bemoaned the sluggish pace of operations, and demanded a 'Second Front Now!'

Although it fell well short of being a honeymoon, that interim of respect and admiration held up for roughly four years, sometimes guarded, and sometimes effusive.[65] From Barbarossa to the cover of the VE Day issue of *Time* which showed GI Joe, Tommy, and Ivan cheerily bearing victory banners, the strata of hostility that ran beneath the praise and admiration in American popular culture and official pronouncements bubbled to the surface only now and then. For several months after Nazi banners were hurled onto pyres in Red Square, despite squabbles over sharing in the military government of Italy, the Soviet abandonment of the Polish Home Army, the Grecian turmoil, and uncertainty regarding eastern Europe's future, the post-war diplomatic landscape seemed relatively calm to the world at large. Then, in the spring of

1946, the cleavage between East and West wrenched open, revealing a chasm in keeping with Churchill's vision of a hellish cauldron, and erasing the benign images of the Grand Alliance and the 'Big Three', and replacing them with the fierce kabuki faces of the Cold War which prevailed for almost half-a-century.[66]

# 12

## Stalingrad and Researching the Experience of War[1]

ANTONY BEEVOR

Stalingrad was one of the most monstrous and inhuman battles ever known. It was further dehumanised by both sides in their propaganda. Since the military development of the campaign had already been thoroughly established, thanks principally to the work of John Erickson and Manfred Kehrig, the point of researching the subject further was to try to find a way to describe accurately the true physical conditions of this battle, and the terrible psychological pressures on the soldiers caught up in it. These included not just fear of the enemy, but also fear of execution by their own side. Soldiers and civilians were crushed pitilessly between the two totalitarian regimes. Red Army snipers at Stalingrad, for example, were ordered to shoot starving Russian children, who had been tempted with crusts of bread by German infantrymen to fill their waterbottles in the Volga.

This is why history from above – the decisions of Stalin or Hitler and their generals – needs to be combined with history from below. It is the only way to demonstrate the direct consequences of their decisions and the consequent suffering of those trapped in the terrible maelstrom created by their propaganda.

The attempt to recreate the experience of battle can come only from a wide range of sources, which naturally vary in validity and in reliability. They include war diaries, reports of prisoner interrogations, officers' and soldiers' letters home, doctors' accounts, chaplains' reports on morale, private diaries, accounts by war correspondents, reports by evacuees written a few weeks after the event, accounts written years later, interviews with survivors and so on. In the case of Stalingrad, one can even learn a good deal from certain novels, but this is a question I will come back to.

The basic reason for researching in breadth as well as in depth is the way personal accounts can often explain things that appear inexplicable in the official documents. Another good argument for a broad approach, especially in the Russian archives, is that you are likely to find material in one archive which in another is still classified as secret and closed.

For example, the GlavPURKKA files of the Red Army political department in the old Party Archive or Marxist–Leninist Institute, and now called RGASPI,[2] have certain documents that are not released in the Central Archive of the Ministry of Defence – TsAMO – out at Podolsk.

The list of sources is almost endless, and the only general point to be made is that very little can be classified in terms of reliability and validity, except in the most general terms. An officer's evidence on the overall situation will probably be worth more than a soldier's because he usually had a better opportunity to gain accurate information. And a staff officer's account is likely to be even better informed, but he will of course know less about the true state of conditions at the front and he may well have more to hide. Letters from soldiers, on the other hand, are very important for other reasons. They offer a good indication of levels of morale at different moments, assuming that there are enough of them. They also provide just about the only evidence of what officers have been telling their men. Of course, one always has to bear in mind how much the letter writer may have worried about censorship. All one can say is that, up until 1943, it seems that German Feldpost censorship was a lot less vigilant than its Soviet counterpart.

In many ways one has to be even more cautious about the interrogation reports of prisoners, for the obvious reason that a frightened prisoner is likely to tell his interrogator what he wants to hear. It was very noticeable, as evidenced both in the Russian and German archives, how ready soldiers were to speak. This may be because the interviews with those soldiers who refused to answer were not recorded. On the eastern front there was no Geneva Convention nonsense of sticking to name, rank, and number. I will never forget one protocol of interrogation by the chief of intelligence of the 62nd Army at Stalingrad working through an interpreter. At the bottom of the page there was a scribbled note to say that the interrogation had been terminated because the subject had died of his wounds.

Many of those who refused to answer were almost certainly shot, but much depended on the time and circumstances. On the basis of the five hundred or so interview reports of prisoners selected by the interrogators from the Seventh Departments of Stalingrad Front and Don Front, it appeared that most German prisoners were keen to talk, partly out of fear, but also – especially towards the end of the battle – out of disillusionment and a sense of betrayal. A number of German officers, including the first battalion commander to surrender, provided very useful testimony as to the physical and psychological state of their men.

Double-checking on many sources is often impossible. So one often has to rely on one's own nose for what is true and what might be false.

If still unsure, then you can resort in your text to an implicit code of likely veracity, almost like an auctioneer's catalogue – with 'it is said that' being roughly equivalent to 'school of'.

Academics are naturally suspicious of using interviews with veterans and eyewitnesses so long after the event. This is absolutely right when it is a matter of dates or locations. Yet general impressions and some personal details are seldom forgotten, even after sixty years. Old men, who can hardly remember what happened two weeks before, retain extraordinarily vivid memories from wartime, partly because they were so unforgettable, but also because the war, and especially a battle like Stalingrad, was the most intense experience of their whole life. I was struck by the way that Soviet veterans who had been in both the battle of Stalingrad and the fight for Berlin, retained much clearer memories of Stalingrad. At the end of the war, they remembered events like crossing the German frontier for the first time and the moment of victory, but much less of the battle itself.

The great advantage of personal testimonies is the way they can explain otherwise mystifying details in official reports. For example, when studying the Soviet reports on the invasion of East Prussia in January 1945 for the Berlin book, I was mystified why so many German women, attempting to commit suicide after being gang-raped, failed to cut their wrists properly. It was only after a German woman wrote to me about the book just after publication, and I rang her back, that she told me how her first cousin had tried to slit her wrists after suffering multiple rape. From what she told me, it was clear that the vast majority of women had assumed that you should cut straight across the wrist, but that did little more than sever the tendon. Most, like the cousin of this woman, managed only to cripple their hands. To sever the artery you needed to cut diagonally.

In the German archives in Freiburg, the Bundesarchiv-Militärchiv, I found that the most interesting reports were those of doctors and priests attached to the Sixth Army. They were outsiders within the military community, as well as naturally acute observers of the human condition. The letters of Kurt Reuber, who was a priest serving as a doctor with the 16th Panzer Division, were particularly perceptive. I will never forget the image of Reuber's eccentric commanding officer deep in his earth bunker under the steppe, playing an abandoned piano obsessively 'even when the walls trembled from bombardment and soil trickled down'.

When describing the fighting, there were two realities. Life out in the steppe was very different, of course, from the street fighting, in the city. For a start, fighting in the steppe was no cleaner than in Stalingrad itself. 'We squat together', wrote Kurt Reuber, 'in a hole dug out of the side of a gully in the steppe. The most meagre and badly equipped dugout. Dirt and clay. Nothing can be made of it. Scarcely any wood for bunkers. We're surrounded by a sad landscape, monotonous and melancholic. Winter weather of varying degrees of cold. Snow, heavy rain, frost then sudden thaw. At night you get mice running over your face.' In fact things were much worse, but presumably Reuber did not want to distress his family. Mice even started to eat the frost-bitten toes of sleeping men who could feel nothing in their feet. Trench foot and frostbite became a major problem. Often up to half the men were suffering from dysentery. 'The plague of lice was frightful,' a corporal wrote, 'because we had no opportunity to wash, change clothes or hunt them down.' And a deadly combination of hunger, cold and stress greatly reduced their powers of resistance to infection. Soon typhus, diphtheria, scurvy and a whole range of diseases gained a hold.

The fighting out in the Don-Volga steppe was in many ways like the trench warfare of the First World War, but with modern variations. Russian patrols went out at night to snatch sentries for interrogation – they called them 'tongues'. Reconnaissance groups or snipers would go forward in snow suits and lie out in snow hides in no man's land. Loudspeaker units broadcast tango music and messages recorded by German communists for Don Front's 7th Department for propaganda. Leaflets were also dropped. These had little effect when they had been written in heavy Stalinist clichés by Soviet officers, but when the German communist writer and poet Erich Weinert took over, the effect was much greater. Weinert exploited German sentimentality and a desperate homesickness, with poems such as 'Denk an dein Kind!', illustrated with a picture of a little boy crying over a dead German soldier, and crying out: '*Papa ist todt!*' Many soldiers broke down weeping when they picked this leaflet up. It brought home to them the hopelessness of their situation far better than all the politico-military bombast from the Soviet authorities.

It is, however, images from the fighting in the city that will endure most in the memory. This represented a new form of warfare, concentrated in the ruins of civilian life. The detritus of war – burnt-out tanks, shell cases, signal wire and grenade boxes – was mixed with the wreckage of family homes – iron bedsteads, lamps and household utensils. Vasily Grossman wrote of the 'fighting in the brick-strewn, half-demolished rooms and corridors of apartment blocks, where there might still be a vase of withered flowers, or a boy's homework open on the table.' In an observation post, high in a ruined building, an artillery spotter seated on a kitchen chair might watch for targets through a convenient shell-hole in the wall.

German infantrymen loathed house-to-house fighting. They found such close-quarter combat, which broke military boundaries and dimensions, psychologically disorientating. During the last phase of the September battles, both sides had struggled to take a large brick warehouse on the Volga bank, near the mouth of the Tsaritsa, which had four floors on the river side and three on the landward. At one point, it was 'like a layered cake' with Germans on the top floor, Russians below them, and more Germans underneath them. Often an enemy was unrecognisable, with every uniform impregnated by the same dun-coloured dust from pulverised brick and masonry.

German generals do not seem to have imagined what awaited their divisions in the ruined city. The decision to assault Stalingrad had deprived them of their great *Blitzkrieg* advantages and reduced them to the techniques of the First World War, even though their military theorists had argued that trench warfare had been 'an aberration in the art of war'. The Sixth Army, for example, found itself having to respond to Soviet tactics, by reinventing the 'stormwedges' introduced in January 1918: assault groups of ten men armed with a machine gun, light mortar and flame-throwers for clearing bunkers, cellars and sewers.

The close-quarter combat in ruined buildings, cellars and sewers was soon dubbed *Rattenkrieg* (rat war) by German soldiers. It possessed a savage intimacy that appalled their generals, who felt that they were rapidly losing control over events. 'The enemy is invisible,' wrote General Strecker to a friend. 'Ambushes out of basements, wall remnants, hidden bunkers and factory ruins produce heavy casualties among our troops.'

German commanders openly admitted the Russian expertise at camouflage, but few acknowledged that it was the relentless bombing by their own aircraft that had produced the ideal conditions for the defenders. 'Not a house is left standing,' a Lieutenant wrote home. 'There is only a burnt-out wasteland, a wilderness of rubble and ruins which is well-nigh impassable.'

The plan of the Soviet commander, General Chuikov, was to funnel and fragment German mass assaults with 'breakwaters'. Strengthened buildings, manned by infantry with anti-tank rifles and machine guns, would deflect the attackers into channels, where camouflaged T-34 tanks and anti-tank guns, waited half-buried in the rubble behind. When German tanks attacked with infantry, the defenders' main priority was to separate them. The Russians used trench mortars, aiming to drop their bombs just behind the tanks to scare off the infantry while the anti-tank gunners went for the tanks themselves. The channelled approaches would also be mined in advance by sappers, whose casualty rate was the highest of any specialisation. 'Make a mistake and no more dinners,' was their unofficial motto.

Much of the fighting, however, did not consist of major attacks, but of relentless, lethal little conflicts. One of Chuikov's officers wrote that the battle was fought by assault squads, generally six or eight strong, from 'the Stalingrad Academy of Street Fighting'. They armed themselves with knives and sharpened spades for silent killing, as well as submachine guns and grenades. (Spades were in such short supply that men carved their name in the handle and slept with their head on the blade to make sure that nobody stole it.) The assault squads sent into the sewers were strengthened with flame-throwers and sappers bringing explosive charges to lay under German positions.

A more general tactic evolved, based on the realisation that the German armies were short of reserves. Chuikov ordered an emphasis on night attacks, mainly for the practical reason that the Luftwaffe could not react to them, but also because he was convinced that the Germans were more frightened during the hours of darkness, and would become exhausted. The German *Landser* came to harbour a special fear of the Siberians from Colonel Batyuk's 284th Rifle Division, who were considered to be natural hunters of any sort of prey.

'If only you could understand what terror is,' a German soldier wrote in a letter captured by the Russians. 'At the slightest rustle, I pull the trigger and fire off tracer bullets in bursts from the machine gun.' The compulsion to shoot at anything that moved at night, often setting off fusillades from equally nervous sentries down a whole sector, undoubt-edly contributed to the German expenditure of over 25 million rounds during the month of September alone. The Russians also kept up the tension by firing flares into the night sky from time to time to give the impression of an imminent attack. Red Army aviation, partly to avoid the Messerschmitts and Focke-Wulfs by day, kept up a relentless series of raids every night on German positions. It also served as another part of the wearing-down process to exhaust the Germans and stretch their nerves.

But what of the civilians? Soldiers at least had some sort of purpose and fairly regular rations to keep them going. The civilians trapped in Stalingrad had nothing. How over ten thousand civilians, including a thousand children, were still alive in the city's ruins after over five months of battle, is still the most astonishing part of the whole Stalingrad story.

The sight of pitiful civilians could produce strange and illogical emotions in Wehrmacht soldiers. 'Today I saw many refugees coming from Stalingrad,' a sergeant wrote home:

A scene of indescribable misery. Children, women, old men – as old as grandpa – lie here by the road only lightly clothed and with no protection from the cold. Although they're our enemy, it was deeply shocking. For that reason we can't thank our Führer and the Good Lord enough, that our homeland has still been spared such terrible wretchedness. I have already seen much misery during this war, but Russia surpasses everything. Above all Stalingrad. You won't understand this quite like me, one has to have seen it.

The German confusion of cause and effect emerges here with striking clarity. The invasion of the Soviet Union to destroy the Bolshevik threat was, in fact, to bring Communist domination to the centre of Europe for nearly half a century.

The many thousands of women and children left behind in the city sought shelter in the cellars of ruins, in sewers and in caves dug into steep banks. There were apparently even civilians cowering in shell-holes on the Mamaev Kurgan during the worst of the fighting. Many, of course, did not survive. The writer Konstantin Simonov, on his first visit, was astonished by what he saw:

> We crossed a bridge over one of the gullies intersecting the city. I shall never forget the scene that opened out before me. This gully, which stretched to my left and right, was swarming with life, just like an ant-hill dotted with caves. Entire streets had been excavated on either side. The mouths of the caves were covered with charred boards and rags. The women had utilised everything that could be of service to keep out the wind and the rain and shelter their children.

Simonov wrote of the 'almost incredible' suffering of all those in Stalingrad, whether soldier or civilian, but then quickly dismissed any notion of sentimentality – 'these things cannot be helped: the struggle being waged is for life or death'. He then went on to describe the body of a drowned woman washed up on the Volga shore holding on to a charred log 'with scorched and distorted fingers. Her face is disfigured: the suffering she underwent before death released her must have been unbearable. The Germans did this, did it in front of our eyes. And let them not ask for quarter from those who witnessed it. After Stalingrad we shall give no quarter.'

A large element in research depends as much on luck as on instinct, and I was indeed very lucky. When, in 1995, I set off for the major archives in Germany, Austria and Russia, I was not optimistic because I did not imagine that I would uncover what I really sought. I expected to find vast quantities of reports devoid of human element, but little in the way of first-hand accounts. I was less interested in details of strategy and manoeuvre, although they also had to be covered so as to set the experience of soldiers in a proper context.

At the Bundesarchiv-Militärarchiv at Freiburg-im-Breisgau, I expected little more than statistics and a dry record of events from the surviving war diaries and files. These had been flown out before the airfields of Paulus's encircled Sixth Army were overrun by the Russians. But even the quartermaster's statistics – the ration returns – brought out a less well-known aspect of the battle. The Sixth Army's front-line divisions had over 50,000 Soviet citizens serving in their ranks, many armed and fighting in the front line against their fellow citizens. There may, according to some sources, have been another 20,000 or more with army troops and auxiliary units. Some had been brutally press-ganged through starvation in prison camps; others were volunteers. During the final battles, German reports testify to the bravery and loyalty of these *Hiwis* fighting against their own countrymen. Needless to say, Beria's NKVD became frenzied with suspicion when it discovered the scale of the disloyalty.

In 1995 a taboo still lingered at that time over the subject in Russia. An infantry colonel with whom I happened to share a sleeping compartment on the journey down to Volgograd (the former Stalingrad), refused at first to believe that any Russian could have put on German uniform. He was finally convinced when I told him of the ration returns in the German archives. His reaction, for a man who clearly loathed Stalin for his purges of the Red Army, was interesting. 'They were no longer Russians,' he said quietly. His comment was almost exactly the same as the formula used over fifty years before when Stalingrad front reported on 'former Russians' back to Moscow.

Also in the Freiburg archives, along with the reports from doctors and German military chaplains, there was a thick file of transcripts from over a hundred letters written to wives or parents in mid-January 1943. The soldiers and officers writing these letters knew that this would be their last one likely to reach home, because the Russians were closing in on Pitomnik airfield. These letters were intercepted and seized on Goebbels's orders, because he wanted them to be used as the basis for a heroic account of German sacrifice. This material, which serves as an interesting indication of the different currents of emotion – the contrast between the modest and the bombastic is striking – has still been surprisingly little used by German historians, except perhaps to show that the letters quoted in that great bestseller of the 1950s, *Last Letters from Stalingrad*,[3] were almost certainly fakes.

In another section of the archive, I found the reports which officers and soldiers flown out of the *Kessel*, or encirclement, had been made to write. These men, usually two from each division, were mostly those selected for Hitler's Noah's Ark. His idea was that he could efface the disaster of Stalingrad by recreating a new Sixth Army with symbolic seeds from the old. Their personal reports, written almost immediately after arrival, struck me as particularly valuable, considering the circumstances in which they were written.

They had no senior officers to fear. They knew that the officers who asked for the reports were desperate for reliable information on what had happened, while they themselves clearly felt a need to testify, because they owed it to all those comrades they had left behind. The confused mixture of relief and survivor guilt among all those who were flown out is very striking. In fact, I was most interested to find that those officers flown to freedom out of the hellish encirclement did not condemn the captured generals, such as General von Seydlitz, who sided with the Russians in a vain bid to start a revolution against Hitler. They could appreciate the anger of those captured senior officers who felt betrayed by Hitler and guilty for having in turn persuaded their own soldiers to fight on uselessly. But I found that junior officers, taken prisoner after the surrender who had somehow survived the years of Soviet labour camps, could not forgive those generals who collaborated with their captors.

Interviews with veterans and eyewitnesses, especially those conducted over fifty years after the event, can be notoriously unreliable, as I said earlier; but when the material is used in conjunction with verifiable sources, they can be extremely illuminating. I was exceptionally fortunate to be put in touch with several of Sixth Army's staff officers who had been flown out on Paulus's orders just before the end. General Freytag von Loringhoven, whom I interviewed in Munich, was also the panzer commander who first reached the Volga on the northern edge of Stalingrad in August 1942. Even more important, was Winrich Behr who wanted to set the record straight after Alexander Stahlberg's book, *Bounden Duty*.[4] He told me the true story of his mission in January 1943, when he was sent by Paulus and Field Marshal von Manstein to Hitler in an attempt to persuade him to allow the Sixth Army to surrender. His account of his meeting with Hitler, surrounded by his staff in the headquarters bunker at Rastenburg, provided the most fascinating morning of my life.

Among the other soldiers and officers I went to see (some of these introductions were arranged through a serving officer in the Bundeswehr) was Colonel Pfeifer, who had been a young battalion commander captured with the 60th Motorised Infantry Division at Stalingrad. He had returned to Germany in 1954 after eleven years of Russian prison camps totally deaf. I had to talk to him through his wife, because he could lip-read her mouth far more easily than my badly enunciated German. He had personally reported to Sixth Army headquarters the fact that the Russian prisoners of war, starved of rations by their German captors in the *Kessel*, were resorting to cannibalism. There is still nothing to show that Paulus himself was informed, and I would not be surprised if his chief of staff, General Schmidt, had kept him in the dark on purpose. Schmidt would have known Führer headquarters would have been outraged if Russian prisoners had been released because of the lack of food.

The longevity of some survivors was astonishing, especially those who had suffered up to twelve years in the Soviet prison camps. A stroke of luck – a sudden hunch of looking in the local telephone directory – revealed that Professor Girgensohn, the Sixth Army's pathologist, was still alive and living only four hundred yards from the archives in Freiburg. Girgensohn was another who wanted to set the record straight before he died. He was furious at inaccurate reports of his work carried out on the spot. He had been flown into the encirclement to study the dramatic rise in deaths of Sixth Army soldiers occurring neither from enemy action nor disease. His own analysis, on the basis of the fifty autopsies he carried out towards the end of the battle, was that the combination of extreme cold, starvation and stress had had a disastrous effect on the metabolism. In such conditions, he concluded, the body evidently absorbs only a small part of the nutritive value of any food consumed. Girgensohn was one of the few who survived many years in the military Gulag after the surrender. His testimony at last provides a satisfactory explanation for the phenomenon that had baffled the medical conference held on the subject in Berlin in the early part of 1943.

At times I felt like an ambulance-chaser. Whenever I met a German, I asked with indecent haste whether they had a relative who had been at Stalingrad. One of my most valuable sources was the uncle of a German woman I met. He insisted on remaining anonymous and refused to allow me to use a tape recorder. He had hoped to avoid the war – he was twenty years old when it broke out – by remaining in the United States in 1939. But he was threatened with the withdrawal of his passport if he did not return for military service, and as the heir to no less than five castles as well as the bearer of a rather well-known name, he felt obliged for his family's sake to come back. He had absolutely no need to persuade me of any anti-Nazi credentials or to justify his record. He was simply irritated by most of the books published on the subject in Germany. In general terms, those of the older generation had sought to justify the Wehrmacht, while those of the younger generation wanted to condemn it in a blanket fashion. As one of the Luftwaffe officers based at Pitomnik airfield, he was able to correct me on many points, to confirm others and to provide a host of small insights. His account of the final surrender within Stalingrad and the appalling conditions in the infamous camp at Beketovka was unforgettable. It lent both substance and visual form to many of the written accounts, which had all been evasive over one terrible aspect. Starving German and Rumanian prisoners were reduced to cannibalism, cutting slivers of flesh from the mounds of frozen corpses.

He took me up into a mountain village nearby to introduce me to the private soldier who had saved his life. This soldier, whose local dialect he had immediately recognised on hearing his voice, worked in the so-called prison infirmary. He had passed him crusts taken from the hands of those who had died, lacking the strength to eat their pathetic ration. The two of them – one a count the other a peasant farmer – spoke with the distant wonder of survival. Neither of these men complained of the cruelty of their fate, nor, considering their experiences, did they display much hatred. They remembered the Russian women for their strength and humanity and despised most of the Russian soldiers, especially the guards, for unpredictable brutality and drunkenness. Towards the end of our day together, the count asked me if I had read Theodor Plievier's novel *Stalingrad*,[5] published in East Germany in 1945. I said that I had. I asked what he thought of it. He told me that purely for the physical descriptions of suffering, it was very accurate. Plievier, a German Communist of 'the Moscow Emigration', had been allowed by the NKVD authorities to tour the Soviet prison camps, interviewing German prisoners on their experiences during the battle of Stalingrad. He had been one of the many questioned by Plievier in great detail, and when he finally had a chance to read the book many years later, he had found it most impressive. I was also to find how accurate in their descriptions of conditions two Russian novels about the battle were: *Front-line Stalingrad* by Viktor Nekrassov,[6] who had fought in the battle as a platoon commander in Colonel Batyuk's division of Siberians, and Vasily Grossman's *Life and Fate*,[7] which many people rate as the greatest Russian novel of this century. Grossman, a novelist, worked as a war correspondent in Stalingrad during the battle, and came to know the soldiers and snipers of the 62nd Army well. Obviously a novel can never provide a valid historical source, but these accounts offered valuable background descriptions.

In Moscow, later that autumn, I was prevented mainly by bureaucratic problems from getting access on that visit to the central Ministry of Defence archive out at Podolsk, but this proved a blessing in disguise. Professor Anatoly Chernobayev, the editor of the journal *Istorichesky Arkhiv*, advised me to go back to the old Marxist–Leninist Institute (now the Russian State Archive for Social and Political History), where I had worked several years before on the French Communist Party for *Paris After the Liberation*.[8] Chernobayev was right. There was a great deal on the fate of Stalingrad civilians, both at the hands of Beria's NKVD and the Germans. There were also captured letters, diaries, notebooks and *samizdat* from German troops and their allies, all of which had been passed by Red Army Intelligence to the Department of Agitation and Propaganda.

Another excellent piece of advice was to go through private collections in the Russian State Archive of Literature and the Arts. The papers of Ilya Ehrenburg contained captured private documents sent to him by soldiers at the front. The papers of Vasily Grossman included all his notebooks, with the original jottings made when he covered the battle of Stalingrad as a journalist. What was interesting was to contrast his sturdily optimistic vision of Soviet Communism in the notes – a wartime need to believe – with the final version of *Life and Fate*, after he had finally realised in 1949 that the Stalinist regime, the self-proclaimed scourge of Nazism, was deeply anti-Semitic itself.

In the Central State Archive, there were all the reports on the extraordinary story of General von Seydlitz-Kurzbach's rather naive dealings with the NKVD after the surrender. Seydlitz proposed forming an army corps from German prisoners captured at Stalingrad. He urged the Russians to arm them and fly them into Germany to start a revolution against Hitler. Beria vetoed the proposal, certain that it was a trick. But Seydlitz's energetic anti-Nazi efforts did him no good. Beria suddenly had him charged with war crimes when he was no longer useful.

Before travelling down to Volgograd, I interviewed a number of participants in Moscow. The most important was Lev Bezyminski, a Red Army intelligence office who was reserve interpreter at Paulus's surrender. Bezyminski provided me with several personal accounts in manuscript, of which by far the most valuable was that of his former colleague, Major Nikolai Dimitrivich Dyatlenko, the key NKVD officer-interpreter attached to Don front headquarters. Dyatlenko's account (verified later by material I found in the Russian Ministry of Defence Archive) gave a fresh view of several important aspects: the Soviet offer of surrender to Paulus in the second week of January 1943, the interrogation of captured German generals, the use of German communists at Don front headquarters and numerous other details.

In Volgograd, I inspected the main sites of the battle, interviewed civilian survivors and veterans from the battle, and worked on the mass of letters taken from German bodies, as well as the collection of letters from Red Army soldiers in the battle. It was the civilian aspect, a scale of suffering which we never really were able to imagine in the West, that impressed me most. Unlike many of the soldiers' stories, which were sometimes boastful, sometimes self-serving, I believed almost every detail that I heard from civilian survivors. Their terrible accounts were delivered with deep sadness, but little trace of self-pity.

The next spring, I returned to Germany to finish the huge volume of material at Freiburg, then moved to Potsdam, to consult some published works and manuscripts in the Militärgeschichtliches Forschungsamt library, and finally went to Vienna, where I found several interesting personal collections of unpublished typescripts from survivors in the Austrian State Archives.

During this time, the last problems were sorted out over access to Red Army files held at the Russian Ministry of Defence Central Archive out at Podolsk, an establishment set up in 1936. Negotiations over access the previous year had been conducted at the Ministry of Defence with the responsible officer on the general staff, which directly controls the archives. He told me flatly that the way the system worked was for me to tell them my subject, and that they would then select the files. It would have been futile to protest.

I explained that I was interested in depicting the experience of soldiers on both sides during the battle. To give an indication of the sort of material I was looking for, I mentioned the reports by doctors and chaplains attached to the German divisions. This prompted a bellow of laughter from the Russian colonel. 'There were no priests in the Red Army!'

'Ah, yes,' I replied, 'but you had political officers.' This provoked more of a grunt than a laugh. 'So you want to see the political department reports,' he said. 'We will see.'

Stalingrad, as the byword for Soviet heroism, is a particularly sensitive subject. This is especially true in post-Communist Russia when all political camps like to use Zhukov and the Red Army (untainted by Stalinism because it had been persecuted in the purges) as symbols of Russian unity and greatness. When I was interviewing veterans in Russia, I soon learned that the one thing to avoid at all costs was becoming bogged down in a political argument. Any hint of criticism of Stalin, and even the most anti-Stalinist of them would go into an all-round defensive position. A criticism of Stalin seemed to undermine their sacrifice.

Richard Overy, in his book *Russia's War*,[9] emphasised that the astonishing capacity of the Russians to withstand suffering had little to do with Communist Party propaganda. 'The Tsarist armies', he writes, 'between 1914 and 1917 averaged 7,000 casualties a day, compared with 7,950 a day between 1941 and 1945... The distinction between the "we" and the "I" was symptomatic of a deeper social outlook in Russian life, where collectivism was preferred to individualism. These cultural traditions were borrowed and enlarged by Soviet Communism.' Orlando Figes disagreed with this collectivist explanation. He underlined the effect of the blocking detachments of NKVD troops and Komsomol groups under their control armed with machine guns.

Undoubtedly the biggest challenge in writing about Stalingrad was to provide some sort of answer to that fundamentally difficult question: Did the Red Army manage to hold on against all expectations through genuine bravery and self-sacrifice, or because of the NKVD and Komsomol blocking groups behind, and the ever-present threat of execution by the Special Detachments, soon to become known as SMERSH? Figes is right to point to the panic and the appalling degree of coercion. But Overy is also right to seek to explain the astonishing degree of self-sacrifice. We cannot tell for sure whether a minority or a majority of soldiers panicked in the early stage of the battle for the city in late August and September. In that early period, before the Political Department of Stalingrad Front felt able on 8 October to make the sinister claim: 'The defeatist mood is almost eliminated and the number of treasonous incidents is getting lower,' the proportion might well have amounted to more than a minority. But equally, there can be no doubt about the astonishing resolution of many, if not most, Red Army soldiers to hold on to their diminishing foothold on the west bank of the Volga. No remotely similar feat was performed by any Western army in the Second World War; in fact the only comparable defence is the French sacrifice at Verdun.

The debate is even more important than it appears on the surface. Young Russians today cannot understand the suffering of the Second World War, as the colonel on the train to Volgograd argued passionately. They will understand it even less as their country gradually picks itself up economically. Yet if they cannot understand it, how will young European and American historians be able to comprehend such things in the future? Will they – hoping to imitate some historians of German forces on the eastern front like Goldhagen and Bartov – set out to analyse the number of party or Komsomol members, the percentage of cadres, intellectuals, factory workers or peasants, breaking them down by age, and marital status, and forming their conclusions almost exclusively on archival statistics? Well, the answer is that they won't be able to. The Soviet system, unlike the bureaucratic Wehrmacht, simply did not bother itself with the personal details of its soldiers. Only when the NKVD began to suspect an individual of 'treason to the Motherland' was such information recorded.

One of the obvious questions is how much important material is still hidden in the former Soviet archives. This was brought home to me two years after *Stalingrad*[10] came out. Professor Oleg Rzheshevsky, the president of the Russian association of Second World War historians, came to London for a seminar and very kindly brought me a copy of a book entitled *Stalingradskaya epopeya*.[11] This glossy volume, which had just been published by the KGB's successor organisation, the FSB, is supposed to contain choice selections from the NKVD files on Stalingrad. But most of the material is anodyne in the extreme. There are a few tantalising documents, but in fact one is left fuming at the glaring omissions. Most striking of all, there is nothing about the NKVD's treatment of former Red Army *Hiwis* captured in German uniform at Stalingrad. Were they executed, as some accounts claim, with clubs and rifle butts to save bullets, even crushed with tanks? Or were the bulk of them transferred to the Gulag to be worked to death on a special punishment regime? How many were executed? And how many managed to take Red Army uniforms from corpses and then reintegrate themselves into the Red Army in the chaos? I long to know, but I fear that we never will find out. I suppose this is why the Russian archives are so frustrating and so fascinating.

# 13

## Women and the Battle
## of Stalingrad

REINA PENNINGTON

The battle of Stalingrad was one of the largest, longest, and most important battles in history. For half a year, from the beginning of Operation Blau in late June 1942 to the surrender of the German 6th Army in February 1943, the Stalingrad region was the focus of the war on the eastern front. Stalingrad was a large industrial city that sprawled in a narrow ribbon for fifteen miles on the west (right) bank of the Volga river – it covered nearly forty miles if the major suburbs are included. It was the home of several immense factory complexes, many of which had been converted to produce military equipment such as tanks. But the battle included much more than just the city; it encompassed three Soviet fronts and a German army group. The battle was the first major instance of modern urban warfare, but it also included the large-scale use of tank forces and manoeuvre warfare. This battle marked the first major defeat of the German army in the Second World War, and was arguably the turning point of the war. In John Erickson's view, 'Stalingrad set the Soviet Union on the road to being a world power'.[1] Field Marshal Keitel, Hitler's chief of staff, later confessed that Stalingrad was the moment at which Germany 'played [its] last trump, and lost'.[2] The price of winning the battle was high; by mid-September, each side had more than half a million troops committed in the region; Soviet strength increased to well over a million on the three-front axis by the start of the counter-offensive in November 1942.[3] Total Soviet casualties during the battle were more than one million, with nearly half a million dead or missing in action.[4] Thus a great deal of attention has been devoted to the study of this battle. A simple search of the Worldcat (an index of the world's largest library consortium) brings up more than fifteen hundred books with the keyword 'Stalingrad'. These books include histories, memoirs, and several novels, in several languages. At least three English-language bestsellers have focused on the battle of Stalingrad, including *Enemy at the Gates*, *War of the Rats*, and *Stalingrad, the Fateful Siege: 1942–1943*.[5] Despite this scrutiny, women's participation in the battle of Stalingrad has been given very little attention. Even so, the alert reader will find that women are mentioned in practically every book dealing with the battle, particularly in Russian-language sources. Often their presence is noted in an almost offhand way through the use of the simple words 'men and women'.[6] For example, a Soviet writer describing the unveiling of the post-war monument on Mamaev Kurgan pointed out: 'The monument is a tribute to the men *and women* of the Soviet Union who won the victory by their staunchness, indomitable courage, and with their blood' [emphasis added].[7] Such references might seem almost perfunctory, but they are uniquely characteristic of the Red Army. No writer describing Western battles in the Second World War would use the phrase 'men and women', because Western women were generally far from the front lines of battle; the situation was quite the reverse in the Soviet armed forces.

The number of women who were present during the battle of Stalingrad is uncertain. Marshal Vasilii Chuikov, commander of the 62nd Army, which was the main defensive force in the city, mentions that there were 'more than a thousand women in units of the 62nd Army who received decorations'.[8] That would be consistent with the fact that in 1943–5, there were an average of 2000–3000 women soldiers in a typical field army, with around 20,000 women soldiers on a front.[9] There were thirteen Soviet field armies plus air armies on the three fronts that were active during the height of the battle, plus 8000 women in local air defence.[10] Thus it can be estimated that a minimum of 20,000 and a maximum of around 60,000 military women participated in the battle. The number of civilian women is much harder to estimate, but probably ran in the high thousands during the early phase, diminishing throughout the battle.

Some authors, including some of the leading generals from the battle, make a particular point of emphasising women's roles. Marshal A. I. Eremenko, commander of the Stalingrad front, wrote: 'There can hardly be found a single military specialty with which our brave women did not cope just as well as their brothers, husbands and fathers.'[11] Chuikov noted: 'Women soldiers proved themselves to be just as heroic in those days of fighting as men.'[12] In his 1960 book on the battle, Chuikov devoted an entire chapter, 'Women in the Defence of Stalingrad', to women's role in the battle.[13] But only a few rather obscure Soviet books have focused specifically on women at Stalingrad, the best of which is L. P. Ovchinnikova's 1987 *Zhenshchiny v soldatskikh shineliakh*. These sources point out the diverse roles played by women. For example, V. S. Murmantseva, a noted academic author on military women, notes that 'entire units and subunits of women took part in the battles for Stalingrad: anti-air divisions, aviation regiments, communications subunits. Women fought at the walls of the tractor factory, the Red October metallurgical factory, at Mamaev Kurgan, and on the streets of the city.'[14] Soviet women filled a variety of roles: *razvedka* (scout, intelligence staff, or observer); *sanitarka* (medical orderly/medic); *saninstruktor* (medical instructor/NCO); *sviazistka* (signaller/communications personnel); *telephonistka* (telephone operator); *zenitchitsa* (anti-aircraft personnel). English-language materials are sometimes confusing in their translations of these terms; for example, female medical personnel are often simply lumped together as 'nurses', while a *razvedka* in anti-aircraft artillery (AAA) had very different duties from one in the army.

In her book about women at Stalingrad, A. D. Zarubina notes:

> In the ranks of the defenders of Stalingrad and the army which surrounded the German forces, there were many Soviet women. They were doctors, nurses, and medics in medical battalions, company *saninstruktory* – medical workers of all ranks and all depths of the front – from evacuation hospitals to the front lines of defence and the ranks of the attacking subunits in the offensive. They were *sviazistki* on front, army, corps, division, and regimental staffs, *sviazistki* in battalions and companies. They were *zenitchitsi* and artillery observers. They were administrative workers in defending and attacking units – soldiers and sergeants in administrative units, sergeants in regimental depots, and cooks. At the same time, during the defensive period of fighting there were women both in the ranks of the militia, and among the scouts from the population who gave invaluable help to the Soviet command.'[15]

Even the sources that emphasise women's participation are selective and incomplete. Most overlook women's roles as fighter pilots, tank drivers, and snipers, for example. This has led some writers to assume that women did not fill certain roles during the battle.[16] But that was not the case, as is obvious from even a relatively brief examination of the sources. Yet only a few authors, such as Ovchinnikova and Murmantseva, make a point of discussing women's participation in designated combat roles. At least twelve women who received the Soviet Union's highest military decoration, the Hero of the Soviet Union, were active at Stalingrad. They included five medical personnel – M. S. Borovichenko, V. O. Gnarovskaia, V. S. Kashcheeva, Z. I. Mareseva, and Z. A. Samsonova; one radio operator – E. A. Stempkovskaia; three dive-bomber pilots – Mariia Dolina, Nadezhda Fedutenko, Klavdiia Fomicheva; two dive-bomber navigators – Galina Dzhunkovskaia and Antonina Zubkova; and fighter pilot L. I. Litviak.

Individual women can be identified in virtually every military role, and there are undoubtedly many others who have not yet been recognised. Soviet policy at the time was only beginning to publicly acknowledge the variety of ways in which women were participating in combat.[17] For example, women fighter pilots were active at Stalingrad from mid-September, but that fact is rarely mentioned in memoirs of the time, and remains unknown to many people to this day.[18] Women's combat roles were not publicised among either Western or Soviet journalists. When journalist Alexander Werth was allowed to visit Stalingrad a few days after the German surrender, he noted that 'women, and even some children, had lived through it all; the women had been busy washing clothes and doing odd jobs for the Red Army'.[19] Werth never described women actually fighting in the battle, although after-wards he talked with a woman in Kotelnikovo who told him her youngest sister had been killed while serving in the air defence at Stalingrad.[20] Similarly, famous journalists such as Simonov and Grossman describe nurses and communications personnel, but not the fighter pilots or snipers. But it should not be surprising that women were driving tanks and flying aircraft at Stalingrad; women had filled every sort of combat role from the very first days of the war, in the ranks of the Red Army and as civilians. Although the number of women would increase dramatically by early 1943, when it reached a peak of about 800,000, their participation was already widespread by 1942. German soldiers make a number of passing references to the presence of female Soviet soldiers during the first year of the war. One German soldier wrote to his family in July 1941: 'When I go back I will tell you endless horror stories about Russia. Yesterday, for instance, we saw our first women soldiers ... and these pigs fired on our decent German soldiers from ambush positions.'[21]

Women's involvement in the battle of Stalingrad was inevitable. As John Erickson has noted, in the conditions on the eastern front of multiple urban sieges and urban assaults, 'the war came to many young girls and women with terrifying suddenness'.[22] Such was the case in Stalingrad, but even more so than with cities such as Kiev and Leningrad that were besieged in the early weeks of the war. By the time the front lines of battle came to Stalingrad, there was a high concentration of women in the city. Thousands of women and children had been evacuated from western areas to cities along the Volga, which initially were far in the rear area. In addition, women had replaced many men in Stalingrad factories before the battle began.[23] A. S. Chuianov, chair of the Stalingrad city defence committee, noted that 'in the first year of the war many thousands [of men] ... went to the front. Their replace-ment became a most urgent problem. Tens of thousands of women came to the workshops and 13,000 became tractor drivers.'[24] In addition to working in war-related industry, women played an early role in constructing defences. Murmantseva notes that women were the primary workforce in building defensive fortifications. This work began as early as September 1941, when a new rail line was constructed from Stalingrad to Vladimirovka that was dubbed 'the women's line' owing to the large number of women who worked on it. Additional lines and roads were built during the winter of 1941–2 which would later prove essential in Soviet transportation into the battle area. A major project was the construction of three defensive lines around the city that extended 478 kilometres.[25] Miles of trenches, fire points, tank traps, barricades, and ditches were constructed.[26] A woman, Mariia Nikolaevna Somova, was commissar for the construction of the defensive line.[27] Photographs from this period clearly show the preponderance of women working on the defences.[28] In addition, one author notes, 'After work women stayed at the factory, they stuffed drum magazines for submachine guns with cartridges, prepared "Molotov cocktails", filled sacks with sand for the barricades, built anti-tank strong points, and studied various military specialties – they prepared for defence.'[29] Four rings of anti-tank ditches extended twenty to thirty miles outside the city, but with their hasty and incomplete construction would not prove sufficient to hold back the German forces.

By mid-July it became clear that Stalingrad was in danger of German attacks, and the city was put on a wartime footing; the Stalingrad front was created on 17 July.[30] During this intensely hot summer period, when the Germans were fighting to cross the Don river, the involvement of residents of Stalingrad in defence preparations was dramatically increased. By August 1942, district party committees had mobilised about 200,000 women and men.[31] The civilians working on the city defences were subject to enemy attack throughout this period, primarily by air. Fourteen-year-old Nina Grebennikova, interviewed by Antony Beevor, had her back broken when she was buried by a bomb explosion while performing such work. Grebennikova was taken to a hospital, where she would once more find herself being bombed during the 23 August attack. She was finally evacuated from the city on 28 August, along with other children from the hospital.[32]

Many women sought a more active role and applied to enter military service. Ovchinnikova describes the thousands of requests received during the spring of 1942 by the Komsomol regional committees and the *voenkomaty* (local military commissariats) from young girls asking to be sent to the front.[33] Many civilians, mostly young women, were recruited in April 1942 for local anti-aircraft defence (PVO) units.[34] A Komsomol call-up brought more than 8000 female volunteers to the 9th Stalingrad PVO Corps.[35] In addition to thousands of local girls, groups of volunteers from the Astrakhan oblast, the Stavropol *rai*, the Bashkir ASSR and other places filled the ranks of the Stalingrad PVO corps. Many of these young girls had to buck the opposition of their

family to join the military, even in local PVO. They became instrument
mechanics, range-takers, signallers, radio operators, and observers.
Women had not previously served in PVO in any numbers, and their
arrival caused some consternation. Raisa Aleksandrovna Gal'chenko
served as an instrument mechanic in the 1079th PVO regiment. She
recalled that when they arrived at their unit in early April 1942, their
presence was clearly a surprise to the male soldiers: 'Soldiers were all
around us. In that first moment a lot of joking retorts could be heard
when the anti-air gunners recognised that girls would be serving together
with them.'[36]

Many girls were assigned to VNOS (air observation, warning and
communication) posts, scattered on the approaches to Stalingrad. Post
commander Valentina Ivanovna Mordvintseva of the 14th independent
VNOS battalion described what VNOS duty was like. Her unit served
in Kalmykiia, where posts were situated about 15–20 kilometres apart
in the steppe. Each post held a crew of five people, primarily young
women. The girls built a bunker and a stove, and drove several miles
to a well for water supplies.[37] Mordvintseva comments:

> But the most difficult thing of all was to sustain the 24-hour watch.
> Two hours you stand on the roof, not taking your eyes from the
> binoculars for a minute. Then you go below and sit at the telephone.
> If we noticed an aircraft in the sky, we had to instantly identify the
> type of aircraft, its altitude, speed, and direction. Hardly was the
> signal 'Air!' given, than everyone at the post joined in the work. Every
> minute we were aware of what sort of responsibility we had. And
> what about repairing telephone communications between posts? At
> that time enemy saboteurs were breaking through on the steppe.
> Hardly was communication lost, than one of the girls went out on
> the line. She walked through the deserted place, where maybe she
> would meet an enemy face to face.[38]

The Russian term for a PVO 'observer' is *razvedchik*, which can also
mean 'scout'. Ovchinnikova explains the difference:

> The word *razvedchik* is usually connected with the picture of fearless
> actions in the rear of the enemy, dangerous crossings of the front
> lines, searches for 'tongues'. Hundreds of girl-volunteers, entering
> into PVO service, began to learn the profession of *razvedchik*. But
> this military labour turned out to be something else entirely. Here
> there were no difficult and dangerous raids, exchanges of gunfire, or
> chases. Everything looked much more prosaic. Soldiers with bin-
> oculars in their hands went up on the roof of the living quarters and
> factory shops, on the heights of the burial mounds, on wooden

towers in the steppes. *Vnosovtsi* (there was such a term) were the
guardians of the sky. They had to be the first to notice enemy aircraft
and report to the PVO staff. At that time the *razvedchiki* did not have
modern sophisticated, sensitive instruments. Violators of the airspace
were determined according to aircraft silhouette, and at night, by
sound.[39]

Women were already heavily represented in communications units by
the summer of 1942. Senior Sergeant Mariia Semenova Kaliberda of
the 65th Army noted that by June 1943 the 129th Separate Signal
Regiment was already eighty per cent women.[40] Kaliberda noted that
women in signals faced some of the same obstacles as women in PVO:
'We wanted to be equal – we didn't want the men saying, "Oh, those
women!" about us. And we tried harder than the men. Apart from
everything else we had to prove that we were as good as them. For a
long time we had to put up with a very patronising, superior attitude.'[41]

In the summer of 1942 the Red Army was permitted to conduct a
fighting retreat to avoid disastrous encirclements such as those that had
occurred during the first summer of the war. Nevertheless, it was
sustaining huge losses at this time; in the Don river area, only 105
soldiers survived the fighting from one division originally 13,000 strong.[42]
Some women were already apparently active in combat roles in the late
spring of 1942 on the approaches to Stalingrad. A senior German NCO
in the 389th Infantry Division (51st Corps, 6th Army) reported in May
1942, when the 389th was advancing toward the Don river, that his
regiment clashed with a 'bandit battalion' of women soldiers led by a
red-haired woman. He said, '[T]he fighting methods of these female
beasts showed itself in treacherous and dangerous ways. They lie
concealed in heaps of straw, and shoot us in the back when we pass
by.'[43]

Three reserve armies, including the 62nd Army, were rushed into
action on the new Stalingrad front, but they had practically no air-
defence capability, so local PVO had to cover strategic points like the
Don river crossings.[44] Marshal Eremenko praised the dedication of the
women working under the most dangerous conditions in AAA.[45]
Chuikov noted that 'in the Stalingrad PVO Corps the majority of the
combat crews were women, whether at AAA guns or at the instruments
of searchlight installations', and pointed out that the combat effectiveness
of those crews was equal to other AAA units he had observed.[46]
Ovchinnikova notes: 'AAA guns and machine guns were installed on
the roofs of the factory shops and the railroad stations, in public
gardens and in city streets. But most of all the air-defence batteries
were situated on the approaches to the city.'[47] They were soon to find
themselves on the front lines of battle. One medical NCO, Valeriia

Osipovna Gnarovskaia, first went into combat in July 1942 at Stalingrad with the 244th Rifle Division of the 62nd Army. The unit was surrounded during the retreat towards Stalingrad but broke out. All personnel were actively involved in the fighting and Gnarovskaia was credited with killing twenty-eight enemy soldiers, apparently with a submachine gun and grenades. Soon afterwards she contracted typhus and was sent to the hospital, returning to her unit in spring 1943. She was later killed on 23 September 1943 in a famous exploit; to protect a medical aid post from an advancing German tank, she threw herself under the tank and set off a string of grenades. She was credited with saving seventy wounded soldiers and was posthumously awarded the Hero of the Soviet Union.[48]

Women also served as interpreters and interrogators. In the summer of 1942, a captured detachment from the 29th Motorised Division of the 4th Panzer Army was interrogated by a female political officer from south-western front HQ, a Lieutenant Lepinskaia.[49] An interesting story is told by Colonel Aleksandr Utvenko, commander of the 33rd Guards Rifle Division (62nd Army), who reported on a battle on the west bank of the Don river in mid-August. His unit was nearly surrounded and had to break free in small groups. Utvenko reported that the situation was so bad that some of his men were shooting themselves to get out of the fighting. When one Russian soldier began walking toward the German positions, an interpreter on Utvenko's staff, referred to only as Galya, reportedly cried, 'Look at him! The snake is going to surrender!' and promptly shot him.[50]

Communications personnel were subject to all the same risks as other soldiers. In battles against the 62nd Army west of the Don river near Kalach, the Germans captured a group of communications personnel, and reported that the group consisted of a male officer and mostly female personnel.[51] Radio operator Elena Stempkovskaia provides one example of the sort of role played by women in the earliest phases of the battle.[52] She had served in the 21st Army since January 1942, and although she served in communications, she had many opportunities to learn how to fire rifles and light machine guns. She actively took part in the fighting whenever she was not occupied with transmitting messages. In late June 1942 she took part in the bloody retreat of that unit on the south-western front; her battalion (2nd battalion/216th regiment/76th rifle division) was reduced to twenty-five soldiers. When the Germans overran her position, Stempkovskaia destroyed her transmitting equipment, and is said to have shot three Germans who entered the battalion HQ. One of the few survivors reports that she helped cover the continued retreat of her unit. Some sources indicate that she died while firing a machine gun; others state that she was captured, tortured and executed.[53]

By 12 July the South western Front was 'practically ripped to pieces'.[54] On 28 July, however, the famous Stavka Order No. 227 was issued, entitled 'Not a step back!' (*ni shagu nazad*). Stalin had determined that no retreat would be permitted beyond the city of Stalingrad. One purpose of the order was to buy time while the city defences were strengthened. Although the order pertained to the Red Army, many civilians took the words to heart and vowed to remain in the city and continue fighting or working. Walter Kerr (a reporter for the *New York Herald Tribune* who was in Russia in 1942) mentions that it 'had something of an exhilarating effect' because everyone, including the women, '[was] told and believed that what was coming was the decisive struggle, that whether the war was won or lost would be determined here, by them'.[55] Militia units (*narodnoe opolchenie*) were formed for the purpose of combat, and 'fighting battalions' (*istrebitelnye batal'ony*) were set up to provide security against saboteurs, spies, etc.; more than 50,000 volunteers filled out the ranks of these *ad hoc* units by late July 1942.[56] Women are reported to have served alongside men in all these units in Stalingrad.[57] In such extreme circumstances, women were joining local militias all over the country. In Odessa, there had already been a militia battalion of 900 women which fought alongside the Red Army.[58]

By late July, the Red Army had slowed the progress of the German forces, but the German 6th Army was reinforced and continued its seemingly relentless advance. In early August, most of the Red Army forces in the Don bend had been destroyed or were in retreat; by the last part of the month, German units broke through to the Volga river north of the city.[59] The massive German air raid on the city that began on 23 August 1942 was a terrifying experience for Stalingrad inhabitants. Hundreds of German bombers pounded the city the first day, and as many as 40,000 people were killed. Panic was widespread among civilians and soldiers. Army nurses watched in horror as one Soviet division commander followed the old Roman practice of decimation as a punishment for cowardice and desertion: he walked down the line of his troops and shot every tenth man until he had emptied his revolver.[60]

On a day when the summer temperatures soared to over one hundred degrees, fires broke out all over the city; some would not be extinguished for weeks; and, as Antony Beevor notes, 'with virtually all the fathers away at the front, or now mobilized, women were left to cope with the appalling aftermath'.[61] Vlasa Kliagina was working on an anti-tank trench south of the city when the 23 August raid began; when she returned home that night, it was a smouldering ruin. She found her daughter sheltering in a cellar, but her young son had vanished, never to be seen again.[62] Many women lost their children; many children were orphaned during the attacks. Thousands of women died, in the factories, at the defensive construction sites, or in their homes.[63] In the attacks on that

day and in the weeks that followed, German Stukas strafed ferry vessels
and the landing areas where civilians hoping to evacuate were massed;
it was said that 'the shoreline was slippery with blood'.[64] Many reported
on the dead bodies in and around the Volga, especially those of women
and children killed during their attempt to cross the river.[65] Soviet
soldiers often reported their grief at seeing the bodies of women killed
in the attacks.[66] Others witnessed first-hand the abuse of women and
children by Germans.[67] German soldiers too often mention the casualties
among civilian women.[68]

Many women evacuated, or attempted to evacuate, from Stalingrad.
The sources vary as to the extent of the evacuations, and as to whether
civilian evacuations were at times prohibited.[69] The city's pre-war
population was about half a million, but had swelled from an influx of
refugees from other areas. Most sources agree that these refugees made
up the majority of those evacuated from Stalingrad, with residents and
workers of the city comprising a much smaller percentage. M. A.
Vodolagin, who was party secretary of the Stalingrad oblast and a
military commissar of a militia corps, says that 300,000 civilians and
wounded were evacuated by 10 September; Chuianov gives a general
figure of 400,000 evacuated under fire.[70] In the process, many of those
assisting the evacuation were killed at their posts, including crews of
transports, party officials, and medical personnel.[71] Many evacuating
civilians were also killed in attacks by air, artillery, and even shots from
tanks aimed at river craft. Ironically, some Germans claimed they would
not hinder civilian evacuations.[72]

Hundreds of women in late August served in emergency first-aid and
evacuation groups to try to deal with the mass casualties and to assist
evacuation.[73] Murmantseva notes that by the time the battle began,
'75,000 women and girls from the Stalingrad oblast had completed
military-medical training. When the bitter battle began, there were
already 500 girls in Stalingrad hospitals daily – female military workers
and nurses worked for the care of the wounded. As many as 100
volunteer detachments composed of girls took part in unloading
wounded from medical trains.'[74] A special women's detachment of those
who could swim was created to assist on the shore. Due to the shortage
of boats, women volunteers scavenged boards and logs and constructed
makeshift rafts, then ferried people across the river on them.[75] Women
had been in charge of children's homes for orphans and children
evacuated from places like Leningrad in the pre-battle period.[76] Women
like Komsomol director Anastasia Modina tried to help the orphans,
leading them to shelter; many had to be persuaded to leave the dead
bodies of their parents; a few could not be persuaded to move and had
to be left where they were.[77] Modina and her charges were evacuated
within a few days. She was credited with saving the lives of over 400

orphaned children.[78] As V. I. Levkin, a party leader in Stalingrad notes, women were both rescuers and the rescued:

> During heavy bombings Komsomol members saved the lives of women, children and old people and organised temporary accommodation for them in dugouts. 'Aid and rescue groups' were set up in all districts. They were recruited from hundreds of Komsomol members and other young people who constantly risked their lives to save orphaned children from ruins and blazing houses, helped wounded soldiers, officers, women and old people and ferried them across to the Volga's left bank.[79]

AAA units were heavily involved in the Soviet attempts to defend against the massive German raids. As the Germans drew ever nearer the city, the young girls working at VNOS posts were in extreme danger. Members of 14th independent VNOS battalion in Kalmykiia suffered a terrible fate when it was surrounded by German troops on 31 August. The crews of three posts were gathered at the village of Khalkhuta, preparing to transfer, when German tanks attacked. The eighteen soldiers – thirteen women and five men – tried to form a circle defence but could not hold out against the heavily armed Germans. The VNOS troops were captured and forced to dig a trench, and then lined up beside it. The Germans produced a map and demanded that someone show them the shortest route to Yust. One by one, as the soldiers refused to answer, they were led to the trench and shot. Only Vera Nikonova survived. Nikonova was wounded in the arm and the back, but lay as though dead amid the corpses of her comrades until the Germans left. She then crept from the pit and began crawling toward a neighbouring post. It took her five days, but she was eventually found and taken to a hospital.[80]

One AAA battery was covering the Latoshinksy railway/ferry crossing on the Volga shore. Anna Kuz'minichna Iakovleva says that the AAA crews were well aware of the importance of their role, and stayed at their posts while railway crews loaded cars onto the ferry. There were concentrations of equipment and supplies in the area, as well as large numbers of evacuees. The battery fought until its guns were destroyed and most of its personnel dead or wounded.[81]

Many young girls stayed at their posts for days on end, or until they were out of shells. One such unit, the 1077th AA Regiment, operated north of Stalingrad in the Spartanovka area near the tractor factory. Rimma Sergeevna Davydenko recalled that her unit was taken by surprise by the rapidly advancing German tanks, and quickly shifted to trying to fire at the tanks rather than the aircraft. Every available person was put to work carrying shells, which were being used up at a fantastic rate, and bandaging the wounded.[82] The women from these gun crews who survived were evacuated on 25 September and reassigned to other AAA units.[83]

Raisa Aleksandrovna Gal'chenko remembers 4 September as an especially difficult day. Her battery was located on the western outskirts of the city, and fired at both aircraft and tanks that day. 'Shells were needed,' she recalls. 'All the girl instrument technicians began to bring up shells. We ran to the vehicle which was standing in a strip of woods. Here were located boxes of shells. Of course, if a shell hit the body of the vehicle, then everything would blow sky high. But do you really think about the danger during a battle? You carry shells, which weigh 16 kg, turn the warhead up and you run to the gun. ... The *zenitchiki* were now on the very front line. Those were terrible hours.'[84] Her unit fought until it was out of ammunition and its guns destroyed; at that point the crews were sent across the Volga, only to return soon after to a new position near the barricades factory.

These heroic actions served to delay the German advance while Red Army units regrouped and civilians fortified the city. Hube's panzer division faced admittedly stiff resistance from the Red Army and militia forces fighting to the north of the city.[85] Chuikov wrote: 'The troops of the 62nd Army will never forget how the women AAA crews stood their ground on the narrow strip of land in the defence of Stalingrad and fired on enemy aircraft to the last round.'[86] Levkin recalls the heroic actions of an AAA battery, typical of the many units that were cut off during the German advance:

> Lieutenant Skakun's AAA battery will never be forgotten. Having lost contact with AAA regimental command it independently fought against enemy air and land forces for over 24 hours. Dive-bombers attacked it from the air and heavy tanks from the ground. The ground, air, flames, smoke, the metallic roar of bomb explosions, the whine of shells and machine-gun rounds all merged into chaos. The battery was manned by AAA gunners, instrument operators, stereoscopic range finders and scouts, all women. They fought side by side with the gunners ... On the evening of the following day four unharmed soldiers and their wounded commander got through and described how the girls had not taken cover for a moment although there had been moments when it was near madness not to take cover.[87]

One Red Army officer told Vasily Grossman of his anguish in watching AAA crews who refused to take cover even when attacked by tanks and Stukas.[88] Professor Nikolai Viktorovich Goncharov told Antony Beevor of one girl who stayed at her post for four days without relief.[89] German units reported resistance from the AAA batteries operated by young women.[90] Some historians, basing their opinion on selected German sources, are dismissive of the capabilities of these units; some accounts say that untrained civilian women futilely fought to the death in AAA positions, and were found 'lying dead in their bloodstained cotton dresses'.[91] One panzer division report that gave the women a higher evaluation stated: '[R]ight until the late afternoon we had to fight, shot for shot, against thirty-seven enemy anti-aircraft positions, manned by tenacious fighting women, until they were all destroyed.'[92]

Many civilians were involved in attempting to stave off the attack by the 16th Panzer Division in the north.[93] On 23 August, some of the worker's units had been hastily deployed to the northern regions of the city, along with elements of the NKVD garrison and some Red Army units.[94] Some women, such as Ol'ga Kovaleva, fought in these militia units. Kovaleva was the first woman in the country to become a steelworker at an open-hearth furnace; she had worked at the Red October factory since 1933. When most of the men in her shop formed a militia unit and went out to fight on 24 August, Kovaleva joined them, although they protested: 'the men can manage this without you'.[95] Savkin, the unit commissar, only noticed that Kovaleva was with the unit after it was deployed in the field. He hardly recognised her, for instead of wearing her usual overalls or men's trousers, she had for some reason put on a grey woman's suit and a bright scarf. Savkin says, 'I had to repeat many times, "Go away, Ol'ga!" before she answered, looking at me intently with her dark eyes: "I'm not going anywhere. And you don't have the right to expel me." It was hard to argue with her. This was a brusque, severe woman. I thought that this was typical of her, not to give in, and I decided to leave it'.[96] The reported opposition to Kovaleva's participation would indicate that it was unusual for women to fight in the militia; however, women had volunteered for militia units by the thousands since early 1941.[97]

On the morning of 25 August the unit received machine guns and a suicidal assignment: to attack and retake a farm held by the Germans. They attacked across an open field and many of the militia were mown down, but Kovaleva was among those who reached the farm. A few minutes later, Savkin stumbled across her corpse in the grass. 'She lay face down, her arms sprawled out. The scarf had fallen off her head, the wind was blowing her hair around. In her outstretched right hand was a rifle, and in the left, a grenade. Her face was bloodstained, the left eye knocked out.' Kovaleva was one of more than one hundred people, including the battalion commander, who were killed in the attack.[98] Her story is repeated in many sources.[99]

However, Kovaleva was not the only female factory worker to take a leading role in the militia. A worker named Piotr Nerozia noted that his superior at battalion headquarters was a woman named Denisova, who ordered him to transfer guns to the tractor factory.[100] A woman mechanic from the tractor factory served as a battalion commissar.[101] One German corporal reported that female prisoners were taken during the fighting north of the city on 23 August. He referred to them as 'soldiers in skirts whose faces are so repulsive that one can scarcely bear to look at them'.[102] In the desperate days of late August, military personnel sought out the assistance of civilians, especially help with first aid and transporting the wounded. On the night of 25 August 1942 at the tractor factory a military commander asked the Komsomol to provide help in carrying out the wounded to a river crossing; Lidia Plastikova, the local party secretary, went out under fire and shelling, along with twenty-five girls, and got all the wounded to the crossing and across the Volga.[103]

Most civilians who could not assist in factory work or defence were allowed to evacuate. When General Eremenko arrived in the city in early August 1942, he noted the crowds of evacuees on the Volga shore waiting for ferries, and the many women who were washing clothing or making ersatz tea as they waited.[104] But the intense German attack only strengthened the resolve of some civilians, including women, to remain in the city. By 25 August, Levkin writes that 'the Komsomol district committees were besieged by young men *and women* with only one wish: to be sent to war ... during that period about 75,000 people poured into the Stalingrad Front's units' [emphasis added].[105] Even in early September, when Germans entered the city outskirts, another 4000 young men and women from all over the region answered Komsomol appeals to defend the city.[106] Kerr mentions that by 10 September, when the Germans were expected to break into the city at any time, thousands of civilians were continuing work on dugouts and trenches and helping to stockpile military supplies. He described the various tasks of the population: '[F]or girls, there were errands to be run. Their mothers sawed wood, cleared the streets of debris, righted overturned trucks, carried telephone poles, pushed heavy carts, and helped soldiers pull the guns.'[107] Women were still involved in work on city defences as late as mid-September.[108]

September and October would mark the most intense period of street fighting; the defending 62nd Army was slowly pushed back until it held only a few small bridgeheads on the Volga. The fighting was vicious and relentless; every yard, every room, every house was a battlefield. Yet thousands of women and children remained in Stalingrad throughout the battle, living in the harshest conditions imaginable. One writer described the smell of the city during this time: 'It was a distinctive odour of hot iron and charcoal and burned brick and corpses rotting under the rubble, sometimes separately, sometimes all intermingled in a heavy caustic stench.'[109] When General Chuikov arrived in the city in mid-September as the new 62nd Army commander, he was beset by civilians, including old women and children.[110] Estimates of the total number of civilians trapped in the city vary widely, from as few as 3000 to as many as 50,000; estimates of the survivors at the end of the battle also vary from 1500 to 10,000.[111]

Most civilians survived in underground shelters. Konstantin Simonov reported his surprise at the number of shelters when he visited the city in late September: 'I will never forget that picture. The ravine stretches far off to the left and the right. It swarms like an anthill, it is pitted with caves. Whole streets have been dug out in it. The entrances to the caves are covered with scorched boards and rags – the women have dragged here everything they can use to shelter their chicks from the rain and wind.'[112] Many sources mention the difficult life of the 'women who lived from hand to mouth with their children on the Volga banks' throughout the course of the battle.[113] Professor Goncharov told an interviewer that his grandmother got separated from the family during the 23 August attack; she managed to survive in a bunker for the next five months, but was not reunited with the family until after the war ended.[114] Food and water were more difficult to obtain than shelter; it required constant foraging to find food, and that meant exposure to fire. Children were the best foragers owing to their size and nimbleness; Beevor describes how 'on the outskirts of the town, children crept out, like wild animals at night, to search for roots and wild berries'.[115] Dead horses, of which there were many, were eagerly sought out as food by both civilians, and later, by the trapped German army. Others attempted to steal grain from the German-held grain elevator; many were shot by German guards in the attempt.[116] Beevor describes the thousands who managed to survive in the rubble, often suffering from food poisoning or bad water.[117]

Such hard conditions were not unique to Stalingrad. At relocated factories in the Ural Mountains, workers were living year-round in hastily constructed dugouts. In one tank factory alone 8000 women workers lived in such conditions.[118] Women throughout the Soviet Union faced severe shortages of shelter, heat, and food. Women typically have better survival rates than men in such conditions. In Leningrad, it was found that among factory workers, men generally succumbed to starvation more quickly than women.[119] However, the women in Stalingrad were living in a battle zone on top of all the other difficulties. It appears that starvation was a lesser danger for civilians in Stalingrad than being caught in the crossfire or targeted by enemy or sometimes even Soviet soldiers. Katrina Karmanova was trapped with her sixteen-year-old son in a German occupation zone. While trying to get to the Volga, they saw another family making a run for the river; a German sniper killed the parents and a son before sparing a little girl.[120] One

German sergeant of the 398th Infantry Division reported that during fighting in late September north of the city, in the worker's settlements for the Barrikady factory, he saw Russian women trying to get to shelter on the German side who 'were cut down from behind by Russian machine gun fire.'[121]

Many civilian women provided what help they could to nearby Soviet troops. Kerr mentions women acting as water bearers in mid-September for the 95th Division under Gorishny near Mamaev Kurgan, describing how the troops of the 95th Division got some relief in the cooler night air 'though five or six hours might pass before the women with the yokes on their shoulders came by'.[122] Another famous story is that of an old woman named Mariia Gavrilovna Timofeeva, 'mother of the 12th Trench mortar battalion', who at night came up from her underground hideout in a drainpipe. She would often bring some porridge to the soldiers who were holding a house on that street, or do a bit of washing or sewing for them. She once promised a treat of cabbage soup, having somehow obtained a head of cabbage and some tinned beef. As she carried the soup to the soldiers, the Germans began firing, and although she was mortally wounded, the soldiers say she managed to reach them without spilling a drop of the soup before she died.[123]

A few women survived through prostitution. Craig reports that two Russian women organised a cellar brothel right on the battlefield in the area of the 284th Division. In a small room with a single mattress, a young, pale, and sickly blonde and a brunette about thirty years old, notable for always wearing bright red lipstick, sold their services to the soldiers. They had found a gramophone and played music, including an Argentine tango; 'everyone who came to the cellar learned it by heart'.[124] Other women, more desperate and with less elaborate quarters, also sold their bodies to soldiers – Soviet or German, depending on the area where they were living – to obtain food for themselves or their children.[125]

Conditions were equally grim in the German-held sections of the city, but there were relatively fewer civilians in those areas. Orders were given in early September that civilians be cleared out of German-held portions of the city. Reportedly a large number of refugees left voluntarily in mid-September, but their prospects were dismal. Refugees were subject to attack (especially from artillery) when crossing areas of active fighting; if they survived, there was faint hope of their finding shelter and food in occupied areas. One German NCO described it as a 'scene of indescribable misery'.[126] One estimate is that 3000 civilians were executed by Germans during the fighting and another 60,000 civilians transported to Germany as forced labour.[127] It is impossible to determine the number of Jews and communists arrested and/or executed by the Germans in the region of Stalingrad. However, a Sonderkommando unit followed the 6th Army into the area and is known to have executed two truck-loads of children on 25 August. The unit remained in the area until the end of September.[128] Many women and girls undoubtedly died as result of the actions of this unit, as well as from direct action by Germany army units. Nevertheless, some civilians remained even in German-occupied portions of the city. In mid-September, eleven-year-old Natasha Kornilova and her mother had both been wounded during the air raids. Natasha had to drag her mother to a concrete shed, where they were trapped for many weeks behind German lines. Natasha went to the German field kitchens for scraps of food and cared for her mother as best she could. After three months in occupied territory, Natasha and her mother were liberated in January 1943; both were suffering from starvation.[129]

Women were apparently seen commonly enough in the city for some Germans to disguise themselves as women, either to try to escape from the city, or in order to act as spies in Soviet zones. Journalist Ronald Seth relates the story of a Sergeant Yershov who came across an odd-looking woman; when he stopped 'her' for questioning, it could be seen that 'under the kerchief tied about the head, the rough-stubbled face of a man glanced with fear ... and beneath the skirt protruded German jack boots. "Don't shoot! I'm a woman" was the only Russian "she" knew.'[130] Seth also reports an incident in the northern part of the city where an 'old woman' was living in a cliff cave. Each morning she went down to the river with two pails, speaking to no one, and 'everyone was too busy to notice her'. She spent some time getting water and doing a little washing. Coincidentally, every morning after her trip, there would be a well-aimed artillery attack on the sector. One morning a Sergeant Korin was bathing in the river when he heard an odd noise, and noticed that the woman's appearance was somehow not right. He sneaked up behind her and found there was a radio transmitter in one of the buckets. He attacked and strangled 'her'.[131]

Children, especially orphans, worked for both Soviet and German units in Stalingrad. In exchange for food, children attached themselves or were co-opted to assist German soldiers for such potentially dangerous tasks as fetching water. According to Antony Beevor, 'for the promise of a crust of bread, they would get Russian boys and girls to take their water-bottles down to the Volga's edge to fill them. When the Soviet side realized what was happening, Red Army soldiers shot children on such missions.' He supports this statement by noting the precedent set during the siege of Leningrad, when Stalin issued orders 'that Red Army troops were to kill any civilians obeying German orders, even if they were acting under duress'.[132] Beevor also cites a report from the 37th Guards Rifle Division stating that when the Germans forced civilians to retrieve the dead, 'our soldiers opened fire no matter who tried to carry away the fascist corpses'.[133] Children assisted Soviet soldiers if they could.[134] The story of fifteen-year-old Sasha Fillipov was made famous in the movie *Enemy at the Gates*. Sasha began the dangerous work of serving the Germans, then crossing the lines and reporting what he learned about them to the Russian forces.[135] In late December the Germans discovered Sasha's espionage activity, and executed him, along with a teenage girl and another teenage boy; all three were publicly hanged from acacia trees on Brianskaia Street. Sasha's mother witnessed the execution; her husband could not bear to watch.[136] Less is written about young girls who worked to assist the army, but as is obvious from the fact that a girl was executed at the same time as Sasha Fillipov, there were girls as well as boys involved in extremely dangerous scouting work for the army.

Ovchinnikova relates the remarkable story of Liusia Rodyna, who at the age of twelve went on seven scouting missions behind German lines. Rodyna's history was tragic but not uncommon. A native of Leningrad, she watched her mother starve to death during the first winter of the blockade. Rodyna was evacuated from Leningrad in the spring of 1942 and ended up in a children's home in Stalingrad. Within a few months, she was once more living in a war zone. The children's home was collocated with an army hospital, and through her contacts with the wounded, Rodyna found herself adopted as a 'daughter of the regiment' by an unspecified unit.[137] She undertook her first scouting mission in August 1942, when the Germans had not yet crossed the Don river. She pretended to be the daughter of a female scout named Elena Alekseeva. They were taken across the Don by the soldiers, and set off on a four-day mission to assess German troop strength. No one paid any attention to them as they headed west; other refugees were also on the road. Rodyna and Alekseeva witnessed German soldiers shooting a wagon filled with wounded Red Army soldiers; a Red Army nurse was trying to cover the wounded with her own body, but all were killed. Their return trip was more difficult, as the Germans were stopping anyone moving east. Rodyna and Alekseeva travelled at night through gullies and ravines, with little water or food, and made their way back to the Don. They gave a signal and were picked up by their unit and debriefed.[138]

In late August, twelve-year-old Rodyna was sent on a solo mission into a German-held area in the north of Stalingrad, near Rynok. Soviet soldiers took her to an area where they thought it was safe to cross, but it turned out to be an area patrolled by the Germans. Rodyna was captured; after being interrogated she was judged harmless and assigned to work in a central mess kitchen. She was forbidden to leave, but by counting the number of meals and cups of coffee that were picked up by field kitchen units, she estimated that some two thousand German troops were being served. After about two weeks, a sixteen-year-old Russian girl arrived, Taisa Chepusova, who said she was looking for her grandmother. Rodyna fed and sheltered her, and they made a plan to get back to Soviet territory. The two managed to get approval to go with other women to bring back watermelons from fields near the Volga, where they slipped away. When they came to a Soviet position, they both knew the proper password; it turned out that Chepusova was also a Soviet scout.[139]

Levkin describes a more formal process of recruiting civilian scouts for the army; he says that 'the Front's military council ordered the regional Komsomol Committee to select three hundred Komsomol members who knew the city and its outskirts well, to perform special missions. These young patriots accompanied military units and reconnoitered in the enemy's rear.'[140] Chuianov notes that 'the modest Soviet woman Fedos'ia Mikhailovna Pirogova, mother of two children, voluntarily went on scouting missions in the enemy rear eighteen times under assignment to the staff of a military unit of the 64th Army'.[141] Nurses might also sometimes act as scouts. Chuianov mentions a Leonida Zaveriukha, apparently a civilian nurse, who received the Order of the Red Star for performing several scouting missions to bring back information on German weapon emplacements.[142] Anna Remnyeva from the barricades factory is credited with going on three scouting missions behind enemy lines for the 39th Guards Rifle Division; she won the Order of the Red Star.[143] Evdokiia Dmitrieva went on fourteen reconnaissance missions before she was killed crossing a minefield.[144] Many other female scouts were killed in the line of duty.[145] Levkin mentions in particular Klava Panchishkina and Anya Obryvkina who 'endured all the hardships and privations of partisan life' and were eventually captured, tortured, and executed.[146]

Many women continued party work throughout the battle.[147] Vodo-lagin mentioned the work of a local press, whose chief editor was R. P. Ternovaia; it published a series of brochures for the benefit of the militia with titles such as 'How to fight enemy tanks'. More than 175,000 copies of these brochures were produced.[148] A photo from a 1943 Soviet publication shows three women in civilian clothing working in a small space by the light of a shell lamp; the caption reads, 'Setting the type of the Red Army paper printed in Stalingrad in the basement of a bombed house'.[149]

It is in their role as medical personnel, however, that military women at Stalingrad are most often remembered. The essential participation of women in the medical services has been widely recognised in both Soviet and Western sources. They are truly examples of courage under fire, for many of these women served in the very front lines of the battle, going out to retrieve wounded men and their weapons even in the thick of the fighting. One of the monuments on Mamaev Kurgan shows a female medic carrying a wounded soldier on her back.[150] Few Westerners associate the roles of nurses and medics with such dangerous conditions.

Chuikov writes about an orderly from N. F. Batiuk's 284th Rifle division, describing the techniques used by medics to move heavy wounded men, even under fire:

> In Batiuk's division there was an orderly, Tamara Shmakova. I knew her personally. She became famous for carrying seriously wounded soldiers from the very front lines of battle, when it seemed that it was impossible to even lift a hand above the ground. Crawling up to a wounded soldier on all fours, Tamara would lie alongside him and bandage him. Determining the degree of his wound, she would decide what to do with him. If he was so badly wounded that it would be impossible to leave him on the battlefield, Tamara took measures for his immediate evacuation. Usually it takes two people with or without a stretcher to carry a wounded man from the battlefield. But Tamara most often managed this alone. Her evacuation method consisted of this: she would lie alongside the wounded man and, like an ant, dragged off her living cargo on her back, often one and a half times or twice her own weight. When it was impossible to lift a wounded man, Tamara spread out a groundsheet, rolled the wounded man onto it, and again on all fours, would drag behind her, like a tugboat, the groundsheet with the wounded man. Tamara Shmakova saved many lives. Many are alive today who owe her for their salvation.[151]

Medical orderly Guards Junior Lieutenant Tamara Stepanovna Umny-agina served with a rifle division from the first week of the war. She emphasised the unique character of the battle of Stalingrad:

> But the most terrible experience of all was still to come – Stalingrad, that was most terrible … there was no battlefield at Stalingrad, the entire city was the battlefield – streets, houses, cellars. You just try to carry a wounded man out of there! My body was one big bruise, my trousers were covered with blood. The sergeant-major told us: 'Girls, there are no more trousers, so don't ask for them.' But our trousers were covered with blood; when they dried they stood up, stiffer from blood than they would have been from starch – you could cut yourself … in Stalingrad there wasn't a gram of earth that wasn't soaked in human blood. Reinforcements would arrive. Such young, handsome fellows they were. And in a day or two they would all be dead, not one of them would be left … this was 1942, you see – the hardest, most difficult period. On one occasion ten of us

were left out of three hundred at the end of the day. And when we were down to ten and the battle subsided, we began to kiss each other and wept because we had happened to survive. Someone dies before your eyes … and you know, you see, that there is nothing you can do to help him, that he has minutes left. You kiss him, stroke him, say some consoling words to him. Say goodbye to him. And there's nothing else you can do to help him … Those faces remain in my memory even today. I see them – all those lads, all of them. Somehow the years have passed and you might think that I would forget someone at least, one face at least. But I haven't forgotten anyone, I remember them all, I see them all.[152]

Grossman commented on the 'supreme heroism' of nurses in November 1942 in the city in Gurt'ev's Siberian division, naming quite a few and remarking the 'astonishing morale' of this division. He noted 'the touching meeting between grey-headed Colonel Gurt'ev and Zoia Kalganova, a battalion Red Cross nurse, when she returned after having been wounded for the second time. "My dear girl, welcome back," he said warmly as he moved forward swiftly with arms outstretched to meet the girl with her wan face and close-cropped head. It was the way a father would greet his own daughter.'[153] Beevor rates the medical orderlies, 'mainly female students or high-school graduates with only the most basic first-aid training', as 'the very bravest figures on the Stalingrad battlefield'.[154] He interviewed Zinaida Georg'evna Gavrielova, who at the time of the battle was an eighteen-year-old former medical student and commander of a 62nd Army sanitary company comprising about one hundred personnel. She noted that her orderlies had to be 'physically and spiritually strong'.[155] That strength is apparent in the achievements reported for many of these women medics. Natal'ia Kachuevskaia is remembered for rescuing twenty wounded soldiers in one day, as well as for using grenades against the enemy.[156] Chuikov credits Valia Pakhomova with carrying more than one hundred wounded from the field of battle.[157] Similarly, V. Zhitkova carried ninety-seven soldiers and officers with their weapons from the battlefield, for which she received the Order of Lenin.[158] Medical orderly Anna Bondarchuk was renowned for her work during the worst of the street fighting in Stalingrad, when she carried 120 wounded men plus their weapons to safety. She was also awarded the Order of Lenin.[159]

While the most famous medics are those involved in the bitter street fighting within the city of Stalingrad, medical personnel served in situations that were just as dangerous in the more fluid environment on the fronts flanking the city. For example, Marionella (Gulya) Koroleva was a twenty-year-old nurse with the 214th Rifle Division (24th Army on the Don front under Rokossovskii). She was a volunteer and left behind a baby son in order to serve with the army. She died in service, posthumously receiving the Order of the Red Banner for rescuing more than one hundred wounded soldiers and killing fifteen Germans.[160] Another woman on the Don front, M. Kukharskaia, was designated as the front's best orderly; she carried 421 men from the field of battle – 277 with their weapons.[161]

Another duty of medical personnel was to accompany the wounded who were being ferried across the Volga – an extremely hazardous mission. Nurses and medics were crossing the river two or three times a day in mid-September.[162] Lieutenant Vera Maksimovna Berestova, who served in the medical services, noted: 'I was at the front from the first day to the last … I ferried across the Volga the wounded out of Stalingrad during the shelling and bombing, in barges and launches or over thin ice on dog sledges throughout the entire fighting … once I fell into the half-frozen Volga. I swam to the shore and pulled a wounded man out as well.'[163]

Konstantin Simonov wrote about orderlies he met in mid-September on a night crossing of the Volga. On the overloaded ferry there were several girls from a medical battalion; Simonov was sitting next to a twenty-year-old Ukrainian girl named Viktoria Shchepenya, who was going back into the city for the fourth or fifth time. 'With nowhere to put medical facilities in this burning city,' wrote Simonov, 'the physician's assistants and orderlies get the wounded and take them straight from the forward positions through the city to the river, load them on boats and ferries, and once they are on the other side, return for the new casualties awaiting aid.'[164] Shchepenya told him that she had already been wounded twice. He mused, 'in fifteen minutes she will be walking past those burning buildings and somewhere, on one of the outlying streets, among the ruins, as shrapnel hums around her, she will get the wounded and take them back, and if she is lucky she will return again, for the sixth time'.[165] Similarly, Sergeant Jakob Pavlov described the impression made on him when he met a female orderly returning from an escort trip when he crossed into Stalingrad on a steamer on 15 September 1942.[166] Soviet female medical personnel were also unique in that they often participated in the fighting. Most of them carried weapons and whenever they were not tending the wounded, or some-times in order to defend the wounded, they fought alongside the regular infantry soldiers. This makes the role of Soviet medical personnel vastly different from anything in the West, and shatters the stereotype of nurses and orderlies working in the relative safety of rear-area hospitals.

Mariia Sergeevna Borovichenko is an example of a woman classified as a medic but who often acted as a scout and combatant. In 1941, when she was sixteen years old, she broke through to Soviet lines during the capture of Kiev; she found herself with the 5th Airborne

Brigade, commanded by Aleksandr Il'ich Rodimtsev.[167] She refused to be sent to the rear, and as she had brought valuable intelligence on German troops, Rodimtsev allowed her to stay. She worked as a medic and a scout, and was credited with often taking part in the fighting. On at least two occasions she took German soldiers prisoner, and loved to brandish her trophy German pistols.[168] She became known in the brigade as 'Mashen'ka from Mishelovka' after her native village, and remained under Rodimtsev's command for the next two years. Borovichenko seemed to be completely fearless; her battalion commander described her as 'a worrisome and reckless girl'.[169] Rodimtsev later wrote a compelling little biography about her, and described a number of incidents when he met her or heard of her exploits.[170]

Rodimtsev became commander of the 13th Guards Rifle Division, and in that famous unit, Borovichenko participated in the battle of Stalingrad from 14 September 1942 to 2 February 1943. The 13th Guards took 30 per cent casualties in the first twenty-four hours; by the end of the battle only 320 out of 10,000 would remain alive.[171] Rodimtsev saw Borovichenko twice at Stalingrad. He came across her first during the intense fighting on 24 September; she was cursing the Germans for having shot up her medical bag.[172] He didn't see her again until late January, when the division was fighting stubborn German opposition in the factory region; she was with her by then constant companion, a medical assistant named Mikhail Kravchenko (they were known as 'Masha and Misha'). They told Rodimtsev they planned to be married after the battle.[173] Two days later, Rodimtsev learned that Kravchenko had been shot dead by an enemy sniper; Borovichenko was there, and killed the sniper with grenades.[174] By the end of the battle, she had received several decorations, including the Order of the Red Star and Order of the Red Banner. Borovichenko herself was killed a few months later at the battle of Kursk; she was shielding a wounded man with her body during a tank attack when she was fatally wounded in the chest by a shell fragment.[175] Borovichenko was posthumously awarded the Hero of the Soviet Union.[176]

Another medic who received the Hero of the Soviet Union was Zinaida Ivanovna Mareseva of the 38th (later 73rd Guards) Rifle Division of the 64th Army. Stalingrad was Mareseva's first introduction to combat. She was one of the medical orderlies who helped ferry wounded across the Volga. Like Borovichenko, Mareseva was later killed at Kursk. It is not clear whether Mareseva actually participated in fighting, although she was credited with stopping a panic among some soldiers who were guarding the wounded by leading them in attack with a pistol.[177] Medical NCO Vera Kashcheeva arrived on the Stalingrad front in spring 1942 and later served as a medic in the 39th Guards Division in the ruins of the Red October factory. She helped ferry wounded across the Volga, and is also reported to have participated in the fighting; she later became a Hero of the Soviet Union.[178] *Saninstruktor* Zinaida Aleksandrovna Samsonova also began her service during the battle of Stalingrad. There is little information on her activities at Stalingrad; in later battles she is noted as firing her submachine gun and throwing grenades. She was killed by a sniper in 1944. Although not made a 'Hero', she was immortalised in a poem by the famous Iulia Drunina, who served in the same battalion with Samsonova.[179]

Women doctors and surgeons were common in the Stalingrad region. They worked in difficult and often appalling conditions. Chuikov described his visit to the medical facilities on the shore of the Volga on his arrival in the city on 11 September 1942: 'Many things are being done improperly; there are wounded lying out in the open, bandages are not being changed, they are not being given water.' But when he saw the medical personnel, he says, 'I realise that the doctors, nurses, and orderlies can do no more than they are doing. They are constantly on their feet, they are not sleeping, they're probably hungry, and so exhausted that they are not able to work any faster. They are worn out.'[180] Doctor Elena Ivanovna Variukhina of the 713th mobile field hospital said, 'in particular I remember Stalingrad ... There were so many wounded that we worked round the clock, all sense of time lost.'[181]

Army doctors and nurses risked their lives working at the front; some were killed when air attacks hit field hospitals.[182] For example, on 23 September, a mobile field hospital unit and surgical stations at crossing no. 62 were bombed by the Luftwaffe despite their red crosses; a female doctor was killed, along with nurses and many wounded.[183] One unnamed nurse working in Stalingrad had become the lover of Captain Hersch Gurewicz (who was interviewed by Craig). While performing her duties she stepped on a land mine. Her arms and legs were blown off; when Gurewicz saw her as she was being evacuated, he was certain she was dying. However, it turned out that she survived, and after the war married and had children.[184] Famous generals such as Chuikov and Smekhotvorov took care to mention a number of female doctors and other medical personnel by name.[185]

Women also served in less glamorous roles, such as cooks and laundresses, that still entailed considerable risk. Chuikov noted that during the heavy fighting on 13 September the field kitchen serving his command post suffered a direct mortar hit. Chuikov says that the kitchen staff, a cook and a waitress named Tasia, were very grateful to be sent in the first group to a new command post location.[186]

Women signallers and telephone operators were almost omnipresent in Stalingrad. When Chuikov arrived at his command post then located on Mamaev Kurgan to take over command of the 62nd Army in mid-

September, he noted: '[T]here are two people in the dugout: General Krylov with a telephone receiver in his hand, and Elena Bakarevich, the telephonist on duty, a blue-eyed girl about eighteen years old ... Bakarevich is sitting near the entrance with two receivers at her ears and is answering someone: "He's busy on the other phone." ... The telephone rings all the time.'[187] Bakarevich was often present in the bunker when no one else but senior staff members were there. It was she who placed desperate calls to and from field commanders and to Moscow.[188] Hundreds of women like Bakarevich served at every level of the Red Army. Simonov commented on meeting young girls who were telegraph operators in a bunker who were 'pale through lack of sleep, work[ing] the keys of their apparatus, tapping out dots and dashes'.[189] When Jakob Pavlov first reported to the bunker of his regimental commander, he purportedly made special note of the women present: 'At the far end of the cellar he could now see two girl telegraph operators tapping busily at their keys. So the women are really in this, too, he thought ... here are these girls in the midst of the fighting. Here in the fortress, sharing all the risks with us men.'[190] Lena Peretolchina and Klavdiia Shtonda served in communications in the 140th Mortar Regiment; both survived the battle and went all the way to Berlin by the end of the war. Peretolchina described their working conditions:

> In Stalingrad, no one built bunkers or shelters for them; they themselves, each for herself or together, dug trenches in the earth, put a thin covering over them out of whatever came to hand, and in those trenches they huddled for months. They were often even buried right where they worked. In October, when the enemy destroyed all our headquarters bunkers, the working and living conditions in Stalingrad became even more difficult. They worked in stuffy, cramped shelters, rested under open sky, ate whatever they could get, and for months didn't know what such a thing as hot water was.[191]

To be a simple telephone operator with front-line units in the Red Army meant risking your life. One female veteran recalled working in a bunker on Mamaev Kurgan on 13 September when a shell or bomb hit their position. She helped drag a young girl named Mariia Guliaeva from the wreckage, bandaged her legs, and then helped carry her to a first-aid station, only to discover that Guliaeva was already dead from a chest wound they hadn't seen.[192] Chuikov wrote about another *sviazistka* who died in the line of duty: 'I know of a case when at an intermediate post near Basargino Station only one girl signaller remained – Nadia Klimenko. When all her friends were either killed or wounded, Klimenko did not leave the post and to the last minute reported on everything that was happening on the field of battle.' The report was cut off; Klimenko's fate remains unknown.[193]

Because of the heavy shelling, telephone land lines were constantly being cut; linesmen took heavy casualties, and the female telephonists helped to perform this repair work. Chuikov mentions frequent breaks in the lines and problems with radio communications as well. 'All the signallers we had were thrown into repairing communications. Even the duty telephone operators in our bunker many times had to leave the phones and try to find and repair the breaks in the lines.'[194] Chuikov remembers the valour of Shura Sheshen'ia, a young communications worker. On 13 September 1942 she was working on Mamaev Kurgan during extremely heavy enemy attacks. The communications lines were being constantly cut, and all the linesmen had gone out to work on the lines. Not one had returned or even 'switched in' from the lines. Sheshen'ia persuaded the communications company commander to let her attempt to repair the lines. He reluctantly agreed, and she succeeded in switching in on the line several times, but at noon on 14 September she was killed.[195]

Red Army communications personnel deployed around the city were also in extreme danger. Fania Reznik was operating a radio transmitter in Iablonovaia Gully on 31 August 1942 when she was killed, along with another girl. Reznik had remained at her post, relaying critical information on enemy movements, even when she heard approaching enemy bombers;[196] and there are several tales of girls like Anna Suchatova, trapped at communications posts during a German advance, who called in fire on their own position.[197] Women in communications, though classified as noncombatants, endured all the hardships of war and saw its effects; signaller Antonina Fedorovna Valegzhaninova recalled of Stalingrad, 'One battle stands out in my memory. There were scores of dead ... they were scattered over a huge field like potatoes brought to the surface by a plough.'[198]

One facet of the city fighting in Stalingrad was the creation of strong points amid the ruins of the city. The so-called garrisons that held the strong points usually included women signallers or medical orderlies; they were exposed to the same risks and privations as the soldiers. Civilian women also did what they could to help the army. Anton Kuzmich Dragan, a company commander in Rodimtsev's 13th Guards Division, told Chuikov about an incident on the night of 20 September:

> That night, risking her life, a woman crossed over to us from enemy territory, a resident of Stalingrad, and reported that the Germans were preparing a tank attack. She told us many valuable things about the disposition of the enemy subunits. I remember her name – Mariia Vadeneeva. I want to note that residents of the city often helped us

with information and water supplies. Unfortunately, the names of these brave patriots remain unknown. I remember only one more young girl-scout, whom the soldiers called Liza; she was killed during the bombing.[199]

A female medic, Liuba Nesterenko, served in Dragan's company; she was killed during the fighting, and is remembered for dying with a bandage in her hand, trying to help a wounded soldier even with blood streaming from a wound in her own chest.[200]

The most famous strongpoint in Stalingrad was held by another member of Rodimtsev's 13th Guards, Sergeant Jakob Pavlov of the 42nd Regiment. On 28 September Pavlov occupied a damaged building in the central part of the city; 'Pavlov's House' would hold out for fifty-nine days. A large number of women were hiding in the three basements, along with a few old men and children – people who had tried to reach the Volga crossings but had to take shelter owing to the intensity of the fighting. There were several wounded civilians, and soldiers being tended by a medic. There were around sixty people in the house, including Pavlov's team but not including occasional snipers and scouts.[201] Pavlov put one of the women in charge of the civilians.[202] Pavlov's team spent five nights digging a communications trench to battalion headquarters so that meals could be brought in. This was dangerous work and the soldiers who dug 'complained that it was a hundred times worse than fighting' because of German fire. 'But we shouldn't have finished the trench in the short time we did if it hadn't been for the women in the basement, who all did their share, and more,' according to Pavlov.[203] There was also at least one military woman with Pavlov's team; Chuikov and Chuianov both mention Mariia Ul'ianova, a nurse in the 42nd Infantry Regiment, who was in Pavlov's House during the entire period and was awarded a Medal for Valour.[204]

Chuikov relates an interesting story that occurred in late October which is worth relating in detail:

In the second half of October the situation in Stalingrad had grown so bad, and the distance between the front lines of battle and Volga had grown so short, that the military council of the army had to transfer some units and establishments to the left bank, in order to avoid needless losses. It was decided first of all to send women to the left bank. Commanders and chiefs of staff were ordered to suggest to women soldiers that they temporarily go to the left bank, in order to rest there and return to Stalingrad after a few days.

This decision by the military council was taken on 17 October, and in the morning of the 18th, a delegation of women soldiers from communications came to see me. The delegation was led by Valia

Tokareva, a native of Kamyshin. She asked me point blank: 'Comrade commander, why are you sending us packing out of Stalingrad? We all want to die or to beat our sworn enemy with everyone else. Why are you making a distinction between the women and the men? Do we really work any worse than them? Do as you like, but we won't cross the Volga...' As this conversation was taking place on 18 October, the day when we transferred to a new command post, I told them that at the new command post we would not be able to fully deploy all the communications equipment, that the situation forced us to use lighter and other types of communications, portable radios, and that was the only reason I was allowing them to be sent to the left bank, that it was truly temporary, until we had prepared a working space for the heavier types of equipment. The women's delegation agreed to carry out the order of the military council, but demanded that I give my word of honour that as soon as conditions necessary for their work came about, we would transfer them back to Stalingrad.

They crossed the Volga on 18 October, and beginning 20 October any time Krylov, Gurov or I called by telephone to the left bank, the signallers gave us no peace. 'We've had our rest,' they said. 'When will you bring us back to Stalingrad?' Or, 'Comrade commander, when are you going to keep your word ...'

We kept our word. At the end of October, along with the communications equipment, we brought them back to the bunkers we had prepared, with which they were extremely happy.

That was the kind of women we had at the front.[205]

Another Soviet division that was renowned for fighting against the most extreme odds was the 138th Division commanded by I. I. Liudnikov. Photographs taken during the battle show some of the women under Liudnikov's command.[206] Many of the references are amazingly offhand. Craig, for example, refers to the state of Liudnikov's division in early November: 'Liudnikov's forces now numbered only several hundred men *and women* capable of resistance' [emphasis added].[207] Liudnikov himself wrote about a nurse who worked on the front lines, despite having been wounded herself. 'One day Serafima Ozerova, a divisional HQ nurse and wife of the communication company commander, came to see me. One of her eyes was bandaged (she had been wounded by a mortar splinter during a crossing) and the other was wet with tears. "Ah, well," I thought, "here she comes again to plead with me not to send her into the rear and separate her from the division and her husband."' Instead, she was asking him to talk to the wounded who were becoming restless.[208]

It is clear then that women performed a wide variety of roles that all involved risking their lives, and many fought at times as well. In addition, some women were full-time combatants. There were few women in 1942 who were regarded as strictly infantry troops, although many medical personnel, machine gunners, etc. often filled infantry roles.[209] But according to Soviet historian Murmantseva, many women served in rifle (infantry) units at Stalingrad, including female submachine gunners, machine gunners, mortar operators, and scouts. Murmantseva gives one example of a submachine gunner named Nina Koroleva on the Stalingrad Front: 'Once in battle Nina noticed that an enemy machine gun was firing in the path of an attacking platoon. The girl threw herself forward and with the butt of her submachine gun wiped out the whole crew of an enemy firing position. The bold accomplishment of the submachine gunner cleared the way toward the attacking platoon. Unfortunately, in this battle Nina Koroleva was wounded by a grenade fragment and was disabled.'[210]

Women fighter and bomber pilots were also active at Stalingrad. Three regiments of female pilots had been formed in 1942, and two of the three participated in the battle. The 586th Fighter Aviation Regiment sent one squadron to fight at Stalingrad, and the 587th (later 125th Guards) Bomber Aviation Regiment flew combat missions, though it arrived only at the end of the battle. The third 'women's' regiment, the 588th (later 46th Guards) Night Bomber Aviation Regiment, was not involved at Stalingrad, but took part in heavy fighting during the same period on the Southern Front, which was closely connected with events at Stalingrad.

The 586th Fighter Aviation Regiment (FAR), a mostly-female PVO unit, sent a squadron of eight pilots and their ground crews to Stalingrad on 10 September 1942 as replacements to aviation regiments there that had endured heavy losses. The squadron was split in two, with four pilots (Raisa Beliaeva, Ekaterina Budanova, Liliia Litviak, Maria Kuznetsova) assigned to the 437th FAR, and the other four (Klavdiia Nechaeva, Klavdiia Blinova, Antonina Lebedeva, and Ol'ga Shakhova) assigned to the 434th FAR in the 16th Air Army.[211] Some of the members of their ground crews included Mariia Konkina, Valentina Krasnoshchekova, Zoia Mal'kova, Sofiia Osipova, Inna Pleshchivtseva, Valentina Skachkova, Faina Tkachenko, Nina Shebalina, Aleksandna Eskina.[212] A ninth pilot, Anna Demchenko, apparently arrived somewhat later.[213] Although they had not yet flown in combat, these women were skilled pilots; most had served before the war as instructor pilots at the Chkalov central air club.[214]

This was a time when the Germans had almost complete control of the air around Stalingrad; the only aviation forces available to the Red Army were badly understrength. The regiments to which the women pilots had been sent were based on the east (left) bank of the Volga, and they were often tasked with attempting to protect the Volga crossings from enemy attacks. Kuznetsova later remarked on the fact that the Soviet pilots were almost always outnumbered.[215] The 434th had already twice suffered such losses that it been withdrawn from the front for replenishment. The women arrived as the 434th was being sent into Stalingrad for the third time.[216] On 13 September, the same day that Chuikov arrived to take command of the 62nd Army, the Germans began their intense assault on the city itself. Fighter pilots flew as many as five sorties a day, an almost superhuman pace considering the extremely hot weather conditions and the demands of air combat.[217]

Inna Pleshchivtseva (married surname Pasportnikova) emphasised the extremely dangerous conditions at Stalingrad.[218] The Germans knew the location of the airfields and often attempted to shoot down Soviet aircraft during take-off or landing; the Soviets simply didn't have enough aircraft to prevent this. German aircraft often bombed and strafed the airfield itself, so that the ground crews were always at risk.[219] In addition, the pilots and their crews had to contend with clouds of dust, tumbleweed, mosquitoes, blazing heat (in which they were constantly burning their hands on the hot metal tools and portions of the aircraft) and, later, heavy frost at night.

The male pilots fighting in these intense conditions were surprised, to say the least, that women were among the replacement pilots they were receiving. Members of both the 434th and 437th reacted with disbelief, or even hostility. The commander of the 437th, Major Khvostikov, is reported to have said, 'This is combat, not a flying club! There are air battles every day. We're waiting for real pilots, and they sent us a bunch of girls.'[220] The 434th and 437th were not quite sure what to do with these inexperienced pilots. They were hesitant to send them on the most dangerous combat missions, where new pilots were just as much 'cannon fodder' as new recruits on the ground. Inna Pasportnikova takes a slightly different point of view on why men were reluctant to let the women fly with them: 'When we arrived at a male regiment, men did not want to fly with us, because of the responsibility, and also because they were afraid for themselves. They were afraid that the female wingmen would not cover them.'[221] So the women did not receive training by flying with experienced pilots. One pilot in the 437th recalled:

There were four of them in our regiment. Four girl-pilots ... Quite often one or another would ask to be wingman to the most active male fighter pilots, especially young Liliia Litviak. She appealed to many, including me. And we, every time, politely refused. Personally, to me it would have been unbelievably difficult to go through the death of such a wingman in combat. And after all, a woman! ... The girls, however, got along without male leadership, and fought well in their own flight.[222]

In the 434th, at least, it appears that it was not just female pilots who were withheld from going on the most intense combat missions. A. F. Semenov, then a pilot with that regiment, noted that 'such [inexperienced] pilots were charged with covering transport aircraft, flying to intercept enemy reconnaissance aircraft, and alert duty at the airfield ... Youth should go into combat by degrees.' However, some of the new pilots, including Vladimir Mikoyan (son of the famous aircraft designer, Anastas Mikoyan), chafed at the restrictions. When A. A. Novikov, the commander of the air force, happened to visit the regiment while he was at the Stalingrad Front, Vladimir Mikoyan and Klavdiia Nechaeva complained to him that they were not being allowed into combat. Novikov commented: 'I think that young pilots should more often be assigned as wingmen to experienced fighters.' Semenov says that the regiment began allowing the young pilots to fly the more dangerous air combat missions, but 'for this accelerated lesson, some had to pay with their lives'.[223]

In fact, within a few days, both Nechaeva and Mikoyan were killed. Twenty-year-old Klavdiia Nechaeva died on 17 September 1942. She was returning from her fifth mission of the day and preparing to land, her leader landing first as usual, when two German Focke-Wulfe fighters began to attack his vulnerable aircraft. Nechaeva engaged them, drawing them away from her leader, but was killed in the fight.[224] Eighteen-year-old Vladimir Mikoyan was killed the day after Nechaeva.[225] Nechaeva, the only female pilot to die at Stalingrad, was just one among many pilots lost in the 434th during this period.[226] The 434th's losses were so severe that by 3 October it was once more sent to the reserves for replenishment, and in November was redesignated as the 32nd Guards in recognition of its performance in combat.[227]

The women in the 437th fared somewhat better. On 13 September 1942, on her second combat mission, Liliia Litviak shot down two enemy aircraft. Her first kill was a German Junkers-88 bomber; the second was made jointly with Beliaeva against a Messerschmitt-109 fighter. The pilot of the Me-109 was captured by the Soviets and brought to Litviak's airfield for questioning. The German pilot turned out to be a baron and a three-time winner of the Iron Cross. He asked to be introduced to the pilot who had managed to shoot him down. When Litviak was brought to the dugout, he was certain the Soviets were playing some sort of joke on him. He refused to believe that the tiny blonde girl before him could have defeated him in battle, until Litviak began to relate the details of their air engagement, which only the two of them could know.[228] Such a story sounds apocryphal but appears in published and archival materials and was personally recounted to the author by Litviak's mechanic.[229]

Litviak's accomplishments on 13 September mark the first time in history that a woman pilot achieved an air-to-air kill. However, until several decades later, no Soviet source made note of this fact. Litviak's achievement was probably overlooked in the hectic battles of Stalingrad. She was no longer flying with a 'women's' regiment (and so was less visible to the press); she made her first kills only three days after arriving at the 437th; and Litviak's squadron was transferred to another regiment within a month (giving the 437th chain of command little incentive to acknowledge or publicise her kills). These factors contributed to the lack of recognition for Litviak's victory.[230] The participation of women fighter pilots in the battle of Stalingrad was publicly recognised only in late January 1943 when the magazine *Ogonek* printed a photo of Litviak, Budanova, and Kuznetsova, and mentioned that they had destroyed a German bomber near Stalingrad (understating their tally).[231] In April another brief *Ogonek* piece credited Litviak and Budanova with twelve combined kills, and again mentioned their participation at Stalingrad.[232]

Litviak was not the only woman to 'begin her combat tally' at Stalingrad. Raisa Beliaeva shot down at least two German planes during her weeks in Stalingrad, and once was forced to jump from her own burning aircraft.[233] Lebedeva and Budanova are also credited with scoring kills.[234] The women served for only a few weeks with the 434th and 437th regiments. By October, the 437th group was transferred to the 9th Guards Fighter Aviation Regiment, which was renowned for its famous pilots, several already Heroes of the Soviet Union. It is interesting that members of this regiment highly praised the skill of the women pilots and showed no reluctance about flying with them.[235]

The 586th itself was indirectly involved in the battle of Stalingrad in December 1942. A group of four pilots, including Beliaeva and Burdina, was detailed to escort a VIP transport aircraft to one of the main airfields near Stalingrad. Nikita Khrushchev, the political officer for the Stalingrad Front, was on the transport. He invited the fighter pilots along for a visit to a camp for some of the German prisoners of war from the battle.[236] The 587th Bomber Aviation Regiment (later 125th Guards), a mostly-female dive-bomber unit, flew its first few combat missions at Stalingrad in late January 1943. Like the fighter pilots, the bomber crews found that the men's crews in a regiment collocated with them were at first sceptical of their abilities. As part of the 16th Air Army on the Don Front, the 587th got its first introduction to combat flying on 28 January, bombing Germans trapped inside the 'ring'. Most of its targets were in the area near the tractor factory, north of the city, where there was determined resistance. The conditions were bitterly cold; armourer Evgeniia Zapol'nova recalls having to work barehanded at temperatures far below zero.[237] Five women in this unit, who performed their first combat flights at Stalingrad, later received the Hero of the Soviet Union: pilots Mariia Dolina, Nadezhda Fedutenko, and Klavdiia Fomicheva, and navigators Galina Dzhunkovskaia and Antonina Zubkova.[238]

There were also women serving in mostly-male aviation units. Antony Beevor interviewed private Klavdiia Vasilevna Sterman, who served with a night fighter regiment that fought at Stalingrad beginning in early August; its improvised base was frequently attacked by enemy aircraft; many civilians in the area were killed. When the regimental commander was shot down in enemy territory, a peasant woman dragged him from the wreckage and cared for him; he was picked up the next morning by other pilots from the unit.[239] The unit was apparently disbanded by late August, since Beevor notes that Sterman was by then with the 'survivors of a disbanded aviation regiment' on the east shore of the Volga who witnessed the evacuation of thousands of wounded. He says that Sterman and others attempted to assist with the wounded, and Sterman 'vowed that as soon as they reached Moscow, she would apply to transfer to a front-line medical unit'.[240] There were undoubtedly many women like Sterman serving in aviation units as ground crews during the battle, as there were throughout the war.[241]

The role of female snipers at Stalingrad has raised some controversy. Because the Central Women's School for Sniper Training was not created until May 1943, some writers have suggested that there were no female snipers at Stalingrad. Such a view not only overlooks anecdotal evidence to the contrary, but also the general context of women's participation as Red Army snipers. Female snipers operated from the very beginning of the war.[242] Galagan, for example, describes the case of N. A. Pribludnaia, who became a sniper in the summer of 1941 and ended the war in Berlin.[243] Sniper Mariia Ivanovna Morozova [Ivanushkina] reported that at the very start of the war, she attended a course on rifle firing composed of forty women, all young girls, conducted by the local military registration and enlistment office. Then after a rigorous selection process, she was enlisted in the army and sent to a women's sniper course near Shchelkovo. 'We learned to mount and demount the sniper's rifle with closed eyes, to determine wind velocity, to evaluate the movement of the target and the distance to it, to dig in and to crawl. We could do it all.'[244] The well-documented sniper team of Kovshova and Polivanova attained a total of more than 300 kills with the 1st Shock Army in the northern region of Russia before their death in August 1942. Prior to that, they had been responsible for founding a 'sniper movement' in their regiment and trained at least two dozen new snipers, including many women.[245] The famous sniper Liudmila Pavlichenko, who scored 309 kills in less than one year, had already been invalided out of service in June 1942. She was accepted as a volunteer during the summer of 1941 on the basis of a marksmanship certificate she had earned before the war. Pavlichenko served in a sniper's platoon during the battles for Odessa and Sevastopol. She was an instructor in a sniper training movement during the spring of 1942. Her tally had included thirty-six enemy snipers.[246] As these cases show, women could easily become army snipers even before the Central Women's School for Sniper Training existed. In fact, by November 1942 the number of female students was large enough for special sniper training courses for women to be established at the Central Sniper School in Moscow; the separate women's school was later created in order to formalise the process through which many hundreds of women had already become snipers.[247]

The most famous story of a female sniper at Stalingrad is that of Tania Chernova, who was interviewed by author William Craig. She arrived in Stalingrad on 23 September with the 284th Division, the famous unit of Siberians commanded by the equally famous Colonel Nikolai Batiuk. She was twenty years old at the time. Craig relates that she had previously fought with partisans in Belorussia and Ukraine, and had already killed several Germans. Her attitude was one of vengeance; she was eager to get into the fighting at Stalingrad.[248]

Chernova became a student at the 'sniper school' of the 62nd Army, an impromptu affair started in the Lazur Chemical Plant in late September. One of the instructors was Vasily Zaitsev, who had arrived on 20 September with Batiuk's division; in his first ten days, he killed forty Germans, and had become a media hero.[249] Chernova was one of some thirty students who trained with Zaitsev. Craig writes:

> Tania relished her new life. Undaunted by her ordeal on the Volga and in the sewer pipe, she had become a professional soldier, living in foxholes, drinking vodka, eating with a spoon she kept in her boot. She slept curled up beside strangers; she bathed in pails of water. She also learned how to take cover in the front lines, how to track the enemy through the telescopic sight and, most importantly, how to wait for hours before firing a single shot that killed.[250]

Craig describes one mission that Chernova conducted while in training. The division HQ had ordered a small group to destroy a German HQ that had been identified in a location between the Red October Plant and the Stalingrad Flying School. Chernova and five others infiltrated enemy territory at night, found the building, and began ascending a stairwell. Chernova was the last in line. A German soldier appeared and she scuffled with him; she gave him a blow to the groin that forced him to drop his pistol. She slammed her knee into his face; he bit her thumb. She got a choke-hold on him, then one of her comrades appeared and clubbed the German in the head with his rifle butt, killing him. Her team had placed the dynamite, and ordered her to light the fuse. They then ran for cover as the building exploded.[251]

Craig says that Zaitsev and Chernova were lovers.[252] Despite their alleged romantic relationship, not all was rosy between Zaitsev and Chernova. On one occasion she violated an order not to shoot without permission. She had spotted a German column, screamed 'Shoot!' to her comrades, and they killed seventeen German soldiers. However, German survivors called in a strike on her position and several of her friends were killed. When she reported to Zaitsev, he reportedly slapped her hard and blamed her for the casualties.[253]

During the Russian counter-offensive in mid-November, Chernova was seriously wounded. Craig reports that she had been sent with three others to kill General Paulus, although it turned out that they had been given bad intelligence about the location of his bunker. Her team included another young woman, who moved clumsily and stepped on a mine. The woman was only lightly injured, but Chernova received a serious abdominal wound. Zaitsev got her to an emergency aid station; at first it looked as though she would die, but by the next day she was stabilised enough to be evacuated across the Volga. According to Craig, Chernova was furious at the 'damned cow' whose stumbling had caused her to be invalided out of the war.

In three months of service at Stalingrad, Chernova achieved eighty kills.[254] Craig says that when he interviewed an ageing Chernova, she told him that she believed for many years that Zaitsev had been killed during the battle; she said she had only learned in 1969 that he had lived. Craig reports that she was stunned when she learned he was married.[255] Zaitsev does not mention Chernova in his memoirs. However, in a 1991 interview with David L. Robbins (author of *War of the Rats*) Zaitsev acknowledged that 'one of our female snipers was Tania Chernova ... she was a fine sniper'. Robbins says that Zaitsev was reluctant to discuss Chernova and only talked about her briefly, when his wife could not hear. Robbins also noted that Zaitsev was a very proud man, more interested in talking about his own exploits than those of other snipers.[256] It seems possible that Zaitsev may have omitted Chernova from his memoirs in consideration for his wife, and also not to distract too much attention from his own accomplishments.[257] In his memoirs Zaitsev does mention one female sniper in a couple of passing references to the sniper pair of Afinogenov and Shcherbina. They had been working in a sector where Zaitsev was assigned a mission to take out an enemy bunker and bring back a 'tongue' to be interrogated. Zaitsev writes, 'We armed ourselves with only light weapons – sub-machine guns, grenades, knives. Afinogenov crawled first, behind him

Shcherbina, then Stepan Kryakhov and me. We were afraid of one
thing: that on the path to the bunker we would run into a mine field.
But everything worked out fine. Apparently this time soldier's luck was
with us.' When they arrived at the bunker, Afinogenov slashed the
guard's throat, then he and Shcherbina remained above on guard while
Zaitsev and Kryakhov entered the bunker and killed all the sleeping
soldiers but one, whom they forced to return with them for interrogation.[258] Zaitsev writes about one other encounter with the pair in
which he instructs them in sniper technique.[259] Zaitsev makes no
distinction at all between Shcherbina and the other snipers. Aside from
Shcherbina (whose first name he never mentions), the only women who
appear in his book are nurses and administrative staff.

Two other women who were active as snipers during the battle of
Stalingrad are mentioned in an article by J. David Truby: a Yugoslav
partisan recalled a Soviet woman in his unit known only as 'Vera' who
had killed thirty-two Germans at Stalingrad, eighteen afterwards, and
an additional eighteen while serving in Yugoslavia; and an American
OSS officer said that in Poland in 1945 he picked up a hitchhiking Red
Army soldier with a sniper rifle who turned out to be a young woman;
she claimed to have killed thirty Germans and wore a decoration for
the battle of Stalingrad.[260]

The Soviet counter-offensive that began on 19 November is one of
the most remarkable events in military history.[261] There was a tremendous
build-up of Soviet forces; there had been about half a million Red Army
troops involved during the defensive phase of the battle, but that
number was increased to well over a million by the beginning of the
offensive.[262] Within a few days the German 6th Army was surrounded,
and over the next few weeks the Red Army concentrated on extending
its control of region to the north, west, and south of Stalingrad, before
it began eliminating the German troops in the city. One particular
branch that played a key role during this phase was armour, which was
just beginning to come into its own in the Red Army. There were
many women serving in armour units as medical personnel and in
communications, but at least one woman also served in armour at
Stalingrad as a combatant.

Ekaterina Petliuk was a tank driver who served from the autumn of
1942 to February 1943 on the Don Front, participating in the immense
Soviet counter-offensive. Petliuk was assigned as a driver-mechanic in
the T-60 light tank, which carried a crew of two. She served with a
succession of tank commanders who were wounded and replaced. An
athletic girl, before the war Petliuk had participated in rifle training and
jumping from a parachute tower. She had dreamed of being a pilot, but
although she had completed her private licence with an air club in 1938,
when the war began she could not gain admittance to military flying

school. She managed to get into tank training school, where she says she found the lessons easy, owing to her previous training in aircraft systems.[263] Petliuk described the demands of driving a tank, which she says required 'considerable physical strength'. She was very short, and had to take apart her seat and set it up so that she could reach the pedals, but unfortunately this resulted in leaving a metal edge that constantly jabbed her in the back. The T-60 had many shortcomings and was in general uncomfortable for its crews.[264] Petliuk recalled how bitterly cold it was during the counter-offensive and subsequent operations:

> I wore a quilted jersey and quilted trousers. This clothing did not save me. How to describe that feeling of cold? The driver-mechanic sat in a strong draught. The air got drawn inside so that it could cool the engine and the water in the radiator, and was drawn outside by the ventilator. When the tank was moving you had a feeling that you were in a windtunnel. In spite of warm clothing, it seemed to me that I sat in a gauze blouse and the wind blew right through it. The cold penetrated to your bones. Your hands and feet literally cramped up. Take a tool in your hand, and the fingers stick to the iron. But here is what was striking in those days. Not one of us got a cold or got sick.[265]

The T-60 was not nearly as capable as the T-34 medium tank, and 'therefore the brigade commander gave missions connected with the delivery of fuel, of reserve units, of evacuating wounded from the field of battle' rather than acting as a main battle tank.[266] However, Petliuk's T-60 was often under heavy enemy fire as it accomplished its missions. Without a two-way radio, she often had to drive right up to disabled friendly tanks as they were still being fired upon to determine whether there were survivors who could be rescued. Petliuk recalled one episode when she and her commander evacuated a wounded T-34 commander who had been hit in the eye. The T-60 was too small to bring wounded inside, so her tank commander, a Lieutenant Gubanov, crawled out on the chassis and held on to the wounded soldier while Petliuk drove for safety. Shells were bursting all around as Petliuk manoeuvred at full speed. They made it to a medical station, Gubanov having turned blue with the cold.[267]

Another typical mission was to rescue supply vehicles that got stuck in the snow. Petliuk's tank was sent to find some fuel trucks that were desperately needed by her tank brigade; a blizzard was raging and the trucks had become bogged down. Petliuk used her tank to pull one truck after another. 'It was exhausting work. You drag one machine all of 200 metres and go for another. The trucks go only a short distance and again get stuck. You have to do everything all over again. And the snowstorm does not abate. And so we worked the entire night.'[268] But the fuel trucks reached the brigade by morning and the tanks were able to proceed with the offensive.

Petliuk often suffered from bruises and slight concussions when shells burst near the tank. Once she was hit in the leg by shrapnel while carrying food from a field kitchen to her tank. The tanks crews jumped into their machines and began to fight, and Petliuk somehow managed to keep driving, even though she said it felt as though her leg had simply stopped working. Her commander at that point, a Lieutenant Fedorenko, was hit in the face while looking out of the hatch. He kept firing until they ran out of shells, and then she took him to a hospital, where he later died.[269]

Another tankist who would become a Hero of the Soviet Union also began her career at Stalingrad, although not in combat. Irina Levchenko started the war in 1941 as a medic, but achieved a transfer to a T-60 medical brigade operating with a tank battalion in the Crimea. She began learning how to fire the gun in the T-60. After recovering from battle wounds, she enrolled in the Stalingrad Tank School, arriving in July 1942 when the battle had already begun but had not yet reached the city. Levchenko was evacuated with the rest of the school to the Ural Mountains. She later served as a tank platoon commander in the T-34 and ended the war with the rank of Lieutenant Colonel.[270]

Women also served in armour support units. Sixteen-year-old Antonina Mironovna Lenkova had been evacuated from Leningrad with her mother and sister to work on a collective farm near Stalingrad in late 1941. She answered a call for volunteers by the Stalingrad Komsomol Regional Committee. On 10 November 1942, she was sent with about twenty-five girls to a reserve regiment on the left bank of the Volga near Kapustin Yar. Due to her experience driving tractors on the collective farm, she was assigned to a field-armour repair shop. 'We were a factory on wheels,' she noted:

> Lorries carried milling, boring and grinding machines and lathes, power generator sets and vulcanising equipment. Each machine tool was operated by two people and each person worked twelve hours without a moment's break. His companion took his place while he ate. If it was the turn of one of them to serve in a duty detail, that meant the other worked 24 hours at a stretch. Assembly work was hardest of all. Shifts were unknown: it was one's duty as a soldier to assemble an engine in a day. Work did not cease even during bombing raids. Men died with the arms round an engine.[271]

The work took a heavy physical toll, which only manifested when the war was over. Lenkova noted, 'After only a few days of civilian life my joints swelled, my right hand became terribly painful and impossible to use, my eyesight grew even worse. I had a prolapsed kidney and a displaced liver and, as became clear later, my vegetative nervous system was completely ruined ... for me university became a second Stalingrad.'[272]

Women also assisted indirectly in the success of Soviet tank operations. General Rodin (26th Tank Corps, 5th Army, South western Front) noted that a civilian woman played an instrumental role in the famous seizure of the bridge at Kalach during the Soviet counter-offensive. As Rodin's units were advancing towards Kalach, they stopped at the village of Ostrov for refuelling and regrouping. They questioned the local people about German strength at Kalach, where the Germans had built a strong bridge. The bridge was essential as the rivers had not yet frozen sufficiently to support tanks. Rodin recalled, 'At 2 a.m. a woman was brought to the commander's hut. She had come from Kalach to purchase food. The commander himself interrogated her with the view to eliciting full details about the strength of the forces guarding the bridgeheads. "Did the sentinels at the bridge examine your papers?" he enquired. "No," replied the woman. "Do German machines cross the bridge with their lights on?" "Yes."' A few hours later, Lieutenant Colonel Filippov's group set off for Kalach, lights blazing.[273] Filippov would become famous for his audacity in capturing the bridge, but without the intelligence provided by an unknown woman, his attack might have failed.

Communications personnel continued to play just as vital a role during the counter-offensive phase of the battle. E. I. Obukhova, a radio operator with the 5th Tank Army on the South western Front, was commended for her dedication to duty during a two-hour continual bombing of the command post by enemy aviation on 21 November 1942; her actions under fire ensured essential communications. She was awarded the Order of the Red Star.[274]

Medical personnel too were in the front lines with the fast-advancing Red Army. A photograph shows nurse Anna Dasiuk aiding the wounded during an attack across an open, snowy field; Dasiuk, the wounded men, and several soldiers with rifles in the background are all wearing winter camouflage – a reminder of the harsh weather conditions of the time.[275] Nikolai Anisimov, deputy commander for the rear areas of the South western and then Stalingrad Fronts, related the tale of Natasha Kachuevskaia, a *saninstruktor* in one of the regiments of the 34th Guards Division of the 28th Army on the Stalingrad Front. Her unit faced stiff opposition during the early stage of the counter-offensive; the nineteen-year-old Kachuevskaia carried twenty wounded from the field of battle in one day. At the first-aid station, she found that some Germans had infiltrated into the rear of her unit. She hid the wounded in a dugout, and from a nearby trench tried to fight off the Germans with only a rifle and some grenades. She was mortally wounded, but managed to set off several grenades just as the Germans approached the trench, taking several of the enemy with her into death.[276]

Yet another role filled by women at Stalingrad was that of sapper. Little information on this area is available, but an intriguing photo from the 1943 book *Stalingrad* is captioned 'Lance-sergeant K. T. Ivanov, awarded Order of the Red Banner, and Private P. O. Zhezheria, both Guards sappers. Swept up hundreds of German mines and cleared the road for the Soviet tanks.' No other information is given. Both are in white winter camouflage; Zhezheria is clearly female.[277] This is the only specific reference to a woman sapper at Stalingrad that has so far been found by this author.

In December and January, the Red Army continued its operations in increasingly harsh weather conditions, but in an increasingly favourable military situation. P. I. Batov, 65th Army commander, describes the difficulties with weather in this period: 'At that time the enemy was far better off, with his trenches, dugouts and shelters ... our troops had neither firewood nor water.' He noted: 'The cold reigned supreme in dugouts and command and observation posts. Even at Army command post the women telephonists' greatcoats froze to the earthen floor overnight while they were resting after shifts.'[278] There were also problems finding reliable transportation for the wounded. Batov credits Masha Terenina, a *saninstruktor* with the 1311th Regiment of the 173rd Division, with recommending dog teams with travois as 'the best way to deliver the wounded across the open spaces on the field of battle to evacuation points'.[279]

As the Red Army advanced, most local inhabitants welcomed their liberation from German occupation. When Werth visited Kotelnikovo in early January 1943, he noted that 'the women told the usual story of how they had hidden in cellars and trenches during the last German occupation'.[280] The inhabitants described their treatment during periods of German occupation. One woman told Werth that 'the local population, especially young girls ... would be forced to carry bricks, and dig, and build fortifications'. She also mentioned that she heard that there were many women raped in some towns.[281] Kotelnikovo was spared some of the worst atrocities, as it was very near the front lines and the Germans were occupied with military matters, 'but right away [the Germans] nevertheless shot two workers at the grain stores, and also four peasant women who had been found harbouring a Russian officer'.[282] Women in such villages were relieved to see Soviet military forces again.

Sometimes, however, the Red Army encountered Soviet citizens who had collaborated with the Germans; some were treated quite harshly.

One Russian sergeant reported that when his unit was advancing toward Rostov in January 1943, both women and men of a Cossack steppe village attacked his unit with farm tools, shouting 'We don't want any Russians here.' The Red Army unit was ordered to destroy the village; all the inhabitants were killed.[283] A female Soviet intelligence officer captured by the Germans six months after the battle is quoted in German records as stating that some Russian civilians (*Hiwis*) who had worked for the Germans were executed by the NKVD in the aftermath of the battle.[284]

As the battle wound to its conclusion, women's presence at Stalingrad began to increase in new ways. Journalists, writers, and entertainers were allowed to visit. On 4 February 1943, the British journalist Alexander Werth was flown to Stalingrad with some other Western journalists, including an American named Janet Weaver and a Chinese woman called 'Miss Tsi Pang'.[285] They were present during an extended tour of the environs of Stalingrad, and present when German generals were interviewed. Rokossovskii mentions that the Polish author Vanda Vasilevskaia visited his command post around Christmas.[286] By New Year's Eve 1943 entertainers including ballerinas were allowed to perform for the 62nd Army on the shores of the Volga.[287]

The battle of Stalingrad finally ended on 2 February 1943. Tankist Ekaterina Petliuk is said to have danced in the streets of Stalingrad when soldiers were holding impromptu celebrations all over the city.[288] She went on to fight a few months later at the battle of Kursk, the largest tank battle in history, and was eventually seriously wounded and invalided out of service, but she survived the war – just one of the thousands of women who had fought to defend Stalingrad.[289]

Even at this point the work of the medical personnel was far from done. Tamara Umnyagina remembers:

> When everything was over in Stalingrad we were given the task of evacuating the most seriously wounded in ships and barges to Kazan and Gorky ... we found so many more wounded, in the ground, in trenches, in dugouts, in cellars – there were so many of them, it's impossible to tell you. It was horrible! We had always thought as we carried the wounded out of the battlefields that no more of them were left ... but when the fighting ended there were so many of them that it could be hardly believed.[290]

Women continued to be involved in the aftermath of the battle. The German generals encountered women among their captors. Beevor mentions that after the surrender, General Schmidt was forced to apologise to a mess waitress whom he had humiliated.[291] Werth mentions a similar incident; he says a Russian soldier told him that the German generals still had 'plenty of cheek'. He recounted a story about a female military barber who was sent to shave them every morning (undoubtedly they were not trusted with razors). The soldier told Werth, 'One of them got fresh with her the very first day, and pinched her bottom. She resented it and slapped his face. He got so scared of having his throat cut, he won't shave any more, and is now growing a beard!'[292] Perhaps the generals came to adopt the views of one German officer from Stalingrad, who reported that soldiers should not look down on women in the Red Army, stating: 'The Russian woman has long been prepared for combat duties and to fill any post of which a woman might be capable. Russian soldiers treat such women with great wariness.'[293]

Lower-ranking Axis POWs encountered many Soviet women as they were marched to camps. Lieutenant Felice Bracci, a POW of the Italian Eighth Army, told an interviewer that he was questioned by a female officer who spoke fluent Italian.[294] He also reported that, as he was marched away from Stalingrad, Russian peasant women would often give him bread and frozen potatoes.[295] A German doctor from the Sixth Army reported that after the surrender, a female Red Army surgeon who came to examine German wounded offered to trade food for watches.[296] Later that spring, another female doctor allowed German medical personnel to forage for fresh greens to offset scurvy among the German wounded, although she pointed out that the local civilians were even more affected.[297] Other Germans similarly reported kind treatment by Russian women. As the 297th Infantry Division was forced to retreat into the city during the encirclement in November, some Russian women helped treat the wounded. One German officer wrote: 'Two Stalingrad women rubbed my frozen legs for an hour to prevent the effects of severe frostbite. Again and again, they looked at me with compassion and said, "So young and yet he must already be dying!"' Others in his group came across several Russian women who traded bread for horsemeat.[298] More often German POWs were treated harshly by their guards and civilians alike.[299] Women sometimes approved, and sometimes reviled the abuse of German prisoners. At Kotluban, thirty miles north-west of Stalingrad, a group of Russian nurses was watching a long procession of German POWs when they saw some Russian soldiers shoot some of the prisoners for no apparent reason; reportedly the nurses 'shook their fists in outrage at their own soldiers'.[300]

We must broaden our views about the battle of Stalingrad; it was not an all-male event, as it is stereotypically depicted. Thousands of women – military and civilian, combatant and noncombatant – participated in the battle from start to finish, day in and day out. In his 1959 book, Marshal Chuikov made the following statement about women and the battle of Stalingrad:

Remembering the defence of Stalingrad, I can't overlook one very important question which, in my opinion, is still weakly covered in military literature, and at times unjustifiably forgotten in our reports and work on the generalisation of the experience of the Great Patriotic War. I have in mind the question about the role of women in war, in the rear but also at the front. Equally with men they bore all the burdens of combat life and together with us men, they went all the way to Berlin.[301]

Unfortunately, sixty years after the end of the battle and forty-four years after Chuikov's book appeared, women's roles are still overlooked. The recent movie *Enemy at the Gates* deliberately downplayed the role of women at Stalingrad; although it showed a number of women in uniform, none of them, not even the so-called snipers, ever killed an enemy; they were more often seen putting on make-up or panicking under attack. Such an image hardly seems consistent with reality. Whatever their roles, the women who participated at Stalingrad are described as soldiers (*boets* or *voin*).[302] They regarded themselves as soldiers; A. Vasilenko, who served in the Red Army at Stalingrad in an unknown capacity, signed a letter to her mother 'with the warmest greetings of a Red Army fighter'.[303] This essay is only a preliminary investigation into this historical event, but it shows how much information can be obtained from published sources. Much more work remains to be done in the archives. We will not truly understand the complexity of such an important historical event as the battle of Stalingrad until we learn more about the participation of women and the ways in which the Red Army military experience differed from anything known in the West.

## 14

## *Forgotten Battles of the Soviet–German War, 1941–45*

DAVID M. GLANTZ

For almost twenty years after the Second World War ended in 1945, most Westerners still perceived the Soviet–German portion of the war as a mysterious, prolonged, brutal, and utterly incomprehensible struggle waged on an unimaginable scale with unprecedented ferocity between Europe's bitterest political antagonists and largest and most formidable armies. History portrayed this struggle as a series of prolonged offensive operations, such as German operations Barbarossa and Blau and Soviet operation Bagration, conducted in alternating fashion, and begun by or culminating in violent, dramatic, and equally incomprehensible battles at Moscow, Stalingrad, Kursk, and Berlin, which took place in a theatre of war distinguished by its immense size, complex terrain, and severe climactic extremes. The paucity of English-language literature about the war prompted Western historians to perceive it as a mere backdrop for far more dramatic and significant battles in western theatres of war, such as El Alamein, Salerno, Anzio, Normandy, and the Bulge.

In the early 1960s, however, and for decades thereafter, John Erickson lifted the veil of obscurity that cloaked this forgotten war. In 1962 his seminal study, *The Soviet High Command*, provided unprecedented details about the Red Army's development from 1918 through 1941, and a decade later his equally massive and now classic tomes, *The Road to Stalingrad* and *The Road to Berlin*, detailed the Red Army's role in the Second World War in equally rich detail. These three volumes, whose factual content have withstood the test of time, single-handedly created the field of modern Soviet military studies in the West.

By rediscovering the forgotten war, Erickson provided necessary context for all subsequent study of the Red Army during peace and war. His unprecedented mosaic of this war established high standards against which all future work would be measured, and the methodologies he pioneered enabled those who followed to complete his work by filling in the 'blank spots' in what he himself recognised as an incomplete mosaic. This short chapter, which fills in some of those 'blank spots', serves as modest tribute to John's pioneering efforts.

*

Popularly termed the War on the German Eastern Front by Westerners and the Great Patriotic War by Russians, the Soviet–German War began on 22 June 1941 and ended on 9 May 1945. Since the war's end, for analytical purposes, Russians have subdivided the war into distinct periods and seasonal campaigns. The First Period of the War, which lasted from 22 June 1941 to 18 November 1942, encompassed German Operation Barbarossa in 1941 and Operation Blau (Blue) in 1942, interrupted by the Red Army's successful defences at the gates of Leningrad, Moscow and Rostov in December 1941 and partially successful offensive in the winter of 1941–2. Although the Wehrmacht retained the strategic initiative throughout much of this period, the Red Army managed to produce the first turning point in the war with its victory at Moscow, which ensured that Germany could no longer win the war on Hitler's initial terms.

During the Second Period of the War, which lasted from 19 November 1942 to 31 December 1943, the Red Army seized the strategic initiative with its twin strategic offensives in the Rzhev (Operation Mars) and Stalingrad (Operation Uranus) regions and held it during its ambitious but only partially successful winter offensive in 1942–3. After relinquishing the initiative to the Germans in the spring of 1943, the Red Army regained the initiative once and for all with its dramatic victory at Kursk in July 1943 and its subsequent advance to and across the Dnepr river by year's end. While the Red Army's victory at Stalingrad indicated that Germany would lose the war, its victory at Kursk ensured German defeat would be total.

The Red Army retained the strategic initiative throughout the Third Period of the War, which lasted from 1 January 1944 to 9 May 1945. Conducted on an ever-increasing scale and often without pause, the Red Army's simultaneous and successive offensives in the Ukraine, Belorussia, the Balkans, Poland and Germany culminated in final Red Army victory at Berlin in May 1945.[1]

Newly released Russian archival materials and more careful study of existing German records now make it possible to fill in many of the 'blank spots' in Erickson's epic portrayal of the Red Army at war. In short, by exploiting the methodologies Erickson pioneered while rediscovering this forgotten war, we can now add a wide range of hitherto concealed 'forgotten battles' to his rich operational mosaic.

## The Summer–Fall Campaign, 22 June–5 December 1941

Although most histories portray Operation Barbarossa as a virtually seamless Wehrmacht advance from the Soviet Union's western frontiers to the gates of Leningrad, Moscow and Rostov, archival materials now indicate that, from its very beginning, the Soviet *Stavka* (High Command) consciously and repeatedly sought to halt this German juggernaut. Pursuant to Stavka directives, from late June through early September 1941, the Red Army launched a series of counter-attacks, counter-strokes, and, in at least one case, a fully-fledged counter-offensive. Collectively, these operations represented a concerted though clumsy effort by the Stavka to implement its 1941 State Defence Plan, which required Red Army *front* commanders to react vigorously and offensively to enemy invasion.[2] At a minimum, these operations included:

- The Kelme, Raseiniai, Grodno, Brest, Brody, and Dubno counter-strokes (late June 1941)
- The Sol'tsy, Lepel', Bobruisk, and Kiev counter-strokes (July 1941)
- The Staraia Russa, Smolensk, and Kiev counter-strokes (August 1941)
- The Smolensk, El'nia, and Roslavl' counter-offensive (September 1941)
- The Kalinin counter-stroke (October 1941)

The counter-strokes the Stavka conducted in late June included poorly co-ordinated, futile, and often suicidal counter-attacks by its North western Front's 3rd and 12th Mechanised Corps at Kelme and Raseiniai in Lithuania, its Western Front's 6th, 11th and 14th Mechanised Corps near Grodno and Brest in Belorussia, and its South western Front's 4th, 6th, 8th, 9th, 15th, 19th and 22nd Mechanised Corps near Brody and Dubno in the Ukraine. Only the violent assaults in the south, which Army General G. K. Zhukov, the chief of the Red Army general staff, personally supervised, had any noticeable effect on the precipitous German advance.[3]

Undeterred by its initial defeats, the Stavka tried once again to orchestrate co-ordinated counter-strokes during July. In the north two North western Front shock groups attacked the vanguard of German Army Group North's LVI Motorised Corps near Sol'tsy south-west of Lake Il'men' on 14 July and, despite heavy losses, managed to delay the German advance towards Leningrad by about one week.[4] Along the Moscow axis, on 6 July the Western and Central Fronts launched multiple counter-strokes aimed at containing Army Group Centre's forces along the Dnepr river. These futile ventures included the spectacular defeat the Red Army's 5th and 7th Mechanised Corps suffered in the Lepel' region, the famous but pathetically weak 'Timoshenko offensive' against Guderian's Second Panzer Group along the Sozh river, and a marginally successful counter-stroke near Bobruisk, all of which failed to halt Army Group Centre's advance to Smolensk.[5] In the south, multiple counter-attacks by the South western Front failed to halt the German advance on Kiev.[6]

Despite its July failures, the Stavka continued conducting extensive offensive operations in August. In the north, the Northern Front's 48th Army and North western Front's 11th, 34th and 27th Armies ferociously assaulted Army Group North's X Army Corps near Staraia Russa on 12 August and delayed the German advance for yet another week.[7] Along the Moscow axis, on 20 July the Western Front employed five *ad hoc* shock groups in intense, poorly co-ordinated, but partially successful assaults aimed at rescuing Red Army forces encircled around Smolensk.[8] Simultaneous Red Army assaults west of Kiev also failed.[9] Despite these failures, these Red Army efforts prompted Hitler to abandon his headlong advance on Moscow for one month and instead attack 'softer' targets in the Kiev region.

Still convinced that its Red Army could halt Hitler's Barbarossa juggernaut, in late August the Stavka ordered the Western, Reserve, and Briansk Fronts to launch massive offensives in the Smolensk region to destroy Army Group Centre and prevent German forces from reaching Moscow and Kiev. However, this offensive too ended in bloody failure and so weakened Red Army forces along the Moscow axis that it contributed directly to the Red Army's disastrous defeats in early October, when the German army advanced toward Moscow in Operation Typhoon.[10] Finally, during Operation Typhoon, a special operational group commanded by N. F. Vatutin, the North western Front's chief of staff, counter-attacked near Kalinin in mid-October, and, while failing to recapture the city, it prevented the German Ninth Army from severing the strategically vital Moscow–Leningrad railroad line.[11]

While proving that the Red Army's strategic defence in 1941 was not as haphazard, improvised, and passive as previously described and that the German advance was not as seamless and inexorable as presumed, these forgotten battles also cast new light on why German forces suffered defeat at the gates of Moscow in early December 1941.

## The Winter Campaign, December 1941–April 1942

Accounts of the Battle of Moscow and the Red Army's winter offensive of 1941–2 largely ignore three major failed Red Army offensives along the southern flank of the battle for Moscow, two north-west of Moscow, one south of Leningrad, and one in the Crimea. The forgotten battles in this campaign include:

- The Liuban' (Leningrad–Novgorod) offensive (7 January–30 April 1942)
- The Demiansk offensive (1 March–30 April 1942)

- The Rzhev-Sychevka offensive (15 February–1 March 1942)
- The Orel–Bolkhov offensive (7 January–18 February 1942)
- The Bolkhov offensive (24 March–3 April 1942)
- The Oboian'–Kursk offensive (3–26 January 1942)
- The Crimean offensive (27 February–15 April 1942)

South of Moscow the Western Front's 10th Army and Cavalry Group Belov, which were attacking on the front's left flank, reached the region east of Kirov in late January 1942, forming an enormous wedge separating Army Group Centre's Fourth and Second Panzer Armies. North of Moscow the Kalinin Front's 4th Shock, 29th and 39th Armies, which were operating on the Western Front's right flank, lunged south toward Viaz'ma in Army Group Centre's rear. Exploiting this opportunity to envelop and destroy Army Group Centre's forces operating east of Smolensk, in early February the Stavka ordered Group Belov and the 50th Army to swing northward towards Viaz'ma and link up with the Kalinin Front's forces advancing from the north. Simultaneously, the 10th Army was to sever communications between the German Fourth and Second Panzer Armies.

Although this pincer movement toward Viaz'ma failed after months of fruitless seesaw fighting, the 10th Army's advance toward Kirov isolated Army Group Centre's Second Panzer and Second Armies in an immense salient anchored on the cities of Belev and Bolkhov. Believing that the eradication of this salient was vital to the success of its winter offensive, the Stavka ordered the Briansk and South western Fronts to eliminate it. However, since the so-called Orel–Bolkhov, Bolkhov, and Oboian'–Kursk offensives failed, they were literally ignored in subsequent histories of the war.[12]

To the north the Stavka ordered its Leningrad and Volkhov Fronts to lift the Leningrad siege in early January 1942 by conducting concentric assaults across the Neva and Volkhov rivers against Army Group North's Eighteenth Army. Although the Volkhov Front's 2nd Shock Army and 13th Cavalry Corps pierced Wehrmacht defences, German forces encircled and destroyed the Red Army force by early July 1942.[13] This failed offensive too languished in utter obscurity for over forty years.[14] Similarly, failed Red Army offensives at Demiansk and in the Crimea also disappeared from the pages of history.[15]

## The Summer–Fall Campaign, May–October 1942

The Red Army also reacted far more offensively than previously described during the spring and summer of 1942. After besting the Wehrmacht around Moscow only six months before, the Stavka refused to abandon the initiative to the Germans in the spring. Instead, it began the campaign with strong offensives at Khar'kov and in the Crimea in May. Even after both of these offensives failed, when the Wehrmacht began Operation Blau, the Stavka ordered its operating forces to resist the German advance ferociously.

During July and August the Stavka ordered the Red Army to conduct numerous, often massive counter-attacks and counter-strokes against Wehrmacht forces advancing in southern Russia and supporting offensives in other key regions. However, since most of these operations failed and were literally subsumed by the Germans' heady advance towards Stalingrad and the Caucasus, they were largely forgotten. These forgotten battles include three major Red Army counter-strokes near Voronezh and others near Siniavino, Demiansk, Rzhev, Zhizdra and Bolkhov further to the north:[16]

- The destruction of Soviet 2nd Shock Army at Miasnoi Bor (13 May–10 July 1942)
- The reduction of encircled Group Belov (Operation Hannover) (24 May–21 June 1942)
- The destruction of Soviet 39th Army southwest of Rzhev (2–27 July 1942)
- The defence of the Donbas region (the encirclement of Red Armies) (7–24 July 1942)
- The Voronezh–Don counter-offensive (4–26 July 1942)
- The Zhizdra–Bolkhov counter-stroke (5–14 July 1942)
- The Demiansk offensive (17–24 July 1942)
- The Rzhev–Sychevka offensive (30 July–23 August 1942)
- The Siniavino offensive (19 August–15 October 1942)
- The Demiansk offensive (10–21 August 1942)
- The Bolkhov offensive (23–9 August 1942)
- The Voronezh counter-stroke (12–15 August 1942)
- The Voronezh counter-stroke (15–28 September 1942)
- The Demiansk offensives (15–16 September 1942)

While existing Russian accounts claim otherwise, new archival information indicates that Wehrmacht forces encircled and decimated the bulk of at least five withdrawing Red armies (the 28th, 38th, 57th, 9th and 24th) during the first month of Operation Blau and the Red Army's defence of the Donbas region.[17]

The largest but most historically obscure Red Army counter-actions during Operation Blau occurred in the Voronezh region in July, August, and September.[18] While Russian sources have briefly described the ill-fated offensive by the Briansk front's new 5th Tank Army west of Voronezh in early July, these sources understate the strength, duration, and ambitious intent of what can be termed the Voronezh–Don offensive. Ultimately, the Voronezh phase of the operation lasted for several weeks and involved as many as seven Red Army tank corps equipped with up to 1500 tanks. Furthermore, the Stavka co-ordinated the 5th Tank Army's assault west of Voronezh with major counter-strokes by the Stalingrad Front's 1st and 4th Tank Armies along the approaches to the Don river west of Stalingrad.

The three offensives the Red Army conducted in the Rzhev, Zhizdra and Bolkhov regions, which were timed to coincide with operations at Voronezh and perhaps also at Demiansk and near Stalingrad, were designed to accomplish more than simply tying down German reserves.[19] For example, the August offensive at Bolkhov included a massive assault by the western front's new 3rd Tank Army and several separate tank corps, while the western and Kalinin Front's August–September offensive near Rzhev, which was orchestrated by Zhukov and achieved moderate success, was a virtual dress rehearsal for an even larger counter-offensive in the same region later in the year (Operation Mars).

Although the Leningrad and Volkhov Fronts' offensive at Siniavino in August and September 1942 failed disastrously, it prevented German forces from capturing Leningrad and tied down the German Eleventh Army, which could have been put to better use elsewhere on the Soviet–German Front.[20] As a result, the 2nd Shock Army, which the Germans had already destroyed at Miasnoi Bor by early July, was destroyed once again in September near Siniavino.

## The Winter Campaign, November 1942–April 1943

The Red Army's victory at Stalingrad in November 1942 and its subsequent winter offensive towards Khar'kov and the Donbas region in early 1943 remain the focus of historical accounts of this campaign. These accounts, however, totally ignore the Red Army's Operations Mars and Polar Star and its Orel–Briansk–Smolensk offensive, severely understate the scope of its Donbas offensive, exaggerate its achievements at Demiansk and Rzhev and distort the Stavka's strategic intent in the late winter of 1942–3. Forgotten battles in this campaign include:

- Operation Mars: The 2nd Rzhev–Sychevka offensive (25 November–20 December 1942)
- The Donbas (Voroshilovgrad and Mariupol') offensive (29 January–23 February 1943)
- The Orel–Briansk–Smolensk offensive (5 February–28 March 1943)
- Operation Polar Star (15 February–19 March 1943)

Code-named Operation Mars and orchestrated by Zhukov, the Western and Kalinin Fronts' 2nd Rzhev–Sychevka offensive, which took place from 25 November to 20 December 1942 and was a companion piece to Operation Uranus at Stalingrad, was an attempt to destroy the German Ninth Army and, if possible, all of Army Group Centre.[21] Although Operation Mars failed, it did tie down some German forces in the Rzhev salient and, in the process, so weakened the German Ninth Army that Hitler authorised Army Group Centre to abandon the salient in February 1943.[22] This offensive was completely forgotten, in part to preserve Zhukov's reputation.[23]

The Western, Briansk, and newly formed Central Fronts conducted the Orel–Briansk–Smolensk operation in mid-February and early March 1943 to collapse German defences in central Russia and drive Wehrmacht forces back across the Dnepr river.[24] Although the Central Front's attacking forces reached the Desna river west of Kursk, the offensive faltered in early March after the Western and Briansk Fronts failed to dent German defences around Orel.[25] After the offensive faltered, the Red Army's new front lines formed the northern and western flanks of the infamous Kursk Bulge.

The North-western, Leningrad, and Volkhov Fronts, also under Zhukov's supervision, launched Operation Polar Star in mid-February in an attempt to pierce Army Group North's defences near Staraia Russa, liquidate the German Demiansk salient, lift the siege of Leningrad, encircle and destroy Army Group North's forces south of Leningrad, and, if possible, penetrate German defences at Narva and Pskov.[26] Although this offensive faltered when the Germans voluntarily abandoned the Demiansk salient, the Leningrad and Volkhov Fronts indeed conducted smaller offensives of their own in the Leningrad region.[27] Even though Operation Polar Star failed, it served as a virtual dress rehearsal for the Stavka's January 1944 offensive that ultimately liberated the Leningrad region.

Finally, critical dimensions of the Red Army's Donbas offensive also remain obscure or entirely forgotten. While existing histories claim the south-western front alone conducted the ill-fated offensive, the southern front also took part in the offensive, in the process losing two mobile corps that penetrated deep into the German rear area only to be decimated before they could escape.[28] In addition, the fighting associated with the German forces' withdrawal from the Rzhev salient, whose ferocity Russian historians have routinely exaggerated, also requires further examination.[29]

## The Summer–Fall Campaign, June–December 1943

The Red Army's signal victory at Kursk in July 1943 and its subsequent dramatic exploitation to and across the Dnepr river in the battles for Gomel, Kiev and Kremenchug dominate existing histories of this campaign. However, accounts of these victories mask several bloody Red Army operational defeats, most of which occurred when an overly optimistic Stavka tested the operational limits of Red Army forces completing successful offensive operations.[30] Contrary to persistent assertions that the Stavka routinely focused the Red Army's offensive efforts along a single strategic axis, specifically in the Ukraine, in reality the Stavka required the Red Army to conduct strategic offensives along multiple axes and across a broad front throughout this campaign.[31]

The forgotten battles in this campaign include:

- The Taman' offensives (4 April–10 May and 26 May–22 August 1943)
- The Donbas offensive (Izium–Barvenkovo and the Mius River) (17 July–2 August 1943)
- The Siniavino offensive (15–18 September 1943)
- The Belorussian offensive (Vitebsk, Orsha, Gomel, and Bobruisk) (3 October–31 December 1943)
- The Kiev offensive (Chernobyl', Gornostaipol', Liutezh, and Bukrin) (1–24 October 1943)
- The Krivoi–Rog–Nikopol' offensive (Krivoi Rog, Aleksandriia–Znamenka, Apostolovo, and Nikopol') (14 November–31 December 1943)

The North Caucasus front's Taman' offensive was a continuation of the Red Army's more famous Krasnodar offensive operation aimed at clearing German forces from the northern Caucasus region. Directed for a time by Zhukov, it constituted a prolonged series of unsuccessful assaults against the German Seventeenth Army's fortified defences around the towns of Krymskaia and Moldavanskoe, which anchored Hitler's bridgehead in the Taman' region.[32] Similarly, the South western and Southern Fronts' July offensives in the Donbas were an integral part of the battle of Kursk, designed to collapse German defences in the Donbas and attract vital German panzer reserves away from the Kursk region.[33] Finally, the Leningrad Front's Siniavino offensive was a furious, bloody, but successful attempt to overcome Army Group North's defences on the Siniavino Heights, a target that had eluded Soviet capture for over two years.[34]

The most dramatic forgotten battles during this campaign began in early October when the Kalinin, Western, Briansk, and Central Fronts attacked into eastern Belorussia to capture Minsk, and the Voronezh Front began operations to expand or seize new bridgeheads over the Dnepr river north and south of Kiev. The former continued unabated through December and involved intense and costly fighting on the approaches to Vitebsk, Orsha, and Bobruisk and along the Dnepr river.[35] Existing histories describe fragments of this massive offensive, such as the Nevel' and Gomel–Rechitsa operations, but studiously ignore the offensive's full scope and ambitious intent.[36]

These histories also ignore the Voronezh (later 1st Ukrainian) Front's bitter struggle in October 1943 to seize a strategic bridgehead across the Dnepr river in the Kiev region. During three weeks of bloody but futile fighting, the Voronezh Front's 38th, 60th, 40th, 3rd Guards Tank, 27th and 47th Armies, in conjunction with the Central Front's 13th and 60th Armies, failed to dislodge forces from Army Group South's Fourth Panzer and Eighth Armies, which contained Red Army bridgeheads in the Chernobyl', Gornostaipol', Liutezh and Bukrin regions.[37] In this instance, the Voronezh Front's spectacular victory at Kiev in November erased these failed offensives from both memory and history.

Existing histories also ignore the 2nd, 3rd and 4th Ukrainian Front's equally frustrating failures in their Krivoi Rog–Nikopol' offensive of November–December 1943, which sought to clear Army Group South's forces from the lower Don river region.[38]

### The Winter Campaign, December 1943–April 1944

Histories of this campaign focus exclusively on the Red Army's successful offensives in the Leningrad region, the Ukraine, and the Crimea but ignore failed Red Army offensives after the end of each of these successful offensives and in Belorussia.[39] These forgotten battles include:

- The Narva offensives (15–28 February, 1–4, 18–24 March 1944)
- The Pskov, Ostrov, Pustoshka offensive (the struggle for the Panther Line) (9 March–15 April 1944)
- The Belorussian offensive (Vitebsk, Bogushevsk, Rogachev, Shlobin) (1 January–15 March 1944)
- The 1st Iassy-Kishinev offensive (Targul–Frumos) (2–7 May 1944)

The Narva and Pskov, Ostrov, and Pustoshka offensives, which began after the Red Army successfully completed its Leningrad–Novgorod offensive against Army Group North on 1 March, were an attempt by the Leningrad and 2nd Baltic Fronts to breach the German Panther Defence Line. The Leningrad front's 2nd Shock, 59th and 8th Armies tried repeatedly but unsuccessfully to encircle and destroy Army Group

North's forces defending Narva and thrust deep into Estonia, while the *front's* 42nd, 67th and 54th Armies wedged into the defences of Army Group North's Eighteenth Army between Pskov and Ostrov but were unable to seize either city despite six weeks of heavy fighting. To the south the 2nd Baltic Front's 1st and 3rd Shock, 10th Guards, and 22nd Armies repeatedly battered the Sixteenth Army's defences at and north of Pustoshka but with only limited success.[40]

To the south in Belorussia, from 29 December 1943 to 29 March 1944, the 1st Baltic, Western, and Belorussian Fronts sought to overcome Army Group Centre's defences by launching seven distinct offensives, which ultimately cost the attackers over 200,000 casualties. The 1st Baltic Front attacked north and east of Vitebsk, severed communications between German forces in Vitebsk and Polotsk, and advanced into the western suburbs of Vitebsk, while the Western Front assaulted German defences south-east and south of the city, trying to encircle it from the south. In southern Belorussia, the Belorussian Front captured Kalinkovichi in January, drove German forces back to Rogachev, and almost severed communications between Army Groups Centre and South along the Pripiat' river.[41]

At the southern extremity of the front, after their successful March offensive in the Ukraine, in late April and May 1944, the 2nd and 3rd Ukrainian Fronts tried to breach German and Rumanian defences in northern Rumania and capture Iassy and Kishinev. While the 3rd Ukrainian Front encountered heavy resistance along the Dnestr river and faltered, the 2nd Ukrainian Front attacked on 2 May with a force of almost 600 tanks from its 2nd, 5th Guards and 6th Tank Armies. After four days of intense but totally forgotten fighting (called the Battle of Targul-Frumos by the Germans), the Germans counter-attacked with the LVII Panzer Corps' 'Grossdeutschland' and 24th Panzer Divisions and inflicted heavy losses on the attackers.[42]

## The Summer–Fall Campaign, June–December 1944

The spectacularly successful offensives the Red Army conducted successively in Belorussia, Poland and Rumania during the summer and fall of 1944 sharply decreased the number of forgotten battles during this campaign. Although the Red Army achieved far more than the Stavka anticipated during these massive offensives, in at least two instances, the Stavka could not resist attempting to achieve even more. The result was several more forgotten battles, including:

- The East Prussian (Goldap–Gumbinnen) offensive (16–30 October 1944)

- The East Carpathian offensive (8 September–28 October 1944)

The East Prussian offensive began on the heels of the 1st Baltic and 3rd Belorussian Front's successful Memel' offensive, when Red Army forces reached the Baltic Sea, isolating Army Group North's forces in Courland from Army Group Centre's forces in East Prussia. The 3rd Belorussian Front's 5th and 11th Guards Armies attacked westward toward Königsberg on 16 October and were reinforced by the 31st, 39th and 28th Armies and the 2nd Guards Tank Corps by 20 October. The offensive faltered with heavy losses after nearly a week of intense fighting when it encountered deeply fortified German defences and intense counter-attacks by hastily regrouped German panzer reserves.[43]

In the East Carpathian offensive, which took place in the Carpathian Mountain region and eastern Hungary, elements of the 2nd, 4th and 2nd Ukrainian fronts sought to envelop the First Panzer Army's mountain defences, disrupt communications between Army Groups Centre and South, and encircle German and Hungarian forces defending eastern Hungary. The 1st Ukrainian Front's 38th Army and 4th Ukrainian Front's 1st Guards and 18th Armies attacked through the mountains into eastern Slovakia to link up with the 2nd Ukrainian Front's 6th Guards Tank and 27th Armies and 1st Guards Cavalry-Mechanised Group attacking northward through eastern Hungary.[44] This offensive failed to achieve its ambitious aims when the 38th Army's offensive bogged down in the Dukla Pass, the 4th Ukrainian Front's attack ground to a halt in the mountains, and the 2nd Ukrainian front's cavalry-mechanised group was encircled and badly damaged at Nyiregyhaza north of Debrecen by counter-attacking German panzer forces.[45]

## The Winter Campaign, January–March 1945

Histories of this campaign focus on the massive Red Army offensives in Poland and East Prussia and, to a lesser extent, the offensive to capture Budapest, Hungary. While doing so they ignore one forgotten battle that was planned but never conducted and another that failed to achieve its ambitious goals. These forgotten battles, both of which began at the end of successful offensives, include:

- The Berlin offensive (February 1945)
- The West Carpathian offensive (10 March–5 May 1945)

After the 1st Belorussian and 1st Ukrainian Fronts' forces reached the Oder river, 60 kilometres east of Berlin, in late January the Stavka ordered the two fronts to mount a final assault to capture Berlin in February or early March. However, although both fronts began this new offensive. Stalin ordered them to abandon the effort on 10 February, while the Allied conference at Yalta was in progress.[46] The most probable explanation for Stalin's actions was his desire to shift the axis of the Red Army's main advance from Berlin to western Hungary and Austria and occupy the Danube basin before hostilities ended. Ultimately, the Red Army began its Berlin offensive on 16 April, the day after Vienna fell to the Red Army.[47]

At the same time, the Stavka sought to overcome stiff German resistance in the western Carpathian Mountains in north-western Slovakia by ordering the 1st Ukrainian Front's 60th and 38th Armies to attack southward through Moravska-Ostrava to Brno in concert with the 4th Ukrainian Front's 1st Guards and 18th Armies to link up with the mobile forces from the 2nd Ukraininan Front, which were attacking northward from northern Hungary and later Bratislava, toward Brno.[48] The 1st Guards Cavalry-Mechanised Group and 6th Guards Tank Army, which took part in the 2nd Ukrainian Front's northward thrust, suffered heavy losses when this offensive failed.

## The Spring Campaign, April–May 1945

The Red Army's climactic offensives against Berlin and Prague in April and May 1945 crushed the remnants of the Wehrmacht and shrank the theatre of military operations to such an extent that all Red Army operations were quite obvious. Nonetheless, some fighting during this final campaign was obscured by the dramatic battle for Berlin. The most important of these neglected battles include:

- The battle for Courland (16 February–8 May 1945)

After isolating Army Group North in the Courland peninsula in mid-October 1944, the 1st and 2nd Baltic Fronts besieged this German force until its surrender on 9 May 1945.[49] Although existing histories accurately describe the Courland siege in general terms, they obscure the heavy fighting that occurred when Red Army forces attempted to reduce the pocket – for example, concerted offensives that took place in late October 1944, from 20–24 November and 21–2 December 1944, and in late February and mid-March 1945.

Building on the necessary context provided by John Erickson as he revealed this forgotten war, this brief summary exploits the methodologies he pioneered to begin exposing the war's many forgotten battles. By filling in some of the blank spots in Erickson's rich mosaic of combat operations during the Soviet–German War, it also helps fulfil the promise represented by Erickson's three monumental histories of the war.

# 15

## Ordinary Collaborators:
## The Case of the Travniki Guards

SERGEI KUDRYASHOV

For several decades already arguments among historians have continued concerning how we are to rationally explain the participation of perfectly ordinary people in the Nazi Terror. The murder of millions of 'harmful and undesirable elements' on the eastern front was not carried out by any kind of specially trained German criminals, but by people engaged in a wide variety of peaceful professions, including the most humanitarian, from artists and priests to doctors and teachers. One of the more fruitful efforts at explaining this was carried out by Omer Bartov and a group of German historians. Using separate parts of the Wehrmacht, these authors succeeded in showing the popularity of, and the degree to which ideas of National Socialism had permeated the military.[1] The American historian Edward Westermann carried out similar research on Police Battalion 310.[2] Although it would require further research to establish the degree to which one can extrapolate to include the German armed forces as a whole, including the air forces and the navy, one can definitely say that ideology was one of the main driving forces in the motivation of the atrocities and terror that were perpetrated. At the same time, it is essential that we take into consideration other motives, which Christopher Browning has proven no less convincingly.[3] The subjects of his work are ordinary policemen, who showed no particularly distasteful qualities before the outbreak of the war. They did not uphold the ideas of National Socialism, and were far from exhibiting any passion for the party's struggle for the Aryan race. However, this in no way prevented them from carrying out monstrous orders and mercilessly killing innocent people. Their motivation turns out to be quite prosaic, i.e. the habit of obedience, the necessity of carrying out orders, and the desire to advance their careers in the service, or simply the desire to act 'like everyone else'.

But how can one explain the behaviour of collaborators who took part in executions and shootings, including those who engaged in these activities voluntarily? They had been brought up under a different regime, and had no understanding of Nazi ideology before the onset of war, but nonetheless accepted the rules of the occupying power and committed acts of evil to the same degree as the representatives of that power. I discussed this question on many occasions with John Erickson, and we agreed that it would be useful to take one group of collaborators who worked together in the same place, and look into their motivations, their careers and what became of them as a whole. To this end I used documents available in the archives of the Russian Federal Security Services as well as in the former archives of the KGB in other parts of the former Soviet Union. Sadly, I was unable to bring this work to a conclusion during John's lifetime, but I am glad that I am able to present its first results in a book dedicated to his memory.[4]

The subject of our research, then, is the 'Travniki men', or the 'Travniki guards'.[5] These were the names given to the recruits and graduates of a special training camp run by the SS,[6] which was set up on the territory of a former sugar factory in the region of Travniki, which is around 30 kilometres from the Polish town of Lublin. But before we turn to the analysis of facts and figures, we must touch on the question of the reliability of the sources we are using, a question that always arises where the KGB[7] archives are concerned. It is no secret that the Cold War gave rise to particularly intense conflict between the special services, who did not shy away from using dirty methods, lies and slander against each other. It is, therefore, not surprising that any appearance in the West of documents from the KGB gives rise to doubts as to their authenticity. This is particularly true with regard to various legal proceedings. Because all KGB documents were considered to be 'classified', the Soviet authorities, should the necessity arise, would present copies of selected pages of a file, and not the document in its entirety. This would almost always provoke the reasonable objection from lawyers regarding the content of the other pages. What, for example, if the other part of the document contained contradictory information? And what if the pages that have been presented are themselves fakes? Since the collapse of the Soviet Union, however, when a part of the KGB's historical archives became accessible to historians, it has been possible to establish their authenticity and compare them with other collections. Now it is possible, with a great degree of certainty, to confirm that the Soviet security apparatus (NKVD – SMERSH – KGB) was not engaged in the falsification of wartime documents. The main reason for this was that there was no sense or point in doing so. In the first place, any falsification of documents demands enormous effort. It is not only important to create a document, but to make it convincing, and to do this it is necessary to create what would virtually amount to a new archive (i.e. to fake real existing German materials, change numbering, dates, etc.). With modern criminal investigation methods it is very simple to expose such falsifications. Secondly, Soviet investigators had such a huge quantity of various materials at their disposal (from German archives to evidence from witnesses and the accused) that there was simply no need to provide more materials. One must add here that in the case of the Travniki men, their guilt was, in accordance with Soviet law, assumed from the very beginning because they had broken their military oath, had served as armed men in the SS and performed the function of police officers. Therefore it was necessary for the investigators to prove to what extent the accused had participated in punitive and repressive actions, and whether they had acted under duress or volunteered their services. The court would pronounce its verdict on the basis of whether the accused had taken part in shootings, and also with regard to the degree of activism displayed by the individual concerned. In a situation where a guilty verdict was going to be delivered in any case, and the only difference was whether this meant a prison term or execution, the fabrication of yet another accusing 'document' lost any kind of meaning at all.

The question of the authenticity of KGB materials was particularly intensely discussed at the time of the trial of John Demjanjuk ('Ivan the Terrible') in Israel (1986–8), where evidence was presented in the form of Demjanjuk's personal Travniki card. The defence declared the card a forgery, and that it had been made by the KGB in order to smear the good name of an honest American citizen. Demjanjuk's defence also promised to 'submit an entire book of KGB-forged documents from the war'. That book, however, never materialised,[8] and it is not difficult to explain why. In the end, it was precisely documents from the archives of the former KGB that helped the Israeli lawyer to obtain the release of his client.[9]

Another aspect of the problem is the following: to what extent can we trust the evidence presented by Travniki guards when we know that Soviet investigators in Stalin's time used physical methods of coercion? Of course, the historian must always regard his sources in a critical manner, and must check them and compare them with other materials. Once again, in the case of the Travniki guards, we are dealing with a large number of legal proceedings many of which took place after the death of Stalin. A number of the trials in the sixties and seventies were conducted openly, with debate between the opposing sides, and with the accused enjoying legal representation. At the time of these hearings much of what was discussed concerned the very same events that were dealt with in the trials in the forties and fifties. It is a simple though time-consuming matter to compare all these materials. One may also point out that investigators in the forties did not have any particular need to obtain evidence by beating it out of the defendant. It was particularly important for them to collect together all the information on the Travniki guards who were in hiding in the USSR or had surrendered to its allies. As a result, each and every Travniki guard was repeatedly interrogated in order to obtain as much material as possible about their conscription, names and surnames. It was clear to the investigators that those under investigation would be tried all the same, and that in such a situation resorting to physical violence would hardly bring about any significant benefits. Our proposition that Travniki guards in the forties and fifties were not subjected to beatings also gains support from the fact that a number of them determinedly rejected the accusation that they had participated in mass killing. They rejected the accusations both when under investigation and during their trial, and it must be said that it was not always the case that Soviet investigators were able to prove that they had participated in such actions. If the Travniki guards had been subjected to violence (as suspects had often been in the thirties) it would have been very difficult, if not impossible, for them to continue to reject the accusations. All this allows us to confirm that the body of documents on the Travniki guards that is to be found in the KGB archive is an important and reliable source, which will assist in the investigation and answering of our principal questions.[10]

The construction of the dedicated SS training camp at Travniki commenced in September 1941. In October Karl Streibel became its head, and the first recruits began their period of training. The necessity of creating such camps was brought about by the severe shortage of personnel that the German army came up against in the very first days of Operation Barbarossa. Casualties at the front, the huge expanses of territory captured and the length of supply lines, the quelling of local resistance and ambitious plans for the 'racial purification' of the occupied territories required more and more soldiers. To make up the shortfall the German command turned to the local population. In a circular, the Reichsführer of the SS and chief of the German police Heinrich Himmler made direct reference to the Ukrainian and Baltic peoples as being ethnically preferable.[11] Together with the *Volksdeutsche*, they, as a rule, were the first groups from which recruits were chosen, first from among those in the POW camps, and, a little later, from among the local population.

There was a standard procedure for recruitment in the camps. The prisoners were lined up on the parade ground, and were addressed by one of the police officers, who would invite them to become members of the German police. Volunteers would be formed into a group, and sent to the Travniki camp. Sometimes it would be done by simply inviting the stronger and fitter of the prisoners to the camp headquarters and offering them the opportunity of serving in the police force. In the

course of post-war hearings, a number of guards stated that right up to
their arrival at the SS camp, no one asked them what they themselves
wanted, and they themselves had no idea what they would be required
to do. It is clear that under such circumstances the degree to which the
recruits could be said to be 'volunteering' is diminished, as is the extent
of their personal activism. But even if one agrees with the version of
events that proposes the forced transfer of certain Travniki guards to
the SS camp, one has to say that they were presented with a clear
choice when it came to signing their personal questionnaire (*Personalbogen*)
and conscription papers (*Dienstverpflichtung*). A personal file was kept for
each recruit and this was given a number, and in the top-left corner a
picture was attached that bore this number. Beneath the picture would
be a thumbprint. All the basic information concerning the recruit would
be listed in the completed questionnaire. Each form would end with a
special three-line pronouncement, signed instead of swearing an oath,
which stated that the future *Wachmann* had given true information about
himself, that he was of Aryan stock and had no Jewish relatives, and
that he had never been a member of either the Communist Party or its
youth wing, the Komsomol. The terms of duty stated that each signatory
must serve in the SS and the German police, and was also obliged to
observe all the service's rules and regulations. It is important to point
out that the texts of the declaration and terms of service were not in
Ukrainian, but in Russian (with spelling mistakes) and German (without
mistakes).

The purpose of the Travniki camp was to prepare personnel
(*Wachmänner*) for the various subdivisions of the SS, mainly for the
guarding of concentration camps and death camps. Those who were
trained there were to guard and escort prisoners, to prevent them from
escaping, or to seek out those who had escaped. When needed, they
would be used to quell resistance among the local population, to fight
against partisans and engage in punitive actions. An overwhelming
majority of Travniki men took part in various anti-Jewish actions and a
number of them, some voluntarily and some under duress, participated
in mass shootings. In other words, the Travniki guards fulfilled all the
functions of the SS units and the German police in the war years.

The instructors and teachers at the camp were Germans, while
*Volksdeutsche* were brought in as interpreters. Only after some time had
elapsed did it become possible for those who had 'graduated' from the
camp and, moreover, distinguished themselves in their subsequent
postings, to be chosen to occupy posts in the lower echelons of the
camp hierarchy. Those arriving at the camp for the first time were
organised into study groups. The period of training was short, from
two to three months. The training programme was basically designed
to instruct trainees in the constitution of the guard service, marching

drill, firearms and physical training, the regulations concerning searches and arrests, and the rounding-up of partisans and the Jewish population. There was instruction in the German language and even fascist marching songs. There were also regular sessions of political study in the traditional Nazi style, with an accent on anti-communism and anti-Semitism. The kindling of hatred toward Jews was a major aspect of the training process. According to one witness, they were directly told: 'This race is to be destroyed.'[12]

The SS camp at Travniki had the structure of a military command post, based on an SS Guards battalion. The battalion consisted of a headquarters and several companies (between five and eight). Each company consisted of three platoons, each of which had three divisions of between eight and twelve persons. At any one time, 700 persons could be undergoing training. The commander of the guard battalion (Streibel) was also the commander of the camp as a whole. On enrolling in the school, the trainee would become a soldier in the battalion, which meant that he could be trained on a full-time basis, and in conditions that were as close as possible to the real thing. In the area of Travniki itself, alongside the training camp was a labour camp (*Zwangsarbeitslager*) where Soviet POWs and Jews were held. In the beginning, it was a rather small camp, but after a series of large scale anti-Jewish actions and deportations, towards the beginning of the autumn of 1943, around 6000 prisoners were being held there,[13] for the most part Jews. Almost all the trainees at Travniki took part in guarding this camp and thus learned the 'necessary skills' of their trade. On 3 November 1943 the overwhelming majority of the prisoners in the camp were shot.[14]

Upon enrolling in the school, the new recruits were accorded the titles Wachmann SS and Security Police and, on completion of their training, were assigned to posts in the various subdivisions of the SS and police, including the death camps at Auschwitz, Belzec, Majdanek, Sobibor and Treblinka. They were issued with firearms – Soviet-made rifles. In cases where a guard had served successfully and had sufficient knowledge of the German language, he would be promoted, and could become an Oberwachmann or Gruppenwachmann. Most received such a rank on completion of a short additional course of training, which again took place at Travniki, and some, especially *Volksdeutche*, were able to obtain the rank without further training.

The SS training camp at Travniki ceased its activities in June 1944, as a result of the Red Army advance. On 24 June the entire SS Guards battalion, together with the officers at the camp, left for the region around Krakow. There they forced the Polish population to build defensive fortifications and organised and guarded labour camps. In autumn 1944 and at the start of winter 1945 a small contingent of Travniki guards was sent to reinforce various nationalist groups such as the Ukrainian National Army, Vlasov's divisions and so on. In January 1945 the battalion was evacuated from Polish territory to the area around Dresden, in Germany. In accordance with orders from the command, the guards gave up their weapons and were set to work alongside the Germans, clearing up, burying and burning the corpses of the city's inhabitants who had been killed during the bombardment of the city by the Allied air forces. On 20 April 1945, with Soviet forces drawing near, the Travniki men were evacuated to Czechoslovakia, to the area of Karlsbad, where they were not given any particular duties and with the end of the war, the battalion disbanded.

In the course of two years and eight months, slightly less than 5000 persons had undergone training at the SS camp at Travniki. This is one of those rare cases in the history of the Second World War when it is possible to establish quite accurate figures. According to the archives of the camp itself and the results of the work of investigators, 5082 questionnaires were completed during the existence of the camp. It follows that one may assume that precisely this number of guards received their identification number. In actual fact, however, the true number of graduates of the training programme was 100–120 less than this figure. This is because, strange as it may seem, the administration of the camp was not carried out as accurately as it might have been, and there are gaps in the numbering of the questionnaires. It is not entirely clear whether this is as a result of mistakes made by a clerk, or whether certain numbers were deliberately reserved for a given group of trainees. There are two questionnaires for some guards, and as for others, we know their name and number and nothing more. However, even taking into account such lapses, it is possible to identify around 80 per cent of Travniki guards.

The overwhelming majority were from Soviet territory, and over half of them were Slavs. The main ethnic groups from which the guards were drawn were Ukrainian and German (*Volksdeutche*). Then there were Poles, Russians, Latvians and Lithuanians. There were also individuals with Tartar, Georgian, Armenian and Azerbaijani surnames. With the odd exception, the group consisted of men between the ages of eighteen and twenty-eight, with the majority of them coming from rural areas. I have been unable to find a single guard who had undergone higher education, though it is also true to say that none of them was illiterate.

What motivated these people when they agreed to serve in the German security police? This question was put to almost all Travniki guards in the course of the post-war trials. As a rule, if they had been POWs, they would cite the very harsh conditions in the camps, hunger and the desire to survive at any cost as the main factors that drove them to do what they did. Some feared that the Germans would punish them if they refused. Others said that they had lost their faith in the eventual victory of the Red Army. On the surface, it is easy to understand the state these young people must have been in, worn out by hunger and finding themselves faced with a difficult choice. However, we must also pay attention to the fact that German officers, while recruiting for the police, had contact with thousands of POWs, but each time chose only a few dozen of the volunteers.[15] It would follow that even the very harshest of conditions left a degree of freedom of choice, however small. It is another matter, however, when local citizens asked to serve as Travniki guards. In such cases, the self-interest involved is clear to see – the desire to stand out, to move up through the ranks of the service, to work and to receive the associated rewards, financial or otherwise. There is one surprising case where a sixteen-year-old teenager, Stepan Kopytyuk, concealing his true age, voluntarily became an SS guard. This young man was sent to serve as a guard at the notorious Janow camp in Lvov, where he took part in the beating and shooting of prisoners. Stepan's father tried to persuade his son to desert, but he refused and continued to serve in the battalion practically until the very end of the war, deserting only when he found himself in Czechoslovakia. The young man was not captured until 1951. At his trial, it was clear that he had not forgotten about his promised share of plunder and had taken part in sharing out possessions that had been confiscated from deported and executed Jews.[16]

To what degree did the Travniki guards think about the tasks they were entrusted with, and did they understand that in signing up to serve in the SS they were getting involved in something wrong? And if they understood, did they see any way out? Testimonies given by Travniki guards, both during investigation and during their trials, and their activities after the war, both in the Soviet Union and in the West, lead us to definite answers to these questions. In the first case, we can see that even the most ill-informed, hoodwinked and terrorised recruit could see, within one or two weeks of serving in the SS guard battalion, to what ends he was to be used. The German command never concealed these ends from their guards, and did use them in police, punitive, anti-Jewish and anti-partisan operations. Those who had agreed in the beginning and subsequently changed their minds, found themselves in a situation where the only way of avoiding carrying out their duties was to desert. During the war, 469 Travniki guards deserted, which accounts for around 9 per cent of the entire body of men. More likely than not, the true figure is actually slightly higher, because some of the guards deserted their posts in the last weeks of the war, too late for the German authorities to be able to register them. Of course, it would be a mistake to attribute all desertions to opposition to Nazi policy. The deserters included those who had run away from the Germans fearing punishment for thieving and drunkenness, as well as those who were desperately trying to change their documents and names in order to avoid capture by the Red Army. However, one cannot doubt that a certain percentage of deserters (though it is difficult to say how many there were) escaped from the Germans so as to avoid 'dirty work', and even joined up with the partisans.

Very many German documents bear witness to the fact that, concerning suicide and desertion, the SS command had the very same kind of disciplinary problems as they did with other national military groups, such as the ROA (*Russkaya Osvoboditel'naya Armiya* – Russian Liberation Army), the Kaminsky Brigade or the Eastern Legions.[17] In this sense, the Travniki guards were not some kind of monolithic, ideologically motivated force. Regardless of the fact that they were, in terms of age, social origins, place of training, place of service and rank very similar to each other, we find every possible shade of human behaviour in their motives and activities. Of course, for those who wanted to gain a position for themselves, advance through the ranks, and be rewarded for their efforts, the nature of service in the SS gave them all the opportunities they could wish for. And here it is extremely difficult to explain why people who had previously had nothing to do with any kind of crime became involved in evil actions together with the Nazis. I could find no evidence in the archives of any of the Travniki guards having joined the Germans on ideological or political grounds, and many of them only became acquainted with Nazi ideology at lectures in the camp school. Nor were there any committed nationalists, nor any convincing grounds to suspect the Travniki guards of having anti-Semitic sympathies before they entered the service of the SS. Nonetheless, none of this in any way got in the way of the greater part of the guards accepting the rules they were required to observe, or obediently carrying out the orders of the German command. The Travniki guards understood very well that they were required and expected to behave in a clearly defined manner with regard to Jews. As the guards themselves expressed in no uncertain terms, they were trained to work in camps where people who had no right to live were exterminated,[18] and behaving badly toward Jews was 'systematic and without any particular cause.'[19] Judging by much of the evidence, those at the school (though not all) were invited or ordered to take part in the shooting of Jews even while still undergoing training. The Travniki guards themselves believed that this was done as a way of testing them out, because there would always be a German officer attentively observing the executions. Other guards took part in shootings only on completion of their course of training.

In the course of the subsequent investigations, the majority of *Wachmänner* denied that they had taken any active role in mass killings, insisting that they had been standing guard or simply escorting the victims to the place of execution, while the shootings themselves were carried out by Germans. At the same time, they were quite prepared to admit that they had regularly beaten prisoners with rifle butts and rubber sticks, assuming, quite reasonably, that they would be punished less severely for such activities. Judging by trials that I know of, Soviet investigators and prosecutors were often unable to prove that the accused had personally taken part in mass executions. However, during their time serving in the various SS groups, at death camps and labour camps, Travniki guards became embroiled in many 'minor incidents', when they were required to employ repressive measures, up to and including killing. For example, they might be charged with the duty of preventing prisoners from escaping. If they did escape, then they had to shoot at them. Captured escapees were often shot, and some Travniki guards would do this voluntarily. After the escape of three Jews from a labour camp attached to an aviation factory 50 kilometres from Lublin, all the Travniki men guarding the camp took part in the search for the escapees. They caught only one, and brought him back to the camp, where the German commander 'invited volunteers from among the *Wachmänner* to shoot him. There turned out to be no shortage of volunteers, all the prisoners in the camp were lined up, and that Jew was shot in front of them.'[20] Here is another example. While prisoners were being marched, the guards had to drive on those who had fallen behind the column with their rifle butts. If they were covering a large distance, a number of prisoners would tire and be unable to continue. In such a case they would be shot. One of the Travniki guards reckoned that he had killed more than a hundred people in this way.[21]

Apart from this, a considerable proportion of guards took part in 'minor actions', such as shooting one or two Jewish families, a group of Jews in hiding, a partisan or several partisans. Many Travniki guards were incriminated in precisely these kinds of incidents in Soviet trials. When investigators came across such information in their preliminary investigations, they would try to establish in as fine detail as possible precisely what had happened. The time and place of the events would be established, the identities of those who had taken part, who shot at whom, what they did afterwards and so on. They would conduct cross-examinations and confront the accused. When necessary, the guards would be interrogated many times. As a result of this, we have today descriptions of incidents that have such detail and accuracy as to prevent any doubts arising about their authenticity. The reactions and behaviour of Travniki guards are notable. Here is a description of one of the shootings that came to light in the case of Aleksei Kulinitch. In September, 1942, eight Wachmänner headed by a German commander killed eleven citizens – eight men, one woman with a child of two or three years of age and a young girl of thirteen, who were being held in the local prison. One of the men was Polish, and the remainder were Jews. At around three o'clock in the afternoon Travniki guards took their victims to be shot, but while in transit the Pole attempted to escape. The guards started shooting and killed him. The remaining ten people were taken to the place of execution and were ordered to undress and lie on the ground close to one another. The men took off their jackets, trousers and boots, but the women burst into tears, and were shot in their dresses. They let loose a volley, at almost point-blank range, into the backs of their victims' heads and in the chest. The woman with the child was shot last of all. She was on her knees, pleading with the Travniki guards not to kill her child, whom she was holding in her arms. They shot both her and the child in that position. Afterwards, the Travniki guards returned home, and the local police dug a hole in the ground and buried the corpses.[22] The accused confused some details of the events, but remembered the order of the shootings surprisingly accurately. They recounted the shootings as if they were describing some kind of routine 'work', which simply had to be done. There was no hint of doubt, no hesitation and no pity – they were ordered to do it and they did it. I have been unable to find any case in the archives of documentary evidence where any of the Travniki guards who served the Germans until the end of the war failed, or moreover refused, to take part in executions.[23] Even if one member of a team of guards did not participate in an execution when the others did, then the reasons were far from moral. For example, one of the accused stated that he had not taken part in a shooting because 'it was his day off'.[24] Another, who had avoided participation in one particular shooting, said that if the Germans had ordered him to shoot Jews, then he 'would of course have carried out the order'.[25]

It is difficult to establish whether Travniki guards experienced any sense of guilt, or whether they were tormented by their consciences after the war. At trials in the USSR, some of them said that they lived constantly with the thought that they would one day have to answer for their actions. However, it is very difficult to say how genuine such pronouncements were. One can say for sure that Travniki guards were afraid of being exposed and did everything possible to conceal their pasts. They changed their names, forged their personal documents, filled out forms incorrectly and often changed their place of residence. While some collaborators, having fled to the West (Ukrainian Nationalists, members of Vlasov's ROA, Latvian, Lithuanian and Estonian legionnaires and so on), conducted themselves in quite an active manner in the Cold War years, talking of their 'necessary' co-operation with the Nazis in the name of 'the struggle against communism',[26] Travniki guards attempted to melt into the local population, and lived quietly and unnoticed. Arguments about their 'tragic youths', 'the struggle for freedom' and 'KGB plots' only started to come to the surface when they were under investigation. Those Wachmänner who attempted to hide on Soviet territory experienced the most unsettling of lives. The Soviet special services pursued them right up to the last days of the Soviet Union itself.

Having turned up in the filtration camps, many Travniki guards passed themselves off as prisoners in Nazi concentration camps, or as eastern workers. If Soviet counter-intelligence officers were unable to bring to light any compromising information after initial interrogations, then the SS guard in question, concealing his past, was quite likely to be recruited once again into the Red Army, and sent back from the front upon demobilisation. In precisely such a surprising way, individual Travniki guards were, in the course of a few years, able to serve in both the German and the Soviet armies, and even received decorations from both sides. This, however, helped none of them. Soviet investigators tirelessly investigated all camp guards, and a detailed card index was built up on each and every Travniki guard, and, beginning in 1944, the long process of bringing them to trial was set in motion. Judging from my own approximate data, there were over 140 trials in the Soviet Union between 1944 and 1987. It is entirely possible that the actual figure is slightly higher, but unfortunately, because of secrecy, not all the relevant materials are available to the modern researcher, and it is impossible to give accurate figures at this time. There was also one trial held in Warsaw in 1954. In the mid-1970s a West German court initiated proceedings against the head of the SS camp, Karl Streibel, and his subordinates. The trial, which took place in 1976, found nothing criminal in their actions, and they were acquitted.

Co-operation between Western and Soviet special services in the exposing and investigation of war criminals did not last for long. The allies handed over Soviet citizens who had borne arms on behalf of the German army to the USSR authorities only until 1948. Among the deportees, Soviet counter-intelligence uncovered several dozen Travniki guards. With the onset of ideological and political confrontation, forced extradition came to an end, and one can therefore say that the Cold War quite literally saved many of the Nazis' accomplices from any kind of litigation. Nonetheless, over forty years, the KGB regularly informed their Western colleagues about possible war criminals living in their countries. The social climate began to change in the 1980s, and, as a result, special investigation departments were set up in the USA, Canada, Great Britain and Australia, which set about looking into the suspicious pasts of many of their citizens, including former Travniki guards. These departments carried out an enormous amount of work, but nowhere did their efforts bear fruit in terms of a guilty verdict where Travniki guards were concerned. A unique, very public and contradictory case was the trial of John Demjanjuk in Israel.

Demjanjuk, concealing the fact that he had served in the SS, settled in the USA. When American investigators became interested in him they turned to Israeli specialists and former death-camp inmates for assistance. Some of the former prisoners, on seeing his photograph, recognised him as one of the most brutal of guards at the Treblinka camp, who was known by the nickname of 'Ivan the Terrible'. The fact that he had concealed information about himself on arriving in the USA, along with the testimony of witnesses, was enough to persuade the American court that Demjanjuk should be extradited and passed into the hands of the Israeli justice system. On 25 April 1988 he was sentenced to death, but on 29 July 1993 he was acquitted. It turned out that he had been confused with another SS guard, Ivan Marchenko, whom the prisoners at Treblinka had dubbed 'Ivan the Terrible' because of his sadism and cruelty. The Jewish lawyer who had won Demjanjuk's release called the whole process a 'Soviet plot', despite the fact that he had obtained the most valuable documents in the defence of his client from the Soviet authorities, including the KGB. If such a plot had indeed existed, then the lawyer would not only have not received any of the documents, but would not have been granted even an entry visa for the USSR. Because Demjanjuk had been acquitted of the main charge, his right-wing supporters announced that he was completely innocent and had nothing to do with the SS or the Travniki.[27] This contradicts the archives and the testimony of Travniki guards who mention Demjanjuk. Had the will been there, it would, even in the 1980s, have been possible to find his former colleagues from the SS Guards battalion, but in the conditions of ideological confrontation that prevailed at the time, and with the absence of diplomatic relations between Israel and the Soviet Union, co-operation between lawyers was practically impossible. Ironically, Demjanjuk spent around eight years in prison, five of them spent in the expectation of being sentenced to death, roughly the same length of time that former Travniki guards who had not personally taken part in killings had spent in Soviet prisons prior to their amnesty.

Considering the fate of these young people who came to be the Nazis' cohorts, it is a simple matter to explain it all away as the result of the upheaval of war and to consider them to be victims of circumstance. But that is not how it was. That particular version of events is contradicted by the fact that tens of thousands of POWs refused to serve in the German police and army. Even in the most difficult circumstances there is still a choice, and the Travniki guards made their choice consciously, first by signing their questionnaire, then by swearing allegiance, and subsequently by training with an SS battalion. Above all it is important to understand that, however things might have turned out for the Travniki guards themselves, it is not *they* that were the victims, but those whom they watched over and escorted, those whom they beat up and killed. Travniki guards were selected and trained for entirely concrete purposes, and therefore they were an important supporting element of Nazi policy. They assisted the Third Reich in carrying out one of its central tasks – the annihilation of the Jewish population and their political opponents. Without the aid of collaborators such as the Travniki guards, the Nazis would never have succeeded in killing as many as they did.

Translated from Russian by Trevor Goronwy

# 16

## The SS-20 Missile –
## Why Were You Pointing at Me?

JAMES CANT

### Introduction

I spent many of my teenage years in the early 1980s worrying about matters well beyond my control. Apparently not content with the usual travails of adolescence, I sought to understand the fractious nature of UK politics, the perennial bad health that afflicted my home city of Glasgow and the Cold War – especially the Cold War. It seemed that the BBC current affairs programme *Panorama* used the same map to illustrate Glasgow whenever the city was featured in one of its programmes. It was always covered by a large red dot. One week this would signify its politics; another week its incidence of cardiac mortality. But this all seemed rather incidental as the final red dot represented the expected effect of a nuclear blast.

We were assured – Russian efficiency was more highly thought of in those days – that everything within a ten-mile radius of the centre of Glasgow would be incinerated. Glasgow was far from being alone on the map of red dots; they obscured most British towns and cities. But as an angst-ridden youth whose family home lay only seven miles from the centre of Glasgow, it was that unwelcome rosette that caught my attention. The author of my demise – I was frequently told – would be the SS-20 missile.

My nemesis would eventually become my old friend as I sought to discover *why* the Soviet Union had decided to develop the missile whose deployment so fuelled the fires of the Cold War and led – in no small part – to the disintegration of the Soviet state.

### The SS-20 Missile[1]

The SS-20 medium-range ballistic missile (MRBM) was considered to be one of the definitive weapons of the Cold War. The perceived threat posed by the SS-20, and the systems subsequently deployed to counter its strengths (among them Pershing II and Cruise missiles), were pivotal to East–West relations during the 1970s and 1980s. The SS-20 deployment therefore affords a unique prism through which to examine Soviet defence decision making of that era.

First deployment of a new Soviet mobile MRBM, the RSD-10, began in 1976. The RSD-10 soon became known by the US designation SS-20. The system was developed to redress a perceived NATO advantage in the sphere of theatre nuclear weapons (TNFs), an advantage that was expected to be enhanced by the new generation of such weapons systems then being developed by the United States. The SS-20 boasted impressive performance attributes and was viewed with considerable concern by NATO analysts. It was a mobile missile, transported on something that resembled the large cranes we see rumbling through the streets from time to time. Naturally this mobility made it much more difficult to track and destroy than static, silo-based systems. Consider how difficult it was to track down a few mobile Scuds in the open expanse of the Iraqi desert during the 1991 Gulf War, with a monopoly of air and satellite cover, using the best troops the West had to offer. How much less chance would there have been of detecting – let alone attacking – the many hundred missiles scattered and concealed across the Soviet Union and throughout the Warsaw Pact. Not that the missiles had to venture far from home – their estimated range was 4000 kilometres, which meant that they could be targeted on Western Europe and much of China from within the Soviet Union itself. It gave the Soviet Union the 'swing capacity' to threaten its erstwhile Communist neighbour in the East and Europe in the West with a single missile force. While the chances of detecting the SS-20 were slim, the chances of destroying it before it was launched were slimmer still. Unlike most Soviet missiles of the Scud era the SS-20 was powered by solid fuel. This was an enormous leap forward for the Soviets, who for years had lagged behind the US in this vital aspect of missile technology. Liquid fuel was inherently volatile. Loading it into missiles took many dangerous hours. For most Soviet missiles, once primed, they had to launch within a few hours or the perilous fuelling process had to be reversed. Flight time from the western Soviet Union to Great Britain was estimated to have been in the region of 15–20 minutes. Upon arrival, the missile could deposit three 150 kiloton warheads on given targets with a degree of accuracy unsurpassed by any previous Soviet missile systems. Its Circular Probability of Error (CEP) was a mere 400 metres.

The deployment of a new generation of theatre systems (SS-20s, Pershing and Cruise) by both sides ensured TNFs came to hold a place of vital symbolic political importance in the ensuing East–West confrontation and the deep divisions within Western Europe itself.

Their deployment was the principal symptom and cause of a dramatic deterioration in East–West relations, to a degree that had not been in evidence for almost two decades.[2] The SS-20's impact upon the Soviet Union's geopolitical relations meant it possessed a unique degree of political importance among Soviet weaponry developments. It came to be viewed as a definitive weapon system of the period. Its decade-long development cycle and apparently uneventful progression through the decision-making chain corresponded precisely with the period that has been characterised as the 'golden era' of defence resource allocation and civil-military relations[3] and also witnessed the acknowledged rise of Brezhnev himself to a position of pre-eminence within the political leadership. The Soviet Union's decision to develop and deploy the SS-20 missile afforded researchers an unsurpassed opportunity to investigate the characteristics of the bureaucratic and interpersonal dynamics that formed the basis of Soviet defence decision making at the height of Brezhnev's tenure.

## *Researching the SS-20*

Russian archival sources can offer only limited information about the true nature of Soviet defence decision making because so much was based upon interpersonal relations and complex institutional interaction. Decisions taken on the basis of a telephone call between top officials or within the confines of a smoke-filled room frequently left little or no documentary record. Against this backdrop, the recollections of key figures within the former Soviet ruling elite were vital in piecing together the Soviet leadership's decision to develop the SS-20 missile system.

Professor Erickson was the key to this process. Through him, I was able to make contact with several key players – American and Russian – pivotal to the story of the SS-20. Among these was Dr Greg Varhall (Lieutenant Colonel USAF, ret.), an arms-control expert who served for three years as an advisor to the Office of the Secretary of Defense on the US delegation at the Nuclear and Space Talks in Geneva. He also backstopped the DST talks and the ABM treaty in Washington and also served as an American INF (Intermediate Nuclear Forces) treaty inspector who oversaw the elimination of INF weapons including the SS-20 in the Soviet Union. His Russian opposite number for much of this process was Dr Alexander G. Savel'yev, the vice president of the independent Institute for National Security and Strategic Studies in Moscow. He participated in the Soviet–American Nuclear and Space Talks in Geneva as an advisor to the Soviet delegation and as the representative of the Academy of Sciences of the USSR. General Lieutenant Nikolai N. Detinov was a high-ranking official in the Central

Committee's Defence Secretariat. He played a critical role in the formulation of the Soviet position at arms-control negotiations from their inception in the late 1960s until the early 1990s. Detinov was one of the genuine 'back-room boys' to whom Brezhnev would adjourn to consult during his summit meetings with US presidents. He was involved in the SALT talks in 1969–72 and participated directly at the Vladivostok summit, between First Secretary Brezhnev and President Ford in November 1974, and the Helsinki conference of 1976. He subsequently participated in the next generation of arms-control negotiations, the Soviet–American Nuclear and Space Talks (START, INF and DST) in 1985–91.

The information I received from these people was priceless; but I was only able to gain access to these high-level contacts because of John Erickson's reputation on both sides of the former Iron Curtain. He was held in uniquely high esteem by both sides, in part for the depth of his knowledge of Russian military affairs, but also for the personal integrity that characterised all of his work. The result was a sense of trust and candour from the sources usually characterised by guarded reticence. This was also evident in the record of interviews with a remarkable array of former Soviet officials, which came to be known as the 'Edinburgh Conversations'.[4] Its participants represented a veritable *Who's Who* of the Soviet defence leadership. The unstinting respect afforded to John Erickson by both sides extended to the 'Erickson Partnership'; and it was a 'partnership' in the truest sense. John Erickson never failed to stress the fact that he was, with his wife Ljubica, involved in a joint effort of academic research that spanned several decades. No one who had the pleasure of watching the partnership in action could doubt the sincerity or the accuracy of his view. When I first wrote to John Erickson, it was much more in hope than expectation. I was delighted just to receive a reply. What I did receive was so much more: numerous informal tutorial sessions in Edinburgh, which taught me more in an afternoon than I could read in a month.

## The Development of the SS-20

So why did the Soviet Union decide to develop the SS-20? There are many theories.

'Hawks' portrayed the SS-20's deployment as further evidence of the Soviet Union's insatiable hunger for global hegemony. Richard Perle was particularly aroused by the issue and was a firm advocate of deploying Cruise and Pershing II missiles in response. Other commentators characterised the Soviet action as a direct response to the many hundreds of medium-range nuclear systems that surrounded its borders, both East and West, and its visceral fear of another surprise attack.

Another theory highlighted the SALT treaties as an unwitting catalyst. They had placed numerical limitations upon both sides' long-range nuclear forces. Medium-range theatre forces had been a thorny issue on which neither side could agree. Eventually they had been dropped from the SALT agendas in pursuit of, albeit limited, consensus. This had apparently angered the Soviet leadership, who viewed NATO's superiority in this field with considerable concern. Soviet diplomats confided to their American counterparts that Brezhnev had been forced to 'spill blood' to gain the military's acceptance of this key omission from SALT II – in this context, was the development of the SS-20 a *quid pro quo*? Moreover, with superpower proliferation capped in long-range systems a new competition via their shorter-range siblings was the inevitable consequence. So, it was argued, that as the ink dried on the SALT II treaty, attention was turned with an almost indecent haste to the development of the SS-20 by the Soviets – and Cruise and Pershing II by the Americans.

'Missile spotters' had their own explanation for the SS-20 – a macabre sense of recycling the weapons of Armageddon. The SS-20, they argued was the 'son' of the SS-16 ICBM. The SS-16 was an unsuccessful project, which was now banned under SALT II in any case because of intercontinental range. Components and technology were then reconfigured to develop the medium range SS-20. Indeed both missiles were portrayed as part of a family of missiles, all supposedly emerging from the Nadiradze Design Bureau, which had apparently been granted monopoly status in seeking to develop solid-fuel missiles.

Military strategists argued that the SS-20 was designed to meet the emerging desire for a more sophisticated response to war with the West. Rather than coming out with all guns blazing from the outset, a significant revision seemed to emerge in Soviet nuclear strategy from the late 1960s onwards. This caveat acknowledged that war with the West might not go nuclear from the outset. The invulnerability of systems like the SS-20 – and the second-strike capability that it afforded – was a prerequisite of this more measured response.

These explanations seemed to make sense and dovetailed well together in terms of timing and rationale. The development of the SS-20 appeared a measured and logical response to the geopolitical context: the perceived threat to the USSR and the availability of relevant technology. But did the evidence that emerged from the Russian side support any of these interpretations? Did one factor predominate or was there a complex interaction between them? How many of them were false avenues, representing Western analysts' desire to seek to rationalise Soviet actions rather than the (un)known facts? Further research into these causal factors corrected a number of important technical and factual details but, for the most part, reaffirmed their *prima facie* validity as explanatory rationales for the development of the SS-20. It also demonstrated – ironically – that the missile's development owed much to coincidence and good fortune within the defence sector, which was riven with personal rivalries and alliances and institutional agendas.

## Was there a New Soviet Strategy for Theatre Conflict?

The nature of the operational demands placed upon Soviet TNFs by the evolving theatre nuclear strategy was traditionally credited as being of prime importance to the development of the SS-20. This development was claimed to have heralded a new era in theatre strategy because, for the first time since the deployment of nuclear forces, the Soviets accepted the possibility that the onset of a future conflagration with the West might not lead to the immediate use of nuclear weapons. While Soviet strategy did indeed evolve to incorporate the *possibility* of a conventional introduction, this course remained but one option of many and the shadow of nuclear engagement continued to loom large. Even in the event of a conventional introduction there was little confidence that conflict would remain at this level for any length of time. The relative weakness of NATO conventional forces and the Limited Nuclear Options (LNO) considered in the strategies of Flexible Response and the Schlesinger Doctrine coalesced to engender the belief that NATO would be forced to escalate to the employment of nuclear weapons.

Moreover the process of evolution that served to produce this revision was itself protracted, and occurred in the face of considerable opposition emanating from members of the military 'old guard'. The more detailed consideration of the nature and extent of the strategic revision afforded by interviews with former members of the Soviet elite reinforced this interpretation. Considerable ferment existed within the upper echelons of the military over the likely nature of a future conflict. In addition it was paralleled by a process of disengagement on the part of the political leadership in the formulation of strategy and doctrine which accelerated during the course of Brezhnev's tenure. Western scholars were largely unaware of the level of opposition from Defence Minister Marshal Grechko and his allies towards the concepts of conventional or limited nuclear conflict with the West. They remained wedded to the notion of a pre-emptive nuclear strike as soon as conflict appeared imminent. While Western accounts often portrayed Grechko as possessing a sceptical attitude towards the merits of *détente* and as an advocate of the retention of military expenditure at maximum levels, few gauged the true extent of his ideological conservatism.[5]

Grechko stridently attacked the notion of a second strike posture and its attendant ideological and technological ramifications, while the head of the Strategic Rocket Forces, Tolubko, was attested to have maintained a similarly hardline perspective. Nor was Grechko averse to confronting powerful vested interests in the pursuit of the adoption of his favoured strategic principles. His opposition to mobile ICBMs, and the assured retaliation strategy they would have engendered, placed him at loggerheads with the political leadership and the proponents of strategic innovation within the General Staff. In addition to this, his attempts to prevent the development of mobile ICBMs placed him in opposition to Ustinov and the Defence Council as a whole.[6]

General-Colonel Danilevich[7] was in a position to offer a definitive account of the evolution of Soviet nuclear strategy. His career as a general staff officer spanned more than a quarter of a century and included Brezhnev's reign. Danilevich characterised the Soviet strategy of the early 1960s as a period of 'nuclear euphoria',[8] premised upon the mass employment of nuclear forces in pre-emptive strikes. However, a sense of conservatism and realism returned to Soviet strategic analyses with the advent of the Brezhnev regime, accompanied by an appreciation of the likely effects of nuclear exchange. The strengthening of the SRF (Strategic Rocket Forces), particularly the addition of SLBMs, and evolving US strategic concepts enabled the development of more sophisticated strategic concepts by Soviet military planners. Danilevich singled out the deployment of the SS-11 in 1970 as a watershed event. Its markedly superior response ability, allied to the 'over the horizon' radars developed at this time, enabled Soviet planners for the first time to consider an assured second strike option.[9]

Danilevich acknowledged the impact that such Western concepts as Flexible Response and the Schlesinger Doctrine had upon the development of Soviet strategy despite their repeated rejection in Soviet public pronouncements. By the mid-1970s, the principle of graduated responses was increasingly coming to hold sway within Soviet nuclear strategy.[10] Add to this the growing influence of the concept of a conventional introduction to a future conflict which was 'officially documented' in the 1974–6 period. Its possible time span increased from a matter of hours to 7–8 days, to its final form, the advance to the Rhine, an operation that was anticipated to be of several weeks' duration. While Danilevich expressed his confidence that Soviet forces could prevail in such an exchange he, like the vast majority of his colleagues, anticipated an eventual strategic nuclear escalation.[11]

The pursuit of a more sophisticated array of strategic options was confined to an elite group *within* the general staff and neither research institutes outwith the general staff's direct authority nor the service branches themselves were involved in these rarefied proceedings. The establishment of strategic principles was effectively devoid of input on the part of the political leadership as Brezhnev and his colleagues increasingly disengaged from the formulation of military policy. When called upon to 'press the button' at the culmination of a large-scale exercise, a visibly shaken Brezhnev repeatedly sought assurances from the officers present that he was not being tricked into 'starting the real thing'. This provided an eloquent expression of the near-complete withdrawal of the General Secretary from the process of military decision making in general and matters nuclear in particular that marked the last decade of his tenure.

Nor were those responsible for weaponry production involved in the intellectual debate as to how they might be used. Dmitry Ustinov was undoubtedly the 'magnate' of military production and possessed a sound grasp of weaponry's technical aspects. But he showed little interest in the affairs of military science and made no attempt to avail himself of the direction of strategic development pursued by the general staff. By the time of his accession to the post of Defence Minister in 1976, Ustinov had firmly established himself as the pre-eminent figure in the formulation of Soviet weaponry procurement policy and consequently his personal policy preferences became the key determinant of the form of defence decision making. Ustinov appears as a rather enigmatic figure. He was possessed of a sound grasp of the technical aspects of weaponry development, but generally lacked an appreciation of their associated military implications. He was a figure who facilitated the development of a raft of new weaponry technologies while a First Deputy Chairman in the 1960s, yet presided over the growth of stifling production practices in the following decade. Paradoxically, he retained a fearsome reputation from his wartime activities and his authority was unquestioned by defence industrialists. Yet at the same time his relations with them contained a certain ambivalence. This led to a leniency and the acceptance of systems whose performance fell well short of optimum operational capabilities and the manufacture of surplus stockpiles through additional production runs that were superfluous to require-ments. This dichotomy came to the fore as Ustinov's rise endowed him with still greater influence upon the decision-making process and reached a critical juncture in the wake of his appointment as Minister of Defence. As General Danilevich observed, 'he acted as the client, the contractor and the customer. In practice, his position was such that he was often forced to compromise with himself. He stood on the edge of the blade and waffled in both directions.'[12]

Moreover, analytical assessments of the likely effects of a nuclear conflict were purposely ignored by the political leadership and directors of defence enterprises throughout the 1970s. This contrasts sharply with the traditional portrayal of Soviet military thinking as the linear process of doctrinal and strategic formulation via a continual and unconstrained interaction between the military and political hierarchies. Against such a background, where the revision process continued apace, virtually devoid of direction on the part of the political leadership, opponents of the revision enjoyed considerable latitude in the expression of their scepticism, as was reflected in the military press. The ensuing revision was thus gradual in nature and cautious in extent and was associated with a generational transition within the military leadership itself.

### Deficiencies of Existing Theatre Forces

Despite this disagreement on the future course of nuclear strategy, both conservatives and innovators alike would have recognised the gross deficiencies in the existing TNF force of SS-4s/SS-5s and the merits of the development of a system possessed of the operational capabilities displayed by the SS-20. Those who expected that any conflict would be nuclear in character from the outset would welcome a system whose rapid response ensured it could meet the requirements of the launch-on-warning strategy that had been adopted in 1969. The vast majority of their colleagues who acknowledged the *possibility* of a conventional introduction anticipated eventual resort to nuclear employment. Rapid response was of equal importance to the proponents of such a strategy in the event of such a contingency. During the conventional period the SS-20's mobility and solid-fuel propulsion would have endowed it with the attribute of mobility, which would have markedly improved its survivability – essential to preserve TNF potential during the anticipated period of attack by NATO conventional forces.

Thus wherever they stood on the broad spectrum of anticipated nuclear strategy, Soviet military planners would be expected to have favoured the development of a new TNF system possessing the type of performance capabilities with which the SS-20 was endowed. Defence Minister Grechko's reported opposition to the development of mobile and solid-fuelled systems was said to have stemmed from his suspicion that possession of them might have tempted the political leadership to forsake a first-strike policy. This would serve as ample testament to the vehemence of Grechko's views on this issue, as the pursuit of such a weaponry procurement policy premised solely upon such a desire would have denied the Soviet Union a valuable enhancement of its strategic potential. One might assume that Grechko's views would have engendered considerable disquiet, even among fellow strategic conservatives who would have been expected to have recognized the potentially vital role that a force of SS-20s might play within the European theatre *regardless* of the means and timing of escalation to nuclear employment. Thus while the nature and extent of the revision of Soviet theatre strategy requires reappraisal, the potential importance of the SS-20's role within either strand of operational principles remains undiminished. There was therefore an apparently strong strategic rationale for the development and deployment of a new generation of TNFs, endowed with attributes of mobility and enhanced responsiveness to meet the operational needs perceived to exist by Soviet strategists of various hues.

## The Politics of Defence

Intra-elite relations and institutional rivalries lay at the heart of Soviet weaponry procurement. This was increasingly the case during the development cycle of the SS-20 itself, which coincided with a vital transitional period in Soviet intra-elite relations and defence decision-making behaviour. Brezhnev's tenure had been marked at the outset by its collegiate style of decision making. The pursuit of such elite consensus was particularly prevalent in the realm of defence policy. This new approach manifested itself in the sphere of strategic formulation, through the re-affirmation of the traditional Soviet precept of 'mixed forces'.[13] The military leadership in particular enjoyed an enhanced status within the Soviet ruling elite in the immediate aftermath of Khrushchev's ouster. The appointment of Marshal Grechko as Minister of Defence in 1967, in preference to Ustinov, served to add still more lustre to the military leadership's status and marked the zenith of its influence upon Soviet defence decision making.

In terms of resource allocation, the first decade of Brezhnev's tenure was justifiably characterised as a 'golden age' for the Soviet defence sector. Both the military services and the defence industries benefited from the extraordinary generosity displayed by the party leadership in the realm of weaponry procurement. Traditional branches of the military continued to enjoy significant levels of patronage while the decade witnessed a remarkable growth in the nuclear arsenal of the Strategic Rocket Forces. The expansion of Soviet strategic forces occurred on such a scale that, by the end of the 1960s, the Soviet Union had effectively overcome the United States' huge advantage in strategic forces and had forced the United States' entry into the SALT process.

The military hierarchy's achievement of effective autonomy in the development of military science and the formulation of strategy coalesced with the zenith of their influence upon the weaponry pro-curement process. This took a tangible form in the role played by the Scientific-Technical Committee of the general staff. It operated autonomously within the general staff until the mid-1960s, overseeing the issuing of contracts for weaponry production by individual service branches and possessing the right to veto on technical grounds. The Scientific-Technical Committee was also responsible for the detailed planning and direction of military research programmes as a whole and the committee's support was a prerequisite to the sanctioning of new projects by the chief of the general staff. Following restructuring in the mid-1960s, the committee was incorporated into the general staff's Directorate for Armaments and was placed under the authority of the Deputy Defence Minister for Armaments. The Directorate of Armaments continued to play a pivotal role in shaping weapons programmes and funding until the mid-1970s and its recommendations to the general staff and to the VPK formed the basis of the funding allocation provided to development projects by the Minister of Defence, the general staff, and the VPK. By the close of the 1960s the general staff had attained a position of pre-eminence in the determination of military procurement policy and enjoyed *de jure* authority upon this vital aspect of defence decision making.

Ironically, while the impressive degree of autonomy in the deliberation of military science was consolidated over the coming decade through Brezhnev's disengagement from the process, so too did the military suffer a dramatic diminution in its ability to influence the course of the weaponry procurement process for much the same reason. In this arena, the dominant position was assumed by Dmitry Ustinov and his cohorts within the defence production sector. Ustinov's growing influence in the determination of defence policy was built upon a long association with both the defence sector and Brezhnev himself. This was signalled by Ustinov's rise to prominence in the development of the Soviet Union's SALT negotiating position. It is instructive to note that, although Ustinov at this point possessed neither the status accorded to a minister nor state committee chairman, it was he who chaired the Big Five. This was despite the membership of both the Defence and Foreign ministers and the heads of the powerful VPK and KGB on this committee. This served as testament to his considerable influence in defence decision making at the end of the 1960s and was to prove portentous as still more power was assumed by Ustinov throughout the 1970s. Ustinov's progress was at the expense of Defence Minister Grechko in particular and the general staff in general. Indeed, Grechko's attainment of full membership status of the Politburo in 1973 was largely devoid of policymaking, as that body had, by then, relinquished effective control of defence decision making.

The dramatic deterioration in Brezhnev's health in the early 1970s served to accelerate the devolution of decision-making authority upon a *troika* of the governing elite, in which the military leadership found itself increasingly marginalised. The Vladivostok summit of November 1974 was identified as the last major event at which Brezhnev was able to function in a competent manner. Brezhnev's health quickly deteriorated, and culminated in a major heart attack in 1976. This effectively signalled the end of Brezhnev's participation in a functioning leadership capacity. From this point onwards Ustinov, Gromyko and Andropov emerged as the principal figures who filled the power vacuum left by Brezhnev's incapacitation. Their associated sections of the Soviet bureaucracy similarly expanded the scope of their activities and assumed responsibility for defence procurement policies. Emergent policy proposals were accorded Politburo acceptance as a matter of course. The new leadership quorum possessed effective autonomy in the formulation of Soviet policy, thus reducing significantly the influence of the military hierarchy. Professor Mstislav Keldysh, the President of the Academy of Sciences, also played an ever-increasing role in the process of weaponry procurement. Keldysh had served as the General Secretary's principal advisor on matters of military doctrine and strategy, and had been instrumental in the formulation of the Soviet Union's revised retaliatory strategy in 1969. His substantial influence upon the General Secretary was well attested and he increasingly acted as a spokesman for Brezhnev as the General Secretary's health declined.

While it is impossible to offer a precise time scale of the cyclical fluctuations of military influence upon defence policymaking, is clear that it reached something of a zenith during the Soviet Union's large-scale strategic build-up in the mid-to-late 1960s and was accompanied by a consensus among the political and military leadership in support of this policy option. However, the strategic revision, which emerged at the close of the decade, coincided with planning for the next generation of missile systems. At this point there seems to have been a divergence of interests between the military leadership and the defence industrialists. Significantly, the defence industry's interests prevailed apparently without exception on the occasion of such a *contretemps*. The Defence Industry Department of the Central Committee was identified as the principal vehicle through which the defence industrialists sought to bend weaponry procurement policy to their own ends. Ministers responsible for armaments production, chief designers and political officers dominated the proceedings of this committee. In its proceedings, the interests of the defence industry held sway with the department over those of the general staff or the Ministry of Defence without exception.[14]

Ustinov's emerging ascendancy among the defence decision-making elite was accompanied by the growing influence of the principal players of the Soviet defence industries. This eclipsed that enjoyed by either the Ministry of Defence or the general staff, whose reduced station was further evidenced by its increasing domination of policy preferences and the VPK's near-monopolistic supply of technical information to the Soviet leadership. Increasingly the VPK alone oversaw development programmes from their inception through their technical and strategic evaluation to their culmination through the determination of the size and location of the production run.

The procedural reforms that emerged in the wake of Ustinov's accession to the post of Minister of Defence in 1976 served to swing the balance of power still further in favour of the defence industries. While Grechko's personal influence within the leadership had diminished markedly in the years prior to his death the General Staff Directorate of Armaments Orders had played a central role in shaping weapons programmes and funding prior to 1976. At this point in time Ustinov introduced a revised process which reduced the general staff's role and greatly expanded the VPK's influence. Henceforth funds were allocated directly to the VPK and individual service branches applied to the VPK for funding in addition to the traditional source, the Ministry of Defence. The Directorate of Armaments was removed from the general staff's authority and made an independent Ministry of Defence Directorate headed by Deputy Minister of Defence Shabanov. Significantly however, its *executive* role was removed and replaced by a mere *advisory* one. While General Detinov stressed the continued role played by the Scientific-Technical Committee in the wake of the reorganisation, his military counterparts were unswerving in the import they accorded this development. The direct allocation of funds to the VPK unleashed the military-industrial complex and circumvented the general staff's role in weaponry procurement policymaking. Both the VPK and the Central Committee Defence Department were viewed as having been motivated principally by their desire to represent the interests of the defence sector.

The vested interests of the defence sector had broadly coalesced with those of the military leadership during the rapid build-up of strategic forces during the second half of the 1960s. The adoption of more sophisticated strategic concepts held attendant requirements in terms of strategic force structure and weaponry performance, which placed a heavy emphasis upon qualitative advances within the next generation of Soviet missile systems. By this point in time, however, the design conservatism that was endemic throughout the long-established sections of the Soviet defence sector had also permeated through the ballistic missile sector. The tangible result was that the missile design bureaux mirrored the defence sector as a whole through the production of a host of weapons systems that were often ill-equipped to perform the designated tasks of Soviet strategy. As the 1970s progressed and the sectional interests of the defence producers became increasingly dominant via Ustinov's associated rise to pre-eminence, the practice of weapon-system replication became endemic in Soviet defence production. Design conservatism combined with sectional self-advancement to ensure that the defence sector produced numerous units of weapons systems of often dubious operational merit. The preference for quantitative increase over qualitative improvement in Soviet defence production behaviour grew inexorably and reached its culmination by the end of the decade. However Ogarkov's subsequent fate seemed to provide a further indication of the inherent strength of the defence sector's institutional interests.

The bureaucratic and intra-elite relations which formed the backdrop to defence decision making are vital in understanding Soviet weaponry procurement of this era. This was all too often neglected by Western analyses of the SS-20. The SS-20's development cycle was peculiar, indeed perhaps unique, and sat 'on the cusp' of an evolving transition. The programme's inception coincided with the zenith of the military leadership's input into the defence decision-making process, while the course of its development through to the point of deployment coincided with a dramatic diminution in the military's input into weaponry procurement. The SS-20 undoubtedly met the operational requirements of evolving Soviet nuclear strategy. It possessed performance characteristics that offered flexibility and invulnerability on a scale that was unrivalled by any previous Soviet system. It provided the Soviet Union with the ability to match NATO's TNF potential for the first time and dramatically reduce Moscow's susceptibility to a surprise 'decapitating' strike. Yet this weapon emerged almost incidentally from the Soviet procurement system. While it might be overstating the case to describe the SS-20 as 'an accident of birth', it is ironic that it matched the operational requirements defined by the Soviet military at a time when their influence upon the procurement process lay at its lowest ebb.

# 17

# Cold Wars New and Old
# Post-Cold War Perspectives on the
# Washington Conference, 1921–1922

PAUL DUKES

This essay is divided into four parts: 1) an introduction on the Cold War; 2) a discussion of the Washington Conference, 1921–1922; 3) an analysis of post-Cold War appraisals of the conference; and 4) a consideration of how the conference may be fitted into a broad geopolitical context. In this manner, it seeks to illustrate the manner in which historical interpretation evolves with the passage of time, including a dialogue between the past and the present. Further to this end, there is a postscript on the impact of '9/11' and its sequel.

I

Now that it is deemed to be over, we need to ask the question: was it *a* Cold War or *the* Cold War? An early use of the term was detected in 1983 by Fred Halliday in the fourteenth century when, describing the struggle between Christians and Muslims, a Spanish observer Don Juan Manuel wrote: 'War that is very strong and very hot ends either with death or peace, whereas cold war neither brings peace nor gives honour to the one who makes it.'[1] In 1968, however, Ernest R. May had observed:

> Ultimately, what frustrates any search for past parallels is the fact of technological progress. The thought may cross one's mind that the Cold War resembles the contest between Christians and Muslims; [or that it] is comparable to the European religious wars of the sixteenth and seventeenth centuries. But any such thought founders when one reflects on the political, economic, and military capabilities of princes such as Harun al Rashid and Charles V, when compared with those of Leonid Brezhnev and Lyndon Johnson.

In fact, there may be only one nation in all history that has had anything like America's post-1945 experience, and that is its contemporary and adversary, the USSR.[2]

The use of the term 'superpower' adds emphasis to May's definition. Here, the derivation is more recent: at least, there is widespread agreement that it was coined by W. T. R. Fox in a book published in 1944. Entitled *The Super-Powers*, the work bore the subtitle: *The United States, Britain and the Soviet Union — Their Responsibility for Peace*. Later, in 1980, Fox asked how he had come to make what now seemed to be the elementary mistake of including Britain along with what he had described as the other two 'peripheral' powers. This peripheral designation was one of the major reasons for Fox's palpable misconception in 1944, when there was still considerable acceptance of Europe as the centre of the world and Britain as a fully qualified member of the Big Three.[3] Arguably, too, the christening preceded the birth, so to speak, since one of the essential attributes of a superpower, the ability to wreak global destruction by means of nuclear arms, had yet to be created. Moreover, in 1944 the British Empire had not appeared close to collapse. Let us recall one of Churchill's declarations at Yalta at the beginning of 1945, that while the Union Jack flew over the territories of the British Crown, he would not allow any piece of British soil to be put up for auction. At the end of the Second World War, let us also recall, in addition to 'Cold War' and 'superpower', a third term was still to be coined or given new usage: decolonisation. Only later, during the Cold War, could the international relations of the post-war period be clearly discerned as an ideological struggle between 'democracy' and 'communism', with the peripheries taking over from the erstwhile centre as the previous empires gave way to the USA and the USSR. Moreover, it was not until the end of the Cold War that the unequal nature of the struggle could be clearly discerned. According to informed post-Soviet estimates, the USSR's GNP in 1990 was no more than one third of the USA's, at least one calculation putting it at little more than a seventh.[4] On the other hand, although the sombre fact is sometimes ignored or forgotten, Russia's ability to make an enormous contribution to any nuclear war remains; and arguably, the danger of such an eventuality through accident rather than design is even greater than before. Meanwhile, the ideological struggle has shifted from 'democracy versus communism' to 'democracy versus terrorism'.

## 2

Useful perspectives on the Cold War may be gained through an examination of its antecedents as well as of its sequel. Let us take as an example the Washington Conference on the Limitation of Armaments of 1921–1922 – 'one of the most significant, and overlooked, diplomatic meetings in American history', in the authoritative estimation of Walter LaFeber.[5] Far less well known than the Paris Peace Conference, it therefore needs some description.

In his inaugural address of 4 March 1921, President Warren G. Harding declared, 'We must strive for normalcy' in order to reach stability. As far as international relations were concerned, he rejected the Versailles peace so passionately defended by his predecessor Woodrow Wilson, declaring that 'a world supergovernment is contrary to everything we cherish' (although during the campaign he had talked of an 'association of nations'). In particular, Harding stated: 'The League Covenant can have no sanction by us.' In general, he stressed that to retain American sovereignty inviolate was not selfishness, but sanctity – neither aloofness nor suspicion of others, it was 'patriotic adherence to the things which made us what we are'. On the other hand, under his leadership, the government of the USA would confer and take counsel with other nations in order 'to recommend a way to approximate disarmament and relieve the crushing burdens of military and naval establishments'.[6]

Meanwhile, other nations were also attempting to adhere patriotically to the things that had made them what they were. Both in Europe and Asia, however, there could be even less return to normalcy than in the USA. For the First World War had brought vast changes to virtually every quarter of the globe. On the continent of Europe, three empires – the Austrian, the German and the Russian – had fallen (not to mention the partly European Ottoman), while the French had lost much of its strength. And if the sun was not yet setting on the most powerful of all empires – the British – it had certainly passed its zenith. In Asia, the sun was rising on Japan, seeking to assert its power throughout the Pacific region, at sea and on land, especially in China, which still awaited a new dawn.

By 1921 the USA was already becoming the world's strongest power, taking over from Great Britain. The new order was made brutally clear by Warren G. Harding's Secretary of State Charles Evan Hughes at a meeting with the British Ambassador Sir Auckland Geddes in mid-April. Hughes had earlier sent Geddes a note requesting British support versus Japan on a minor matter concerning the small Pacific island of Yap, which was a significant communications centre. Geddes observed that his government's reply would no doubt make some mention of His Majesty's obligations as set out in the Anglo-Japanese Alliance of 1902. According to the ambassador, the Secretary of State stood up as if stabbed, with his face turning the colour of 'the light rings in boiled beet-root', and began a lengthy invective charged with high emotion:

'You would not be here to speak for Britain! You would not be speaking anywhere! England would not be able to speak at all, it is the kaiser [all this grand crescendo moving to a shouted climax] – the kaiser who would be heard, if America, seeking nothing for herself, but to save England, had not plunged into the war and [screamed] won it!! And you speak of obligations to Japan.' Hughes declared that the Versailles treaty had removed all previous obligations.[7]

The Anglo-Japanese Alliance of 1902 had recognised the interests of both powers in China and provided for the defence of those interests. Renewed in 1905 and 1911, it was due to expire in 1921, and therefore constituted one of the most important subjects for discussion at the British Imperial Conference in the summer of that year. In his opening address on 21 June, Prime Minister Lloyd George declared: 'Friendly co-operation with the United States is for us a cardinal principle, dictated by what seems to us the proper nature of things, dictated by instinct quite as much as by reason and common sense.' At the second meeting, the South African premier Jan Smuts observed that the British Empire 'emerged from the war quite the greatest Power in the world, and it is only unwisdom or unsound policy that could rob her of that great position'. To his mind, it seemed clear 'that the only path of safety for the British Empire is a path on which she can walk together with America ... The most fateful mistake of all ... would be a race of armaments against America.' Smuts was conceding then, that the world's 'greatest power' was sufficiently in decline to need the support of her transatlantic partner.[8] There was much talk at about this time of the necessity for close English-speaking relations led by Great Britain and the USA. In the view of one commentator, they inhibited the long drift 'into a long series of wars which will sap the vitality of the white races and expose the civilised world, as we know it, to incursions from the barbarians of our epoch'. However, as the historian Denna Frank Fleming observed later: 'It was true that Great Britain was so impoverished by the war that she could ill afford to undertake a new rivalry, yet she could hardly be expected to relinquish without a struggle her century-old control of the seas.'[9]

Over in the USA, on 29 June 1921, the US House of Representatives followed the Senate to pass a resolution that had first been introduced the previous December by Senator William E. Borah, one of the most implacable foes of the League of Nations and a sceptic concerning one of President Wilson's later policies, expansion of the navy. Borah proposed that the USA should collaborate with Japan as well as the British Empire to reduce naval building for the next five years by as much as a half. A congruence of interest was leading towards the realisation of the idea put forward by President Harding in his inaugural. On 2 July the British Imperial Conference formally called for a conference specifically concerned with the Pacific and the Far East. On 8 July US Secretary Hughes sent cables to the American ambassadors in the UK, Japan, France and Italy instructing them to find out more generally if the governments would participate 'in a conference on limitation of armament ... to be held in Washington at a mutually convenient time'.[10] Through all the diplomatic interchanges, the new realities of international power politics shone through, with the American, not the British, capital at the centre.

On 21 July 1921 the US minister at Stockholm was handed a note composed by the Soviet Russian 'Commissar of the People for Foreign Affairs' Georgii V. Chicherin and dated 19 July, Moscow. Addressed to the governments of Great Britain, France, Italy, the United States of America, China and Japan, it began with the observation that the news had come to the Russian Government through the medium of the organs of the foreign press that a conference of the sovereign powers of the Pacific or possessing interests there would be convoked immediately at Washington. In its capacity as one such sovereign power, the Government of the Russian Socialist Federal Soviet Republic could not conceal its surprise on learning that the intention existed of assembling a conference of that character without its participation. Both the Russian Republic and the Democratic Republic of the Far East[11] should have been invited. Instead, however, 'the powers in question declare that they themselves will take in consideration the interests of Russia, without the presence of this latter, reserving to themselves to invite eventually a new Russian Government replacing the present government to accede to the resolutions and agreements which will be adopted there'. The Russian Government could not consent to the other powers arrogating to themselves the right of speaking for it, the more so as there was no intention of subjecting the counter-revolutionary government which might replace it to the ostracism aimed at the Russian Government. Such an attitude could be interpreted only as a new manifestation of the interventionist system as well as clearly favourable to the counter-revolution. The Russian Government formally declared that it would not recognise any decision which might be taken by the conference in question as long as this assemblage took place without its participation.

While 'The Russian Government would greet only with joy all disarmament or diminution of the military burdens which crush the workmen of all countries,' on the other hand, 'A policy aiming to leave Russia out of the collective resolutions of the different Powers upon questions which concern her, far from favouring the removal of the rivalries which trouble the world at the present time, will only aggravate them and increase them with new complications.'[12]

The Washington Conference met from November 1921 to February 1922 without the participation of Soviet Russia. (The tenor of Chicherin's remarks suggests that such participation might well have been counter-productive.) The conference's results reflected the relative influence of the powers that were involved. A series of treaties set limits on the number of capital ships of the major naval powers; replaced the Anglo-Japanese Alliance with a guarantee of stability in Asia by the USA, Japan, Great Britain and France; and gave the force of international law to the principles of the 'Open Door' of equal economic opportunity for all in China.

3

Having discussed the Washington Conference of 1921–1922, we now move on to post-Cold War evaluations, beginning with those in English. Now that the struggle between the two superpowers and their allies was over, there were hopes for a new world order in general and more objective historical appraisal in particular. Of course, the focus of our attention had not been entirely neglected in academic analysis during the period 1921–91, but there was no publication on it that included in a substantial manner the policies of both future superpowers. This omission was not so surprising in view of the circumstance that Soviet Russia was not a participant in the Washington Conference and received only minor mention there. However, the same circumstances applied to the Paris Peace Conference, which produced two substantial works devoted to the Russian question.[13] The absence of any comparable work on the Washington Conference should probably be ascribed to the comparative neglect of this subject as a whole. Even up to now, the most comprehensive works remain two that were both published in the 1920s.[14]

In a survey of successive lessons drawn from the conference in 1994, Ernest R. May began by noting that, throughout the 1920s, the agreements made in Washington – most famously on the 5:5:3 ratio for the capital ships of the American, British and Japanese navies – were taken to be examples of how the cause of peace could be advanced by 'bold risk-taking'. In the 1930s and 1940s, however, arms experts moved towards recommendation of the calibration of force levels to potential threats, now looking upon the decisions taken in 1921–2 as 'exemplifying wishful thinking'. In the early Cold War period, emphasis was given to 'the need to nail down details, to police performance, and to depend as little as possible on simple good will'. Later during that conflict, however, as tension between the superpowers lessened somewhat, American and Soviet statesmen took up arms-limitation negotiation as a means of averting the final showdown. Drawing on the work of historians, the political scientist Hedley Bull pointed out how the Washington treaties on the limitation of capital warships had encouraged the development of alternative armaments such as aircraft carriers and submarines. Comparable consequences might ensue if the American and Soviet negotiators concentrated exclusively on intercontinental nuclear weapons. Then, with the consolidation of *détente* in the 1980s, other political scientists cited further historical studies of the Washington Conference to argue for the advisability of sustainable public support for arms limitation agreements in the USA at the same time as warning against agreements making the assumption of 'a constraint like public opinion on the Soviet side'.

May observed that, while most of the academic discussion of the Washington Conference had concerned arms control, the agenda in 1921–2 was in fact much larger, including Pacific and Far Eastern questions as well. In post-Cold War retrospect, he noted, we can also more clearly perceive its broader setting in a series of attempts to create a post-First World War new international order following the failure of the 'comprehensive effort' at Paris in 1919. May continued: 'Dealing with problems piecemeal rather than with any thought-through formula, the successors of the Paris peacemakers developed regional arrangements. The Treaty of March 1921, ending a war between Russia and Poland, allowed the new, revolutionized Russia to isolate itself temporarily from the great power system in which Tsarist Russia had been an integral force.' Washington followed from November 1921 to February 1922, then Lausanne in July 1923, isolating the former Ottoman Empire, and Locarno in October 1925 seeking 'to transform the former great power system into a regional system'.

However, moving towards a conclusion, May suggested that these interconnected systems turned out to be fragile owing to their dependence on 'the great storage battery of the North American economy', which ran dry at the end of the 1920s. May asserted, the short life of this new order should not lessen its interest or relevance:

> There are in the 1920s parallels with contemporaneous efforts to create regional systems and comprehensive regimes, such as those for the oceans and environment. The fact that the earlier new order came to such a quick end is itself instructive, for it suggests the need to worry whether the current systems and regimes could withstand a shock comparable to that which ushered in the Great Depression.
>
> Like those who convened in Washington in November 1921, we who live in the 1990s face a future more full of uncertainty than the futures faced by our immediate forebears. We have no clear sense of what will be the sides or stakes in the future.

There was even some doubt that future competition would concern nations rather than civilisations, May added, following Huntington, whose assertions we shall discuss below.

Coming to the end of his Foreword to the book on the Washington Conference from the particular point of view of naval rivalry, East Asian stability and the road to Pearl Harbor, May commended the individual contributions to the study of 'the specifics of past attempts to construct new systems of relationships crossing national and cultural boundaries'. Just as earlier works stimulated strategic thought from the beginning of the Second World War to the end of the Cold War, so the present volume 'ought to help the thinking of those who are trying to see their way into a post-Cold War world'.[15]

There should be widespread agreement with Ernest R. May that the past can help us to understand the present, and that, in particular, his comments on the Washington Conference of 1921–1922 and successive interpretations of that event throughout the decades of the twentieth century constitute a stimulating aid to comprehension not only of them but also of the beginning of the first decade of the twenty-first century as well as of the conference itself. However, with respect to one of the leading international historians of the Cold War period, we can also make use of his remarks to discuss one of the barriers to such comprehension: historiographical unilateralism.

A case can be made for suggesting that even he, with the advantage of post-Cold War perspective, is not beyond criticism in this respect. Let us consider the observations that he makes and does not make about the Soviet side of the superpower equation. First, if the Washington Conference is to be taken as an example of the necessity of 'clearly sustainable public support', it is perhaps worth noting that such Russian public opinion as existed at the time of the conference, both Red and White, was unhappy about the lack of an invitation to participate in it. Secondly, the treaty of Riga of March 1921 obliged rather than 'allowed' Soviet Russia 'to isolate itself temporarily from the great power system in which Tsarist Russia had been an integral force'. Thirdly, in the reference to the international relations following the conference, there is a somewhat surprising omission: Genoa and Rapallo. (There is scant mention in the book, too.)

In the search for balance, let us look at the post-Soviet side as set out in the shape of A. Iu. Sidorov's book on the foreign policy of Soviet Russia in the Far East, 1917–22, published in 1997.[16] Sidorov emphasised the inadequacies of Soviet historiography, which he found not to be not so much quantitative as qualitative. That is to say, ideological preconceptions warped the conclusions of even the most serious scholars. However, Sidorov also noted the absence of any overall study of the Washington Conference, Soviet or post-Soviet, even though there had been many references to the 'Washington System'. In his excellent work on the foreign policy of Soviet Russia in the Far East, 1917–22, however, he himself devoted little more than ten pages to the conference.

In his conclusion, Sidorov underlined the importance of the Far Eastern Republic as a 'buffer' during the period of the Washington Conference, a role enhanced by its 'bourgeois' democratic nature. The FER assisted Soviet Russia to achieve its basic aims in the Far East, the restoration of territorial integrity and resumption of influence in Mongolia, without war against Japan. Meanwhile, 'uninvited Russia' maintained a useful dialogue with both Japan and China. Although the Soviet regime did not welcome the new world order established by the Washington Conference, 'the key Russian interests were completely taken into account'. By the end of 1922, on the eve of the formation of the Soviet Union, Soviet Russia had achieved the status of a leading power in the Far East.[17]

*Pace* Sidorov, perhaps we should not dismiss completely the views of Soviet historians in spite of their ideological preconceptions, but at least take the example of E. I. Popova's study of evaluations of the Washington Conference published in 1971.[18] From that vantage point, she suggested division of Soviet historiography on the conference into three phases: from 1922 to the mid-1930s; from the mid-1930s to the mid-1950s; and from the mid-1950s to the early 1970s. (In parentheses, perhaps, we should note that 'mid-1950s' could be a euphemism for the death of Stalin, while the early 1970s were part of another although not so deep 'freeze'.) According to Popova, the first phase was characterised by illumination of the Washington system, with special emphasis on the role of Soviet diplomacy and the importance of the Chinese revolution. However, under the influence of the dominant Soviet historian M. N. Pokrovsky, there was too much emphasis on commerce, and under the influence of American historiography, too much concentration on Japan. Moreover, the new role of the USA was imperfectly understood. The second phase was marked by the comparative neglect of the conference, although a considerable amount of attention was paid to the triangular relationship of the USA, Great Britain and Japan. The third phase strongly reflected the influence of the Cold War, with an exaggeration of the part played by the USA in the Allied intervention in Soviet Russia. Following Soviet practice, Popova asserted that great progress was being made, as she went on to summarise the understanding that had been achieved by 1971.

For Popova, the conference marked the emergence of the USA as a leading world power, with an emphasis on its own national security rather than the security of Asia and the Pacific. Thus, the USA aimed at establishing naval predominance at the same time as arranging an informal 'association of nations' as prefigured in the conference treaties.

Meanwhile, the internal debate between isolationism and globalism concurrent with the conference reflected domestic US circumstances, including close relations between the government and monopolies. Externally, the conference indicated imperialist contradictions, especially between the USA and two other powers, Japan and Great Britain. Emphasis was given throughout the 1920s to agreement with Japan in order to defend Asia from revolutionary and independence movements.

Giving up the alliance with Japan at the conference, Great Britain began to cultivate the 'special relationship' with the USA which, in spite of ups and downs, continued throughout the 1920s and beyond.

The conference also marked a significant moment in the USA's 'special relationship' with China, the nature of which had been indicated by the earlier enunciation of the concept of the 'Open Door'. Top priority had to be maintenance of enough stability to keep the door open. Finally, the conference reflected the clash of interests between the imperialist powers and Soviet Russia, which spoke out against unequal treaties and expansionist intervention. Nevertheless, the USA came near to the recognition that was finally accorded in 1933.[19]

Looking at the observations of May, Sidorov and Popova from the vantage point of the early twenty-first century, we may now see them as to some extent complementary and converging, even though their standpoints and emphases differ. At the very least, they show how interpretations evolved through the decades from the 1920s onwards, throwing light on the history of those decades as well as on the conference itself.

Of course, the great hopes held out for the Washington Conference went unrealised. It did not so much promote arms limitation as clear the decks, so to speak, for rearmament. Nevertheless, if the cause of peace was promoted to a restricted extent and for a limited time, it helped to promote a post-war system of international relations reflected in, at the same time as obscured by, the First World War and the Russian revolution, and their sequel. The decline of the European 'great powers' and the emergence of the USA and then the USSR as superpowers did not reveal themselves fully until after the Second World War.

Needless to say, with ideological preconceptions on both sides, the historiography of the Cold War period was prone to distortion. Hence, the great hopes for a fuller measure of objectivity from 1991 onwards.

4

Let us turn finally to broader geopolitical perspectives. As with history in a more restricted space and time, our understanding is increased if we bear in mind the inevitability of a dialogue between the past and the present. From the sixteenth century onwards, tsarist Russia and colonial America developed as transcontinental and transoceanic frontiers of Europe. In America from almost the beginning, there was an intimation of 'Manifest Destiny'. Later, in 1776, the Declaration of Independence at the beginning of the American revolution marked a conscious attempt to break away from Europe, amplified in the debates leading to the framing of the Constitution in 1787. Alexander Hamilton put the argument forcefully for the development of an American navy: 'Let Americans disdain to be the instruments of European greatness! Let the thirteen States, bound together in a strict and indissoluble Union, concur in erecting one great American system, superior to the control of all transatlantic force or influence, and able to dictate the terms of the connection between the old and the new world!'[20] Already, the cast of mind was apparent that would lead through the enunciation of the Monroe Doctrine to some of the views expressed at the time of the Washington Conference. Then indeed, as we have seen, the USA was able 'to dictate the terms of the connection between the old and the new world'.

Continuity of world outlook in the Russian case is less easily established, since the revolution of 1917 appeared at the time to be a bigger discontinuity than 1776. The debate about the nature of Soviet as opposed to tsarist Russia was still going on at the time of the Washington Conference. However, the collapse of the end product of that revolution, the Soviet Union, in 1991, put new life into the search for lines of filiation and the essence of the Russian spirit. To cut a very long story extremely short, we may resort to three triads. The first is tsarist, explicitly set out in the reign of Nicholas I by his minister Count Uvarov: Orthodoxy, Autocracy, Nationality – that is to say Russian Christianity, separate from the Western since the Middle Ages; the unlimited power of the tsar; and the distinctive character of the people. The second, Soviet version – never of course actually set out – could be defined as Marxism–Leninism; the Communist Party of the Soviet Union; and Nationality. (Allowance has to be made here for the role of Stalin and other leaders.) Thirdly, as yet in process of formation in the post-Soviet period, we might suggest Orthodoxy; Democracy; Nationality – although the 'democratic' nature of the Russian polity is at least as subject to reservations as that of most of its peers elsewhere. Each of these triads, needless to say, could be discussed at far greater length. Moreover, comparisons suggest themselves, not least with successive stages of American 'Manifest Destiny'.[21]

Throughout the nineteenth century, Russo-American relations were mostly but by no means exclusively via Europe.[22] An exception was tsarist infiltration down the west coast of North America, helping to bring about the enunciation of the Monroe Doctrine. At the end of that century, however, relations were more explicitly carried on via Asia, too, when John Hay directed his Open Door policy largely at Russian activities in China. Still transcontinental and transoceanic, Russian and American empires were now clashing more on the Pacific than on the Atlantic. Hence, the significance of the Washington Conference for the 'uninvited guest', Soviet Russia. With the consolidation of the Soviet Union, the Far East was fully incorporated and played a significant part until the collapse of 1991.

Five years afterwards, Samuel P. Huntington enlarged upon his suggestion that 'culture and cultural identities, which at the broadest level are civilization identities, are shaping the patterns of cohesion, disintegration, and conflict in the post-Cold War world'. The survival of the West would depend on 'Americans reaffirming their Western identity and Westerners accepting their civilization as unique not universal'. As for the former major adversary: 'While the Soviet Union was a superpower with global interests, Russia is a major power with regional and civilizational interests.' So we should 'accept Russia as the core state of Orthodoxy and a major regional power with legitimate interests in the security of its southern borders'.[23]

A year later, in 1997, Huntington's erstwhile collaborator, Zbigniew Brzezinski, went even further in his observation that 'the American global system emphasizes the technique of co-optation (as in the case of defeated rivals – Germany, Japan, and even lately Russia) to a much greater extent than earlier imperial systems did'. While Russia remained 'a major strategic player, in spite of its weakened state and probably prolonged malaise', its 'only real geostrategic option' was Europe, and 'not just any Europe, but the transatlantic Europe of the enlarging EU and NATO'.[24]

In 2001, Dmitri Trenin wrote: 'Russia-Eurasia is over. To the west of its borders, there lies an increasingly unified Europe, a natural place for Russia's own integration *as a European country* in an appropriate form. To the east lies an increasingly interconnected Asia, where Russia must either establish itself *as a country in Asia* or face the mounting pressure to withdraw west of the Urals. To the south, there is the challenge of Islamic activism whose source is both internal and external.' Within this configuration, the Far East was unique among Russian regions in maintaining the stability of its borders. Yet it was there and in Siberia that Russia's geopolitical destiny was likely to be tested and even decided. In particular, economic degradation and depopulation might separate the Far East from European Russia. Pressure from a developing China increasing in population would constitute the largest threat to the strong attachment of Russian citizens to their unified state.[25] In a sense, this was a latter-day version of the situation facing the Russian

Far East at the time of the Washington Conference, 1921–1922, although the greater threat then was not from China but from Japan.

The events of 9/11/2001 and their sequel have brought to an end the hopes for a new world order of the post-Cold War period on which this essay has concentrated. As a brief postscript, however, let us glance at the manner in which these events have given added emphasis to some of the remarks of Huntington, Brzezinski and Trenin on the geopolitical context, and suggested yet another perspective on the conference itself, adding to those put forward by May, Sidorov and Popova. While the primary focus has been on the problems of the Middle East stemming from the dissolution of the Ottoman Empire at the end of the First World War (as well as from the medieval struggle between Christians and Muslims), the inclusion of North Korea in the group of 'rogue states' developing Weapons of Mass Destruction recalls the Far East power configuration of 1921–2. Now as then – even more – the USA is exercising preponderant influence, while Russia again finds it difficult to have its voice fully heard in the international forum. Arguably, too, in their concentration on WMD, today's powers have repeated the error of their predecessors who singled out capital ships to the neglect of lesser forms of armament. Moreover, there is palpable evidence that the UK has yet to accept fully the diminished role in world affairs foreshadowed at Washington.

Observations of this kind must be treated as preliminary, for historical investigation as a dialogue between the past and present works best when 'today' is stretched sufficiently to allow a clearer perspective – as, so to speak, the wood begins to emerge from the trees. Yet however mature post-9/11 perspectives on the Washington Conference become, they too will ultimately be viewed, like those of the post-Cold War 'yesterday', as the creatures of their time.

# 18

## The New Central Asia
## Challenges for the Region

SALLY N. CUMMINGS

In 2001 John Erickson wrote of the substantial geo-economic and
geopolitical challenges Central Asia poses both for the governments of
this region and for external players: 'The formation of the international
coalition to wage war on terrorism transformed what had been long-
standing "Eurasian manoeuvres", competition for political and economic
influence, jostling for privileged positions to exploit huge regional
energy resources, into a series of turbulent gyrations. The sanctity of
"Heartland" was not only invaded, some of the invaders were actually
invited in, obligingly paying their way.'[1] Among John Erickson's vast
knowledge and interests was also Central Asia and he spoke often with
me of the destabilising forces that had emerged in the region. This
chapter outlines four such key challenges to Central Asia: the development of Caspian reserves; the involvement of national and multinational interests in the region; the response to transnational non-state
forces and actors; and the protracted and complex nature of state- and
nation-building in Central Asia.

For most of the 1990s Central Asia was praised by the West for its
general stability. With the important exception of Tajikistan and its
bloody civil war (1992–7), none of the four remaining post-Soviet
Central Asian states – Kazakhstan, Kyrgyzstan, Turkmenistan and
Uzbekistan – experienced civil war in the aftermath of the Soviet
implosion in 1991. By the end of the 1990s, however, transnational
drugs trafficking and criminality, international terrorism and border
disputes had come to dominate discussions of the region. This
evolution has prompted key analysts of the region to 'take stock',[2]
and to suggest that the next years will prove decisive for the stability,
good governance and development of market economies.[3] Issues of
state-building, in the context of international actors and threats, have
supplanted those of securing sovereignty which dominated the
euphoria of independence.[4]

## *The Development of Caspian Reserves*

The development of Caspian reserves, although to many the most intractable of the four challenges at the outset of the 1990s, had made considerable progress by the end of the decade. This is partly because interested actors, particularly corporations and governments, have at times managed to view the extraction of Caspian resources as positive-sum on the condition that they co-operate in the fields of extraction and transportation.

Initial comparisons of the Caspian reserve base with those of the Persian Gulf have been dismissed as illusory; the International Institute of Strategic Studies in 1998, for example, suggested that claims of recoverable oil reserves had been overestimated.[5] The Caspian reserve base is now mainly compared to that of the North Sea. John Roberts writes that, at some 40–60 billion barrels of oil (around 4 to 6 per cent of world proven recoverable oil reserves) and 10 to 15 trillion cubic metres (7 to 10 per cent of world proven recoverable gas reserves), 'the oil and gas resources of the Caspian region are significantly higher than those of the North Sea, and may even be double those of the North Sea'.[6] The Oxford Institute for Energy Studies also concludes that the North Sea rather than the Middle East is a useful point of comparison. Precise estimates of the Caspian reserve base continue to vary;[7] the Petroleum Finance Company claims that the US government has published inflated and unsubstantiated numbers.[8]

Gawdat Bahgat, who concurs that Central Asian resources are more likely to resemble those of the North Sea, nevertheless underscores, as do others, how two recent discoveries 'have triggered upward revisions of Caspian oil and gas potential and added a sense of optimism that the Caspian region can play a vital role in meeting world energy demand'. They were discovered offshore from Azerbaijan and Kazakhstan, particularly Shah-Deniz and Kashagan. Kashagan is considered one of the largest oil discoveries in the world in the last several decades, with some estimating a potential to produce up to 2 million barrels of light crude a day once the field is fully developed.[9]

The principal obstacles to drawing the full potential of the Caspian came, however, not from production but from transportation.[10] Within a decade, however, even if 'there is no guarantee that [the combination of old and new] lines will prove sufficient to avert the need for what is commonly called a "Bosporus bypass"', 'a major portion of the Caspian conundrum is now resolved'.[11] There are four significant oil export pipelines in operation at the time of writing: the Atyrau-Samara line (a Soviet-era line running from Atyrau to Samara); the Baku-Novorossiysk line (another Soviet-era line running from the oil terminals outside the

Azerbaijani port (and capital) of Baku to Novorossiysk through southern Russia); the Baku-Supsa line (opened in late 1998 with first deliveries in 1999, it runs from Baku to the Georgian Black Sea port of Supsa); and, the Caspian Pipeline Consortium (CPC) Tengiz–Atyrau–Novorossiysk line, opened in October 2001 and running from the giant Tengiz oilfield in Kazakhstan to the Russian Black Sea port of Novorossiysk. The Baku–Tbilisi–Ceyhan line under construction will comprise the first pipeline route to bypass Russia and provide direct access to a deepwater port.

## The Involvement of National and Multinational Interests in the Region

Caspian reserves have been the principal reason for interest by external powers. The US has sought to diversify its suppliers and so reduce its dependence on the Persian Gulf and increase its strategic regional interests relative to both Russia and Iran. Multiplying oil and gas pipeline routes serves both these goals. Russia has both security and commercial interests in the region. Under Yeltsin, Russia largely disengaged from Central Asia,[12] which allowed these states to anchor their newly discovered sovereignty by diversifying their foreign relations. When Vladimir Putin became prime minister in 1999, Russian post-communist foreign policy toward Central Asia became more pro-active than at any time previously, and its involvement has been largely pragmatic.

Under Putin the change in relations between Russia and Central Asia has been manifested in four main ways. First, Russian foreign policy, as expressed in the new foreign policy concept of summer 2000, is driven by a strong sense of pragmatism, and notes 'the limited resource support for the foreign policy of the Russian Federation, making it difficult to uphold its foreign economic interests and narrowing down the framework of its information and cultural influence abroad'.[13] Second, Putin has attempted to breathe new life into the Commonwealth of Independent States (CIS) which by the mid-1990s had become largely a dormant organisation, a victim partly of its overambition and lack of functional specialisation.[14] Third, an elaborate Caspian policy emerged, which was specifically mentioned in the new Russian foreign policy concept and which was presided over by a newly created special presidential representative for Caspian affairs – Viktor Kaluzhny, former minister of energy, who has travelled frequently to the region. In July 2000 a joint company composed of LUKoil, Gazprom and Yukos was created to develop Caspian Sea resources.[15] Fourth, relations became characterised by a new mix of multi- and bilateralism.

Turkey's interest in the region was at once historical, linguistic, cultural and ethnic but also economic. Its interest in Central Asia, argues Gareth Winrow, was, however, poorly conceived and co-ordinated, even if it remains an important player in the region.[16] In practice, Turkey's own economic problems and political uncertainties have prevented it from playing a major role in Central Asia. As in Russia's case, Iran's engagement in the former Soviet south has been primarily motivated by pragmatic interests, which included reducing Iran's international isolation by recultivating cultural and religious links, maintaining its good relations with Russia and encouraging new economic and commercial deals. And like Russia, Tehran conceives its relations with this part of the world as successful.[17] Edmund Herzig underscores elsewhere that a 'normalization of US–Iranian bilateral relations will have the most significant and far-reaching effect on the character of Iranian–Central Asian security relations'.[18]

The arrival of a US military presence in Central Asia, as part of the war in Afghanistan but set to remain for some time, has disrupted the *modus vivendi* that was being established between the great powers. For John Erickson, the increased competition between powers has transformed Eurasia and Central Asia in particular 'into the world's geostrategic cockpit', with the US presence threatening Russian political and economic dominance. He also emphasised how the US presence, 'when coupled with the warming American-Indian strategic relationship and growing Indo-Japanese contacts, with American troops in South Korea and Japan, could intensify Chinese fears of encirclement'.[19] The US presence is having repercussions for relations between Central Asian states as well, in particular heightening competition between the two regional rivals, Kazakhstan and Uzbekistan, and strengthening Uzbekistan's role as the US's primary strategic partner even in the context of human-rights abuses by Uzbekistan.[20]

The five Central Asian states continue to see their security alignments in flux, constantly renewing relationships with outside powers without committing to any one power in particular. According to a US State Department poll among populations in Kazakhstan, Kyrgyzstan and Uzbekistan, all three continue to place more long-term trust in Russia than in the USA, China, their neighbours or even the UN, probably because Russia continues to hold 'the image of stability and restraint', while the US remains unfamiliar.[21] Majorities in all three take issue with a permanent US military presence, while all three oppose a diminishing influence of Russia. Both Uzbekistan and Kyrgyzstan felt the campaign justified, with as many as 71 per cent (compared to 50 per cent in Kyrgyzstan) in Uzbekistan supporting it, demonstrating how, as the US poll writes, '[O]nly in eager ally Uzbekistan do a majority voice strong support.'[22]

## *Transnational Problems*

Russia's heightened role in Central Asia coincided with the region's insurgency events of 1999 and 2000. The insurgency events underscored the degree to which the security environment in Central Asia had deteriorated, particularly in Kyrgyzstan, Tajikistan and Uzbekistan, all of whom share a border with Afghanistan. In February 1999 Tashkent accused the Islamic Movement of Uzbekistan (IMU) of the attempted assassination of Uzbekistan President Islam Karimov. While he escaped unharmed, thirteen people were killed. After the bombings, the Uzbek government successfully pressured the United States to list the IMU as an international terrorist group. IMU insurgents crossed into Kyrgyzstan from Tajikistan in the summer of 1999 and 2000, holding several settlements hostage. The group seems to have become part of the al-Qaeda network, operating in their own camps in Afghanistan and safe havens over the border in Tajikistan. Even if IMU's military leader, Juma Namangani, and many of his fighters were reportedly killed in late November 2001,[23] the large number of young unemployed and disaffected continue to provide a pool of new recruits, and also to groups that preach more radical forms of Islam, such as Central Asia's largest Islamic group, Hizb-ut-Tahrir (Party of Islamic Liberation). 'Whatever the fate of Hizb-ut-Tahrir, other radical groups seem certain to emerge from the turmoil of the transitions that Central Asian states are still undergoing.'[24] The Hizb-ut-Tahrir, which promotes unity among its believers in the creation of a new caliphate and a utopian vision of Islam without corruption and poverty, has attracted followers by its ostensible refusal to use violence, 'a claim that deserves more complete exploration',[25] however. Following massive arrests, adherents of the movement have gone underground in Uzbekistan, but their numbers are increasing in the border regions of Kazakhstan and Kyrgyzstan. Evidence revealed in 2003 points to how terrorist groups are being trained in the region.[26]

One major source of finance for insurgency groups comes from drugs cartels. Afghanistan, by the close of the 1990s, was supplying 80 per cent of Europe's heroin and the northern trafficking route through Central Asia has become the principal transit point: 'Tajikistan's chief narcotics control official estimates that only about one-tenth of the drug traffic across his country is successfully interdicted.'[27] Drugs money has become a major source of financing of organised criminal groups (including partial funding of al-Qaeda), which sometimes also have links to local or international terrorist and sometimes extreme religious groups. The international community, especially the US, has been accused of largely ignoring this source of drugs trafficking.[28] Drugs cartels and security services in both Afghanistan and Central Asia often work together. 'If eyewitness reports are at all credible, then Tajikistan and Turkmenistan already meet some of the definitions of "narco-states".'[29] There has been little co-ordination of anti-drug-trafficking efforts. Central Asian states, in particular Uzbekistan and Turkmenistan, have often been unwilling even to seek regional solutions. Turkmenistan, under its 1995 policy of positive neutrality, refuses to join coalitions.

Retrenchment rather than co-operation has also marked these governments' reaction to water and border disputes. Central Asia's downstream users – Kazakhstan, Uzbekistan and Turkmenistan – are dependent upon Kyrgyzstan and Tajikistan, where the majority of upstream water resources from the Syr Darya and Amu Darya (both of which flow to the Aral Sea) is found, but also in Afghanistan and China.[30] Competition for water is increasing rapidly, but the Central Asian states have failed to come up with an effective regional approach since they have four key problems: the absence of coherent water management; the failure to abide by or to adapt water quotas; non-fulfilled agreements and payments; and uncertainty over future infrastructure plans.[31] Even if water is unlikely to lead to war between the five states, it adds significantly to the tensions between them.

The collapse of the Soviet Union also opened a number of border disputes, which largely stem from the Soviet demarcation of Central Asian borders that took place in the 1920s. These demarcations did not coincide with ethnic configurations, and frequent redrawing made little improvement. Upon independence, some borders took on international importance, others lost their significance as major transportation and industrial routes. Border communities in some cases were keen to resurrect old ties; in other cases governments were concerned about borders being too porous in the context of the new security threats of drugs trafficking and international terrorism. Demands for visas have also often made movement difficult, and Uzbekistan has mined its borders, notably with Tajikistan and Kyrgyzstan. Uzbekistan, especially, unilaterally closed boundaries. The most complicated border negotiations involve the Ferghana Valley both because several enclaves exist and because the three countries which share it – Uzbekistan, Tajikistan and Kyrgyzstan – all have historical claims and economic interests in it.[32]

These new security threats have not to date, as may have been predicted, furthered the cause of either Central Asian regional co-operation or co-operation between external actors. Argues Roy Allison: 'The conditions for such regional alignments have been changing since the incursions of Islamic insurgents into Kyrygzstan and Uzbekistan in summer 1999 and 2000. So far the security assistance programmes extended by external powers to the Central Asian states reflect competitive policies more than they express common co-operative efforts.'[33]

It remains unclear how much practical assistance NATO's Partnership for Peace programme (PfP) can supply to Central Asia. The Shanghai Forum,[34] which uniquely involves the two great powers of Russia and China, in addition to the four Central Asian states (minus Turkmenistan), endeavoured to deal with issues related to trade, water and the violation of borders by opposition groups. But experience suggests that Russia and China have often had goals at odds with those of the Central Asian members. Similarly, insurgencies have often sparked accusations by states against their neighbours for failing to undertake adequate pre-emptive measures.[35]

## State- and Nation-building in Central Asia

Although external players and transnational problems have posed key challenges to Central Asia, arguably the greatest challenge has come from within these borders in the form of nation- and state-building, and in forging a new relationship with a population defined by new state boundaries. The place of Islam in this new relationship, different in each of the five states, is complex.[36] As Shirin Akiner notes: 'There is a schizophrenic attitude towards Islam in post-Soviet Central Asia. On the one hand, there is general agreement that Islam is an integral part of the national culture; on the other, there is widespread fear of the rise of so-called "fundamentalism". This dichotomy is born of a lack of genuine familiarity with the religion.'[37] The existence, as noted in the previous section, of terrorist groups with Islamist labels and goals, both indigenous and with links to wider Islamic terrorist organisations, is of grave concern to the region's governments. But this concern has in general led to a blanket-wide repression of religious forces generally, including moderate and non-Islamic ones. This has destabilising consequences. Ahmed Rashid observes: 'The growing popularity of militant Islam in Central Asia is primarily due to the repressiveness of the Central Asian regimes.'[38] Similarly Yaacov Ro'i writes: 'Their [Islamic parties'] persistent repression by hardline regimes has served no purpose, except perhaps to make their intransigence more resolute.'[39] The governing elites in all five states have at various times and for various purposes legitimated their action by appealing to Islam, at the same time as often repressing non-state-sponsored Islamic movements.

Overall, we cannot either dismiss or take at face value the politicisation of Islam. While Islam is used by leaders to legitimise their repressive practices, at the same time threats from IMU and Hizb-u-Tahrir cannot be ignored. Still again, the automatic equation of terrorist and Islamist groups is highly misleading and obfuscates the region's traditional mix of conservative, modernist and radical elements.

The control of political and economic life has become the hallmark of these repressive regimes. Even the two liberalisers of the region, Kazakhstan and particularly Kyrgyzstan, have since the late 1990s concentrated executive powers in the hands of an ever smaller number of individuals. Their regimes have also become increasingly repressive. In 2002 members of the opposition were arrested in Kazakhstan[40] and in March 2002 in Kyrgyzstan members of the police shot dead five demonstrators in the southern district of Aksy. Uzbekistan's Islam Karimov has been the leader who has most frequently invoked the fight against Islamic radical forces as the justification for repressive policies. Turkmenistan's regime remains dominated by the megalomania and despotism of Saparmurat Niyazov, who used his apparent survival of an assassination attempt in late 2002 to justify further intimidation. Freedom House 2002 ranks the five states as follows (1–7, with 7 denoting least freedom): Kazakhstan and Kyrgyzstan as the relatively more free at 5.5, Turkmenistan as the least free at 7, with Uzbekistan and Tajikistan in between at 6.5 and 6.0 respectively.[41]

Smooth political succession will loom as a major issue in the stability of Central Asian states. The largely Soviet-era leadership that emerged in the late 1980s (with the exception of Kyrgyzstan's leader Askar Akaev) face the critical issue of how best to handle this issue. The Kazakhstani president is mooted to be grooming a successor among his family relatives, such as one of his son-in-laws. By contrast, in autumn 2002 Kyrgyzstan's Askar Akaev became the first Central Asian president to announce officially his intention to leave office after completing his constitutionally granted second term, which ends in 2005.[42] In the absence of legal and political mechanisms of succession, how these leadership transitions will take place in the five states is difficult to predict, and the degree to which succession is orderly and peaceful will likely depend as much, if not more, on whether the successor is legitimated by the elite as well as the population.

Governments have been mired in corruption scandals. Opinion polls, where available, indicate declining trust by the population in the effectiveness and legitimacy of government, particularly due to reports of corruption. The private abuse of public office in these regimes is closely linked to the high personalisation and weak institutionalisation of these regimes. Often top leaders conflate notions of personal and state property – such as by the holding of state funds in personal bank accounts; additionally, state service in all the five states remains highly personalised, where office is dependent either on the goodwill of the key recruiters or on the individual's ability to purchase it. Transparency International's 2002 Corruption Perceptions Index puts Uzbekistan and Kazakhstan in 68th and 88th places, respectively, out of 102 countries.[43]

Irrespective of charges of corruption, economically Kazakhstan has relatively been the regional success story. Since 1997 it has maintained its position as the country with the highest post-communist per capita foreign direct investment (after Hungary); in 2001 it registered a budget surplus, and by 2002 it had been designated as a 'market economy'. Foreign direct investment has helped Kazakhstan to rank highest among Central Asian states in the 2002 United Nations Human Development Index, which looks at 173 countries; it places Kazakhstan 79th, while Turkmenistan ranks 87th, Uzbekistan 95th, Kyrgyzstan 102nd and Tajikistan 112th.[44]

## Conclusions

Russia's strengthening of its commercial and strategic interests in the region have coincided with the heightened possibility of commercial gains from the Caspian, the insurgency events of 1999 and 2000 and the US military presence in the region after 11 September. Russia's involvement in the region is still welcomed by a large majority of Central Asia's population, and is not at odds with the foreign policies of Central Asian states, who also recognise Russia's significant intelligence of the region and its practical offers of assistance. While external actors and non-state security threats are a vital influence on these states' development, the most powerful negative influences on the security of the Central Asian states will, however, continue to be internal. As wider sections of the populations are subject to ongoing economic instability and social deprivation and are ostracised by increasingly hardline regimes legitimised by Russia, China and the West, the medium-term effect will continue to be destabilising.

# 19

## *Rumours as Evidence*

DONALD CAMERON WATT

Rumours are a kind of evidence with which historians have been reluctant to grapple. Partly this is because there is no obvious single archive in any country responsible for collecting them, listing them and which historians can consult and from which they can cite individual or clumps of rumours. Partly it is because as evidence they have an uncertain status; what is a rumour evidence of, apart from its own existence? Is a rumour or a sequence of rumours part of the history of a society or a culture? Should they be seen, if they are political in nature – and it is to this kind of rumour that this paper is dedicated – as part of the political process? How can their nature, given the general assumption that they are generated by some not easily identifiable or documentable process from the lower reaches of society, be reconciled with the top-down study of political policymaking and decision taking that the plethora of political documentation at the disposal of historians of the last century has made possible and which forms the major part of most historical writing on political processes? Do rumours, in fact, come from that uncharted or unchartable area of unreason from which from time to time manifestly irrational mass movements of opinion emerge such as the 'Great Fear' that preceded the French Revolution?

Contemporary historians of the Cold War, for example, already have problems in separating their investigations of the state of public opinion and the press from the evidence from official sources of the efforts by clandestine agencies such as the American CIA or the British Foreign Office Information Research Department to influence and manufacture opinion. Indeed some of them seem to entertain a model of 'public opinion' which posits the 'public' as an entirely passive collection of easily gullible fools whose 'opinion' only amounts to a parroting of 'messages' planted on them by such sinister secret agencies. That extraordinarily over-praised American historian Frances Stonor Saunders has argued that the entire British literary establishment of the late 1950s and early 1960s was nothing more than an echo chamber for the manipulations of the CIA, who were the source of finance of the

London literary journal *Encounter.*[1] Equally the 'discovery' of the 'secret' Foreign Office department, the Information Research Department, which waged the kind of political warfare against the Soviet bloc that the Political Warfare Executive had against Hitler and his New Order in Europe from 1940 onwards, was also regarded as something rather shameful.[2] This appears to have inhibited any attempts to analyse or investigate its effectiveness as an instrument of British policy where its activities were in fact clandestine, that is in the foreign countries whose press it targeted. The Indian press, for example, is fairly open to investigation. A comparison with the materials sent out to influence and perhaps be reproduced in selected Indian newspapers would perhaps be a good opening contribution to matters while Indian historians sort out the nature and the meaning of the term 'public opinion' in an all-Indian context. One cannot help feeling that this is an area in which the much derided Departments of Media and Communications Studies of the non-Oxbridge universities could make a mark that might silence the neophobes of the London press establishment. The press of Latin American countries is equally available for study and was equally targeted.

It is not proposed that this paper should spend too much time on the much neglected field of press history and studies. Its subject is rumour, its nature and prevalence in relation to specific events or policies and to the public debate over these policies, especially in the fields of foreign policy and of international relations.

In the first place it is an error to believe that there is an absence of hard evidence. As with everything else in the historical field there are patches where there is almost an *embarras de richesse.* One case is in the effect of German radio broadcasts to Britain during the Second World War. A recent work by Professor M. R. Doherty demonstrates the richness of materials available not merely on the broadcasts and the broadcasters that were lumped together as the work of 'Lord Haw-Haw' but on their impact on British public opinion, especially in the nature and scale of the rumours they generated.[3] One of Dr Doherty's most cogent arguments is that the propensity of the British public to listen to German propaganda broadcasts in English was a reaction to the gross inadequacies of the information about the war provided by British official information agencies and broadcast on the BBC.

This same point is made with enormous strength by the writer Claud Cockburn, editor of the political newsletter *The Week,* which had an enormous private circulation during the years before and during the Second World War in Britain, in his various memoirs.[4] His is only the best known of a series of private newsletters which, in the late 1930s, flourished in direct proportion to the attempts by the Chamberlain government of 1937–40 to exercise control and direction over the British press. How far this actually succeeded is still a matter that historical research has not agreed upon. Studies such as W. J. West's *Truth Betrayed*[5] or Richard Cockett's *Twilight of Truth: Chamberlain, Appeasement and the Manipulation of the British Press*[6] tended to reflect the official records on which they were largely based. They did not altogether accord with the pictures painted by studies of the British press based at least in part on the archives of the newspaper themselves.[7]

It is, however, true that dissatisfaction with or suspicion of the Panglossian note struck by much of the British press reportage of Hitler and his Germany in the 1930s made it possible not only for Claud Cockburn's *The Week* to flourish but also Commander Stephen King-Hall's newsletter, the *Whitehall Letter* edited by Victor Gordon Lennox, diplomatic correspondent of the conservative *Daily Telegraph*, and the right-wing *Intelligence Digest* to maintain their share of the market.

Claud Cockburn, who under the *nom de plume* Frank Pitcairn, was an assistant editor on the British Communist Party's *Daily Worker* (entirely dependent, Ms Stonor please note, on the subsidy from the Soviet embassy), claimed to have derived a good deal of his information from the former Permanent Under-Secretary in the Foreign Office, Sir Robert Vansittart, and to have been under continuous observation by the myrmidons of MI5, the Security Service. He was almost certainly under the observation of the less experienced Special Branch. But it appears to have been the *Whitehall Letter* that was regarded with most suspicion by the Security Service – not surprisingly, since its assistant editor confided in the 1960s that it derived a great deal of its reports from Vansittart himself and from Reginald 'Rex' Leeper, the head of the Foreign Office press department.[8]

It has been possible now for detailed comparison to be made between the reporting of the ordinary press and the various newsletters and the course of events as we know them from the historical documents. An excellent example is provided by the fully fledged 'war scare' of late January 1939. It was almost entirely ignored by the regular press. *The Week* denied that the scare should be taken seriously and stated that the information on which it was based was largely manufactured (which was true). The *Whitehall Letter* carried extensive reportage. There can be no doubt that the government took it very seriously. They believed reports that Hitler was planning either a direct air assault on London or an invasion of the Netherlands to provide him with air bases from which such an assault could be launched. Lord Halifax approached President Roosevelt directly with the reports, hoping that he could intervene with the Dutch with more credibility than London could. He embarked on talks with the French, which led early in February to an exchange of guarantees between Britain and France. Even more significantly the cabinet abandoned their decade-long resistance to a major commitment to the defence of the Continent, and embarked on a campaign of army expansion that led to the doubling of the Territorial Army as the first step to the introduction of conscription.[9]

With the mention of *The Week* and its rivals, discussion moves inevitably into a different area of what we might call 'rumourology', one not of spontaneously generated rumours, and the light they may shed on the degree of public confidence in government and the effectiveness of, and the credibility placed in, the government's explanations of its actions, but into the area of the manufactured, 'planted' rumour. But before moving on to discuss this new aspect of 'rumourology', there is one further point that emerges from Dr Doherty's admirably detailed exposition. That is that the rumours which plagued the British government and their observers of public opinion after September 1939, in so far as they purported to be based on what Lord Haw-Haw and his minions had said on the air in their broadcasts to Britain, were themselves untrue, in that they commonly attributed to these broadcasts some item of alleged information, some threat to a particular British target of the Luftwaffe, some detail of local knowledge outside London itself, which a detailed examination of the monitoring reports in the German broadcasts showed never to have been broadcast at all. Even Churchill himself was not always guiltless in accepting such rumours as accurate reports of what Lord Haw Haw had said.[10] The implication of all such rumours was the existence of a German espionage organisation in Britain that was so universal and so efficient that it even reported to Berlin such details as the irregular time-keeping of the town-hall clock. In fact, as Churchill was well aware, no such organisation existed. German agents who came to Britain had either been turned into double-agents or executed.

Dr Doherty's work is laid in a period in which the British government was extremely worried about the impact of German propaganda on British opinion and employed a number of different agencies to both collect and evaluate what the public were talking about. There were the Ministry of Information, the Cabinet Office, the BBC, the Home Office, the Security Service, the Foreign Office, a home Morale Emergency Committee, the Prime Minister's Office, the Postal Censorship, to name only a few of the agencies that have left records. Individual MPs sent in rumours that had cropped up in their correspondence with their constituents. There was also the Mass Observation organisation founded in the late 1930s to adapt not the questionnaire beloved of Public Opinion polling organisations such as the American Gallup organisation (which had established itself in Britain in the late 1930s) but the more informal and continuous methods of the British school of social anthropology. The unusual richness of the evidence this has provided him with has made it possible for him to identify and enumerate the large number of rumours that scurried through the undergrowth of distrustful British citizenry and produce a model picture of the milieux in which rumours circulated.

To extend this kind of analysis to the processes of international relations is more difficult. It requires access to a number of different diplomatic archives from different countries, as well as an overview of the international press and some knowledge of how the international community of foreign correspondents of the world's leading newspapers interacted upon each other, given that, apart from the employees of news agencies such as Reuters and the American commercial news agencies, the correspondents all acted for particular national newspapers of very different cultures. There is nevertheless evidence enough both from satires such as Evelyn Waugh's *Scoop* and a plethora of press and radio correspondents' memoirs, papers and diaries on top of a number of biographies and historical studies, to show that to a certain extent the common experiences of the correspondents in particular capitals and on particular battlefields gave them a common culture and common reference points as well as a reflection of the ideological clashes that were besetting European international politics in the 1930s and 1940s.

Indeed Cockburn has explained that he was used by US correspondents to provide them with a plausible base for reports that otherwise rested entirely on the reliability of their contacts and their own professional reputations. They gave him the story so that they could quote *The Week* as a source, since it was Cockburn's acknowledged policy to print rumours as well as authenticated reports (or what he chose to regard as such). One can find in the archives of the various diplomatic services and in the international press, a coverage of the more significant and influential rumours that bedevilled both official and press reportage. In what follows, attention will be directed to the use by the Soviet authorities of rumours for two quite separate but explicit purposes. The first was as a part of political and military intelligence gathering as to the reality and planning of other potentially unfriendly powers. The second was to manufacture evidence for internal security uses.

These can be separated from the planting of rumours as part of political (the American term 'psychological' is more specific) warfare against enemy morale. This will be dealt with later. What is at issue here is the manufacture and planting of rumours in specific instances and for obvious purposes unconcerned with any attack on the morale of a potential enemy. This practice, it should be emphasised, seems to have been established as Soviet practice before Stalin's ascendancy was established; and it does not appear to have been a device that it occurred to him to use. It seems to have originated in the 1920s as part of Djherzhinski's attack on the main sources of foreign subversive attack on the new Soviet regime, the Russian Socialist Boris Savinkov, and the man whom the Soviets regarded, probably wrongly, as the instrument of British Sovietophobia, the former British intelligence agent, Sidney Reilly.[11]

The evidence as to Stalin and Molotov's ignorance of this ploy is of course entirely negative. There are, for example, two occasions on which we have positive evidence of these two men suffering acute anxieties over deductions they had made from, or fears that had been aroused in them of threats of military attack on the Soviet Union, where they did not resort to the use of rumours, and there seems to be no valid reason for their not doing so. The first is in the months of June and July 1939, preceding the conclusion of the Nazi–Soviet pact. Stalin was confronted with a British (and French) guarantee for Poland, which their diplomacy was trying to persuade him to underwrite. At the same time Britain refused to guarantee the small Baltic republics of Latvia, Lithuania and Estonia, as they did Finland. Led by Finland, all four countries had made it publicly plain that they did not wish for such a guarantee, the Finns going so far as to hint that they would regard such action on the part of the Western allies as an unfriendly action. Stalin appears to have conceived the suspicion that the British response in the face of such unanimity was a signal, or even a broad hint, to assure Germany that an attack on the Soviets along the Baltic coast towards Leningrad would not be something to which they would object. His anxiety was communicated to his military commander in the Baltic area, and the Red Army carried out its annual summer exercises not in the Ukraine but in White Russia, close to the hypothetical line of advance of such an attack. It is not impossible that German action was taken to plant such suspicions. The armies of the three mini-republics were led by military men who looked naturally to Germany for their external contacts. Both General Halder, the chief of staff to the German army, and Admiral Canaris, the head of the Abwehr, paid visits to the area in June, on what pretexts was not clear. In military and logistic terms the idea of such attack seems far-fetched, to put it mildly. What does seem clear is that no serious effort was made by Soviet intelligence to investigate the question. In particular, although the capitals of these three republics had been a fertile source for rumours about Soviet intentions since the mid-twenties, there is no record of any rumours having been circulated that had any connection with alleged German plans or with Soviet counter-moves.

The Soviets had equal anxieties about the Anglo-Turkish rapprochement, which had begun in 1936 and was to lead in May 1939 to the issue of a British guarantee for Greece and Turkey, involving the conclusion of an Anglo-Turkish alliance. But they chose to deal with it by direct pressure, culminating in the public bullying and humiliation of the Turkish Foreign Minister, M. Saracoglu, when he came to Moscow in September 1939. Saracoglu was so angry that the conclusion of the Anglo-Turkish alliance followed within the month. Molotov's unsuitability for the role of Foreign Minister has rarely been so convincingly demonstrated; but he was merely doing what his master required of him: to play the thug rather than the relative of Scriabin.

The second example is even better documented both from the Italian documents and from the research the Russians permitted the Israeli historian Gabriel Gorodetzki to undertake in the Soviet archives. In January 1941, shortly after he had replaced Lord Halifax as British Foreign Secretary, Anthony Eden visited Ankara for talks with the Turks. The intention of his visit was to try to use the Anglo-Turkish alliance to persuade Turkey to follow the British example and reinforce the Greeks, who had substantially defeated Mussolini's attack on them and driven the Italian forces back into the dreary wastes of eastern Albania. Mussolini had acted without Hitler's approval let alone his support. The Greeks did not want British military aid – not in the form of troops – opining, rightly as it turned out, that this would bring Hitler's might upon them. This was a view that the Turks shared; they were determined not to bring about a German invasion of Turkey. Eden was not to be deterred; and the Cabinet, not with any enthusiasm, agreed to the dispatch of a British Expeditionary Force to Greece.

The news of Eden's mission was greeted with anxiety amounting almost to despair by Stalin and Molotov. The latter poured out his anxieties to Augusto Rosso, the Italian ambassador in Moscow, whom he seems to have treated as a kind of father confessor. Essentially both his record and that sent to Rome by Rosso agree. Molotov was convinced that the purpose of Eden's visit was to organise a joint Anglo-Turkish re-enactment of the Crimean War with an amphibious attack on Odessa and the Crimean coast. The idea is so far from anything that the British, stretched to the limit in the Eastern Mediterranean and the Middle East, could contemplate as to be ludicrous. It suggests either that neither Stalin nor Molotov had the remotest understanding of what was involved in any amphibious operation in terms of ships, supply trains, logistics and so on (something which their later enthusiasm for a 'Second Front Now' does something to confirm), or that the picture their intelligence had supplied them with as to the British order of battle in the area, or the enormous strain Britain was under in terms of arms and troops at the time, was incompetent in the extreme.[12] The account Rosso gave of his meeting with Molotov can only be described as flabbergasting; the more so when it is contrasted with Stalin's monolithic refusal to believe any of the warnings he received of the approach of Barbarossa and the action he was preparing against the GRU organisation, including the great Ricard Sorge in Tokyo, whose warnings he regarded as British inventions.[13]

If the second of these two examples reveals the weaknesses of both Soviet intelligence and of its direction, it is the first that is the more revealing. The absence of any Soviet excursion into 'rumourology' in June and July 1939 can be contrasted with the effort put into convincing the international press via *The Week* in February and March 1939 that German forces were massing around Klagenfurt, capital of the former Austrian province of Carinthia, in preparation for some kind of venture into Jugoslavia and the Balkans. It does not seem to have had any marked effect on Prince Paul of Jugoslavia. There was then as now a sizeable Slovene minority in Carinthia, and I find it difficult to believe that Jugoslav intelligence did not know the second name of the cousins of every German soldier stationed there. There were no German concentrations in southern Austria. There were troops preparing to go into Bohemia and into Slovakia from the northern Austrian provinces of Ober- and NiederOesterreich; but that was another matter entirely. The German–Italian staff talks which began at the end of March 1939 and continued through the summer concerned themselves with a Mediterranean war against France and Britain. But the Germans had no plans for such a war; and the Italians dreaded it. The degree of Soviet ignorance of the dispositions and the plans of the troops of the major European powers as a whole, not merely of those of their German–Italian opponents, and of the whole issues of railways, mobility, logistics and so on, throw an odd light on the abilities of Soviet intelligence at this time, let alone of the questions asked of them by their political bosses or the assessment of any intelligence reports made by those same bosses. They were, after all, as concerned with the final liquidation of Trotsky at this time as with the military plans and dispositions of the European powers which threatened them at any time with war and invasion.

The clearest case of the Soviet security services fomenting rumours for use in an internal security matter can be seen as part of their campaign against the Soviet High Command of the Red Army which resulted in the purges of the Soviet marshals and their juniors beginning with the trial of Marshal Tukhachevsky and two of the other five Soviet marshals, which was to drag on until the Soviet commander-in-chief in the Far East, Blyukher, was also brought down a year later.[14] I have myself examined elsewhere[15] the coincidence in time of these waves of rumours of secret Red Army contacts with the Reichswehr, with the moves of the NKVD against the Soviet High Command. The rumours originated in Riga, Prague and Warsaw, and reports on them can be found in the British, French, Italian, Hungarian and American printed volumes of diplomatic documents or in their various diplomatic archives in more or less identical terms suggesting a common source. One could almost imagine the Western diplomats had been attending a single press conference in each city. The reports were so far from being true that the Reichswehr had sent to Moscow a veteran of the former period of clandestine Reichswehr–Red Army co-operation to discover if anything could be done to bring about a return to the state of affairs that had 'existed before Stalin had broken off the contacts in the summer of 1933'. He found that none of his former buddies in the Red Army were even prepared to see him at all so scared were they of being caught in the NKVD's plotting, which had already resulted in the arrest of several second-rank military men.

The deliberate invention and circulation of rumours was also part of the methods used by the British Political Warfare Executive against German morale during World War II. (As noted above, the American preference for the term 'psychological warfare', or 'Psywar', indicates more clearly the nature of the war they were fighting and the weapons that they were using.) The British launched these rumours (for which the term 'sib' was used) in part through neutral capitals (Lisbon being very much the preferred launching pad), in part through the various 'black' radio services that were gathered together under the direction of the former *Daily Express* correspondent in Berlin Denis Sefton Delmer. The in-house demi-official history of the Political Warfare Executive prepared after the end of the war,[16] though not released until the turn of the century, was extremely crushing on the subject of the British 'sibs', condemning them as 'foolish and often childish'.[17] More to the point, the author condemned the execution of the policy as amateurish and not based on any thought-out strategy, not based on any psychological need felt by their German audience which might have made them more credible and not based on any research which might have suggested such a basis. It was in his view a case of 'too many cooks spoiling the broth'. The author of this criticism was himself an amateur propagandist, a professional writer from the younger ranks of the Bloomsbury set; and there may well have been personal animosities underlying his criticisms. The praise others have given for Delmer's journalistic expertise, his command of the British popular style of journalism coupled with his long experience of Berlin from 1931 onwards, suggests that he and Garnett would have been unlikely to see eye to eye – though Delmer did not have any great hand in the manufacture of 'sibs'. It is not clear whether, at war's end, any British or Anglo-American agency investigated the German reception of these 'sibs' or their impact on German morale. Such studies of German opinion that have been undertaken, resting as they do on the Gestapo files, do not give 'sibs', of whose existence they may even have been unaware, as playing any part in the impact of British propaganda. It was the universal audibility and very general practice of listening to BBC broadcasts that figures largest in their reports. It was, of course, an offence leading to serious punishment for a German to be discovered listening to the BBC.

Whereas the national historians, especially those who have access to party files, to the private correspondence of political figures both in and out of parliament, will probably never complain about the availability of evidence as to what was actually happening and circulating in the substratum of gossip and rumour in which so much of ordinary life is spent, the international historians will have to take their evidence wherever it emerges from the archives. The wider the net cast, the more likely it is that evidence of the role of rumour in the closed societies of diplomatic posts in police states will merge and that clumps of rumours like those of secret contacts between the German and Soviet military will emerge. This is something with which intelligence agencies engaged in the 'War against Terror' are already familiar. But in the years of the Cold War it is much more difficult to discover the role played by the unvoiced opinions of the publics in the Soviet zone and, it has to be said, very little serious attention has been paid even to the nature and sources of public opinion in the West. The number of times that I have encountered young scholars from the former Soviet ally states of Eastern Europe who seem to have had access to the police and security archives of their own countries gives one hope for the future. But without understanding the state of opinion in all its varieties in Britain in the late 1960s, for example, it is difficult to understand why the Soviet intervention in Czechoslovakia in 1968 came as such a surprise. From first-hand experience I can testify to the fact that even a private luncheon of dyed-in-the-wool British Cold Warriors, which included Robert Conquest, Kingsley Amis and Tibor Szamuely, when asked by a visiting American whether they expected a Soviet intervention answered, all but one, in the negative. (I was the exception, which accounts for my remembering it.) Szamuely replied that the Russians were too stupid to intervene, although he thought they should. I had no doubts; but then I had no doubts that the East German army would act against their rioting fellow citizens in 1989, and said so in print, only to be proved wrong two months later.

The rumours, the *on dits*, the assumptions, the entire actuality and the *mentalités* then displayed can be matched by what was written in the press. But the occasion I remember was entirely private between long-standing friends, who saw themselves as allies against those whom Amis labelled as 'softies', fellow-travellers in emotion even if not in reality, sentimental Russophiles and perennial optimists of short memory. To understand how and why the Gorbachevian implosion of the Soviet Union took everyone by surprise the intellectual ferment of 1968 has to be remembered; but, as they say in pop-music circles about the 1960s, 'If you can remember what it was like, then you weren't there.'

# 20

## The Edinburgh Conversations

LYNN HANSEN

### Introduction

During the four years I spent as an American liaison officer to the Group of Soviet Forces in East Germany I frequently heard the name of Professor John Erickson. He was praised repeatedly as being the person living within the confines of NATO who knew the most about the Soviet armed forces. It was a bit difficult for me to understand how an academic could possibly know more than did we, who were watching the ten divisions of combat-ready ground forces and the 16th Air Army virtually every day. The commander of our unit was frequently invited to attend various seminars and symposia dealing with the Soviet military. He always returned generous in his praise of Professor Erickson when he informed us of the issues discussed at such gatherings. Personally, I paid scant attention to all this, since I was not terribly interested in an intellectual view of Soviet military doctrine, strategy, operational art and tactics. After all, we were not gathering our information from books; we were observing the Soviet front-line forces in contact. Thus, I more or less forgot about the professor from the University of Edinburgh who was so greatly admired by my army colleagues.

Two years after I left that assignment, I was encouraged to apply for an assignment as a US Air Force Research Associate. Air force officers in the rank of Lieutenant Colonel who possessed advanced academic degrees were eligible for such assignments. After much bureaucratic wrangling, I was told I would be assigned to work at Professor John Erickson's elbow at the University of Edinburgh.

I think both he and I were a little surprised at the assignment. Nonetheless, we developed a wonderful relationship, one I shall always treasure. I quickly learned that he did indeed know more about the Soviet armed forces than did we; his knowledge was deeper and more strategic in nature than that we acquired by superficial observation.

After a year with Professor Erickson at the University of Edinburgh I returned to work in the Pentagon and then in the Arms Control and Disarmament Agency in Washington, DC. Eventually, I became a participant in the all-European process known as the Conference on Security and Co-operation in Europe (CSCE). My responsibilities were limited to the security basket of CSCE, where I participated in the Madrid CSCE follow-up meeting (1980–83), the Stockholm Conference on Confidence- and Security-building Measures and Disarmament in Europe (1984–6), and the Negotiations on Conventional Armed Forces in Europe from 1989 to 1993.

During the period of my involvement in European arms-control issues, I maintained contact with Professor Erickson. For most of this period, he was engaged with senior officials in the Soviet government, arranging and conducting a series of academic exchanges known as the 'Edinburgh Conversations' that for a time carried the theme of 'Survival in the Nuclear Age'.

## Setting the Stage

Students of world events now recognise that this was a period of grave danger. Great mistrust of the North Atlantic Treaty Organisation in general and the United States in particular permeated the highest decision-making circles in the Soviet Union. Moscow and Washington were hardly speaking to each other. Before continuing further, I would like to sketch out the seriousness of this period of time in order for the reader to catch a glimpse of the importance of the Edinburgh Conversations in conveying non-hostile intent between West and East when a falsely interpreted message might have led to catastrophe.

Strange as it may seem to the Western mind, there were those in the Soviet Union in the early 1980s who sincerely believed that NATO was preparing itself to launch an offensive war against the Warsaw Pact involving a first strike with nuclear weapons. It is difficult to locate with clarity the source of such views. Some believe it was simply worst-case analysis within the KGB; others believe that the KGB was attempting to enhance its status within the Soviet hierarchy. It seems clear, however, that many of the top Soviet leaders at the time believed that US President Reagan was determined to build up NATO and US forces to the point where they would be capable of launching a surprise nuclear attack. Former Soviet Ambassador to Washington Anatoli Dobrynin notes that Brezhnev, Andropov and Chernenko all thought nuclear war with the United States was a distinct possibility; however, only Andropov, according to Dobrynin, believed the US would launch a surprise first nuclear strike.[1]

This fundamental paranoia seemed to be the motivating factor for many of the positions and actions taken by the Soviet Union. The shooting down on 1 September 1983 of a Korean airliner that had strayed off course and entered Soviet airspace occurred because they had been tracking an American aircraft orbiting outside its territorial limits that they believed was collecting intelligence in support of US attack plans. The unfortunate KAL aircraft blundered across the border in the same general time frame and was therefore believed to be operating for American intelligence agencies.

To make matters worse in the eyes of the Kremlin, the United States and its NATO allies conducted a 'nuclear release exercise' called Able Archer from 2 to 11 November 1983. The purpose of the exercise was to test the communications and command procedures for the use of nuclear weapons and therefore involved a simulation of orders that would have to be given to employ such weapons in wartime. Although this exercise had been conducted regularly for years, the 1983 exercise was more extensive than any preceding ones. It seems clear that some in the Soviet intelligence apparatus misunderstood and calculated that US forces had been placed on alert and that the countdown to nuclear war might actually have begun.

NATO's decision to deploy Pershing-2 and ground-launched cruise missiles (GLCMs) in Europe further exacerbated the Kremlin's fears that the West was preparing to go to war. Western rejection of various Soviet arms-control proposals continued to frustrate Soviet leaders. When NATO began actual deployment of Pershings and GLCMs, the Soviet Union walked out of the nuclear arms negotiations in Geneva and the Negotiations on Mutual and Balanced Force Reductions then taking place in Vienna.

Thus, diplomacy between East and West was fundamentally at a standstill. Both sides seemed to recognise this unfortunate state of affairs, but neither seemed willing to take steps to alleviate the situation. Two sides, armed to the teeth, facing the possibility of nuclear war, were simply not talking to each other.

### The Beginning[2]

In 1980 Lord Ritche Calder visited Moscow in his role as Chairman of the Scotland–USSR Society and engaged his hosts in a rather frank discussion of critical East–West issues. Concerned that he had offended his hosts with his frankness, he was surprised when they suggested that he bring a group of Scots to Moscow a second time again to engage in discussions, which, as he put it, had lost the veneer of politeness.

It was quickly realised that no Scottish group bent on discussing the sensitive subjects of the Cold War would be complete without the participation of John Erickson, who was Professor of Defence Studies at the University of Edinburgh. Consequently, Professor Erickson and nine others visited Moscow for three days in late 1980. In February 1981 three Soviet officials visited Edinburgh to discuss the possibility of initiating more formal exchanges beginning in the fall of the same year.

In subsequent meetings with the Principal and Vice-Chairman of the University, Sir John Burnett, it was determined that Edinburgh would host the first meeting in the autumn. They agreed the theme for the meetings would be 'Survival in the Nuclear Age'.

The first set of Conversations were then held in Edinburgh from 5 to 7 October 1981 with General Sir Hugh Beach (master of the Queen's Ordnance until April 1981, but at the time Research Associate at the Defence Studies Department, University of Edinburgh) added to the British side. A solitary American was present, although not officially a member of the UK group.[3] Professor Burnett headed the UK delegation and Vitaly Kobish of the Department of International Information of the Communist Party of the Soviet Union led the contingent from Moscow. He was accompanied by six others with interests in foreign affairs, history, medicine and cultural relations.

Not surprisingly, much of the discussion centred on the question of nuclear war. Reacting to some rather uninformed views that had been the topic of defence intellectuals in Washington about the possibility of a limited nuclear war being fought in Europe, there was general agreement concerning the impossibility of such a concept being implemented. The group repudiated the idea of Europe becoming a 'theatre of war' or a 'theatre of nuclear weapons'. Of course, reaching agreement on such concepts was important to the Russians, who somehow continued to believe that the West, principally the United States, thought that nuclear war could be limited to Europe. Frankly, I was somewhat surprised to learn that the group also seemed to agree to what was a Soviet proposal in several different arms-control forums, namely *no first use of nuclear weapons*.[4] Yet, I came to learn that participants in the Conversations represented only themselves and not – at least not officially – their governments.[5]

At this initial meeting, there was no table at which the participants sat nor any formal seating plan. These were to be conversations, not two sides declaiming at one another. This precedent was adhered to in subsequent meetings, although the Soviet hosts in the second meeting might have preferred the more formal arrangement. UK media coverage was favourable, with such headlines as, 'Soviet and UK Academics Claim a Breakthrough' and 'Edinburgh Talks Could Reduce Risk of Nuclear War'. An article in a Moscow newspaper by Professor Igor Sokolov, one of the Soviet delegates stated: 'The Edinburgh meeting will undoubtedly make a positive contribution to the strengthening of peace and promotion of fruitful international co-operation.'

## Subsequent Meetings

In all, seven sets of Conversations were held, alternating between Edinburgh and Moscow. I was invited to join the UK group during the second set, held in Moscow from 25 September to 2 October 1982. The nature of the discussions led the UK participants to think that there should be a US observer present. Since I had been a post-doctoral fellow in Defence Studies and therefore associated with the University of Edinburgh, I must have seemed a logical choice to be invited. At the time I was a serving air force colonel assigned to the US Arms Control and Disarmament Agency in Washington.

From the beginning I found it interesting that Professor Erickson chose not to engage in the head to head talks as they were often, particularly in the early years, quite belligerent in nature. He was an academic, not a politician nor a representative of the British government or NATO and did not wish to speak for anyone. Nonetheless, he was the dominant 'behind-the-scenes' person who was consulted by both UK and Soviet participants. It was quite clear that he not only knew more than any of us about the Soviet armed forces, he was also expert at deciphering Soviet innuendo and mood. Without him, the whole project might have unravelled.

The trip to Moscow was stimulating. Professor Erickson, Michael Wescott, Dr John Loraine, Professor Iain McGibbon and I boarded an Aeroflot plane in Glasgow for the flight to Leningrad. Professor Erickson and I sat together and discussed what lay ahead. As an aside, we both agreed that the pilot of the passenger jet must have learned to fly on an old Sukhoi-7 fighter (notorious for its clumsy handling) as he flung his passengers about the sky while landing in Leningrad. From there we boarded the Red Arrow Express – a fast train to Moscow – for the remainder of the trip. John was in a great mood, joking and discussing the coming events with all who could match his staying power.

At the train station in Moscow the following morning we were met by the large black Chaika sedans with curtains on the windows and transported to a Labour Union guest house in the suburbs of Moscow. It was there we were to reside, eat our meals and conduct our talks. The group with which Professor Erickson and I travelled was joined in Moscow by Field Marshal Lord Carver, Sir John Burnett, Nigel Calder (son of Lord Ritchie Calder) and General Sir Hugh Beach. As a lowly colonel, I felt pretty insignificant. However, Professor Erickson made sure that I was accorded almost equal treatment. While the Soviet delegation was intrigued by having both a field marshal and a general on the UK delegation, they seemed almost equally interested in having an American military officer present.

On this occasion (and all subsequent ones) the Soviet delegation was led by Gennadiy Yanayev, an official in the Soviet trade union apparatus, Deputy President of the Soviet Friendship Societies, and a high official in the Communist Party of the Soviet Union.[6] Several other Soviet dignitaries were also involved in the discussions, including Vladimir Semeonov, who was at the time Deputy Head of the Second European Department of the Soviet Foreign Ministry (and later ambassador to Singapore). Georgiy Arbatov, Director of the Institute of US and Canadian Studies and Deputy of the Supreme Soviet; Lev Semeiko, Senior Research Fellow from the same institute; Professor Vladimir Alexandrov, member of the Academy of Public Sciences, and General Konstantin Mikhailov (who was my negotiating partner at the CSCE follow-up meeting in Madrid) participated, among others, in the Soviet delegation.

Soviet participants were particularly interested in having a press release that would portray the character of our discussions. As is usually the case in such situations, the press release was drafted outside the group, discussed with key individuals, and then presented to the group for adoption. Field Marshal Lord Carver took exception to one of the paragraphs in the draft and insisted on changes. This being a discussion under the auspices of the university, Professor Erickson did not feel that the document needed to reflect the view of the UK military. The dispute was rather calmly resolved after a little huffing and puffing. Being an observer, I was not entitled to an official view of the declaration, but worked quietly with Professor Erickson to ensure that its content would not get me into trouble with my authorities in Washington. Among other things, the document noted that the idea of waging nuclear war was unreal and unacceptable: 'The notion of waging nuclear war is sheer madness ... nothing can warrant nuclear war, which would be the ultimate crime ... there would be no victor in such a war, which would mean the end of civilisation.' I was pleased to note that not only the first use of nuclear weapons was condemned, but also the first use of conventional forces. We also understood that the 'no first use' principle could not and should not apply merely to nuclear forces, but also to conventional forces. Of course, the document urged that we continue to meet.

My personal view was that the Conversations had proved to be a useful venue in which to discuss critical issues of the day but that agreement was most difficult to reach; disagreement was generally glossed over in what proved to be rather conventional diplomatic language.

The third set of meetings was then held in Edinburgh between 17 and 22 September 1983. It was agreed that these talks should centre around military/strategic problems, environmental/behavioural constraints and consequences arising from these two issues. This was not a particularly propitious time to hold such a meeting. About two weeks before the Conversations were to convene, Soviet air defence forces shot down a civilian airliner of Korean Airlines. Even though there was some media offence that Soviet generals (Mikhailov and Milshtein) were allowed into the country, the meetings themselves were conducted in relative quiet. As previously noted, Gennadiy Yanayev led the Soviet delegation which, in addition to the two generals, also included Professor V. Afanasiyev, who was editor-in-chief of *Pravda*, Viktor Lynnik, who was said to be a consultant in the Department of International Information (I personally believed him to be KGB) and Andrei Parastaev. The British delegation included two new participants: Sir Ian McGeoch, former Flag Officer Scotland and Northern Ireland (and at that stage Research Associate at the Defence Studies Department) and Aubrey Manning, Professor of Zoology at Edinburgh University.

At the request of my UK organisers, I invited Professor Eugene Rostow – a well-known hawk in Washington who had served as head of the US Arms Control and Disarmament Agency. Throughout the discussions, Rostow repeatedly made the non-use of force commitment in the UN Charter his theme. He and I were now official members of the UK delegation; we participated freely. Nonetheless, it was very clear that East–West relations were at an all-time low, or close to it, and one could not speak of any particular breakthroughs, as all participants were deliberately careful. I did not want, for example, to offend my UK hosts and in particular Professor Erickson. The communiqué did refer to the upcoming Stockholm conference, for which Mikhailov and I had negotiated the mandate at the just-concluded CSCE meeting in Madrid and the talks in Geneva. The closing words of the communiqué read: '[W]e consider these dialogues to be significant, with their significance possibly growing and enhanced by American participation. Continuity of exchange, access and discussion among participants, each distinguished in his own way and exerting a variety of influences, has proved its worth.'

The Stockholm conference kicked off in January 1984 with the Soviet Foreign Minister Andrei Gromyko giving the most virulent anti-American speech in recorded diplomatic history. The deployment of US 'first-strike' nuclear missiles, as Gromyko called NATO's new Pershing-2 missile system, made arms control or any other form of political accommodation impossible. In the meantime I had retired from the US Air Force and had been named as deputy head of the US delegation in Stockholm. In view of this new assignment, the Edinburgh Conversations took on new significance for me.

\*

The fourth set was held in Moscow from 15 to 22 September 1984. Again I was asked to invite an American participant. I chose Ambassador Max Kampelman, for whom I had worked in Madrid and whom I knew to be a vigorous advocate for human rights and fundamental freedoms. While it would be a mistake to say that he opposed arms control, it was clear that the issue had little priority with him. The British delegation, in addition to Professor Erickson, Sir Hugh Beach and Sir John Burnett included Nicholas Soames MP (Churchill's grandson), Admiral Sir John Eberle (Director of the Royal Institute of International Affairs), Mr John Roper, a former MP and at that time member of the research staff of the Royal Institute of International Affairs, and Professor Manning. The Soviet delegation consisted of Georgiy Arbatov, Generals Mikhailov and Milshtein, Dr Lynnik, Dr Lev Semeiko, Dr Alex Yakovlev, Professor Sergei Kapitsa, the well-known physicist, and Genadiy Yanayev.

I was a little concerned that the Conversations this time seemed to reflect the bad relations between the Soviet Union and the United States. They kicked off with a discussion of Soviet abuse of dissidents and its violations of human-rights accords. When Georgiy Arbatov attacked me for my initial intervention, Ambassador Kampelman countered by referring to the Soviet Union as one huge concentration camp. Luckily, a non-emotional intervention by British Admiral Eberle took the edge off the confrontation and the meeting continued in a more diplomatic mode.

Behind the scenes, Professor Erickson was again consulted by all concerned. He was my light and conscience. It was, I think, clear that Dr Burnett, who felt responsible for the success or failure of the meetings, was concerned about the manner in which they had begun. From all I gathered at the time, Professor Erickson was able to reassure him that it was probably good that the meeting began with a rather rough exchange. That seemed to have cleared the air and allowed the participants to continue along a more measured course.

As always, the Soviets had pre-drafted the communiqué even before the meeting began. Professor Erickson found this entirely unacceptable since it was loaded with the usual clichés relating to first-strike missiles, no first use of nuclear weapons, the arms race, and nuclear issues more generally. During the time I and other participants were enjoying an evening at the Soviet circus in Moscow, Professor Erickson and Michael Wescott were redrafting the communiqué to rid it of the Soviet clichés. The draft was later shown to me and I objected to a couple of points, which were then improved during a meeting between Professor Erickson and Dr Burnett. Given the ugly nature of East–West relations, it was, of course, impossible to agree on many substantial points. Nonetheless, a communiqué was issued; I forwarded it to Washington, as I had done on previous occasions.

This set of conversations concerned itself substantially with ecological issues, with Professors Kapitsa and Manning influencing the discussion and this was reflected in the communiqué:

> The participants agreed that, as a spur to securing international agreements, the possible aftermaths of a nuclear conflict should be considered. Medical groups from all countries, whose deliberations were summarised in a recent WHO document, were unanimous that there is no possible adequate response to the unprecedented suffering which would result from a nuclear conflict. Their opinion was accepted. It is now realised that in addition to the other dangers of a nuclear exchange, it would have climatic and environmental effects which would transcend the boundaries of the area of conflict.

Following the close of business Professor Erickson and I then tried to visit the Soviet war museum but found it closed. We were able to walk around the outside displays of tanks and aircraft and took some pleasure in being able to see and touch equipment that had a short time previously been front-line armament. I was struck by the intensity of Professor Erickson's personal involvement in the Conversations this time around. It was clear that this set had disturbed him to a greater degree than previous ones. Although I did not have any direct line into his personal feelings, I knew him well. My sense was that he disliked very much being forced into taking sides or representing one point of view over the other. I knew that for the most part he was very supportive of NATO and even US policies, but wanted the conversations to be more academic in character in a way that allowed varying opinions. The Soviet pre-draft of the communiqué had destroyed this approach.

The fifth set of Conversations was again held in Edinburgh between 12 and 17 April 1986. The Soviet side was unchanged, apart from the addition of Anatoly Masko. The British delegation now included Brigadier John Hemsley, who at the time was a Research Fellow at the Department of Defence Studies, and Bruce Millan (former Secretary of State for Scotland). On the American side Professor Dick Thomas from Texas A&M University's Centre for Strategic Technology attended. Much had changed. In Stockholm, we had actually been negotiating with one another for the first time and it seemed clear that an agreement there was possible. The new Soviet leader, Mikhail Gorbachev, had removed Gromyko as Foreign Minister and replaced him with Eduard Shevardnadze. As a team they seemed to be exploring the possibility of accommodating some of the preoccupations of the West in the area of arms control.

Despite the fact that the United States had launched an air strike against Libya at almost the precise time the Conversations were to commence, the Russian participants did not dwell on the issue. This was the first clue that maybe things really had changed. By this time I had been given the rank of ambassador and was very engaged in the Stockholm negotiations. There, I sensed the possibility for agreement, although there were still many unresolved issues.

Soviet participants in the Conversations struck an almost conciliatory mood. Much was made of the changes in the Soviet Union that were taking place under the banner of perestroika – 'restructuring' is one translation of the word. Although the American participants (Colonel Fred Boli – who had also been a US Air Force Research Associate in Defence Studies – and Dr Dick Thomas from Texas A&M University) were mildly sceptical, it was clear that something was happening.

As turned out to have been the case at each preceding set of talks, Professor Erickson was busy behind the scenes interpreting each delegation to the other and taking steps to ensure that particularly the Scottish media did not give the wrong slant to the Conversations in their reporting. He was particularly engaged in developing a strategy for the usual press conference and the accompanying communiqué. After the press conference it was gratifying to read in *The Scotsman*:

> One of the few places in the world where Russians and Americans were talking civilly to each other yesterday was the third floor room in an Edinburgh Georgian terrace where the University's Department of Defence Studies stores large quantities of blank paper and keeps magazines like *NATO Review* and *Soviet East European* reports in neat piles. This was where delegates to the *Edinburgh Conversations* held a farewell reception.
>
> Nobody mentioned Libya, unless asked. Professor Gennady Yanaev of the Soviet Friendship Society said there had been no formal discussion, but he had given the view that the American attack did not contribute to world stability. Professor Richard Thomas, Director of the Centre for Strategic Technology, Texas, said that he had made the point that it was a pity that the possession of Soviet weaponry allowed Gaddafi to be so bellicose.
>
> But no – nobody had even suggested that the Conversations should be halted. To symbolise the supranationality of it all, Dr. Vyktor Lynnik of the Department of International Information will take back to Moscow a mock Scottish passport and two haggis-like gonks for his daughters. Jaw-jaw has survived war-war.

*Perestroika*, it turned out, became an important issue throughout the Soviet Union even though Russian humorists were quick to poke fun at it. Still, there remained essential gaps in mutual understanding, since East and

West approached peace and stability in quite different ways. Nonetheless participants returned to Moscow for the sixth set of Conversations between and 27 September and 3 October 1987 in a hopeful mood. The British delegation now included Sir Clive Rose (former UK ambassador to NATO), Field Marshal Sir John Stanier, Air Commodore Ted Williams, Brigadier John Hemsley, Group Captain David Bolton, former British Air Attaché in Moscow, and Nigel Calder. Professor Thomas, Colonel Boli, William Taylor from the US office at NATO, and I were from the United States. At this time I was Assistant Director of the US Arms Control and Disarmament Agency in Washington.

In general I was feeling quite positive about East–West relations. A year earlier, we had successfully concluded an agreement in Stockholm that allowed on-site inspections of troops in the field. Several of these inspections had been conducted by many different states, all without incident.

It was nonetheless a little disconcerting to learn that the Russians had drafted a concluding communiqué before we had begun discussing the issues at hand. Again, it was Professor Erickson who had to deal in the first instance with this tricky question.

The issue most jarring to the Soviet mind was President Reagan's Strategic Defense Initiative (SDI), often referred to as 'Star Wars'. I was very sensitive to this issue; I was, after all, now a politically appointed member of the Reagan administration. Of course the Soviet draft had us all agreeing to a condemnation of SDI. With John playing the leading role, a counter-communiqué had been drafted by Western participants, which would then be played off against the Soviet draft. SDI was tied up with the Ballistic Missile Treaty and the final draft included text relating to maintaining the sanctity of that document. In the end, I reluctantly agreed to allow the text, knowing that Washington's view was that SDI did not violate the treaty itself. Professor Erickson and others were greatly relieved.

It seemed to me that this set of Conversations showed rather conclusively that the monolithic nature of the Soviet Union was cracking. Clearly we had engaged in the most far-ranging exchanges to date. On the world stage, the Stockholm Agreement was followed by the Treaty on the Elimination of Intermediate Range Nuclear Missiles, negotiations were back on track with respect to strategic nuclear weapons, and in the Geneva Conference on Disarmament there was progress on eliminating chemical weapons. NATO and the Warsaw Pact were engaged in negotiations aimed at eliminating the asymmetries in conventional forces in Europe. In the confidence-building sphere, work was under way to create the mechanisms to facilitate regular exchanges between American and Russian military officers.[7]

*

Against this background the seventh and final set of Edinburgh Conversations took place in Edinburgh between 4 and 8 December 1988. Although everyone put forth the best effort, it soon became evident that developments in the relationship between East and West had advanced so far that the original need for the Conversations had ceased to exist. Of course, they could have been continued under some other rubric as academic exchanges, but the fire was gone.[8]

## Concluding Observations

To the best of my knowledge, Professor Erickson has not written about the Edinburgh Conversations. In many respects this is a shame. He, more than any of us, understood the spirit and the dynamics of what was taking place. His own peculiar and particular knowledge of the Soviet military and consequently of Soviet politics not only was key to the success of the Conversations but it also gave him a yardstick against which to measure the events that transpired during the seven years in which Russian, British, and American representatives sat in an informal circle and discussed events that might have been disastrous.

While it is true that the Conversations had no official status with any government, they nonetheless provided a venue where key officials could have frank and open exchanges in an environment that allowed one to probe the limits of what might be possible. I believe that this forum, as envisaged by Lord Ritchie Calder and implemented so wisely by Professor Erickson, Sir John Burnett and Michael Wescott contributed immensely to the transition that eventually took place in Soviet politics and policies. Certainly the message was repeatedly given that no one in the West wanted a nuclear war and indeed no one was planning one. The edge was taken off the *Feindbild* (enemy image), allowing serious progress on serious matters.

Having participated in all but the very first of the Conversations I am convinced their success was in huge measure attributable to Professor Erickson. I was always greatly impressed with the respect shown him by all participants, irrespective of what country they represented. His genius could not be hidden, his love for his country was unshielded, and his devotion to academic rigour was as much in evidence here as in his many books and articles.

# NOTES

## JOHN ERICKSON AND RUSSO-SCOTTISH CONNECTIONS

1 This paper was first presented at the John Erickson Memorial Panel, British Association For Slavonic And East European Studies, Fitzwilliam College, Cambridge, 29–31 March 2003.

2 On Robison and many others, see A. G. Cross, *'By the Banks of the Thames': Russians in Eighteenth-Century Britain* (Newtonville, Mass., 1980) and *'By the Banks of the Neva': Chapters from the Lives and Careers of the British in Eighteenth-Century Russia* (Cambridge, 1996).

3 See more generally H. A. and M. T. Brück, *The Peripatetic Astronomer: The Life of Charles Piazzi Smyth* (Bristol, 1988).

4 The contributions by Fedosov, Cross and Hughes are to be found in Mark Cornwall and Murray Frame, *Scotland and the Slavs: Cultures in Contact 1500–2000* (Newtonville, Mass., 2001).

5 See Dimitry Fedosov, *The Caledonian Connection: Scotland–Russia Ties Middle Ages to Early Twentieth Century: A Concise Biographical List* (Aberdeen, 1996).

## Chapter 1   COCK OF THE EAST

1 *The Enterprising Scot*, ed. J. Calder (Edinburgh, 1986), p. 13.

2 C. O. Skelton & J. M. Bulloch, *The House of Gordon*, vol. III, *Gordons Under Arms* (Aberdeen, 1912).

3 Besides J. M. Bulloch's work see Paul Dukes, 'Scottish Soldiers in Muscovy', in *The Caledonian Phalanx: Scots in Russia* (Edinburgh, 1987), pp. 18–23; *idem*, 'Patrick Gordon and His Family Circle: Some Unpublished Letters', *Scottish Slavonic Review*, no. 10 (1988), pp. 19–49; G. P. Herd, *General Patrick Gordon of Auchleuchries: A Scot in Russian Service*, PhD dissertation (University of Aberdeen,

1995); A. Brückner, *Patrick Gordon i yego dnevnik* (St Petersburg, 1878).

4 *Passages from the Diary of General Patrick Gordon of Auchleuchries* (Aberdeen, 1859; reprint N.Y., 1968), the only edition of the English original, is still useful, but contains just a smaller part of the whole; *Tagebuch des Generals Patrick Gordon*, 3 vols. (Moscow–St Petersburg, 1849–53) is the German version by M. C. Posselt, very faulty and incomplete. My own unabridged translation into Russian is in progress: *P. Gordon. Dnevnik 1635–1659* (Moscow, 2000) and *Dnevnik 1659–1667* (Moscow, 2002); I am now halfway through the third of six surviving volumes (1677–8).

5 Judging by some quotations and hints in his journal. In 1686 Gordon recorded seeing *Hamlet* in London, probably the earliest known reference to Shakespeare by a resident of Russia.

6 Patrick Gordon, *Diary*, vol. I, Russian State Archive of Military History (RGVIA), Moscow, Fond 846, opis' 15, no. 1, f. 5.

7 By my count Gordon mentions 127 named Scots alone in volume I of his diary and 118 in volume II, mostly soldiers on the continent. No wonder in some Swedish and Polish units officers preferred Scottish broadswords and pistols, while the Scots pint was used to measure the beer allowance.

8 The patent is dated 2 July 1661 in Warsaw. Gordon, *Diary*, vol. II, RGVIA, Fond 846, opis' 15, no. 2, f. 116 v.

9 *Ibid.*, f. 37 v.

10 See, for instance, Johann Georg Korb, *Diarium Itineris in Mscoviam* (Vienna, 1700) or various translations of this work.

11 *Diary*, I, f. 66.

12 Words of M. C. Posselt, German editor of the diary. *Dnevnik Generala Patrika Gordona* (Moscow, 1892), pt. I, p. 7.

13 *Diary*, II, ff. 20–20 v., 39 v.

14 A. Brückner, *Patrick Gordon i yego dnevnik* (St Petersburg, 1878), p. 134. This is still the best essay on Gordon in Russian.

15 *Diary*, I, ff. 52, 125–125 v.

16 D. V. Tsvetayev, *Istoriya sooruzheniya pervago kostiola v Moskve* (Moscow, 1886).

17 *Diary*, I, ff. 12 v., 44.

18 *Ibid.*, f. 181 v.

19 *Ibid.*, f. 239.

20 His rank then was actually captain lieutenant.

21 *Diary*, II, f. 55. See also R. Romański, *Cudnów 1660* (Warszawa, 1996).

22 *Ibid.*, p. 139. Cf. *Diary*, II, ff. 69–76. Romański wrongly styles Gordon a lieutenant, a rank he never had.

23 The first document of Gordon's Russian period has survived; it is a petition for reward by himself and fellow Scots with a note of the tsar's consent on 7 September 1661. It also runs: 'To Major Patricius is given 40 roubles, 8 pairs [of sables] at 5 roubles a pair, [and] *kamka kufter* [a piece of cloth]' (RGVIA, F. 495, op. 1, no. 27, ff. 2–3).

24 *Diary*, II, ff. 130–130 v. In *Passages from the Diary...* (Aberdeen, 1859), p. 47, based on a transcript by M. C. Posselt, this fragment is heavily censored: '... morose and niggard, and yet overweening and valuing themselves above all other nations'.

25 British archives preserve a number of documents about these visits, some unknown or unpublished. I have found deeds of factory, issued by Patrick Gordon in 1670 and 1686, in the National Archives of Scotland.

26 *Diary*, II, f. 148 v.

27 *Ibid.*, f. 157.

28 King Charles's reply to the tsar, delivered by Gordon, is preserved in the original (Russian State Archive of Ancient Acts (RGADA), Moscow, F. 35, op. 2, no. 98). The parchment is damaged, but the diary gives the full text.

29 *Diary*, III, RGVIA, F. 846, op. 15, no. 3, ff. 100–106.

30 These were the abortive coups inspired

by Tsar Peter's half-sister Sophia and backed by the *streltsy*.

31 *Rasskazy Nartova o Petre Velikom* (St Petersburg, 1891), pp. 104–5.

32 Gordon must have been involved in the adoption of the saltire as a Russian national emblem (naval flag and Order of St Andrew) in the late 1690s, a striking sign of Scottish influence.

## Chapter 2   JOMINI VERSUS CLAUSEWITZ

1 Liddle Hart, B. H. *Strategy the Indirect Approach*, NY 1954.

2 *Military Historical Journal* (VIZh) no. 11, 2002; also *Red Star* (K3) 16.10. 2002 and 7.12.2002

3 A. N. Mertsalov and L. A. Mertsalova, *A. A. Jomini: The Founder of the Theory of Military Science* (Moscow, 1999).

4 *Life and Fate of Professor I. N. Borozdin* (Voronezh State University, 2000); A. Stahel, *Klassiker der Strategie* (Zürich, Pressdek AG, 1995); A. Stachel, *Strategisch Denken*, (Zürich, Hochschulverlag AG, 1997).

5 A. N. Mertsalov, *A Historian on his Forebears and Himself* (Moscow 2001), Appendix no. 14.

6 A. M. Samsonov *Second World War* (Moscow, Nauka, 1990), p. 605. Academician Samsonov thought very highly of John Erickson. See A. M. Samsonov, *Past Memories* (Moscow, Nauka, 1988), pp. 302–315.

7 N. Kudryavtsev, *Napoleonic Echos* (St Petersburg, 1912), pp. 13, 38.

8 S. A. Tyushkevich, *Military Science of the Fatherland* (Krasnodar, Krasnodar University, 2001), p. 54.

9 See B. A. Anikin, *Logistics* (Moscow, 2000), pp. 9–10.

10 See *The History of Military Strategy of Russia* (Moscow, Kuchkovo Pole, 2000), pp. 11, 84.

11 N. P. Glinoetskii, *Historical Study of the Nikolaevskaya Academy of the General Staff* (St Petersburg, 1881), vol. 1. p. 253.

12 K. Clausewitz, *On War*, (Moscow, AST, 2002), vol. I. pp. 22–6, 33, 66.

13 *Ibid.*, p. 410.

14 *Ibid.*, pp. 13, 573–4.

15 *Ibid.*, vol. I, pp. 477, 479; vol. II, pp. 407–11, 422, 431–42.

16 Quotation from *Philosophy of War* (Moscow, Ankil-voin, 1995).

17 *Izvestiya*, 5.1.2003.

18 See G.-A. Jakcobsen '1939–1945', in the book *Second World War: Two Views* (Moscow, Mysl', 1995), p. 67.

19 V. I. Lenin, *The Complete Works of Lenin*, (Moscow, Politizdat), volume XXXVI, p. 292.

20 K. Clausewitz, *On War* (2002), volume II, pp. 410–11, 437–9.

21 Philosophy of War, Soviet Military Doctrine (Westport, 1992), pp. 18–19.

22 *Bol'shevik*, no. 3, 1947.

23 Clausewitz AST, p. 4.

24 A. E. Snesarev, 1865–1937, author of 'The philosophy of war' (pub. 2003) and Head of the Academy of General Staff, 1919–1921.

25 See Protiv reaktsionnykh teorii na voenno-istoricheskom fronte (Leningrad Leninizdat, 1931).

26 A. Mikoyan, *Tak Bylo* (Moscow Izdatel'stvo Vagrius).

27 K. K. Rokossovskii, *Soldatskii Dolg* (Moscow, Voennoe Izdatel'stvo), pp. 164–171.

28 See author's article in *Barbarossa: The Axis and the Allies*, (Edinburgh, Edinburgh University Press, 1994, 1998).

29 N. G. Kuznetsov, *Nakanune* (Moscow, Voenizdat, 1991), pp. 719–29; Rokossovskii, op. cit., p. 253, and others.

30 *Krasnaya Zvezda* (Red Star) 26.9.2002.

31 See G. Hoth, *Tankovye operatsii* (Tank Operations) (Smolensk, Rusich, 1999), p. 236.

32 *Rossiya i SSSR v voinakh XX veka (Russia and the USSR in the Wars of 20th Century)* (Moscow, Olma Press, 2001); ViZh no. 11, 2002; see also author's article 'Stalinizm i voina' (Stalinism and the war), *Rodina*, no. 2, 2003.

33 M. A. Gareev, *Neodnoznachnie stranitsi voiny* (Significant Pages of the War, Moscow, Izdatel'stvo RFM, 1995), pp. 298, 302; Nezavisimoe voennoe obozrenie, no. 30, 2004.

34 Itogi izucheniya v SSSR–RF istorii voiny: Rossiya v XX v. (The Results of the Studies of War in the USSR–Russian Federation) (Moscow, Nauka, 1996), pp. 619–29 Appendix no. 16 to author's book of 2001; Zhukov in the most recent

publications, Voenno istoricheskii arkhiv no. 5, no. 6; D. M. Glantz, *Zhukov's Greatest Defeat* (Kansas, University Press of Kansas, 1999).

35 See *Velikaya Otechestvennaya Voina 1941–1945* Kn. 4, (The Great Patriotic War, 1941–1945, book 4) (Moscow, Nauka, 1999), pp. 302, 314; Istoriya voennoi strategii Rossii (Moscow, Kuchkovo Pole, 2000), pp. 351–67; Voennaya istoriya Rossii (Moscow, Kuchkovo Pole, 2001), pp. 572–87; S. A. Tyushkevich Ukaz Soch. p. 153, pp. 175–6; *Krasnqya Zvezda*, 25.12.2002

36 A. Zinov'ev, *Sovetskaya Rossiya*, 29.10.2002.

37 See S. V. Kudryashov, Velikaya Otechestvennaya voina v noveishikh trudakh angliskikh i amerikanskikh istorikov (Moscow, Institut Rossiiskoi Istorii, RAN, 1996).

38 Compare Krasnaya Zvezda, 10.1.2003.

## Chapter 3 'CATASTROPHES TO COME...'

This chapter is largely drawn from the author's PhD thesis *The Russian and Soviet View of the Military-Technical Character of Future War, 1877–2017* (two volumes, University of Edinburgh, 1991), supervised by John Erickson from 1987 to 1991. On 8 December 1991, seven weeks after the viva (18 October 1991), the break-up of the Soviet Union at the end of 1991 was announced. Although the author intended to revise the thesis for publication, other priorities intervened and it was never published. This chapter is therefore the first opportunity to present an updated summary of its findings.

1 John Erickson, *The Road to Stalingrad: Stalin's War with Germany, Volume 1* (Panther, London, 1985), 'On War Games, Soviet and German', p. 23.

2 See I. F. Clark, 'The First Forecast of the Future', *Futures, the Journal of Forecasting and Planning*, June 1969, pp. 325–30. For some (mainly literary) predictions of future war see his book *Voices Prophesying War, 1763–1984* (Oxford University Press, 1966).

3 Valeriy Bryusov '*Zapadny Front*' ('Western front'), *Russkiye vedomosti (Russian Gazette,*

[a quality newspaper similar to the *Independent*]), no. 290, 17 December 1914, poem dated 30 November, p. 3, col. 1, '*Ot Alp nepodvizhnykh do Pa-de-Kale Kak-budto doroga bezhit po zemle ...*', translated by the author.

4 Cited in Alastair Horne, *Death of a Generation (Neuve Chapelle to Verdun and the Somme)* (Macdonald Library of the 20th Century, Macdonald, London, 1970), p. 72.

5 By 30 November 1914 the British front-line trenches had not even been connected up. See Brigadier General J. E. Edmonds and Captain G. C. Wynne, *History of the Great War Based on Official Documents, Military Operations, France and Belgium, 1915* (Macmillan, London, 1927), pp. vi–vii, 4–5.

6 Ivan S. Bliokh [transliteration, using Nato Stanag system, of his name as rendered at the time in Russian] *Budushchaya voyna v tekhnicheskom, ekonomicheskom I politicheskom otnosheniyakh (Future War in its technical, economic and political relations)* 5 volumes, plus Atlas of diagrams, Tipografiya I A Yefrona, St Petersburg, 1898). *Obshchye vyvody iz sochineniya 'Budushchaya voyna...' (General conclusions from the work 'Future war...')*, which form a sixth volume, are sometimes cited separately. Bloch's work was published in full in French and German the following year. The *General Conclusions* were translated into English as *Is War now impossible? Being an abridgement of 'The war of the Future in its Technical, Economic and Political Relations' by I. S. Bloch with a Prefatory Conversation with the Author by W. T. Stead* (Grant Richards, London, 1899).

This quotation, *Obshchye vyvody*, p. 49; *Is War now impossible?* p. 41.

For a reappraisal by the author, Dr Christopher Bellamy ' "Civilian Experts" and Russian Defence Thinking: the Renewed Relevance of Jan Bloch', *RUSI Journal*, vol. 137, no. 2, (April 1992), pp. 50–56.

7 V. A. Melikov, *Strategicheskoye razvërtivaniye (Strategic deployment)* (Voyenizdat, Moscow, 1939), vol. 1, p. 514, cited in Col. R. A. Savushkin, 'Zarozhdeniye i razvitiye sovetskoy voyennoy doktriny' ('The birth and development of Soviet Military doctrine'), *Voyenno-istoricheskiy zhurnal (Military-Historical Journal) (VIZh)*, 2/1988, pp. 19–26, this ref., p. 23.

8 'Joint', for tri-service and 'combined', for multinational within an Alliance, are the current Nato terms – hence 'Combined Joint Task Forces'. As the late war with Iraq has demonstrated more than ever, modern military operations also have to be inter-agency, involving intelligence and counter-intelligence services, communications intelligence services, Non-Governmental Organisations, national development agencies and so on. Aleksandr Svechin (1878–1938), writing about future total war, recognised this in *Strategiya (Strategy)*, (2nd edn., Voyenny Vestnik press, Moscow, 1927 [first edition was 1925]). Svechin, a former tsarist major general, disappeared in 1938, presumably a victim of the great purge.

9 An allusion to the range of agencies and expertise recruited to the UK Government Code and Cypher School at Bletchley Park during World War II, and also to the BBC, broadcasting to the Home Front and to occupied Europe.

10 Col. A. A. Sidorenko, *The Offensive* (translated under the auspices of the US Air Force, US Government Printing Office, Washington DC, 1976), p. 61. Translated from the Russian *Nastupleniye* (Voyenizdat, Moscow, 1970).

11 The film shown in 1935 recorded the 1934 Minsk manoeuvres. The film of the 1935 Kiev manoeuvres received a wider audience. Ivan Maisky (Soviet ambassador to the UK), '*V Londone*' ('In London'), in N. I. Koritskiy, ed., *Marshal Tukhachevskiy: vospominaniya druzey I soratnikov (Marshal Tukhachevskiy: Memoirs of Friends and Comrades-in-Arms)*, (Voyenizdat, Moscow, 1965), p. 229.

12 Raymond L Garthoff, ed. and trans., *Science and Technology in Contemporary War by General G. I. Pokrovskiy* (Atlantic Books, London, 1959), p. viii.

13 General A. N. Kuropatkin, *The Russian Army and the Japanese War*, trans. Capt. A. B. Lindsay, ed. Maj. E. D. S. Swinton (2 vols., John Murray, London, 1909),

editor's Introduction, vol. 1, p. xi. The book was translated from a 'faint carbon copy of a typescript', which Kuropatkin had been unable to publish. However, much of the same material also appears in Kuropatkin's *Zadachi Russkoy Armii* (*The Role of the Russian Army*), (3 vols., V. A. Berezovskiy, Commissioner of Military-Educational Establishments, St Petersburg, 1910).

14 'I have received ... the letter which Your Excellency was good enough to send me in reply to that which I wrote to him on the subject of the changes that railways will impose on future wars and, above all, on defensive wars.' Jomini to Milyutin, *Egerton MSS 3168*, Department of Manuscripts, British Library, ff. 67–68, letter dated 18 September Old Style, 30 September, New Style, 1866. The drafts of these letters, full of alterations, were retained as a record, the fair copy being sent to the addressee.

15 In his book *Deep Battle: the Brainchild of Mikhail Tukhachevskiy* (Brassey's, London, 1987), pp. 5, 83, the late Brigadier Richard Simpkin (1921–86) suggests that Tukhachevskiy (1893–1937) did not develop an elegant Russian style because, as a down-at-heel Russian aristocrat, his first language might have been French. The present author finds this difficult to believe, partly because Tukhachevskiy was not from the higher aristocracy, but more because the voluminous oceans of material on military matters published in late imperial Russia are all in Russian.

16 N.Z., '*Zadachi kavalerii v sovremennykh voynakh*', *Voyenny Sbornik (Military Collection) (VSb)*, 9/1877, pp. 25–43.

17 *Ibid.*, p. 25, line 7.

18 Interview with Dr Romil K. Tshenin of the Institute of World Economics and International Relations, Soviet Academy of Sciences, on a visit to Edinburgh, January 1989; former GRU officer, using pseudonym Viktor Suvorov, interviewed at the offices of his publishers, Hamish Hamilton, Kensington, London, 18 May 1990.

19 Record of discussions between US Army representatives and the Soviet General Staff, September 1989. The Soviet representatives said they had eschewed

the term *budushchaya voyna* because it implied that (a) future war was inevitable.

20 *Sovetskaya voyennya entsiklopediya (SVE)*, 8 vols., Voyenizdat, Moscow, 1976–8; *Voyenno-entsiklopedicheskiy slovar'(VES)* (Voyenizdat, Moscow, 1983, 1986).

21 Nikonov and G. Tummeltau, '*Budushchaya voyna*', *SVE*, vol. 2 (1933), pp. 834–44.

22 *Vazhneyshuyu chast' voyennoy doktriny*. 'The most important' would have been *samuyu vazhneyshuyu*...

23 *SVE*, vol. 2 (1976), p. 184.

24 Lt. Gen. Makhmut A. Gareyev, 'Soviet Military Doctrine', lecture 18 October 1988 to the Royal United Services Institute (RUSI), London, attended by the author, recorded in *RUSI Journal*, Vol. 133, no. 4 (Winter 1988), pp. 5–10.

25 Thomas S. Kuhn, *The Structure of Scientific Revolutions* (2nd edn, 1st edn was 1962), enlarged, *Foundations of the History of Science*, vol. II, no. 2, International Encyclopedia of Unified Science (University of Chicago Press, 1970).

26 On 'Military Revolutions' see author's entry in Richard Holmes, ed., *The Oxford Companion to Military History* (Oxford University Press, 2001), pp. 587–8. The Russians coined the term 'Revolution in Military Affairs' to cover the paradigm shift created by ballistic missiles with (thermo-)nuclear warheads, but the Americans hijacked it around the time of the 1991 Gulf War to describe the 'revolution' centred around the microchip. By the end of the 1990s, however, the preferred term was 'military transformation' and a Transformation Office was set up in the Pentagon. Cyril Falls, in *A Hundred Years of War, 1850–1950* (London, 1953) noted that observers often described the military changes they were witnessing as 'revolutionary' but that in fact military affairs made continuous and 'on the whole, fairly even' progress.

27 *SVE*, vol. 3 (1977), p. 225, '*prinyataya v gosudarstve na dannoye vremya sistema vzglyadov na tseli i kharakter vozmozhnoy voyny*'...

28 Marshal Nikolay V. Ogarkov, *Vsegda v gotovnosti k zashchite otechestva (Always in Readiness to Defend the Motherland)* (Voyenizdat, Moscow, 1982) (signed to press 26 January), p. 53. '*vozmozhnoy*

*budushchey voyny ... na dannoye*
*(opredelënnoye) vremya'*.

29  *VES*, 1986 edn, p. 240.

30  Rear Admiral G. Kostev, '*Nasha voyennaya
doktrina v svete novogo politicheskogo
myshleniya*' ('Our Military doctrine in the
Light of New Political Thinking'),
*Kommunist Vooruzhennykh Sil (Communist of
the Armed Forces)(KVS)*, 17
(September)1987, pp. 9–15, this, p 10.
'*Na predotvrashcheniye voyny*'. Emphasis
added.

31  '*Oboronitel 'ny kharakter sovetskoy voyennoy
doktriny i podgotovka voysk (sil)*' ('The
Defensive Character of Soviet Military
Doctrine and the Preparation and
Training of Forces'), *Voyennaya Mysl'
(MilitaryThought)(VM)*, 1/1988, pp. 3–13.
Emphasis added.

32  V. Krasnov, V. Daynes, *Russkiy voyenno-
istoricheskiy slovar'* (*Russian Military-
Encyclopædic Dictionary*), (Olma-Press,
Moscow, 2002), ISBN5–224–01493-X,
p. 184.

33  Charles E. Callwell, *Small Wars: Their
Principles and Practice* (HMSO 1896, 1899,
1906). Reprint of the latter with
Introduction by Douglas Porch (Bison
Books/University of Nebraska, Lincoln
and London, 1996).

34  Even after the long experience in
Afghanistan, there was no evidence the
Soviet Army was moving towards
'"doctrine" or force structures specifically
tailored to such operations'. Scott R.
McMichael, 'The Soviet Army,
Counterinsurgency and the Afghan War',
*Parameters*, December 1989, pp. 21–35.

35  Callwell, ed. Porch, pp. 32, 36, 79, 104,
145, 187, 247, 265, 266, 272, 278, 285,
388, 399, 444.

36  A. Kotenev, '*O razgrome basmacheskikh
band v Sredney Azii*' ('The defeat of the
Basmachi Bands in central Asia'),
*Voyenno-istoricheskiy zhurnal (Military-
Historical Journal) (VIZh)*, 2/1987, pp. 59–
64. On p. 63 Kotenev asks 'Why did this
last so long?' [14 years], suggesting a
parallel with the then ongoing Afghan
dilemma.

37  Arvydas Anušauskas, ed., *The Anti-Soviet
Resistance in the Baltic States*, (Genocide
and Resistance Research Center of
Lithuania, Du Ka, Vilnius, 1999),

esp. pp. 61 (four-fifths of partisans), 240–
41.

38  'First Public Subscription to MVD
Journal', Radio Liberty report on the
USSR, 8 September 1989, p. 48 (report
dated 1 September).

39  Author's interview with General
Shabanov on ministerial flight from
Leningrad to Moscow, 18 May 1990.

40  The author reported for the *Independent*
from Chechnya, January to February 1995.

41  *The National Security Concept of the Russian
Federation*, approved 10 January 2000,
replacing that of 1997:
http://www.russiaeurope.mid.ru/
RussiaEurope/russiastrat2000.html

42  *The Military Doctrine of the Russian
Federation*, approved 21 April 2000,
replacing that of 1993:
http://www.freerepublic.com.forum/
a394aa0466bfe.htm

43  *SVE*, vol. 1, pp. 500–501.

44  I. F. Clarke, 'The Great War that never
was, 1871–1914', *Futures*, vol. 16, no. 6,
December 1984, pp. 641–7, this, p. 646.
This issue is discussed further in the
author's article '"Civilian experts"...', see
note 6.

45  A. K. Puzyrevskiy '*Budushchaya voyna v
tendentioznom izobrazhenii*' ('Tendentious
images of future war'), *Razvedchik (Scout)*,
(St Petersburg), no. 410, 1898, pp. 737–
40; no. 411, pp. 755–6, a reprint of
Puzyrevskiy's review in *Varshavskiy
Dnevnik (Warsaw Daily)*, nos. 200, 201
(1898); A. I. Dragomirov, '*Otkritoye pis'mo
G Bliokhu*' ('Open letter to Mr Bloch'),
*Razvedchi*, no. 316, 1898, pp. 976–7.

46  Kuropatkin's recommendation, in W. T.
Stead, prefatory conversation with Bloch,
cited in introduction to English edition
of *General Conclusions* (1899), p. xiii;
popularity in forces in spite of size, cited
in Lt. Col. (GS) Simanskiy, '*Otvet G
Bliokhu na ego trud "Budushchaya voyna"...*'
('*Reply to Mr Bloch on his work...*') (A. A.
Levenson, Moscow, 1898), p. 6.

47  Bloch, *Obshchye Vyvody (General
Conclusions)*, pp. 58–9.

48  V. T. Novitskiy, ed, *Voyennaya
entsiklopediya (Military Encyclopedia)*, (Sytin,
St Petersburg/Petrograd, 18 vols., 1911–
15, publication discontinued at letter 'P'),
vol. 4, pp. 569–70.

49 See the author's article, *Journal of Soviet Military Studies*, vol. 3, no. 3, (September 1990), pp. 491–512.

50 Bloch, *Budushchya voyna*, vol. 4, and the *Atlas of Appendices*, 'Review of the Economic Difficulties in Russia in the Event of War (vol. 4, pp. 153–279); Russia's greater resilience was not an opinion peculiar to the Bloch study. A. Gulevich, *Voyna I narodnoye khozyaystvo (War and the Economy)* (1898) had predicted the same, and is cited in Aleksandr Svechin, *Strategiya (Strategy)* (2nd edn, Voyenny vestnik Press, Moscow, 1927), pp. 32–3, note 1, as a possible source of the Bloch study's ultimate error.

51 'Doktrina voyennaya', in Krasnov and Daynes, *Russkiy voyenno-entsiklopedicheskiy slovar'*, (2002), p. 184.

52 *Ibid.*

53 N. P. Mikhnevich, *Osnovy strategii* (St Petersburg 1913), extract in L. G. Beskrovny, ed., *Russkaya voyenno-teoreticheskaya mysl' xix I nachala xx vek (Russian Military-Theoretical thought of the late 19th and early 20th Centuries)* (Nauka, Moscow, 1960).

54 A. A. Neznamov, *Plan voyny*, in Beskrovny, op. cit.

55 A. A. Neznamov, *Sovremennaya voyna. Deystviya polevoy armii* (1912) in Beskrovny, op. cit.

56 A. A. Neznamov, *Sovremennaya voyna. Chast' vtoraya (Plan voyny, krepost', boyevaya podgotovka armii) (Contemporary warfare. Second part. . .)* (Vysshiy voyenny redaktsionny Sovet, Gosizdat, 1921).

57 E. I. Martynov, *Strategiya v epokhu Napoleona I i v nashe vremya (Strategy in the Age of Napoleon I and in our time)* (General Staff Press, St Petersburg, 1894), p. 297.

58 A. Petrov, *'Zadachi sovremennoy strategii'* ('Tasks of Contemporary Strategy'), *Voyenny Sbornik (VSb)*, 5/1894, pp. 35–64, esp. pp. 49, 50, 53.

59 H. G. Wells, *'War and Common Sense'*, reprinted from the *Daily Mail*, 7, 8, 9 April 1913, pp. 7–9; *The War that will End War* (Frank and Cecil Palmer, London, September 1914), pp. 66–7.

60 E. I. Martynov, 'Neskol'ko slov v ob'yasneniye I razvitiye sochineniya "Strategiya. . ."' ('A Few Words in Explanation and Development of the Word *Strategy*. . .') *Vsb* 7/1894,

pp. 21–41; 8/1894, pp. 232–48, this p. 236 of the latter, emphasis in original.

61 General N. P. Mikhnevich, 'Poyavyatsya-li milionniya armii v budushchey bol'shoy yevropeyskoy voyny (Zametki po povodu stat' i A. Petrova "K voprosam strategii")' ('Will Million-Strong Armies appear in a Future Major European War? (Remarks on A Petrov's article 'On Questions of Strategy')'), *VSb* 2/1898, pp. 260–64, this p. 264.

62 S. Vishnev and A. Shpirt, *'Voyna motorov I rezervov'* ('(A)War of Engines and Reserves'), *Pravda*, 23 March 1941. Includes figures on the 'energy armament' *(energovooruzhennost')* of the world's leading armed forces.

63 Ellsworth L. Raymond, *Soviet Preparation for Total War, 1925–1951*, (PhD, University of Michigan, 1952, available through UMI Dissertation Information service).

64 Komkor (Lt. Gen.) Vladimir Triandafillov, *Kharakter operatsii sovremennykh armii (The Character of Operations of Contemporary Armies)*, (3rd edn, Gosvoyenizdat, Moscow, 1936) (259 pp.), p. 37 in section 'The possible numerical Strength of Mobilised Armies', sub-section 'Small motorized units or million-strong armies?' Cites Svechin *Strategiya* 1st edn., p. 172.

65 See the author's 'Red Star in the West: Marshal Tukhachevskiy and East–West Exchanges on the Art of War', *RUSI Journal*, vol. 132, no. 4 (December 1987), pp. 63–73.

66 Aleksandr A. Svechin, *Strategiya (Strategy)*, (2nd ed., Voyenny Vestnik Press, Moscow, 1927) (Preface to first edition was written in 1925).

67 Mikhail Tukhachevskiy, 'Predisloviye k knige Dzh Fullera, "Reformatsiya voyny"', in Tukhachevskiy, *Izbrannye proizvedeniya (Selected Works)* (2 vols., Moscow, 1964), pp. 147–56.

68 R. Eydeman 'K voprosu o kharaktere nachal'nogo perioda voyny' ('On the Question of the Character of the Opening Period of a War'), *Voyna I Revolyutsiya (War and Revolution) (ViR)*, 3/1931, pp. 11–17, this p. 17. Emphasis (!) in original. Eydeman was one of the editors of the unfinished 1933 *Military Encyclopedia*.

69 Mikhail Tukhachevskiy, *Voprosy*

*sovremennoy strategii* (*Questions of Modern strategy*), (pamphlet, Voyenny Vestnik Press, Moscow, 1926) in *Izbrannye proizvedeniya*, op. cit., vol. 1 (1917–1927), pp. 244–61, this p. 252.

70 Mikhail Tukhachevskiy, *O kharaktere sovremennykh voyn v svete resheniy VI Kongressa Kominterna* (*On the Character of Contemporary war in the Light of the Decisions of the VI Comintern Congress*), in *Kommunisticheskaya Akademiya, sektsiya po izucheniyu problem voyny* (Communist Academy, Section for the Study of Problems of War), Zapiski (notes), vol. 1, (*Izd. Kommunisticheskoy akademii*, Moscow, 1930), pp. 6–29, stenographic record of paper to the Leningrad branch of Komakad, pp. 3, 9, 14, 19. At the end of the Introduction to Fuller's *Reformation of War* (*Izbrannye proizvedeniya*), vol. 2, p. 156, he had stressed that 'the war of the imperialists against us will not savour of a little war'.

71 A. Kokoshin and Army Gen. V. N. Lobov, '*Predvideniye (General Svechin ob evolyutsii voyennogo iskusstva*' ('Foresight (General Svechin and the Evolution of Military Art)'), *Znamya* (*Standard*), February 1990, pp. 170–82, this p. 175, '*Pri strategii "izmora" mogut presledovat' stol' zhe reshitel nye voyennye I politicheskiye tseli, tak i pri "strategii sokrusheniya"*'.

72 Svechin, *Strategiya*, 2nd edn (1927), p. 38, top.

73 *Ibid.*, pp. 46–47 ('*Vedomstvo vnutrennykh del...*' By 1941 this was the People's Commissariat for Internal Affairs – NKVD), 48 (*Aviatsiya, radio-telegraf...*). Home leave was still very rare in the Red Army in the Great Patriotic War, unless you were either very senior, or wounded.

74 Donald W. Mitchell, *A History of Russian and Soviet Sea Power* (André Deutsch, London, 1974), pp. 185–6; *SVE*, vol. 8, pp. 81–2.

75 V. Adm. A. Belomor, *Rokovaya voyna 18?? Goda (otdeleniye ottiski iz zhurnala 'Russkoye sudokhodstvo')* (*The Fatal War of 18?? (Extracts from the Journal 'Russian Seaborne Trade')*), (R. Golik Press, St Petersburg, 1889).

76 'A.K.' [Anon. – probably Belomor, above], *Kreyser 'Russkaya Nadezhda'* (*The Cruiser 'Russian Hope'*), (S. S. Lyubavin, St Petersburg, 1887), translated into English as 'A.K.', *The "Russia's Hope"*.

77 *Der Zükunftskriege im Jahre 18?? ... Vision eines russischen Patrioten von A. Bjelomor. Einzig berechtigte Übersetzung von Karl Kupffer* (*Future War in the Year 18?? ... The Vision of a Russian Patriot by A. Bjelomor...*) (Zweite Auflage, Verlag von Heinrich Minden, Dresden and Leipzig, 1897).

78 'A.K.', *The "Russia's Hope"*, English version, pp. 24, 35, 105 (portee across Persia), 118–19.

79 Belomor, *Rokovaya voyna 18?? goda*, pp. 107–9.

80 *Ibid.*, p. 109.

81 Mikhail Bulgakov, *Rokovye yaytsa* (*The Fatal Eggs*). See Ellendea Proffer, ed., and Carl R. Proffer, trans., Mikhail Bulgakov, *Diaboliad and other Stories* (Indiana University Press, Bloomington and London, 1972), story pp. 48–134. The story is signed October 1924 and was first published in *Nedra*, no. 6 (Moscow, 1925), pp 79–148 (Proffer and Proffer, p xiii).

82 Bulgakov, *Rokovye yaytsa*, trans. Proffer, p. 127.

83 *US Military Intelligence Reports, Soviet Union, 1919–41.* Reel 10. Frames not numbered, original document no. 66/2 (mobilisation), *Mobilisation Plan for Leningrad factories and works*, 5 November 1928, items 5, 10.

84 Aleksey Tolstoy, *Giperboloid inzhenera Garina (Sovetskiy pisatel'*, Moscow, 1939), trans. George Hanna as *The Garin Death-Ray*, (Foreign Languages Publishing House, Moscow, 1955). All editions indicate that the work was written in 1926–7, suggesting that the Garin character had worked in Petrograd (1914–24) and had left the Soviet Union recently. The similarity between Garin's 'Hyperboloid' and the newly-discovered (1957) laser (Light Amplification by Stimulated Emission of Radiation) was explicitly noted in the article on Tolstoy's science-fiction work appended to the 1962 school edition of *Hyperboloid ... and Delita* (1922), (Vologda Book Publishers, 1944), p. 444.

85 Tolstoy, *The Garin Death-Ray*, English translation (1955), p. 100. On intellectual

life in Petrograd, see V. Shcherbin's critical essay in the 1962 Vologda edition, p. 442.

86 English edition (1955), p. 100.

87 *Ibid.*, p. 121. The device is illustrated on pp. 120–121; see also the 1939 Russian language edition, which omits the hole from which the narrowed beam issues.

88 *Ibid.*, p. 122.

89 *Ibid.*, p. 285.

90 Major General of Technical Services G. Pokrovskiy, '*Primeneniye dal 'noboynykh raket*', *Tekhnika Molodezhi*, April, 1944, pp. 7–8, graphic on p. 7. Other graphics show that rockets need to spin to be stable, and the ballistic trajectory of a missile and the relative air density as it arcs into space.

91 *Ibid.*, p. 8, '*massovoye porazheniye*'.

92 Major General of Aviation E. Tatarchenko, '*Nekotorye problemy razvitii vozdushnoy moshchi*' ('Certain Problems of the Development of Air Power'), *Vestnik vozdushnogo flota (Air Force Herald)* (*VVF*), 5–6, pp. 1946, pp. 60–63, esp. p. 61, col. 1, on the development of 'nuclear politics'.

93 'An Absurd Situation', *Vestnik: Soviet Magazine for Politics, Science and Culture*, June 1990, pp. 58–64. Facsimile pp. 61–3 and translation of Kapitsa's 18 December 1945 letter to Molotov, held in the Russian Foreign Policy Archives, ref. no. *13134/19.XII–45g.*, with Molotov's notes in green pencil. In a telephone conversation on 25 December Podtserob, Molotov's aide, told Kapitsa to 'wait a while'.

Western analysts, including Field Marshal Sir Alan Brooke, agreed on the relative ineffectiveness of the first nuclear bombs. See the Tizard Report – Public Record Office (PRO), *Defe II 1251(45)*, 24 October 1945, memorandum by Sir George Thompson, 'Effect of atomic bombs on warfare in the next few years', p. 4; *PRO Defe II 1252, Examination of the Possible Development of Weapons and Methods of War, TWC(46) 3 (Revised)*, 30 January 1946.

94 See Harriet Fast Scott and William F. Scott, ed., and trans., *Soviet Military Strategy*, (3rd edn, Macdonald and Jane's, London, 1975), a translation of Marshal of the Soviet Union Vasiliy Danilovich Sokolovskiy (1897–1968), *Voyennaya Strategiya (Military Strategy)*, (Voyenizdat, Moscow, 1968). This edition highlights changes made to the two earlier editions of 1962 and 1963. 'By 1960, in Soviet terminology, a '*Revolution in Military Affairs*" had taken place.' An article 'The Revolution in Military Affairs and the Task of the Military Press' appeared in *KVS* in November 1963 and the book *Problems of the Revolution in Military Affairs* was published by Voyenizdat in 1965. See Scott and Scott, pp. x, xv, xvii.

95 See for example V. V. Druzhinin, D. S. Kontorov, *Ideya, algoritm, resheniye (prinyatiye reshenii i avtomatizatsiya)* (Voyenizdat, Moscow, 1972), translated (accurately) as *Concept, Algorithm, Decision (Decision-Making and Automation)*, (US Air Force, US Government Printing Office, Washington DC, 1978), V. V. Druzhinin, D. S. Kontorov, *Voprosy voyennoy sistemotekniki (Questions of Military Systems Technology)* (Voyenizdat, Moscow, 1976). John Hemsley's *Soviet Troop Control: the Role of Command Technology in the Soviet Military System* (Brassey's, Oxford, 1982) makes no mention of the latter book but uses the former extensively. Many books on systems technology and automated control systems were published by the Nauka and Radio i svyaz' publishing houses.

96 General Makhmut Akhmetovich Gareyev, *Yesli zavtra voyna? ... (Chto izmenyayetsya v kharaktere vooruzhennoy bor"by v blizhayshiye 20–25 let) (If there is war tomorrow? ... What will change in the Character of Armed Struggle in the Next 20–25 years)*, (Vladar, Moscow, 1995) ISBN 5–86209–008–8 (5000 copies).

97 *Ibid.*, pp 21–3.

98 *Ibid.*, pp. 230–31.

99 Foreign policy concept The Jamestown Foundation, 'New Foreign Policy Guidelines', *Fortnight in Review*, vol. 6, issue 15, 21 July 2000, http://russia.jamestown.org/pubs/view/for_006_015_001 .htm National Security Concept and Military Doctrine, see notes 41 and 42.

100 A. Baumgarten, '*Artilleriyskiye voprosy*' ('Artillery Questions'), *Artilleriyskiy zhurnal* (*Artillery Journal*), 1/1896, pp. 1–32. This, p. 1.

### Chapter 4   RUSSIA, GERMANY AND ANGLO-JAPANESE INTELLIGENCE COLLABORATION, 1898–1906

1 The English-language version of the story was carried in the *Japan Times*, 4.5.2000.

2 The author is grateful to the British Academy, London and the Nihon Shinkôkai, Tokyo for support to carry out research at the *Gaikô Shiryôkan* (GST) and the *Bôei-chô Kenkyûsho Senshi-shitsu* (BKST) in the winter of 2001.

3 See Public Record Office (PRO), Kew: ADM1/7813, p. 207 and GST, File 5.2.2.13–1, 'Nichi-Ro sen'eki kankei. Rokoku Kokkei oyobi Giyû ryô kantai no kankei dôsei zakken,' pp. 86–7.

4 Makino (Vienna) Secret Report no. 42 of June 1904 at: GST, *ibid*, pp. 117–25.

5 Nicholson had previously commanded a ship in the British Mediterranean Fleet which took part in extensive manoeuvres designed to heighten British capabilities in the event of war with France and Russia under the command of Admiral Sir John Fisher. Extensive experiments were conducted by Nicholson and other ships' commanders in the use of radio equipment and the results of these activities were discussed with Admiral Ijuin, commanding the Japanese squadron sent to take part in the Spithead Naval Review, when it stopped over at Malta in May 1902. Ijuin had lengthy discussions with both Fisher and Prince Louis of Battenberg, the senior captain in the Fleet, who was appointed Director of Naval Intelligence (DNI) on Fisher's recommendation in October 1902. See the author's 'British Use of "Dirty Tricks" in External Policy prior to 1914,' *War in History*, 9/1 (January 2002), pp. 60–81.

6 Woroniecki appears to have tried to pass himself off as a Russian named Krimansky, but Makino believed the two to be identical. See Makino Secret Report no. 70 of 28.7.1904 at: GST, File 5.2.7.3, 'Nichi-Ro sen'eki kankei

teikoku ni oite mitteisha shiyô zakken'.

7 John Johnson, *The Evolution of British Sigint 1653–1939* (London: HMSO, 1998), pp. 24–5 and citing authorisation by Sir John Adye at GCHQ, Cheltenham.

8 See PRO: ADM1/7260 and the author's essays on 'Britain, Japan and the "Higher Realms of Intelligence"', 1900–1918' in: I. Gow et al., *The History of Anglo-Japanese Relations, 1600–2000*, vol. III, *The Military Dimension* (London: Palgrave Macmillan, 2003), chaps. 5 and 10.

9 PRO: ADM121/73, p. 383 refers to the transmission of important cables on Franco-Turkish and Franco-Russian relations via Syra; Fisher (Malta) to Admiral Wilson (C.-in-C., Channel), 12.2.1902 and Fisher to Wolfe-Barry, 17.3.1902 in: Fisher Papers, FISR1/3, ff. 89 & 96: Churchill College, Cambridge (CCC).

10 Fisher refuted these judgements by showing knowledge of the secret movement of the French fleet from Toulon to Mytilene in 1901 by means of radio interception when all news had been withheld from the press and foreign consuls. Joint fleet manoeuvres off Gibraltar that autumn demonstrated 'the usefulness of wireless telegraphy … but it has been shown that it should be used in conjunction with some very secret code, as open signals can be taken in with equal ease by an enemy who is within range'. Fawkes to Selborne, 3.9.01: MS Selborne, vol. 28, ff. 250–1: Bodleian Library, Oxford (BLO).

11 PRO: ADM1/7253.

12 See the author's 'Admiral Sir John Fisher and Japan, 1895–1905' in: Sir Hugh Cortazzi, ed., *Britain & Japan: Biographical Portraits*, vol. IV (Folkestone: Japan Library, 2004 forthcoming).

13 *Ibid*. Access at Wei-hai-wei was granted by Admiral Itô, commander-in-chief of the Japanese Combined Fleet in June 1895. PRO: ADM1/7248.

14 Detailed regular intelligence reports about Russian military activities in Central and Eastern Asia were compiled by the War Office in the second half of the century: see PRO: WO32 & WO33.

15 The US armed forces, which had the

largest number of military and naval officers seconded to the Russian front lines during the Russo-Japanese War relied on their British colleagues for translations of important Russian-language materials. The shortcomings on the naval side at least were overcome by the opportunities taken by Commander McCully, who had become the US Navy's principal Russian expert by 1919.

16 The British military attaché in Tokyo reported both to London and Simla, while the Japanese army was permitted to send a military attaché to Simla. He reported in June 1905 that he had received information about Russian movements in the Indian Ocean from the Indian Intelligence Bureau which he believed had been obtained from interception of French or Russian cable traffic passing through Singapore.

17 PRO: Fo83/2096.

18 Gamble to Selborne, 9. & 20.9.1901 provides a list of French construction and a detailed report on the review of the French fleet at Dunkirk to welcome the tsar's visit. Ottley report of 16.9.01 gave a holding reply until he had had time to confirm the Russian construction programme by personal visits to yards on the Neva (3.10.) and on the Black Sea (21.10.01). MS Selborne, vol. 29, ff. 174–7 & 196–209: BLO.

19 'Balance of Naval Power in the Far East', 4.9.1901, which was welcomed without reservations by the Senior Naval Lord, Lord Walter Kerr. This was premised on the perceived inability of the Royal Navy to match either US resources or a combined Franco-Russian threat at sea, which had been accepted by Selborne following his meeting with Admiral Fisher at Malta in April 1901. See MSS.252, Fisher Papers, item 15, vol. 2, item IXa: Royal Navy Museum, Portsmouth (RNMP).

20 Sanderson to Selborne, 22.4.1902 at: MS Selborne, vol. 13, ff. 223–6: BLO.

21 Sanderson to Hardinge, 7.6.1904: PRO: Fo800/2, pp. 218–9.

22 Heenan Report no. 745 to State Department, 24.7.03: National Archives, Washington DC: Record Group 58, M–459, roll 7.

23 See Roosevelt Papers, 1887–1917: Library of Congress, Washington DC; Spring-Rice Papers, Churchill College, Cambridge.

24 Sanderson to Hardinge, 11.6.1904: Hardinge Papers, vol. 7, f. 76: Cambridge University Library.

25 'The Emperor apparently knows and approves. It is possible that forged deciphers are given to him to prejudice him against us.' Spring-Rice to Hardinge, 10.5.1906: PRO: HD3/133.

26 Kurino Tel. No. 31 of 14.1.1904 to Tokyo: GST, file 5.2.7.3.

27 The papers of Lord Lansdowne include a memorandum by Sir Francis Bertie of November 1901 warning against a reinforcement of German dominance of Europe by becoming involved in conflict with Russia and France. They also include a detailed memorandum of 9.9.1901 by Colonel James Grierson, liaison on the international military staff at Peking, identifying Germany as the greatest future threat to the British Empire. Grierson, who was author of the first British military intelligence compilation about Japan in 1887, was on very friendly terms with Fukushima and was appointed Director of Military Operations (DMO) at the War Office on the outbreak of the Russo-Japanese War. PRO: Fo800/115.

28 GST, 'Meiji 34-nen raiden'. The brother of the Emperor Meiji, Prince Komatsu, who was in Europe as his delegate to the coronation of King Edward VII, was effectively snubbed by the kaiser and his wife when he sought to go to Potsdam to confer a high honour bestowed by his brother. He did not fail to note the much more friendly reception he subsequently received from the tsar on his way home.

29 Kurino (St Petersburg) Tel. No. 8 of 29.3.1903 to Tokyo: GST: 'Meiji 35-nen raiden'. The German officer begged Akashi to keep this information secret, otherwise he would find himself in very hot water.

30 GST: 'Meiji 36-nen zai-Eikôshi raiden, 7–12 tsuki'.

31 Minister Inoue (Berlin) Tel. No. 303 of 28.7.1904 to Tokyo: GST, file 5.2.3.24.

32  The supply service of the German navy
was a worldwide organisation established
to provision German warships and
assemble naval intelligence in wartime. It
operated most successfully from neutral
countries and the Russo-Japanese War
provided an ideal testbed for the
subsequent operations of the East Asian
Squadron in 1914. These experiences are
well summarised in a lecture of 1936 to
the German Armed Forces Academy by
Commander Werner Vermehren at:
*Marine Archiv: AIII MND: Akte III-1,
'Etappenwesen-Allgemeines', Heft 5 (1935–
1937).*

33  Iwasaki (Sydney) to Tokyo, 13.12.1904:
GST: file 5.2.2.20. It was claimed that
Hardenflycht had served under the alias
of Count Hoogerwoera as an agent in
London of the French secret service.
After the Baltic Fleet left Indochinese
waters in April 1905, it disappeared for a
time somewhere south of Formosa and
the Japanese navy remained uncertain if
the fleet would sail round Japan to
Vladivostock. The arrival of German
supply vessels at Woosung, however,
confirmed the Russian intention to sail
northward via the China Sea and thus
facilitate the successful Japanese search
in more narrow waters which ended in
the decisive sea battle off Tsushima on
27 May 1905.

34  Inoue Tel. No. 31 of 22.1.1905: GST,
file 5.2.2.17–1.

35  Spring-Rice reported that a German Jew
named Hartyng, who had been chief of
the Russian secret police bureau in Berlin
had been promoted to head a department
of the *Okhrana* in St Petersburg: PRO:
HD3/125. This was interpreted as
evidence of the solidarity of the two
autocrats, whom he described as
'Emperor of the West' and 'Emperor of
the East'. Steps were taken by the War
Office and the Secret Service in 1903
and 1904 to disassociate Britain directly
from Japanese Army secret service
activities and promotion of revolution in
Russia. Information about these was
nevertheless obtained indirectly through
India.

36  Inoue Tel. No. 4 of 4.1.05 and Tel. No.
13 of 8.1.05 in: GST, file 5.2.2.17–1.

37  Inoue Tel. No. 231 of 30.5. and No. 238
of 1.6.1905 in: *ibid.*

38  See Hayashi (London) Tel. No. 203 of
18.7.1904 to Tokyo in: GST, 'Meiji 36-
nen zai-Eikôshi raiden, 7–12 tsuki'.
Minister Inoue had warned in Tel. No.
157 of 10.4.1904 that evidence obtained
in both Germany and Russia indicated
that the latter was making the necessary
preparations to dispatch the Baltic Fleet
to the Far East in June: GST, file 5.2.2.16.

39  Battenberg to Fisher and Selborne,
7.11.1904: Fisher Papers, FISR1/4, f.
139, CCC. Custance had frequently
warned Selborne about the German
threat and this was repeated by Selborne
to Balfour in April 1902. At this time,
Selborne took the first steps to acquire
the land on which the Rosyth naval base
was subsequently built.

40  See Roosevelt Correspondence, series 4.
The Spanish authorities had complained
about French failure to take their interests
in Morocco into proper account about a
year previously and had called on British
support as a party to the agreement on
spheres of influence there: see de Bunsen
(Paris) letter of 27.4.04 to Sir Thomas
Sanderson: PRO: Fo800/2, pp. 195–200.
The Spanish King was a member of the
house of Hohenzollern, but Edward VII
was involved in successful efforts to
arrange his marriage to one of his own
Connaught or Battenberg nieces rather
than to anyone suggested by Wilhelm II.

41  Fisher to Lansdowne, 22.4.1905:
FISR1/4, f. 149, CCC.

42  Balfour to Fisher, 26.4.05: FISR1/4, f.
154. Balfour agreed with Selborne in
correspondence with Lansdowne that
Britain had a duty to protect Japan
should it be likely to be defeated at sea:
see Balfour to Selborne, 30.10.1903 in:
MS Selborne, vol. 34, ff. 41–2: BLO.
Before becoming prime minister, Balfour
found it extremely difficult to believe
Selborne's warning about a German
threat: *ibid.*, vol. 30, ff. 5–6.

43  PRO: HD3/128 & 130–2 show that the
memo was drafted in the War Office in
the autumn of 1905 and subsequently
circulated by Sanderson to the British
missions at Copenhagen, Stockholm and
The Hague for secret consultations

between October 1905 and January 1906.

## Chapter 5  BRITAIN AND RUSSIA, 1914–1917

1 Keith Wilson, *The Rasp of War: the letters of H. A. Gwynne to the Countess Bathurst 1914–1918* (London, 1988), pp. 53–6. What follows began life at a conference on the relationship between Russia and Scotland, organised by Paul Dukes, funded by the British Academy, and held at the University of Aberdeen in May 2002; I am grateful to all three.

2 John Gooch, *The Plans of War: the general staff and British military strategy c.1900–1916* (London, 1974) pp. 198–237.

3 Keith Neilson, *Britian and the last Tsar: British policy and Russia 1894–1917* (Oxford, 1995), is particularly forceful on the continuities that span the apparent divide in 1907; I am heavily indebted to it in what follows.

4 David Dilks, *Curzon in India* (2 vols., London, 1970), I, pp. 103–207.

5 David French, 'The meaning of attrition, 1915–1916', *English Historical Review*, CIII (1988), pp. 385–405.

6 Fisher to Churchill, 16 January 1912, in Arthur Marder (ed.), *Fear God and Dread Nought: the correspondence of Admiral of the Fleet Lord Fisher of Kilverstone* (3 vols., London, 1952–9), II, p. 426. This whole theme has been fully explored by Jon Tetsuro Sumida, 'British capital ship design and fire control in the Dreadnought era: Sir John Fisher, Arthur Hungerford Pollen, and the battle cruiser', *Journal of Modern History*, LI (1979), pp. 205–30; *In defence of naval supremacy: finance, technology and British naval policy, 1899–1914* (Boston, 1989).

7 Nicholas Lambert, 'Economy or empire? The fleet unit concept and the quest for collective security in the Pacific, 1909–14, in Greg Kennedy and Keith Neilson (eds.), *Far-flung lines: essays on imperial defence in honour of Donald Mackenzie Schurman* (London, 1997), pp. 5–76.

8 Dietrich Geyer, *Russian Imperialism: the interaction of domestic and foreign policy, 1860–1914* (Leamington Spa, 1987), p. 260.

9 George Bernard Shaw, *What I Really Wrote About the War* (London, 1931), p. 80.

10 Keith Neilson, '"My beloved Russians": Sir Arthur Nicolson and Russia, 1906–1916', *International History Review*, IX (1987), pp. 521–54.

11 Stephen Graham, *Russia and the world: a study of the war and a statement of the world problems which now confront Russia and Great Britain* (London, 1917), p. 193.

12 Keith Neilson, *Strategy and Supply: the Anglo-Russian alliance, 1914–1917* (London, 1984) is fundamental on these points; see also Keith Neilson, 'The Anglo-Russian alliance, 1914–1917: lessons for the present?', in Dennis E. Showalter (ed.), *Future Wars: coalition operations in global strategy* (Chicago, 2002).

13 Peter Gatrell and Mark Harrison, 'The Russian and Soviet economies in two world wars: a comparative view', *Economic History Review*, XLVI (1993), p. 430; on manpower policies, see also N. Golovine, *The Russian Army in the World War* (New Haven, 1931).

14 Golovine, *The Russian Army in the World War*, pp. 126–7.

15 For these points, see Hew Strachan, *The First World War*, vol. 1, *To Arms* (Oxford, 2001), pp. 1069–70.

16 Kathleen Burk, *Britain, America and the Sinews of War 1914–1918* (Boston, 1985), pp. 44–5, 62–4.

17 Gail Owen, 'Dollar diplomacy in default: the economics of Russian–American relations, 1910–1917', *Historical Journal*, XIII (1970), pp. 251–72; Alexander M. Michelson, Paul N. Apostol, and Michael W. Bernatzky, *Russian Public Finance during the War* (New Haven, 1928), pp. 312–17.

18 D. Jones, 'Imperial Russia's forces at war', in Allan R. Millett and Williamson Murray (eds.), *Military Effectiveness* (3 vols., Boston, 1988), I, *The First World War*, pp. 268–9.

19 Neilson, *Strategy and Supply*, pp. 129–34; *History of the Ministry of Munitions* (12 vols., London, 1922), II, part 8, pp. 20–3.

20 David French, *British Strategy and War Aims 1914–1916* (London, 1986), pp. 69, 105–11.

21 C. Jay Smith, Jr, 'Great Britain and the 1914–1915 Straits agreement with Russia: the British promise of November 1914', *American Historical Review*, LXX (1965), pp. 1015–34; Harry Howard, *The partition*

*of Turkey: a diplomatic history 1913–1923*
(New York, 1966), pp. 123–37.

22 C. J. Lowe and M. L. Dockrill, *The Mirage of Power: British foreign policy 1902–22* (3 vols., London, 1972), III, p. 502.

23 Sir George Buchanan, *My Mission to Russia and Other Diplomatic Memories* (2 vols., London, 1923), II, p. 41.

24 Lord Riddell's *War Diary 1914–1918* (London, 1933), p. 245.

25 Imogen Gassert, 'In a foreign field: what soldiers in the trenches liked to read', *Times Literary Supplement*, 10 May 2002, pp. 17–19.

26 Hugh Walpole, *The Dark Forest* (New York, 1916), p. 295.

27 Buchanan, *My Mission*, II, p. 29.

28 Walpole, *The Dark Forest*, p. 314.

**Chapter 6  MILITARY POLICY, INTERNATIONAL RELATIONS AND SOVIET SECURITY AFTER OCTOBER 1917**

1 J. Erickson, *The Soviet High Command. A Military-Political History, 1918–1940* (London, 1962).

2 *Polnoe sobranie sochinenii*, vol. 9, p. 152.

3 The great exceptions to this were the *narodnik* writer Nikolai Chernyshevskii and the founder of Russian Marxism Georgii Plekhanov.

4 J. Nettl, *Rosa Luxemburg*, vol. 1 (London, 1966).

5 K. Radek, *Der deutsche Imperialismus und die Arbeiterklasse* (Bremen, 1911), reprinted in his *In den Reichen der Deutschen Revolution, 1909–1919. Gesammelte Abhandlungen* (Munich, 1921).

6 G. Zinoviev, *O prichinakh krakha germanskoi sotsial-demokratii* (Petersburg [*sic*], 1917), part 1, p. 6.

7 *PSS*, vol. 27, pp. 299–426.

8 S. Cohen, *Bukharin and the Bolshevik Revolution* (London, 1971), pp. 25–42; R. Service, *Lenin: A Political Life*, vol. 2, *Worlds in Collision*, pp. 118–122 and pp. 139–43.

9 *PSS*, vol. 26, p. 40.

10 *PSS*, vol. 26, p. 161; M. Kharitonov, *Zapiski Instituta Lenina*, vol. 2 (Moscow 1927), p. 120.

11 Nettl, *Rosa Luxemburg*, vol. 2.

12 R. Service, *Lenin*, vol. 2, pp. 241–7.

13 *PSS*, vol. 32, p. 96.

14 *PSS*, vol. 50, p. 186: note to Trotskii and Sverdlov, 1 October 1918.

15 *Ibid.*

16 *PSS*, vol. 50, p. 227.

17 *PSS*, vol. 50, pp. 285–6 and 310. See also V. M. Kholodovskii, 'V. I. Lenin I mezhdunarodnye otnosheniya novogo tipa', in M. A. Kharlamov and others (eds.), *Leninskaya vneshnyaya politika Sovetskoi strany* (Moscow, 1969), p. 93.

18 *PSS*, vol. 37, p. 490.

19 R. Service, *Lenin: A Political Life*, vol. 3, *The Iron Ring* (London, 1995), p. 197.

20 E. H. Carr, *History of Soviet Russia*, part 2, *The Interregnum* (London, 1954).

21 *Devyataya konferentsiya RKP(b) Protokoly* (Moscow, 1972), pp. 13–14.

22 GARF, f.130, op.2, ed. khr.1(5), Sovnarkom, 16 May 1918; f. 130, op. 2, ed. khr. 2(2): Sovnarkom, 20 July 1918.

23 *PSS*, vol. 41, p. 458; and RSsKhIDNI, f. 44, op. 1, ed. khr. 5, pp. 20–1 (Lenin's speech to the Ninth Party Conference).

24 *Ibid.*

25 *Izvestiya Tsentral'nogo Komiteta KPSS*, 1991 (no. 4), p. 171.

26 *Desyatyi s"ezd RKP(b). Mart 1921 g. Stenograficheskii otchët* (Moscow, 1963), pp. 473 and 491.

27 *PSS*, vol. 42, p. 112.

28 J. Erickson, *The Soviet High Command*, p. 153.

29 *PSS*, vol. 43, p. 210.

30 *PSS*, vol. 33, p. 50.

31 R. MacNeal, *Stalin: Man and Ruler* (London, 1988), p. 218.

**Chapter 7  TURKEY IN THE RUSSIAN MIRROR**

1 William Taubman: *Khrushchev. The Man in His Era* (New York, 2002) pp. 324ff. for the context (chapter 13), and *Cold War International History Project Bulletin No. 10*, March 1998, pp. 50–59. But see also Republic of Turkey Ministry of Culture www.discoverturkey.com...*Izmir* for the correction of 'square' to 'street'. Also v. Georges-Henri Soutou, *La guerre de cinquante ans* (Paris, 2002) pp. 118ff.

2 Stanford Shaw: *From Empire to Republic* (5 vols, Ankara, 2000) vol. II, pp. 919–960 and vol. III, pp. 1443–1588. The sources are voluminous.

3 Changing the alphabet of Turkic

languages was a huge enterprise. The latest and most authoritative account of this subject is Geoffrey Lewis: *The Turkish Language Reform. A Catastrophic Success* (Oxford, 2002). The reform has been a battlefield in the Turkish *Kulturkampf* as between Arabic script and Ottoman vocabulary on the one side, with Latin script and (sometimes made-up) Turkic vocabulary on the other. It now has echoes in the Turkic-speaking parts of the old USSR. Things have gone so far, Lewis says, that people cannot read what was written even thirty or forty years ago: classic novels have to be translated into a language readers can read. The process has been accompanied by the usual rise of English, 'the foreign language which it is easiest to speak badly', as a Frenchman remarked. Oktay Sinanoglu: *Bir New-York Ruyasi 'Bye-Bye' Turkce* (Istanbul, 2002) is a long and learned protest at the resulting 'Turklish'.

4 The background to Soviet–Turkish collaboration appears in (ed.) N. G. Kireyev, *Turtsiya mezhdu Yevropoy i Aziyey* (Moscow, 2001), pp. 360f. This book is the best on modern Turkey in any language. It is endlessly informative, takes the subject entirely seriously, and does not wag its finger in the Western European way; v. also Norman Stone, 'Trotsky on Prinkipo', in *Cornucopia* (Istanbul) no. 28, vol. 5 (2003) pp. 57–63. It was characteristic of the close relations of the time between Turkey and the USSR that Trotsky's doings were reported back. He apparently hit upon a variant of rockfish, which was red and had gills in a vaguely hammer-and-sickle form. He called it *sebastes leninii*. Stalin was not to be outdone, and contributed an article on this creature to the *Zoologicheski Zhurnal* in the middle of the Second World War.

5 Alexander Gerschenkron, *Europe in the Russian Mirror* (Cambridge, 1970). Isaac Deutscher had delivered a romantic series, *The Unfinished Revolution*, the previous year, and Carr was fresh from his triumph with *What Is History*, in which he memorably declared that historians of failures were like cricket commentators concentrating on men who scored ducks.

The writer contributed a none-too-respectful obituary of E. H. Carr in *The London Review of Books* (February 1983). John Erickson offered generous support with the resulting unpopularity. Tocqueville says somewhere that if you approve of dictatorship for a people, it means you despise the people. Carr did – he said at the end of his life that all those dead peasants meant progress. As Orwell said, it's all very well saying you can't make an omelette without breaking eggs, but where's the omelette?

6 Richard Friedenthal: *Karl Marx. Sein Leben und seine Zeit* (Munich, 1990).

7 Justin McCarthy: *Death and Exile* (New York, 1995) is the authoritative account but cf. S. Faroqhi et al., *An Economic and Scoial History of the Ottoman Empire* (Cambridge, 1997) vol. II p. 793 and Selim Deringil, *The Well-Protected Domains* (London, 1998). According to *Ethnohistorical Dictionary of the Russian and Soviet Empires* (London, 1994) p. 147, 400,000 Caucasus Muslims emigrated to the Ottoman Empire. Between the wars, half the urban population in Turkey consisted of immigrants; hence widespread popular resistance to proposals that Armenians have a special case.

8 There is a 'Dudayev Square' in Ankara, and a considerable diaspora from the Caucasus in Turkey generally. Between the Wars, Caucasus-exile literature was forbidden, for the sake of good relations with the USSR.

9 In the Cold War period, study of Russia in Turkey became something of a political matter. It is now very obvious that the resulting imbalance should be redressed, given that Russia is Turkey's most important neighbour. Bilkent University (with John Erickson as strong supporter – 'You have winds of history coming through the Caucasus') has established a Russian Centre, the first of its kind in the country. The present essay – necessarily very broad indeed in scope – is intended as an indication of what will be done.

10 The cultural effect of Russia upon Turkey is important, though for political reasons

this has been badly obscured. The greatest poet of modern Turkey was Nazim Hikmet, who modelled his early work on Mayakovski's. There is a penetrating English biography, Saime Goksu and Edward Timms, *Romantic Communist* (London, 1999).

11 Andrew Mango, *Ataturk* (London, 2000) replaces everything else. Lord Kinross's old warhorse biography *Ataturk. The Rebirth of a Nation* (London, 1993) is still, nevertheless, a good introduction to Turkey for anyone coming to the subject for the first time.

12 Horst Widmann, *Bildung und Exil* (Bern, 1973). Ernst Reuter, later mayor of West Berlin under the Stalin blockade in 1948, and before 1933 social democratic mayor of Magdeburg (and ten years before that a member of the Reichstag as a Communist) became professor of town planning in Ankara and had Turkish, within a relatively short time, at such a level as to be placed on the language reform commission (p. 161). This was an extraordinary emigration, not forgotten by the students of its students. It produced some extraordinary memoirs. Fritz Neumark, *Zuflucht am Bosporus* (Frankfurt, 1980) is one of the noblest books in the German language.

13 Udo Steinbach: *Die Turkei im 20. Jahrhundert* (Bergisch Gladbach, 1996) pp. 125f. ('the rules and theories of an old Arab sheikh and the abstruse interpretations of dirty and ignorant clergy have fixed all civil and criminal law in Turkey for five hundred years ... Islam is a rotting corpse poisoning our life.'). In public, Ataturk was careful, and there was no real campaign against Islam – certainly nothing comparable to that in the USSR – except in the sense, familiar to Pius IX, of the persecutor's feeling martyred by the restrictions placed on persecution by the secular state.

14 D. E. Queller and S. J. Stratton: *The Fourth Crusade* (Philadelphia, 1997). The latest account is Jonathan Harris, *Byzantium and the Crusades* (London, 2003) p. 155ff.

15 S. Mardin, *The Genesis of Young Ottoman Thought* (Princeton, 1962) p. 54.

16 Mehmet Fuat Koprulu, *The Origins of the Ottoman Empire* (New York, 1992).

17 An ancient argument, by now, maybe going back to Walter Scott (*Ivanhoe* etc.) and Stubb's *Charters*. An older generation of Russians took an interest, because, for them, combining Liberty and Order was *the* question, and perhaps the answer lay somewhere in English medieval history. For anyone who grew up in the world of the *zemstva* the relationship between state, local government and peasant was bound to be of interest. The Russian-born historian M. M. Postan, who divided his time between the British war economy of 1939–45 and agriculture in the high Middle Ages obviously took his impetus from this. It is encouraging to see that in another form the Anglo-Norman argument comes back – v. e.g. Alan Macfarlane, *The Origins of English Individualism* (Cambridge, 1978) and *The Culture of Capitalism* (Oxford, 1988).

18 V. ed. A. F. Litvina and F. B. Uspensky, *Iz Istorii Russkoy Kultury*, vol. II, book 1, *Kievskaya i Moskovskaya Rus* (Moscow, 2002) p. 480.

19 L. N. Gumilev, *Tysyacheletiye vokrug Kaspiya* (Baku, 1991) and *Drevniye Tyurki* (Moscow, 1967). A good recent survey is David Christian, *A History of Russia, Central Asia and Mongolia*, vol. 1, *Inner Eurasia from Prehistory to the Mongol Empire* (Cxford, 2000) esp. chapter 11 (pp. 277–303). The bibliography is very useful. V. also Dimitri Obolensky, *Six Byzantine Portraits* (Oxford, 1988) pp. 86ff. for the relations of Kiev with the Pechenegs and Kipchak (Turks) – the Byzantines' *Komanoi*, otherwise Polovtsians; A. N. Kurat, *Pecenek Tarihi* (Ankara, 1937) p. 8; N. A. Baskakov, *Russkiye familii tyurkskogo proiskhozhdeniya* (Moscow, 1993) pp. 56–59.

20 A. A. Zimin, *Rossia na poroge novogo vremeni* (Moscow, 1972) p. 99. I owe this reference to Donald Ostrowski, *Muscovy and the Mongols. Cross-Cultural Influence on the Steppe Frontier* (Cambridge, 1998) pp. 56–9 on the sixty Mongol ('Juchid') princes in Muscovite service in the fifteenth and sixteenth centuries. John Meyendorff, *Byzantium and the Rise of Russia* (Cambridge, 1981) pp. 261–2 notes Karamzin's remark as to Russia's debt to

'the khans' and Ostrowski, op. cit., p. 9 for remarks to the same effect. He asserts on pp. 144ff. that the anti-Tatar ideology was made up by the Church in the later sixteenth century, the expression 'Tatar yoke' being unknown before *c.*1575. An earlier and still valuable book is Charles Halperin, *Russia and the Golden Horde* (Bloomington, 1985).

21 Isabella de Madariaga, *Russia in the Age of Catherine the Great* (London, 1981) pp. 508f. is sage on Russian Islam. There is much interesting information in Hakan Kirimli, *National Movements and National Identity among the Crimean Tatars 1905–1916* (Leiden, 1996) and Alan Fisher, *The Crimean Tatars* (Stanford, 1976).

22 Heath Lowry, *The Nature of the Early Ottoman State* (New York, 2003) chapter 7, pp. 115f.

23 *Istoriya Russkoy Kultury*, op. cit., p. 480 for reference to *Svethia Magna* but pp. 425–41 and 621–41 deal respectively with 'the Third Rome' and the introduction of the Double-Headed Eagle around 1500 – both, apparently, in reaction to Habsburg arrogance. The Double Eagle appeared as *Reichswappen* in 1433, but its origins appear to be Babylonian; there is a Hittite example in the Museum of Anatolian Civilisations in Ankara. Alain Besançon quotes the monk, Filotey: '*Grand prince resplendissant, tsar chretien orthodoxe, seigneur de tous, toi qui sieges sur le grand trône, toi, regent des saints trônes divins de la Sainte Eglise universelle et apostolique, Eglise de la Sainte Mere de Dieu, de son Assomption venerable et glorieuse, Eglise qui a repandu la lumière a la place des Eglises de Rome et de Constantinople ...*' and pertinently adds: '*Le tsar en question règne sur des arpents de forets et des champs cultives sur brulis*' ('La Russie est-elle européenne,' in *Commentaire*, no. 87 (autumn 1999) pp. 610–11). He adds that the 'mégalomanie de ce royaume est déjà stupefiante'. Yes: and another possible Russo-Turkish connection?

24 Jean Paul Roux, *Histoire des Turcs* (Paris, 2000) p. 182; Christian, op. cit., p. 248; D. Kitzikis, *L'empire ottoman* (Paris, 1984) p. 70 and *Turk-Yunan Imparatorlugu: Arabolge Gercegi Isiginda Osmanli Tarihine Bakis* (Istanbul, 1996). René Grousset,

*L'empire du levant* (Paris, 1947) is an old classic on the whole subject.

25 Heath Lowry (op. cit.) establishes himself as the latest authority and not very much survives of Paul Wittek's endeavours. Chapter 3 ('Wittek re-visited') p. 33ff. is devastating. Wittek (1894–1978), who became an Ottomanist through service with the Austro-Hungarian army in the Near East in the First World War – he claimed he had learned the language in the troop train through the Balkans – dominated his subject in London. Colin Heywood (*Welt des Islams*, vol. 38, no. 3, November 1998, pp. 387–405) wrote a study of Wittek, somewhat puzzled that such a formidable man should have written what appears to be romantic quasi-fantasy. The first challenge to Wittek came from G. Arnakis, *Oi protoi Othomanoi* (Athens, 1947) but v. also (ed.) A. Bryer and M. Ursinus, *The Byzantine World and the Turks 1071–1571* (Amsterdam, 1991), although it is known to the writer only indirectly.

26 Spiros Vryonis, *The Decline of Mediaeval Hellenism in Asia Minor* (London, 1971), pp. 466f. and *Byzantium: its Internal History and Relations with the Muslim World* (London, 1971), p. 221 (v. especially his essay, 'Byzantium and Islam', pp. 295–240) – an important correction to the statements of the more romantic spokesmen for 'the Byzantine (Orthodox) Commonwealth' such as Meyendorff. Vryonis notes, for instance, that the Byzantine Empire had been weakened long before because of Orthodox exclusivity: for instance, when the (at least symbolically) decisive battle of Manzikert was lost to the Seljuk Turks in 1071, it was because 'many of the Armenians and Syrian Monophysites saw in the Seljuks their delivery' (*Byzantium*, p. 172). The same was ironically true for the Orthodox in 1453. Hagia Sophia, far from being permanently in use as the faithful besought Divine intercession to prevent the final extinction of Constantine's eastern Rome, was kept shut to prevent Latins and Orthodox from coming to blows.

27 Franz Babinger, *Mehmet the Conqueror and His Times* (2nd edition, Princeton, 1968),

p. 787. Urban offered the gun first to
Constantine XI, who did not have the
money.

28 Steven Runciman, *The Great Church in
Captivity* (London, 1968) is a wonderful
antiseptic book; there has never been a
better introduction to the arguments
concerning the Trinity and the *filioque*
clause than Runciman's first thirty or so
pages. There is formidable literature on
the direct transmission of classical
civilisation to the Islamic world (i.e.
without the interruption by Visigoths etc.
that occurred in the West). The great
German orientalist C. H. Becker summed
it up with the phrase: 'No Alexander, no
Mohammed' – meaning that the eastern
Roman world retained a very great deal
of its classical unity and shape, including
Christianity, well into the Muslim era. A
modern, accessible, and also brilliant
recapitulation of this theme is Peter
Brown, *The World of Late Antiquity*
(London, 1971).

29 Vryonis, *Byzantium*, pp. 234f. Anna
Comnena c.1080 divided the population
of Anatolia into three groups – Greeks,
*barbaroi* and *mixo-barbaroi*. Seljuk sultans
had their children baptised, and there was
a great deal of intermarriage. In the 1430s
the language of the Ottoman court was
Greek. It should in fairness be added
that the Vryonis thesis has been
challenged by followers of Koprulu, who
stress the Iranian influences.

30 In Robert Mantran, *Histoire de l'empire
ottoman* (Paris, 1989) p. 328.

31 Two recent outstanding books on the
reactions of non-Western societies to
'capitalism': Richard Pipes, *Property and
Freedom* (New York, 2000) knows the
Russian side especially, and David
Landes, *The Wealth and Poverty of Nations*
(New York, 1998) has first-hand
knowledge (and a great respect for)
matters Ottoman. An old theme: the
contempt of the soldier for the
tradesman? An interesting topic, not to
the writer's knowledge explored, except
implicitly, by Fernand Braudel, is the
comparison of Turkey with Spain –
empire, Islam, minorities, 'backwardness',
civil war. Amerigo Castro, *Espana en su
historia* (Buenos Aires, 1948) and *The

*Spaniards* (Los Angeles, 1980) discussed
those elements, Jewish or Muslim, of the
Spanish inheritance that Francoists (and
Catalan nationalists) denied or detested.
On the 'Europeanisation' of modern
Spain, v. John Hooper, *The New Spaniards*
(London, 1995), a brilliant study which
Turks should ponder.

32 François Georgeon, *Turk Milliyetciliginin
Kokenleri. Yusuf Akcura 1876–1935* (Ankara,
1986), Hakan Kirimli, op. cit., Ilber
Ortayli, *Imparatorlugun en uzun yuzyili*
(Istanbul, 1987); David Kushner, *The Rise
of Turkish Nationalism 1876–1908* (London,
1977), and Jacob Landau, *Panturkism in
Turkey* (London, 1981). Sina Aksin,
*Jonturkler ve Ittihat Terakki* (Istanbul, 1987),
*passim*, is useful for biographies of the
leading figures, Crimeans and Circassians,
who with a Russian education often
looked down on Anatolians. The whole
process needed a shot in the arm from
men who knew Russia. Of contemporary
commentators known to the writer, it
was the Frenchman Anatole Leroy-
Beaulieu, *L'Empire des Tsars et les Russes*
(Paris, 1990) who wrote most
sympathetically about the Tatar attempts
to pull themselves up by the bootstraps.
On p. 74 he notes quite rightly that
reform of the grotesquely out-of-date
educational institutions of the Crimea
(where teachers, themselves ignorant of
Arabic, spent most of their time
administering it in blocks of letters to
pupils who were not finished until they
were thirty) could only proceed because
of Russian insistence – as with the Jews,
he says, '*l'émancipation morale sortant de la
servitude politique*', but v. also Kirimili,
op. cit. p. 22ff. for a description of this
dismal scene, and of the activities of
Ismail Gaspirali to change things. He had
been Turgenev's assistant in Paris, and
ended in Ataturk's Istanbul. He thought
that Russia could become 'the greatest
Moslem nation'. A further formidable
Russian export to Turkey was Zeki
Valide Dogan, whose memoirs
(*Vospominiya*, 2 vols., Urfa, 1994, 2000),
though very informative as to conditions
for a Bashkir intellectual in tsarist
Moscow and as to Lenin's attitudes
towards the Muslim peoples' hope for

independence, are unfortunately silent as to his experiences in republican Turkey. In 1932, when the republicans closed down the old Istanbul university, his institute was closed. He went for a time as an exile in Vienna – the neighbour, in the Berggasse, of Freud, whose sessions he disturbed with loud declamations of Uzbek poetry. There were words.

33  V. note 21 above.

34  Geoffrey Hosking, *Russia. People and Empire 1552–1917* (London, 1998) pp. xix–xx. *Gosudarstvennaya Duma. Tretii sozyv. Stengraficheskiye otchety*, cols. 370–71. I owe this reference to my colleague, Dr Sergey Podbolotov.

35  John P. McKay, *Pioneers for Profit* (London, 1970) pioneered the subject, but he has had many successors.

36  These memoirs have been well utilised in Philip Mansell, *Constantinople. City of the World's Desire 1453–1924* (London, 1995).

37  Mahmut Cetin, *Bogaz'daki Asiret* (Istanbul, 2002) *passim*.

38  Gerasimos Augustinos, *Kucuk Asya Rumlari* (Ankara, 1997) p. 254, and Alexis Alexandris, *The Greek Minority of Istanbul and Greek-Turkish Relations* (Athens, 1992), p. 108, which notes that of 654 wholesale concerns in Istanbul, 528 were Greek.

39  Bernard Lewis, The Emergence of Modern Turkey (2nd edition, London, 1968), and the less-known but formidable Niyazi Berkes, *The Development of Secularization in Turkey* (London, 1998). There had been, for example, three calendars in use – Islamic, Julian, Gregorian; and even the months – lunar in the traditional one – were different (p. vii).

40  *Welt des Islams*, loc. cit., p. 282, on Gotthold Weil, who showed how the enterprise of Ibrahim Mutteferika (originally Hungarian) with printing had to be pushed through with the help of *fetwa* by the religious authority and even a *hatt-i serif* from the sultan, because of objections from the *ulema* and the economic interest of the scribes. Serif Mardin, in a lecture given at Bilkent University in 1999, argued that the resistance came because the authorities feared dissemination of seditious literature among the Greeks. But it is all

part of a general disapproval of modern importations – again, cf. Spain, where even Dutch shipbuilding manuals were banned.

41  Selim Deringil, op. cit. *passim* for the background; v. also Roderic H. Davison, *Essays in Ottoman and Turkish History 1774–1923* (University of Texas Press, 1990), pp. 25, 140.

42  S. Mardin, *The Genesis of Young Ottoman Thought* (Princeton, 1962), pp. 81ff., and M. Sukru Hanioglu, *The Young Turks in Opposition* (Oxford, 1995). The essential argument is about the degree to which Ataturkism was being anticipated before 1914, and how religion was involved – not at all a straightforward question, since 'religion' in this case involves the 'brotherhoods' (*tarikat*) that, under a very superficial external similarity, varied very widely indeed in practice, shading into the Alevis, perhaps a quarter of the population, in whose religious practice men and women are equal and wine is used for ritual purposes. There is a possible comparison between Alevis and Russian 'Old Believers' (whom Gerschenkron, in his *Mirror* lectures, considers, but on the whole rejects, as a 'capitalist' creative minority). But under the Sunni Ottomans, Alevis faced discrimation and were generally poor, even an underclass – v. David Shankland, *The Alevis in Turkey* (London, 2002).

43  Kemal Karpat, *Turkey's Politics* (Princeton, 1959), pp. 18f., and Sina Aksin, *Jonturkler ve Ittihat ve Terakki* (Istanbul, 1987).

44  Ali Kemal remained abroad until 1918, when the British occupation of Istanbul gave him hope of a liberal, multinational and revived Ottoman state. He vociferously attacked the nationalists and was lynched when Istanbul was liberated in 1922.

45  The most recent publication is Yusuf Halacoglu, *The Armenian Deportations* (Ankara 2001).

46  Michael Llewellyn-Smith, *Ionian Vision* (Michigan, 1998) is an outstanding account of this disaster.

47  Stanford Shaw, *From Empire to Republic* (5 vols, Ankara, 2000) is authoritative; but v. also Karpat op. cit., ch. 14, pp. 349ff. on Turkish Communism. Turkey, like

Sweden (and Great Britain, famously) though not nearly on the same scale, handed back refugees to Stalin's mercies. The failure of Communism in Turkey is a good subject. You might very well argue that the two Western statesmen who dealt most intelligently with Communism from a position of weakness were Ataturk and De Gaulle.

48  Peter Hopkirk, *Setting the East Ablaze* (London, 1995) remains the classic account, but cf. Ali Fuat Cebesoy, *Moskova Hatiralari* (Istanbul, 2002), pp. 34, 45f., 52.

49  Mehmet Bardakci, *Sahbaba* (Istanbul, 2000) uses the private papers of the last sultan. As he went into exile, he wanted to do the pilgrimage to Mecca. The British, fearing disturbances, would not allow this, and he went to Italian exile instead (with twenty thousand pounds, out of which he was soon swindled). Ironically, he would have been the only Ottoman sultan to do the Hac. His predecessors were all too busy (or perhaps feared being overthrown) and simply sent wagon-loads of presents instead.

## Chapter 8   THE IDEOLOGY AND REALITIES OF SOVIET WOMEN'S TRACTOR DRIVING IN THE 1930s

An earlier version of this chapter was presented as a paper entitled 'Get on your tractor, baba!' at the annual conference of BASEES, Fitzwilliam College, Cambridge, April 2000.

Gratitude is due to the British Academy, the ESRC and the Carnegie Trust for the Universities of Scotland for funding research trips to Russia during which these data were gathered.

1  John Erickson, 'Women at War', in John Garrard and Carol Garrard, eds., *World War Two and the Soviet People* (London, Macmillan, 1993), pp. 50–76; and his 'Night Witches, Snipers and Laundresses', *History Today*, vol. 40, July 1990, pp. 29–35.

2  *20 let Sovetskoi vlasti: statisticheskii sbornik* (Partizdat TsK VKP (b), Moscow, 1937), p. 48.

3  Tsentral'nyi upravlenie narodnokhoziai-

stvennogo ucheta gosplana pri SNK SSSR, *Sotsialisticheskoe stroitel'stvo soiuza SSSR (1933–1938): Statisticheskii sbornik* (Moscow–Leningrad, Gosplanizdat, 1939), p. 87.

4  Mary Buckley, 'Was rural stakhanovism a movement?' in *Europe–Asia Studies*, vol. 51, no. 2, 1999, pp. 299–314.

5  Mary Buckley, *Women and Ideology in the Soviet Union* (Hemel Hempstead, Harvester/Wheatsheaf, 1989), pp. 108–138.

6  Both *Traktoristy* and *Kubanskie Kazaki* were directed by Ivan Pyrev, released in 1939 and 1949 respectively. For more detailed discussion of the role of cinema, see Richard Stites, *Russian Popular Culture* (Cambridge, Cambridge University Press, 1992), pp. 64–97.

7  *Kolkhoznitsa*, no. 3, March 1935, front cover.

8  *Krest'ianka*, no. 12, April 1936, front cover.

9  *Ibid.*, no. 10, 1037, front cover.

10  *Ibid.*, no. 21, November 1939, front cover.

11  *Ibid.*, no. 8, 1938, inside cover.

12  *Ibid.*, no. 7–8, March 1937, inside cover.

13  Sue Bridger, 'The heirs of Pasha: the rise and fall of the Soviet Woman Tractor Driver', in Linda Edmondson, ed., *Gender in Russian History and Culture* (London, Palgrave, 2001), p. 195.

14  See P. Angelina, *Liudi Kolkhoznykh Polei* (Moscow–Leningrad, Gosudarstvennoe Izdatel'stvo Detskoi Literatury, 1952), pp. 43–9.

15  *Ibid.*, p. 49.

16  Praskovya Angelina, *My Answer to an American Questionnaire* (Moscow, Foreign Languages Publishing House, 1949), pp. 48–9; *Krest'ianskaia gazeta*, 30 October 1937, p. 2.

17  Angelina, *Liudi Kolkhoznykh Polei*, op. cit., p. 52.

18  *Ibid.*, p. 53.

19  *Traktorist-Kombainer*, no. 12, June 1936, p. 17. Archives carry lists of women's tractor brigades and their achievements. For Leningrad oblast see Tsentr Khraneniia Dokumentov Molodezhnykh Organizatsii (TsKhDMO), fond 1, opis' 23, delo 1261, listy 12–20.

20  For details of the 1936–7 plan to train women in mechanised skills, see

TsKhDMO, f. 1, op. 23, d. 1185, ll. 14–28.

21  *Ibid.*, f. 1, op. 23, d. 1185, l. 15.

22  *Ibid.*, f. 1, op. 23, d. 1185, l. 14.

23  *Ibid.*, f. 1, op. 3, d. 158, l. 104.

24  *Ibid.*

25  *Ibid.*, f. 1, op. 23, d. 1120, l. 51.

26  *Ibid.*, l. 54.

27  *Ibid.*, f. 1, op. 23, d. 1261, l. 20.

28  *Ibid.*, l. 33.

29  *Traktor-Kombainer*, no. 3, 15 February 1937, p. 4.

30  *Ibid.*, no. 23, December 1938, p. 6.

31  *Ibid.*, no. 24, December 1936, p. 11.

32  *Krest'ianka*, no. 15, June 1938, p. 21.

33  Angelina, *Liudi Kolkhoznykh Polei*, op. cit., pp. 28–9.

34  *Traktorist-Kombainer*, no. 5, 15 March 1937, p. 7.

35  *Ibid.*

36  T, R, Voroshilova, ed., *Traktoristy-dvukhtysiachniki: opyt raboty luchshikh stakhanovskikh traktornykh brigad Moskovskoi oblasti* (Moscow, Moskovskii rabochii, 1937), pp. 82–5.

37  *Ibid.*

38  *Krest'ianka*, no. 15, June 1938, p. 21.

39  Voroshilova, *Traktoristy-dvukhtysiachniki*, op. cit., p. 86.

40  For fuller details see, Mary Buckley, 'Why be a shock worker or a stakhanovite?' in Rosalind Marsh, ed., *Women in Russia and Ukraine* (Cambridge, Cambridge University Press, 1996), pp. 199–213.

41  *Traktorist-Kombainer*, no. 5, 15 March 1937, p. 6.

42  Buckley, 'Why be a shock worker or a stakhanovite?' op. cit., p. 202.

43  *Traktorist-Kombainer*, no. 7, 15 April 1937, p. 12.

44  Buckley, 'Why be a shock worker or a stakhanovite?' op. cit., pp. 202–03. See, too, Angelina, *My Answer*, op. cit., p. 22.

45  For further discussion see Mary Buckley 'Categorising resistance to rural stakhanovism,' in Kevin McDermot and John Morison, eds., *Politics and Society under the Bolsheviks* (Macmillan, 1999), pp. 160–88.

46  Angelina, *Liudi Kolkhoznykh Polei*, op. cit., p. 45.

47  *Krest'ianskaia gazeta*, 10 February 1937, p. 8.

48  TsKhDMO, f. 1, op. 3, d. 158, l. 10. This includes both 'O Vsesoiuznom sorevnovanii zhenskhikh traktornykh brigad', and 'O podgotovke mekhanizatorskikh kadrov sel'skogo khoziaistva iz zhenskoi molodezhi'. The Komsomol had earlier in June 1935 discussed a conference on work among female youth. See f. 1, op. 23, d. 1120, l. 10 for 'O sozyve soveshchaniia po rabote sredi zhenskoi molodezhi'.

49  *Ibid.*, f. 1, op. 3, d. 158, l. 98. See, too, *Traktorist-Kombainer*, no. 12, June 1936, p. 17.

50  *Traktorist-Kombainer*, no. 5, 15 March 1937, p. 2. *Krest'ianskaia gazeta*, 10 February 1937, p. 8.

51  *Traktorist-Kombainer*, no. 12, June 1936, p. 17.

52  *Ibid.*, no. 5, 15 March 1937, p. 2.

53  *Krest'ianskaia gazeta*, 10 February 1937, p. 8 and 12 February 1937, p. 1.

54  TsKhDMO, f. 1, op. 23, d. 1261, l. 19.

55  *Ibid.*, f. 1, op. 23, d. 1261, ll. 17–18.

56  *Ibid.*, f. 1, op. 23, d. 1261, l. 20.

57  *Ibid.*, f. 1, op. 3, d. 176, ll. 142–3.

58  *Krest'ianskaia gazeta*, 22 May 1937, p. 7. See, too, TsKhDMO, *Ibid.*, which holds 'O Vsesoiuznom sotsial'isticheskom sorevnovanii zhenskikh traktornykh brigad, tractoristok i kombainerok v 1937 godu'.

59  *Krest'ianka*, no. 9, March 1938, p. 1.

60  *Ibid.*, Archival documents summed up in the competition in TsKhDMO, f. 1, op. 23, d. 1261, ll. 1–3 and ll. 28–29.

61  *Krest'ianka*, no. 9, March 1938, p. 2.

62  *Ibid.*

63  *Ibid.*

64  TsKhDMO, f. 1, op. 23, d. 1310, l. 100.

65  *Krest'ianka*, no. 9, March 1938, p. 2.

66  *Ibid.*

67  *Ibid.*, no. 15, June 1938, pp. 20–21.

68  Angelina, *Liudi Kolkhoznykh Polei*, op. cit., p. 59; *Traktorist-Kombainer*, no. 1, January 1939, p. 15.

69  *Traktorist-Kombainer, ibid.*

70  *Ibid.*

71  *Ibid.*, no. 9, May 1939, p. 4.

72  *Ibid.*

73  *Ibid.*, p. 5, See too TsKhDMO, f. 1, op. 3, d. 1357, ll. 1–8.

74  *Ibid.*

75  *Krest'ianka*, no. 9, May 1939, inside cover.

76  *Ibid.*, no. 11, June 1939, p. 22.

77  *Ibid.*, no. 12, June 1939, p. 22.

78 *Ibid.*

79 *Ibid.*

80 *Ibid.*

81 TsKhDMO, f. 1, op. 3, d. 219, l. 59.

82 *Ibid.*, f. 1, op. 3, d. 219, l. 60.

83 *Ibid.*, f. 1, op. 3, d. 219, l. 68.

84 *Ibid.*, f. 1, op. 3, d. 225, l. 56.

85 *Ibid.*, l. 58.

86 *Ibid.*, f. 1, op. 23, d. 1357, l. 72.

87 *Ibid.*

88 *Ibid.*, l. 73.

89 *Ibid.*, l. 74.

90 *Ibid.*

91 *Ibid.*

92 *Ibid.*, l. 75.

93 RGASPI (*Rossiiskii Gosudartsvennyi arkhiv sotsial'no-politicheskoi istorii*), formerly RTsKhIDNI and before that TsPA, f. 17, op. 123, op. 123, d. 10, ll. 1–3.

94 *Ibid.*, f. 17, op. 123, d. 9, l. 11.

95 TsKhDMO, f. 1, op. 23, d. 1357, l. 88.

96 *Ibid.*, f. 1, op. 23, d. 1421, l. 8.

97 Iu. V. Arutiunian, *Mekhanizatory Sel'skogo Khoziaistva*, SSSR v 1929–1957g. (Moscow, Izdatel'stvo Akademii Nauk SSSR, 1960), p. 60.

98 *Ibid.*, f. 1, op. 23, d. 1421, l. 51.

99 *Ibid.*

100 *Ibid.*, l. 52.

101 *Ibid.*

102 *Ibid.*, l. 53.

103 *Ibid.*, f. 1, op. 23, d. 1357, ll. 10–12.

104 Arutiunian, *Mekhanizatory Sel'skogo Khoziaistva*, op. cit., p. 60.

105 Bridger, 'The heirs of Pasha', op. cit., p. 197.

106 For details of 1942 and 1943, see RGASPI, f. 116, op. 1, d. 41, ll. 7–24; f. 116, op. 1, d. 53, ll. 33–6; f. 116, op. 1, d. 85, ll. 1–17; f. 116, op. 1, d. 33, ll. 15–16.

107 Bridger, 'The heirs of Pasha', op. cit., p. 200.

## Chapter 9    THE GERMAN MILITARY'S IMAGE OF RUSSIA

1 Cf. John and Ljubica Erickson, *The Eastern Front in Photographs, 1941–1945*, London, 2001, pp. 9–17.

2 *Mein Kampf*, 63rd edition (München 1933), pp. 742–3. See Ian Kershaw, *Hitler. 1889–1936: Hubris* (London, 1998), p. 249.

3 Cf. *West-östliche Spiegelungen*, ed. Lew Kopelew, vol. 4, *19./20. Jahrhundert. Von der Bismarckzeit bis zum Ersten Weltkrieg. Russen und Russland aus deutscher Sicht*, ed. Mechthild Keller (Berlin 2000); Peter Jahn, '"Russenfurcht" und Antibolschewismus. Zur Entstehung und Wirkung von Feindbildern', in *Erobern und Vernichten. Der Krieg gegen die Sowjetunion 1941–1945*, ed. Peter Jahn and Reinhard Rürup (Berlin, 1991), pp. 47–64; *Das Rußlandbild im Dritten Reich*, ed. Hans-Erich Volkmann (Köln, 1994) (essays by M. Zeidler and J. Förster) and Andreas Hillgruber, 'The German Military Leaders' View of Russia prior to the Attack on the Soviet Union', in *From Peace to War. Germany, Soviet Russia, and the World, 1939–1941*, ed. Bernd Wegner (Providence, R.I., 1997), pp. 169–185.

4 See Winfried Baumgart, *Deutsche Ostpolitik 1918. Von Brest-Litowsk bis zum Ende des Ersten Weltkrieges* (München, 1966), p. 221, n. 45.

5 See the Reich War Ministry's official publication *Die Rückführung des Ostheeres* (Berlin 1936), pp. 17–18 and 5–6 respectively.

6 Minute by Maj. Werner von Fritsch, the future C.-in-C. of the army, dated 28 March 1920. Printed in *Die Anfänge der Ära Seeckt. Militär und Innenpolitik 1920–1922*, ed. Heinz Hürten, Düsseldorf 1979, document no. 46. See Fritsch's letter to Lt.-Col. Joachim von Stülpnagel of 16 November 1924.

7 See Francis Ludwig Carsten, 'The Reichswehr and the Red Army, 1920–1933, in *Journal of the Royal United Services Institution*, 108 (1963), p. 253.

8 *Raum and Volk im Weltkriege* (Oldenburg, 1932).

9 *Ibid.*, p. 10 and pp. 293–8 respectively.

10 *Der Tagesspiegel* (Berlin) of 1 October 1995, p. 23.

11 See Carsten, 'Reichswehr and Red Army', pp. 230–40 (on Blomberg 1928) and pp. 241–4 (on Halm 1930), and Manfred Zeidler, *Reichswehr und Rote Armee 1920–1933. Wege und Stationen einer ungewöhnlichen Zusammenarbeit* (München 1993), pp. 253–8.

12  Bundesarchiv-Militärchiv, Freiburg (hereafter BA-MA), RH 2/2417.

13  HDv 26g, in: BA-MA, RHD 5/26.

14  Heeresleitung, TA (T 3, Va) of 10 May 1935. *Ibid.*, RH 2/1443. In contrast, the competent German military attaché in Moscow, Lt. Gen. Ernst Köstring, though not free of anti-Semitic prejudices himself, spoke of Stalin's 'oriental distrust', punishing potential opponents preventively. See Hermann Teske, *General Ernst Köstring. Der militärische Mittler zwischen dem Deutschen Reich und der Sowjetunion 1921–1941* (Frankfurt a.M. 1965), p. 189.

15  Psychologisches Laboratorium des Reichskriegsministeriums, no. 241/35 of 2 November 1935, betr. Völkerpsychologische Untersuchung 5: 'Die nationale Zusammensetzung der Bevölkerung der UdSSR und die Möglichkeiten für eine propagandistische Bearbeitung', in BA-MA, RH 2/v.981.

16  Generalstab des Heeres, Abt. V b of 10 November 1937. *Ibid.*, RH 2/1440.

17  See Oberkommando des Heeres/Generalstab des Heeres/O Qu IV, Fremde Heere Ost (II), no. 794/39 of 28 October 1939, and OKH/GenStdH/OQu IV/FHO (II), no. 1995/39 of 19 December 1939, in BA-MA, RW 5/v. 351 and RH 2/2106 respectively. Cf. *Germany and the Second World War*, ed. Militärgeschichtliches Forschungsamt, vol. IV, *The Attack on the Soviet Union*, Oxford 1998, pp. 226–33.

18  OKH/GenStdH/OQu IV, Abt. Z.b.V., no. 177/39 of 27 October 1939, in BA-MA, RH 19 III/343.

19  Helmuth Groscurth, *Tagebücher eines Abwehroffiziers 1938–1940*, ed. Helmut Krausnick and Harold C. Deutsch (Stuttgart, 1970), p. 487.

20  Exerpts of that study in OQu IV/FHO (I) of December 1939 and in Chef des Generalstabes, Oberost of 11 January 1940, in BA-MA, RH 2/v. 390.

21  Teske, *Köstring*, p. 202.

22  OKH/GenStdH/OQu III, no. 130/39 of 30 March 1939, in BA-MA, WF–03/13173.

23  See n. 17.

24  See Ingo Lachnit and Friedhelm Klein, 'Der Operationsentwurf Ost des

Generalmajors Marcks vom 5. August 1940,' in *Wehrforschung*, 1(1972), pp. 114–23.

25  See Marcks' assessment of situation Red of 10 September 1940, in BA-MA, 18th Army, 17562/9.

26  *The Attack on the Soviet Union*, p. 268 (contribution of Ernst Klink).

27  Edmund Glaise von Horstenau, *Ein General im Zwielicht*, ed. Peter Broucek, vol. 2, Vienna 1983, p. 525 (1 September 1940).

28  *The Halder War Diary, 1939–1942*, ed. Charles Burdick and Hans-Adolf Jacobsen, Novato, CA 1988, p. 297.

29  Hitler on 9 January 1941. See *Kriegstagebuch des Oberkommandos der Wehrmacht (Wehrmachtführungsstab) 1940–1941*, ed. Percy Ernst Schramm, vol. I (München, 1965), pp. 257–258. Four years ago, Hitler had mentioned Russia's strength and her drive to world revolution (28 January 1937).

30  OKH/GenStdH/OQu IV/FHO (II) No. 100/41, betr. 'Die Kriegswehrmacht der Union der Sozialistischen Sowjetrepubliken (UdSSR),' in BA-MA, RHD 18/210. Cf. *The Attack on the Soviet Union*, pp. 235–7 (contribution of Ernst Klink).

31  BA-MA, RHD 6/19/2, edition of 1942. In July and August 1941, the German army learnt how costly their advance could be. See two assessments of Eighteenth Army on the Russian's strength in defence, in *Ibid.*, RH 20–18/1635.

32  See Jürgen Förster and Evan Mawdsley, 'Hitler and Stalin in Perspective. Secret Speeches on the Eve of "Barbarossa"', in *War in History* (forthcoming). For details of the Luftwaffe's appreciation of the Soviet air force cf. *Halder War Diary*, pp. 321–3 (22 February 1941).

33  Minute of the operations officer (Ia) of Eighteenth Army, in BA-MA, 18th Army, 19601/2. Cf. *The Attack on the Soviet Union*, p. 485 (contribution of Jürgen Förster).

34  *Ibid.*, p. 37 and pp. 519–20 respectively. Küchler, commander-in-chief of Eighteenth Army, had been a critic of the SS murders in Poland and changed after Hitler's triumph in the west. The full text of that address in German has

been printed in Hans-Heinrich Wilhelm, *Rassenpolitik und Kriegführung* (Passau, 1991), pp. 133–140.

35 BA-MA, RH 20-4/114.

36 Olaf Groehler, 'Zur Einschätzung der Roten Armee dutch die faschistische Wehrmacht im ersten Halbjahr 1941, dargestellt am Beispiel des AOK 4', in *Zeitschrift für Militärgeschichte*, 7 (1968), pp. 729–33 (29 December 1940). Cf. Erhard Moritz, 'Zur Fehleinschätzung des sowjetischen Kriegspotentials durch die faschistische Wehrmachtführung in den Jahren 1935 bis 1941', in *Auf antisowjetischem Kriegskurs. Studien zur militärischen Vorbereitung des deutschen Imperialismus auf die Aggression gegen die UdSSR (1933–1941)*, ed. Deutsches Institut für Militärgeschichte (East Berlin, 1970), pp. 150–184.

37 Cited after Ian Kershaw, *Hitler. 1936–1945: Nemesis* (London, 2000), p. 285 (March 1941).

38 See the 'Guidelines for the behaviour of the troops in Russia' of 19 May 1941 and specific army leaflets attacking the peculiarities of Soviet warfare, the distribution of which Hitler had insisted on. Cf. *The Attack on the Soviet Union*, p. 516 (contribution of Jürgen Förster).

39 Directives on the practice of propaganda in Operation Barbarossa of June 1941, in BA-MA, RW 4/v. 578. Cf. Ortwin Buchbender, *Das tönende Erz. Deutsche Propaganda gegen die Rote Armee im Zweiten Weltkrieg* (Stuttgart, 1978).

40 Quote accorded to *The Attack on the Soviet Union*, p. 516 (contribution of Jürgen Förster).

41 *Sieg Heil! War Letters of Tank Gunner Karl Fuchs, 1937–1941*, ed. and trans. Horst Fuchs Richardson, Hamden, Conn. 1987, p. 124. Cf. Stephen G. Fritz, *Frontsoldaten. The German Soldier in World War II* (Lexington, Kentucky, 1995).

42 *Halder War Diary*, p. 446 (3 July 1941).

43 *Ibid.*, p. 506 (11 August 1941).

44 See the memorandum on the 'Influences of Bolshevism of 8 August 1941,' in BA-MA, RH 26–291/18.

45 See Jürgen Förster, 'Zum Rußlandbild der Militärs 1941–1945,' in *Das Rußlandbild im Dritten Reich*, ed. Hans-Erich Volkmann, Köln 1994, pp. 153–4.

46 Cf. Bernd Wegner, 'The Tottering Giant. German Perceptions of Soviet Military and Economic Strength in Preparation for "Operation Blau" (1942)', in *Intelligence and International Relations, 1900–1945*, ed. Christopher Andrew and Jeremy Noakes (Exeter, 1987), pp. 293–311, and *Germany and the Second World War*, vol. VI, *The Global War* (Oxford, 2001) (contribution of Bernd Wegner).

47 Memorandum on 'Dringende Fragen des Bandenkrieges und der "Hilfswilligen"-Erfassung', in: BA-MA, RH 2/2558.

48 See Strikfeldt's lecture on 'Russian man' ('Der Russische Mensch'), in *ibid.*, RH 35/1273, and Dwinger's leaflet 'Do you know Russian man? The Road to overcome Bolshevism' (Kennst Du den russischen Menschen? Der Weg zur Überwindung des Bolschewismus), RH 13/v. 47. Cf. Third Panzer Army, Ic/AO (ABO) of 30 May 1943. 'The political task of the German soldier in Russia under the sign of total war' ('Die politische Aufgabe des deutschen Soldaten im Zeichen des totalen Krieges'), RH 21-3/v. 475.

49 Groscurth, *Tagebücher eines Abwehroffiziers*, pp. 528 and 552 (letters of 18 and 25 October 1942 respectively).

50 Examples of the latter one are the communication of 246th infantry division of 15 December 1943 and the official manual of the army's personnel office, 'What we fight for?' ('Wofür Kämpfen wir?') of January 1944, in BA-MA, RH 26–246/42 and Militärgeschichtliches Forschungsamt library respectively.

51 Cited after Förster, *Rußlandbild*, p. 163.

**Chapter 10   CELLULOID SOLDIERS**

1 The best known are *Feldzug in Polen* (1930), *Feuertaufe* (1940), and *Sieg in Westen* (1941). See more in David Welch, *Propaganda and the German Cinema, 1933–1945* (Oxford, 1983), 186–237.

2 Omer Bartov, *Germany's War and the Holocaust: Disputed Histories* (Ithaca, N.Y., 2003), 15–58.

3 See further in Omer Bartov, Atina Grossmann, and Mary Nolan, eds., *Crimes of War: Guilt and Denial in the Twentieth Century* (New York, 2002), ix–xxxiv, 41–60.

4 See more in Robert G. Moeller, *War Stories: The Search for a Usable Past in the Federal Republic of Germany* (Berkeley, Calif., 2001).

5 Carl Zuckmayer, *Des Teufels General: Drama in drei Akten* (Stockholm, 1946).

6 See further in David Irving, *The Rise and Fall of the Luftwaffe: The Life of Luftwaffe Marshal Erhard Milch* (London, 1973).

7 One may also wonder whether the name Harras was chosen to juxtapose the fictional heroic Luftwaffe general with the much-maligned British Air Chief Marshal Sir Arthur Harris, C.-in-C. of British Bomber Command from 1942 to 1945, who earned the nickname 'Bomber' because of his fervent support for area bombing of German cities.

8 Erich von Manstein, *Verlorene Siege* (Bonn, 1955); Heinz Guderian, *Erinnerungen eines Soldaten* (Heidelberg, 1950). For more see Omer Bartov, *The Eastern Front, 1941–45: German Troops and the Barbarisation of Warfare*, 2nd ed., (New York, 2001), 1–4.

9 Robert G. Moeller, ed., *West Germany under Construction: Politics, Society, and Culture in the Adenauer era* (Ann Arbor, Mich., 1997); Hanna Schissler, ed., *The Miracle Years: A Cultural History of West Germany, 1949–1968* (Princeton, N.J., 2001); Klaus Naumann, ed., *Nachkrieg in Deutschland* (Hamburg, 2001).

10 See Jeremy Noakes and Geoffrey Pridham, eds., *Nazism, 1919–1945: A Documentary Reader*, vol. 3: *Foreign Policy, War and Racial Extermination* (Exeter, 1998), 1199–200, for Himmler's speech to SS officers in Posen on 4 October 1943, and his speech to army generals in Sonthofen on 5 May 1944, which carries a similar message.

11 Omer Bartov, *Hitler's Army: Soldiers, Nazis, and War in the Third Reich* (New York, 1991), 86, 130.

12 The origins of this heroic soldier actually date back to World War I. See Omer Bartov, *Murder in Our Midst: The Holocaust, Industrial Killing, and Representation* (New York, 1996), chs. 1–2. On the crisis of masculinity in post-war Germany see Frank P. Biess, 'The Protracted War: Returning POWs and the Making of East and West German Citizens, 1945–

1955', Brown University PhD diss., 2000.

13 See, e.g., Jost Hermand, Helmut Peitsch, Klaus R. Scherpe, eds., *Nachkriegsliteratur in Westdeutschland 1945–49* (Berlin, 1982).

14 Hans Hellmut Kirst, *Null-acht fünfzehn: Roman*, 3 vols. (Vienna, 1954–5), vol. 1: *In der Kaserne*; vol. 2: *Im Krieg*; vol. 3: *Bis zum Ende: Der gefährliche Endsieg des Soldaten Asch*. The title refers to a World War I machine gun whose name, 08/15, became a German military slang expression for 'standard issue'. The film subtitles in English are, 1: 'In the Barracks'; 2: 'At the Front'; 3: 'Back at Home'.

15 Heinz G. Konsalik, *Der Arzt von Stalingrad* (München, 1989). The novel went through at least forty reprints and is still selling briskly.

16 For full analysis see Moeller, *War Stories*, 149–55.

17 See Bartov, *Murder in Our Midst*, ch. 7.

18 Bernd Boll and Hans Safrian, 'On the way to Stalingrad: The 6th Army in 1941–42', in *War of Extermination: The German Military in World War II, 1941–1944*, ed. Hannes Heer and Klaus Naumann (New York, 2000).

19 Ernst Klee, Willi Dressen, Volker Riess, eds., *'The Good Old Days': The Holocaust as Seen by Its Perpetrators and Bystanders*, trans. Deborah Burnstone (New York, 1991).

20 See note 3, above.

21 Heinrich Böll, *A Soldier's Legacy*, trans. Leila Vennewitz (New York, 1985).

22 W. G. Sebald, *On the Natural History of Destruction*, trans. Anthea Bell (New York, 2003); Jörg Friedrich, *Der Brand: Deutschland im Bombenkrieg 1940–1945* (Berlin, 2002); Günter Grass, *Crabwalk*, trans. Krishna Winston (Orlando, 2002).

23 See especially W. G. Sebald, *Austerlitz*, trans. Anthea Bell (New York, 2001).

## Chapter 11 THE DEVIL HIS DUE

Special thanks are due my colleagues, Professors Chester Dunning and Roger Reese of the History Department at Texas A&M, for their aid and counsel in developing this chapter.

1 For a satirical contemporaneous overview, see 'History of the American Communist Party', in A. Hirschfeld,

*Hirschfeld on Line* (New York, Applause, 1999), pp. 60–61.

2 E.g., see Editors of Fortune, 'The Bear that Shoots Like a Man', in *Background of War* (New York, Alfred A. Knopf, 1937), pp. 251–96; a late Cold War survey of US magazines and newspapers found that conservative American newspapers in the thirties tended to attribute Soviet policy and action to a desire to extend communism more than moderate papers. See table 6, Thomas R. Maddox, *Years of Estrangement: American Relations with the Soviet Union, 1933–1941* (Tallahassee, University Press of Florida, 1980).

3 A pollster in 1939 claimed that 31% of college students surveyed 'would fight against Fascism. The same group would fight for the Communist ideal, not Communism as practiced in Russia'. Betsy Barton, ' "We Won't Fight," Say College Students', *Liberty*, 16:17 (29 April 1939), p. 23.

4 Quoted in Daniel Bell, *Marxian Socialism in the United States* (Princeton, Princeton University Press, 1967), p. 137, who from a Cold War perspective observed: 'Between the romantic image of the communist conjured by the intellectuals and the grubby reality of the sectarian party lay a vast gulf ... a striking illustration of how compelling a myth can be that the intellectuals ignored the disparity between illusion and actuality.' *Ibid.*, p. 138.

5 Catherine Radziwill, 'Stalin Talks About Hitler', in Allen Churchill, ed., *The Liberty Years, 1924–1950: An Anthology* (Englewood Cliffs, Prentice-Hall, 1969), p. 280.

6 Franklin D. Roosevelt, 'The Soviet Union is a Dictatorship', in Benson L. Grayson, ed., *The American Image of Russia 1917–1977* (New York, Frederick Ungar, 1978), pp. 150–52.

7 Preface to his play on the Russo-Finnish War *There Shall Be No Night* (New York, Scribner's, 1941), pp. xxvii–xxviii; in much the same vein was H. M. Harwood's letter to Samuel N. Behrman of 8 December 1939: 'Like most people whose politics are slightly Left Wing, I hoped for something better from Russia; it was apparently ignorance that led me to hope. Since I have never been there,

I could only argue from analogies', like the eventual amelioration of conditions 'in France after the revolution there'; in F. Tennyson Jesse and H. M. Harwood, eds., *London Front: Letters Written to America 1939–1940* (New York, Doubleday, Doran, 1941), p. 103.

8 Louis Fischer, *Men and Politics* (New York, Duell Sloan and Pearce, 1941), p. 432–5.

9 *Ibid.*, p. 436.

10 *Ibid.*, p. 529–30.

11 Joe Morella, Edward Z. Epstein, and John Griggs, *The Films of World War II: A Pictorial Treasury of Hollywood's War Years* (Secaucus, Citadel Press, 1973), pp. 19, and 22–3.

12 In that incident, in October 1939, a prize crew from a German surface raider took a US merchant vessel into Murmansk, and the Soviet authorities rebuffed US queries regarding the situation. The ship was later seized by Norwegian authorities on its way to Germany.

13 E.g., for glimpses of atmospherics at the time, see Jesse and Harwood, *London Front*, pp. 103, 122, 133–4, 150, 153, and 189; and Andrew Barnes, 'Embassies of the Dead', *Coronet*, 9:5 (March, 1941), pp. 113–17; for a detailed analysis of American public opinion and official reactions during the Russo-Finnish War, see Maddox, *Years of Estrangement*, pp. 114–26.

14 A contemporaneous compendium of American communist defences of Stalinist excesses is Earl Browder, *The Second Imperialist War* (New York, International Publishers, 1940), esp. pp. 72, 269–86, and 271.

15 J. Edgar Hoover, 'Enemy Within Our Gates', *American Magazine*, 130:2 (August 1940), pp. 144–5.

16 A recent perspective is Andrew Hemingway, *Artists on the Left: American Artists and the Communist Movement 1926–1956* (New Haven, Yale University Press, 2002).

17 For a post-Cold War view, see Christopher Andrew and Vasili Mitrokhin, *The Sword and the Shield: The Mitrokhin Archive and the Secret History of the KGB* (New York, Basic Books, 1999), pp. 104–34.

18 Donald Rugg, 'American Morale When

the War Began', ch. xi, pp. 189–207, in Goodwin Watson, ed., *Civilian Morale: Second Yearbook of the Society for the Psychological Study of Social Issues* (Boston, Houghton Mifflin, 1942), pp. 191–3.

19 Most visible of the strikes led by Communist labour leaders were those at the Allis-Chalmers plant in West Allis, Wisconsin, and the North American Aviation plant at Inglewood, California.

20 Geofrey P. Megargee, *Inside Hitler's High Command* (Lawrence, University Press of Kansas, 2002), p. 114.

21 Despite some gaffes like the conclusion that the 'initial blitzkrieg [was] over' and the 'battle [was] now in hands of infantry'; 'War in Russia: Secret Maps Record First Seven Weeks of Battle', *Life*, 11:8 (August 25, 1941), pp. 30–31.

22 Joseph E. Davies, *Mission to Moscow* (New York, Pocket Books, 1943 [March – 13th printing]), p. 464.

23 Including comic strips; e.g., Captain Marvel, Jr. went to Stalingrad to help augment the flow of tanks to the front.

24 For a contemporary view, see Michael Evans, 'Outwitting the Censors', *Coronet*, 9:6 (April 1941), pp. 125–6.

25 Ralph Ingersoll, *Action on All Fronts: A Personal Account of This War* (New York: Harper & Brothers, 1942), p. 76.

26 *Ibid.*, p. 120.

27 *Ibid.*, pp. 125–7.

28 *Ibid.*, p. 136.

29 *Ibid.*, p. 100.

30 *Ibid.*, pp. 100–101 and 165.

31 *Ibid.*, p. 101.

32 *Ibid.*, pp. 100 and 166.

33 Alice-Leone Moats, *Blind Date With Mars* (Garden City, Doubleday Doran, 1943), p. 199; she also countered other correspondents' reports of Soviet softening toward religion, and expressed her desire to 'fly back to the warm arms of capitalism'. See *ibid.*, pp. 208, 235, 239, 262, 268, 313, 433, and 445. Later in the war, Edgar Snow dismissed reports of Soviet massacres of Polish elites in *People on Our Side* (New York, Random House, 1944), p. 149.

34 Joseph E. Davies, *Mission to Moscow* (New York, Pocket Books, 1943 [March – 13th printing]) p. 209.

35 Moats, *Blind Date With Mars*, pp. 235–8.

36 Larry Leseuer, *Twelve Months That Changed the World* (New York, Alfred Knopf, 1943), p. 345.

37 *Ibid.*, p. 344.

38 *Ibid.*, pp. 254, and 305–306.

39 Harry B. Henderson and Herman C. Morris, eds., *War in Our Time* (Garden City, Doubleday, Doran, 1942); also see pp. 40–43, pp. 66–9, and p. 255.

40 S. S. Sargent, 'Propaganda and Morale', ch. IX, pp. 166–185, in Goodwin Watson, ed., *Civilian Morale: Second Yearbook of the Society for the Psychological Study of Social Issues* (Boston, Houghton Mifflin, 1942), p. 171.

41 Erwin Lessner and James C. McMullin, 'Russia and Japan Must Fight', *Liberty*, 14 August 1943, pp. 20–21, 44 and 56; the sub-headline was 'An All-out Slugging Fest between Russia and Japan is Coming'.

42 E.g., Genevieve Tabous, 'The Coming French Revolution', *Coronet*, 10:5 (September, 1941), pp. 9–13; *The New Yorker War Album* (New York, Random House, 1942), pp. 59 and 85.

43 Wallace Carroll, in *We're in This with Russia* (Boston, Houghton Mifflin, 1942), p. 46; also see Maddox, *Years of Estrangement*, p. 102.

44 Leslie Balogh Bain, *The War of Confusion* (New York, M. S. Mill, 1942), pp. 97 and 102; Francis L. Bacon, *The War and America* (New York, Macmillan, 1942), pp. 21 and 65.

45 Ely Culbertson, *Total Peace* (Garden City, Doubleday, Doran, 1943), p. 145. Similar statements included 'the history of the remainder of the twentieth century will be written around Russia and the United States', p. 150; 'the horrible abuses of capitalism will become mere annoyances', p. 151; the need for 'the great Communist laboratory' and the 'great American laboratory' and comparison of a war between the two to Harvard bombing Princeton, p. 152; no danger of a communist Germany, Europe or Asia 'as long as Stalin and his group are leading the Soviet Union', p. 156; and 'If we know what we want, if we are guided by what is essentially just to Russia and to her neighbors, and if we are fair in our policy, we need not fear Russia,' p. 162.

46 Joseph E. Davies , 'The Soviets and the Post-War', *Life*, 14:13 (29 March 1943), pp. 49–50.

47 'The Father of Modern Russia', *Life* 14:13 (29 March 1943) p. 29.

48 Francis Sill Wickware, 'Timoshenko: A Great Defensive Leader: He was First Victorious Allied General', *Life* 14:13 (29 March 1943), pp. 99 and 102–105.

49 *Ibid.*, p. 39.

50 *Ibid.*, p. 40; sometimes syrupy adulation also appeared in Luce's *Time*, e.g., cover stories on Shaposhnikov, 'What Will Spring Bring?', *Time*, 39:7 (16 February 1942), pp. 26 and 29; Zhukov, 'Stalin's *Liubimets*', *Time*, 40:24 (14 December 1942), pp. 35–8,: Timoshenko, 'A Peasant and His Land', *Time*, 40:2 (27 July 1942), pp. 20 and 23–4; Vasilevsky, 'Victory is Fighting Word', *Time*, 42:1 (5 July 1943), pp. 25–8; and Novikov, 'Close to the Earth', *Time*, 44:5 (31 July 1944), pp. 18–20; examples of the tenor in other publications are Ralph Parker, 'Pokryshkin – Ace of Aces', *Liberty*, 21:46, (11 November 1944), pp. 26–7, and John H. Craige, 'Russia's Wizard of War', [Vasilevsky], *Liberty*, 21:40 (30 September 1944), pp. 20–2 and 62.

51 Sumner Welles, ed., *An Intelligent American's Guide to the Peace* (New York, Dryden Press, 1944), pp. 118–19; a more detailed apologia is Walter Duranty, 'The Moscow Trials', in Curt Reiss, ed., *They Were There: The Story of World War II and How It Came About by American Foreign Correspondents* (New York, G. P. Putnam's, 1944), pp. 64–5; for a sharp contrast, see Louis Fischer, *Men and Politics* (New York, Duell Sloan and Pearce, 1941), chapter 30, 'The Moscow Trials and Confessions', pp. 502–531.

52 Samuel Stouffer, et al., eds., *Studies in Social Psychology in World War II*, vol. 1, *The American Soldier: Adjustment During Army Life* (Princeton, Princeton University Press, 1949), p. 442.

53 George C. Marshall, *General Marshall's Report. The Winning of the War in Europe and the Pacific* (Washington, D.C., War Department, 1945), p. 107.

54 Henry L. Stimson and McGeorge Bundy, *On Active Service in Peace and War* (New York, Harper and Brothers, 1947), p. 527.

55 George H. Roeder, Jr., *The Censored War: American Visual Experience During World War II* (New Haven, Yale, 1993), p. 129.

56 Thomas R. Maddox, *Years of Estrangement: American Relations with the Soviet Union, 1933–1941* (Tallahassee, University Press of Florida, 1980), p. 36.

57 Nikolaus Basseches, *The Unknown Army: The Nature and History of the Russian Military Forces*, trans. Marion Saerchlinger (New York, Viking Press, 1943), p. 199.

58 Raoul de Russey de Sales, *The Making of Tomorrow* (New York, Reynal and Hitchcock, 1942), p. 285.

59 Quoted in Edgar Snow, *People on Our Side* (New York, Random House, 1944), p. 242.

60 *Ibid.*, p. 258.

61 Basseches, *The Unknown Army*, pp. 117–78. Basseches, however, acknowledged 'the influence exerted on the Red Army leadership' of 'methods of terror … consummately carried out … by … savage means', *ibid.*, p. 219.

62 'Negotiating on Military Assistance, 1943–1945,' in Raymond Dennett and Joseph E. Johnson, *Negotiating With the Russians* (Boston, World Peace Foundation, 1951), p. 8.

63 For details, see John R. Hazard, 'Negotiating Under Lend-Lease, 1942–1945', in Dennett and Johnson, *Negotiating With the Russians*, pp. 36–44.

64 Bacon, *The War and America*, p. 71.

65 For example, in early 1945, just over a third among a cross-section of white enlisted men in the US army expected the US and Britain would fight Russia within twenty-five years; one-quarter believed the US would fight Russia alone, although a special programme to improve attitudes had some moderating effect; Stouffer, et al., *Studies in Social Psychology*, pp. 445, 475 and 479.

66 For an example of the contrast between World War II perspectives and early Cold War depictions of Soviet society in the American media, see Ella Winter, 'Russian Children Fight', *Liberty* (20 February 1943), pp. 22–3 and 73–4 and William Van Varnig, 'What Russian Children are Taught', *Liberty*, 23:51 (21 December 1946), pp. 24–5, and 77–8.

## Chapter 12 STALINGRAD AND RESEARCHING THE EXPERIENCE OF WAR

1 This chapter was originally a Lees-Knowles lecture delivered at Cambridge University in November 2002.

2 Rossiyskiy Gosudarstvenniy Archiv Sotsialno-politicheskoi Istorii (Russian State Archive of Social and Political History).

3 John E. Vetter, *Last Letters from Stalingrad* (McLean, VA, Coronet Press, 1955).

4 Alexander Stahlberg, *Bounden Duty: memoirs of a German officer, 1932–45* (London, Brasseys, 1990).

5 Thomas Plivier, *Stalingrad, roman* (Berlin, Aufbau-verlag GMBH, 1945).

6 Viktor Nekrasov, *Front-line Stalingrad* (London: Harvill Press, 1947).

7 Vasily Grossman, *Life and Fate* (London: Harvill Press 1995 [1980]).

8 Antony Beevor and Artemis Cooper, *Paris after the Liberation, 1944–1949* (London, Hamish Hamilton, 1994).

9 Richard Overy, *Russia's War* (London, Allen Lane, 1998).

10 Antony Beevor, *Stalingrad* (London, Viking, 1998).

11 A. T. Zhadobin (ed.), *Stalingradskaia epopeia: Vpervye publikuemye dokumenty, rassekrechennye FSB RF: Vospominaniia fel'dmarshala Pauliusa. Dnevniki soldat RKKA i vermakhta. Agenturnye doneseniia. Protokoly doprosov. Dokladnye zapiski osobykh otdelov frontov i armii* (Moscow, Zvonnitsa–MG, 2000).

## Chapter 13 WOMEN AND THE BATTLE OF STALINGRAD

1 John Erickson, *The Road to Berlin: Continuing the History of Stalin's War with Germany* (Boulder, CO, Westview, 1983), 43.

2 Richard Overy, *Why the Allies Won* (New York, Norton, 1997), 85.

3 John Erickson, *The Road to Stalingrad: Stalin's War with Germany* (Boulder, CO, Westview, 1984), 558; David M. Glantz and Jonathan M. House, *When Titans Clashed: How the Red Army Stopped Hitler, Modern War Studies* (Lawrence, KS, University Press of Kansas, 1995), 134.

4 Glantz and House, *When Titans Clashed*, 295.

5 Antony Beevor, *Stalingrad, The Fateful Siege: 1942–1943*, 1st American edn (New York, Viking, 1998); William Craig, *Enemy at the Gates: The Battle for Stalingrad* (New York, NY, Penguin Books, 2001); David L. Robbins, *War of the Rats: a novel* (New York, Bantam Books, 1999).

6 A. S. Chuianov, 'A Heavy Ordeal', in *Two Hundred Days of Fire; Accounts by Participants and Witnesses of the battle of Stalingrad* (Moscow, Progress Publishers, 1970), 234.

7 *Ibid.*, 7.

8 V. I. Chuikov and Ivan Grigorevich Paderin, *Nachalo puti, Voennye memuary* (Moscow, Voenizdat, 1959), 261.

9 John Erickson, 'Soviet Women at War', in *World War II and the Soviet People*, ed. John Garrard, Carol Garrard, and Stephen White (New York, St Martin's, 1993), 68. See also Valentina Yakovlevna Galagan, *Ratnyi podvig zhenshchin v gody Velikoi Otechestvennoi voiny* (Kiev, Vysshaia shkola, 1986), 275.

10 L. P. Ovchinnikova, *Zhenshchiny v soldatskikh shineliakh* (Volgograd, Nizhne-Volzhskoe, 1987), 150; Aleksandr Mikhailovich Samsonov, *Stalingradskaia bitva*, 2nd revised and expanded edn (Moscow, Nauka, 1968), 526–9, 557–60.

11 A. I. Eremenko, *Stalingrad* (Moscow, 1971), 293.

12 V. I. Chuikov, 'Razdum'ia o samykh tiazhelykh dniakh Stalingrada', in *Stalingradskaia epopeia*, ed. M. V. Zakharov, Aleksandr Mikhailovich Samsonov, and Vitol'd Kazimirovich Pechorkin (Moskva, Nauka, 1968), 238.

13 V. I. Chuikov, *Vystoiav, my pobedili: zapiski komandarma 62-y* (Moscow, Sovetskaia Rossiia, 1960), 88–94.

14 Vera Semenova Murmantseva, *Sovetskie zhenshchiny v Velikoi Otechestvennoi voine 1941–1945* (Moscow, Mysl', 1974), 177.

15 Anastasiia Dmitrievna Zarubina, *Zhenshchiny na zashchite Stalingrada* (Stalingrad, Stalingradskoe knizhnoe izdatl'stvo, 1958), 10.

16 Beevor, *Stalingrad*, 157–8. Although Antony Beevor makes frequent reference to civilian women in AAA units and to Red Army women in support roles, such as signals and medical duties, he believes that 'very few women served as combat

soldiers in the city' apart from the tanker Ekaterina Petliuk. He does, however, note that many medical personnel took part in fighting and killing Germans.

17 Reina Pennington, *Wings, Women, and War: Soviet Airwomen in World War II Combat*, ed. Theodore Wilson, *Modern War Studies* (Lawrence, KS, University Press of Kansas, 2001), 63–9.

18 Ovchinnikova, *Zhenshchiny v soldatskikh shineliakh*, 5.

19 Alexander Werth, *The Year of Stalingrad: A Historical Record and a Study of Russian Mentality, Methods and Policy*, reprint of 1946 edition edn (Safety Harbor, FL, Simon Publications, 2001), 461.

20 *Ibid.*, 400.

21 Omer Bartov, *Hitler's Army: Soldiers, Nazis and War in the Third Reich* (New York, Oxford University Press, 1991), 154, citing Richardson, *Sieg Heil! War Letters of Tank Gunner Karl Fuchs 1937–1941* (Hamden CT, 1987), 119.

22 Erickson, 'Soviet Women at War', 59.

23 Chuianov, 'A Heavy Ordeal', 224.

24 *Ibid.*, 228.

25 Murmantseva, *Sovetskie zhenshchiny*, 175.

26 V. I. Levkin, 'Young Communists Became Men', in *Two Hundred Days of Fire; Accounts by Participants and Witnesses of the battle of Stalingrad* (Moscow, Progress Publishers, 1970), 242.

27 L. S. Plastikova, 'Stalingradki', in *Oktiabrem rozhdennye*, ed. N. S. Gudkova (Moscow, Politizdat, 1967), 287.

28 Vladimir Ivanovich Atopov et al., *Volgograd* (Moscow, Sovetskaia Rossiia, 1985).

29 Plastikova, 'Stalingradki', 287.

30 Erickson, *The Road to Stalingrad*, 363–4; Samsonov, *Stalingradskaia bitva*, 525.

31 Beevor, *Stalingrad*, 97–8; Murmantseva, *Sovetskie zhenshchiny*, 175.

32 Beevor, *Stalingrad*, 97–8, 105, 111.

33 Ovchinnikova, *Zhenshchiny v soldatskikh shineliakh*, 146.

34 Beevor, *Stalingrad*, 98.

35 Ovchinnikova, *Zhenshchiny v soldatskikh shineliakh*, 150, cites *Istoricheskii podvig Stalingrada* (Moscow, Mysl', 1985), 207. See also Levkin, 'Young Communists Became Men', 243–4, who cites a figure of 7000.

36 Ovchinnikova, *Zhenshchiny v soldatskikh shineliakh*, 146–8.

37 *Ibid.*, 151–4.

38 *Ibid.*, 151.

39 *Ibid.*, 150.

40 Svetlana Alexiyevich, *War's Unwomanly Face*, trans. Keith Hammond and Lyudmila Lezhneva (Moscow, Progress Publishers, 1988), 30.

41 *Ibid.*, 158.

42 Konstantin Mikhailovich Simonov, *Raznye dni voiny: dnevnik pisatelia* (Moskva, Mol. gvardiia, 1975), 96.

43 Beevor, *Stalingrad*, 66, citing Uffz. Hans Urban, 389th I.D., Bundesarchiv-Militärarchiv, Freiburg im Breisgau, RW4/v264, p. 89.

44 Erickson, *The Road to Stalingrad*, 363.

45 Galagan, *Ratny podvig zhenshchin*, 176–7.

46 Chuikov and Paderin, *Nachalo puti*, 250–51.

47 Ovchinnikova, *Zhenshchiny v soldatskikh shineliakh*, 156.

48 Kazimiera J. Cottam, *Women in War and Resistance: Selected Biographies of Soviet Women Soldiers* (Nepean, Ontario, New Military Publishing, 1998), 321–33.

49 Beevor, *Stalingrad*, 87, citing a report of 10 August 1942, TsAMO 48/453/13/ pp. 4–10.

50 *Ibid.*, 91.

51 Simonov, *Raznye dni voiny: dnevnik pisatelia*, 96.

52 Murmantseva, *Sovetskie zhenshchiny*, 180.

53 Galagan, *Ratny podvig zhenshchin*, 191. See also Cottam, *Women in War and Resistance*, 172–4.

54 Erickson, *The Road to Stalingrad*, 360.

55 Walter Boardman Kerr, *The Secret of Stalingrad*, 1st edn (Garden City, NY, Doubleday, 1978), 157.

56 Chuianov, 'A Heavy Ordeal', 225; Erickson, 'Soviet Women at War', 59.

57 Plastikova, 'Stalingradki', 288.

58 Erickson, 'Soviet Women at War', 61.

59 Gerhard L. Weinberg, *A World at Arms: A Global History of World War II* (New York, Cambridge UP, 1994), 422.

60 Craig, *Enemy at the Gates*, 72. Beevor reports this event as well but does not mention the presence of the observing nurses; he gives no citation for his source. Beevor, *Stalingrad*, 117.

61 Beevor, *Stalingrad*, 105.

62 William Craig, *Enemy at the Gates*, 54, 60–61.

63 Chuianov, 'A Heavy Ordeal', 235; Craig, *Enemy at the Gates*, 58, 66.

64 Craig, *Enemy at the Gates*, 70.

65 Konstantin Simonov, *Always a Journalist*, (Moscow, Progress, 1989), 27, 33.

66 Craig, *Enemy at the Gates*, 105.

67 *Ibid.*, 143.

68 *Ibid.*, 166.

69 Beevor, *Stalingrad*, 106–110; Craig, *Enemy at the Gates*, 67; Kerr, *The Secret of Stalingrad*, 133.

70 Chuianov, 'A Heavy Ordeal', 229, M. A. Vodolagin, 'V dni trevog', in *Stalingradskaia epopeia*, ed. M. V. Zakharov, Aleksandr Mikhailovich Samsonov, and Vitol'd Kazimirovich Pechorkin (Moskva, Nauka, 1968), 397.

71 Vodolagin, 'V dni trevog', 397.

72 Beevor, *Stalingrad*, 111.

73 A. S. Chuianov, 'Stalingradskaia partiinaia organizatsiia v dni surovykh ispytanii', in *Stalingradskaia epopeia*, ed. M. V. Zakharov, Aleksandr Mikhailovich Samsonov, and Vitol'd Kazimirovich Pechorkin (Moskval, Nauka, 1968), 364, Vodolagin, 'V dni trevog', 385.

74 Murmantseva, *Sovetskie zhenshchiny*, 177.

75 Plastikova, 'Stalingradki', 289.

76 Vodolagin, 'V dni trevog', 388–9.

77 Craig, *Enemy at the Gates*, 66–7.

78 Levkin, 'Young Communists Became Men', 245.

79 *Ibid.*

80 Ovchinnikova, *Zhenshchiny v soldatskikh shineliakh*, 152–3.

81 *Ibid.*, 161–2.

82 *Ibid.*, 158.

83 Beevor, *Stalingrad*, 160.

84 Ovchinnikova, *Zhenshchiny v soldatskikh shineliakh*, 163.

85 Joel S. A. Hayward, *Stopped at Stalingrad: The Luftwaffe and Hitler's Defeat in the East, 1942–43* (Lawrence, KS, University Press of Kansas, 1998), 189.

86 Chuikov and Paderin, *Nachalo puti*, 251.

87 Levkin, 'Young Communists Became Men', 243–4.

88 Beevor, *Stalingrad*, 107, citing Grossman papers, RGALI 618/2/108.

89 *Ibid.*, 108.

90 *Ibid.*, 106., citing BA-MA, RH27–16/42.

91 Hayward, *Stopped at Stalingrad*, 187. This seems odd, since women had been at PVO posts for several months before the battle, and were in military uniform. However, it is possible that there were incidents where civilians attempted to assist air defence units when their crews became casualties.

92 Beevor, *Stalingrad*, 108 citing BA-MA, RH27–16/42.

93 *Ibid.*, 109.

94 Erickson, *The Road to Stalingrad*, 410–411, A. M. Vasilevsky, 'A Victory to Outlive the Centuries', in *Two Hundred Days of Fire; Accounts by Participants and Witnesses of the battle of Stalingrad* (Moscow, Progress Publishers, 1970), 23.

95 Zarubina, *Zhenshchiny na zashchite Stalingrada*, 24.

96 *Ibid.*, 25.

97 Erickson, 'Soviet Women at War', 59.

98 Zarubina, *Zhenshchiny na zashchite Stalingrada*, 27.

99 Craig, *Enemy at the Gates*, 69; Levkin, 'Young Communists Became Men', 245; Samsonov, *Stalingradskaia bitva*, 138; *Stalingrad* (Moscow, Foreign Languages Publishing House, 1943), Vodolagin, 'V dni trevog', 396.

100 Craig, *Enemy at the Gates*, 59. See also Murmantseva, *Sovetskie zhenshchiny*, 176.

101 Beevor, *Stalingrad*, 109.

102 *Ibid.*, 110.

103 Murmantseva, *Sovetskie zhenshchiny*, 177.

104 Craig, *Enemy at the Gates*, 38.

105 Levkin, 'Young Communists Became Men', 244–5. See also Murmantseva, *Sovetskie zhenshchiny*, 176. See also Simonov, *Always a Journalist*, 31.

106 Levkin, 'Young Communists Became Men', 246–7.

107 Kerr, *The Secret of Stalingrad*, 155–6.

108 *Ibid.*, 159.

109 Ronald Seth, *Stalingrad: Point of Return; the story of the battle, August 1942–February 1943*, 1st American edn (New York, Coward-McCann, 1959), 96.

110 Craig, *Enemy at the Gates*, 86.

111 Beevor, *Stalingrad*, 174–6, 407; Craig, *Enemy at the Gates*, 97, 385.

112 Simonov, *Always a Journalist*, 32.

113 V. A. Grekov, 'The Soldiers of a Great Battle', in *Two Hundred Days of Fire; Accounts by Participants and Witnesses of the*

*battle of Stalingrad* (Moscow, Progress Publishers, 1970), 269. See also Kerr, *The Secret of Stalingrad*, 182.

114  Beevor, *Stalingrad*, 442.

115  *Ibid.*, 179.

116  *Ibid.*, 176.

117  *Ibid.*, 179.

118  Erickson, 'Soviet Women at War', 54, Richard Overy, *Russia's War* (New York, Penguin, 1997), 170.

119  Robert W. Thurston and Bernd Bonwetsch, *The People's War: Responses to World War II in the Soviet Union* (Urbana, University of Illinois Press, 2000), 94.

120  Craig, *Enemy the Gates*, 58, 97–8.

121  Beevor, *Stalingrad*, 162, citing Uffz. Hans Urban, 389th I.D., Bundesarchiv-Militärarchiv, Freiburg im Breisgau, RW164/v264, p. 189.

122  Kerr, *The Secret of Stalingrad*, 180–81.

123  *Russians Tell the Story; Sketches of the War on the Soviet-German Front from 'Soviet War News'*, (London, Hutchinson, 1944).

124  Craig, *Enemy at the Gates*, 169–170.

125  Beevor, *Stalingrad*, 179.

126  *Ibid.*, 175.

127  *Ibid.*, 177.

128  *Ibid.*, 177–8.

129  Craig, *Enemy at the Gates*, 98–9, 107, 317.

130  Seth, *Stalingrad: Point of Return*, 143–4.

131  *Ibid.*, 144–6.

132  Beevor, *Stalingrad*, 177.

133  *Ibid.*, 177, citing TsAMO 148/486/125/163.

134  Kerr, *The Secret of Stalingrad*, 160, *Russians Tell the Story*, 96–7.

135  Craig, *Enemy at the Gates*, 97.

136  *Ibid.*, 285.

137  Ovchinnikova, *Zhenshchiny v soldatskikh shineliakh*, 50.

138  *Ibid.*, 50–52.

139  *Ibid.*, 53–6.

140  Levkin, 'Young Communists Became Men', 247.

141  Chuianov, 'Stalingradskaia partiinaia organizatsiia v dni surovykh ispytanii', 372.

142  Chuianov, 'A Heavy Ordeal', 238.

143  *Ibid.*

144  Levkin, 'Young Communists Became Men', Zarubina, *Zhenshchiny na zashchite Stalingrada.*

145  Plastikova, 'Stalingradki', 289.

146  Levkin, 'Young Communists Became Men', 247.

147  *Ibid.*, 249–250, Murmantseva, *Sovetskie zhenshchiny*, 176.

148  Vodolagin, 'V dni trevog', 382.

149  *Stalingrad, an Eye Witness Account* (London, Hutchinson & Company, 1943), facing 49.

150  Atopov et al., *Volgograd.*

151  Chuikov and Paderin, *Nachalo puti*, 261. See also Chuikov, 'Razdum'ia o samykh tiazhelykh dniakh Stalingrad', 239; Murmantseva, *Sovetskie zhenshchiny*, 178.

152  Alexiyevich, *War's Unwomanly Face*, 241.

153  Vasilii Semenovich Grossman, *Stalingrad Hits Back*, trans. A. Fineberg and D. Fromberg (Moscow, Foreign Languages Publishing House, 1942), 20; Vassily Grossman, 'In the Line of the Main Attack', in *Moscow 1941/1942 Stalingrad: recollections, stories, reports*, ed. Vladimir Sevruk and Aleksandr Mikhailovich Vasilevskii (Moscow, Progress Publishers, 1970), *Stalingrad*, 73, 76.

154  Beevor, *Stalingrad*, 157.

155  *Ibid.*

156  N. P. Anisimov, 'Tyl Iugo-Vostochnogo i Stalingradskogo frontov v bitve na Volge', in *Stalingradskaia epopeia*, ed. M. V. Zakharov, Aleksandr Mikhailovich Samsonov, and Vitol'd Kazimirovich Pechorkin (Moskva, Nauka, 1968), 681.

157  Chuikov, 'Razdum'ia o samykh tiazhelykh dniakh Stalingrada', 239.

158  Levkin, 'Young Communists Became Men', 245–6.

159  Galagan, *Ratny podvig zhenshchin*, 169, Murmantseva, *Sovetskie zhenshchiny*, 177.

160  Galagan, *Ratny podvig zhenshchin*, 164. See also Beevor, *Stalingrad*, 157; Murmantseva, *Sovetskie zhenshchiny*, 121.

161  Galagan, *Ratny podvig zhenshchin*, 169.

162  Seth, *Stalingrad: Point of Return; the story of the battle, August 1942–February 1943.*

163  Alexiyevich, *War's Unwomanly Face*, 239.

164  Simonov, *Always a Journalist*, 28.

165  *Ibid.*, 28–29. This story is repeated in a reprint of Simonov's 25 September 1942 essay in *Stalingrad*, 57–8.

166  Seth, *Stalingrad: Point of Return*, 101.

167  Aleksandr Il'ich Rodimtsev and Petr Severov, *Mashen'ka iz Myshelovki* (Kiev, Izd. detskoi literatury 'Veselka', 1966).

168  *Ibid.*, 46, 56–8, 80, 90.

169 *Ibid.*, 64.

170 *Ibid.*

171 Beevor, *Stalingrad*, 134–5.

172 Rodimtsev and Severov, *Mashen'ka iz Myshelovki*, 132.

173 *Ibid.*, 136–7.

174 *Ibid.*, 138.

175 *Ibid.*, 155–6.

176 Cottam, *Women in War and Resistance*, 227–9.

177 *Ibid.*, 243–5.

178 *Ibid.*, 234–5, Murmantseva, *Sovetskie zhenshchiny*, 178.

179 Cottam, *Women in War and Resistance*, 248–53.

180 Chuikov and Paderin, *Nachalo puti*, 77.

181 Alexiyevich, *War's Unwomanly Face*, 164.

182 Craig, *Enemy at the Gates*, 71.

183 Chuikov and Paderin, *Nachalo puti*, 355.

184 Craig, *Enemy the Gates*, 143, 398.

185 Chuikov, 'Razdum'ia o samykh tiazhelykh dniakh Stalingrada', 239; F. N. Smekhotvorov, 'V boiakh za Stalingrad', in *Stalingradskaia epopeia*, ed. M. V. Zakharov, Aleksandr Mikhailovich Samsonov, and Vitol'd Kazimirovich Pechorkin (Moskva, Nauka, 1968), 343.

186 Chuikov and Paderin, *Nachalo puti*, 190.

187 *Ibid.*, 83–5.

188 Craig, *Enemy at the Gates*, 86.

189 Simonov, *Always a Journalist*, 29; *Stalingrad*, 58.

190 Seth, *Stalingrad: Point of Return*.

191 Chuikov and Paderin, *Nachalo puti*, 256–60.

192 *Ibid.*, 253.

193 *Ibid.*, 252.

194 *Ibid.*, 92–3.

195 *Ibid.*, 254–5.

196 *Ibid.*, 254.

197 Elena Kononenko, 'Ty snami, devchonka v shineli!', *Rabotnitsa*, no. 5 (1965).

198 Alexiyevich, *War's Unwomanly Face*, 10.

199 Craig, *Enemy at the Gates*, 102.

200 Chuikov, 'Razdum'ia o samykh tiazhelykh dniakh Stalingrada', 239.

201 Craig, *Enemy at the Gates*, 119–20; Seth, *Stalingrad: Point of Return*, 161, 173.

202 Seth, *Stalingrad: Point of Return*, 162.

203 *Ibid.*, 169.

204 Chuianov, 'A Heavy Ordeal', 237; Chuikov, 'Razdum'ia o samykh

tiazhelykh dniakh Stalingrada', 239.

205 Chuikov and Paderin, *Nachalo puti*, 262–3.

206 Atopov et al., *Volgograd*, Chuikov, *Vystoiav, my pobedili: zapiski komandarma 62-y*, I. I. Liudnikov, 'There is a Cliff on the Volga...', in *Two Hundred Days of Fire; Accounts by Participants and Witnesses of the battle of Stalingrad* (Moscow, Progress Publishers, 1970), 189.

207 Craig, *Enemy at the Gates*, 157.

208 Liudnikov, 'There is a Cliff on the Volga...', 195–6.

209 Erickson, 'Soviet Women at War', 63, citing Vera Semenova Murmantseva, 'Ratny i trudovoi podvig sovetskikh zhenshchin', *Voenno-Istoricheskii Zhurnal*, no. 5 (1985). By November 1942, however, the Soviet government was forming both an independent volunteer women's rifle brigade and an independent women's reserve rifle regiment in the Moscow military district.

210 Murmantseva, *Sovetskie zhenshchiny*, 180.

211 Pennington, *Wings, Women and War*, 130.

212 *Ibid.*, 109, 129–132. Ovchinnikova, *Zhenshchiny v soldatskikh shineliakh*, 5, 10. See Pennington for a discussion of the anomalies and implications of this event.

213 Ovchinnikova, *Zhenshchiny v soldatskikh shineliakh*, 14.

214 *Ibid.*, 15–22.

215 *Ibid.*, 13.

216 Aleksandr Fedorovich Semenov, *Na vzlete* (Moscow, Voenizdat, 1969), 93.

217 Ovchinnikova, *Zhenshchiny v soldatskikh shineliakh*, 11. Semenov, *Na vzlete*, 94.

218 Inna Vladimirovna Pasportnikova, Interview with author, 15 May 1993, Sredniaia Akhtuba airfield, Russia (near Volgograd); Pennington, *Wings, Women, and War*, 130–32.

219 Ovchinnikova, *Zhenshchiny v soldatskikh shineliakh*, 44.

220 Ovchinnikova, 11.

221 Inna Vladimirovna Pasportnikova, Interview with author, 8 May 1993. Zhukovsky, Russia.

222 P. Golovachev, 'My ikh lyubili', *Geroi i Podvigi*, ed. M. F. Loshchits, 4 vols. (Moscow, Voenizdat, 1963) I: 111–13.

223 Semenov, *Na vzlete*, 96.

224 Ovchinnikova, *Zhenshchiny v soldatskikh shineliakh*, 15. See also G. K. Prussakov et al., *16'aia vozdushnaia: voenno-istoricheskii ocherk o boevom puti 16-i vozdushnoi armii* (Moscow, Voenizdat, 1973), 11–12. Semenov offers a slightly different version of the story; he says her death occurred during a dogfight, but agrees that she saved her leader from an attacking aircraft when two German fighters shot her down. Semenov, *Na vzlete*, 97.

225 Semenov, *Na vzlete*, 99.

226 Prussakov et al., *16'aia vozdushnaia*, 31–2.

227 Semenov, *Na vzlete*, 105.

228 Reina Pennington, ed., *Amazons to Fighter Pilots: A Biographical Dictionary of Military Women*, 2 vols., vol. 1 (Westport, CT; Greenwood Press, 2003).

229 Inna Vladimirovna Pasportnikova, 'Letter 27 August', ed. author (1992), 'Rol' 586 Istrebitel'nogo aviastionnogo zhenskogo polka v Otechestvennoi voine' (Podolsk, Russia, TsAMO, n.d.). For more on Litviak, see Pennington, ed., *Amazons to Fighter Pilots*, 261–5.

230 Pennington, ed., *Amazons to Fighter Pilots*, 263.

231 'Liubimaia doch' sovetskogo naroda', *Ogonek*, no. 4 (817) (31 January 1943), 7. See also Pennington, *Wings, Women and War*, 73.

232 'Vozdushnykh pobed', *Ogonek*, no. 15–16 (828–9) (1943).

233 Ovchinnikova, *Zhenshchiny v soldatskikh shineliakh*, 17.

234 *Ibid.*, 21, 23, 25.

235 Vladimir Dmitrievich Lavrinenkov, *Vozvrashchenie v nebo*, 2nd edn (Moscow, Voenizdat, 1983), 42–3; Pasportnikova, 'Letter 27 August'.

236 Pennington, *Wings, Women and War*, 117.

237 *Ibid.*, 92–9.

238 Cottam, *Women in War and Resistance*; Pennington, ed., *Amazons to Fighter Pilots*, 168–9, 171–2, 517–20.

239 Beevor, *Stalingrad*, 92–3, 442, 449.

240 *Ibid.*, 158.

241 Reina Pennington, 'Wings, Women and War: Soviet Women's Military Aviation Regiments in the Great Patriotic War' (Master's thesis, University of South Carolina, 1993), chapter 6.

242 Galagan, *Ratny podvig zhenshcin*, 24–5.

243 *Ibid.*

244 Alexiyevich, *War's Unwomanly Face*, 13–14.

245 Cottam, *Women in War and Resistance*, 197–9.

246 *Ibid.*, 208–213.

247 Pennington, ed., *Amazons to Fighter Pilots*.

248 Craig, *Enemy at the Gates*, 106–107.

249 *Ibid.*, 121.

250 *Ibid.*, 122.

251 *Ibid.*, 122–3.

252 *Ibid.*, 122.

253 *Ibid.*, 145.

254 *Ibid.*, 236.

255 *Ibid.*, 386, 397.

256 David L. Robbins, interview with author, 2 July 2003, by telephone.

257 The author has observed a similar phenomenon in her interviews with female Soviet veterans; some were eager to discuss their wartime romances in private, but asked that I keep this information off the record. Some had never told their husbands and could not publicly reveal their interest in particular individuals.

258 Vasily Grigorevich Zaitsev, *Za volgoi zemli dlia nas ne bylo* (Moscow, DOSAAF, 1971), 149.

259 *Ibid.*, 204.

260 David Truby, 'Russia's Female Snipers', *Modern Gun*, October, year unknown.

261 Weinberg, *A World at Arms: Global History of World War II*, 449.

262 Glantz and House, *When Titans Clashed*, 295.

263 Ovchinnikova, *Zhenshchiny v soldatskikh shineliakh*, 97–101.

264 *Ibid.*, 103.

265 *Ibid.*, 106.

266 *Ibid.*, 103.

267 *Ibid.*, 104.

268 *Ibid.*, 105.

269 *Ibid.*, 108.

270 Cottam, *Women in War and Resistance*, 215–16, Erickson, 'Soviet Women at War', 66.

271 Alexiyevich, *War's Unwomanly Face*, 145.

272 *Ibid.*, 146.

273 *Stalingrad*, 113–14.

274 Galagan, *Ratny podvig zhenshchin*, 191.

275 *Stalingrad*, facing 112.

276 Anisimov, 'Tyl Jugo-Vostochnogo i

Stalingradskogo frontov v bitve na
Volge', 681.

277 *Stalingrad*, facing 97.

278 P. I. Batov, 'In the Don Bend', in *Two
Hundred Days of Fire; Accounts by
Participants and Witnesses of the battle of
Stalingrad* (Moscow, Progress Publishers,
1970), 157.

279 P. I. Batov, 'Na udarnom napravlenii',
in *Stalingradskaia epopeia*, ed. M. V.
Zakharov, Aleksandr Mikhailovich
Samsonov, and Vitol'd Kazimirovich
Pechorkin (Moskva, Nauka, 1968),
537.

280 Werth, *The Year of Stalingrad*, 394.

281 *Ibid.*, 396–7.

282 *Ibid.*, 413.

283 Craig, *Enemy at the Gates*, 321.

284 Beevor, *Stalingrad*, citing an interrogation
of Klavdia Sveridovna Ribaltshenko by
Gruppe Geheime Feldpolizei 626 on 21
July 1943, Bibliothek für Zeitgeschichte,
Sammlung Sterz, Stuttgart.

285 Werth, *The Year of Stalingrad*, 442, 445.

286 K. K. Rokossovskii, 'Na Stalingradskom
napravlenii', in *Stalingradskaia epopeia*, ed.
M. V. Zakharov, Aleksandr
Mikhailovich Samsonov, and Vitol'd
Kazimirovich Pechorkin (Moskva,
Nauka, 1968), 179.

287 Craig, *Enemy at the Gates*, 307.

288 Ovchinnikova, *Zhenshchiny v soldatskikh
shineliakh*, 97.

289 *Ibid.*, 109.

290 Alexiyevich, *War's Unwomanly Face*, 242.

291 Beevor, *Stalingrad*, 397.

292 Werth, *The Year of Stalingrad*, 441, 446.

293 Beevor, *Stalingrad*, 108, citing BA-MA,
RW4/v. 264.

294 Craig, *Enemy at the Gates*, 305.

295 *Ibid.*

296 Beevor, *Stalingrad*, 409.

297 *Ibid.*, 420.

298 *Ibid.*, 376.

299 *Ibid.*, 410.

300 Craig, *Enemy at the Gates*, 388.

301 Chuikov and Paderin, *Nachalo puti*, 249.

302 Plastikova, 'Stalingradki', 288.

303 Kerr, *The Secret of Stalingrad*, 159.

### Chapter 14 FORGOTTEN BATTLES OF THE SOVIET–GERMAN WAR

1 Prior to 1956, Soviet historians
subdivided the war into four periods by
treating 1944 and 1945 as separate
periods.

2 For a sample of the newly released
documents that support this contention,
see V. A. Zolotarev, ed., 'Stavka VGK:
Dokumenty i materialy 1941 god' [The
Stavka VGK: Documents and materials
of 1941] in *Russkii arkhiv: Velikaia
Otechestvennaia* 16 (5–1) [The Russian
archives: The Great Patriotic War, 16
(5–1)] (Moscow, Terra, 1996), and
'Dokumenty po ispol'zovaniiu
bronetankovykh i mekhaniziriyannykh
voisk Sovetskoi Armii v period s 22
iiunia po sentiabr' 1941 g. vkliuchitel'no'
[Documents on the employment of the
armoured and mechanised forces of the
Soviet Army in the period from 22 June
to September 1941, inclusively] in
*Sbornik boevykh dokumentov Velikoi
Otechestvennoi voiny, vypusk 33* [A collection
of combat documents of the Great
Patriotic War, issue 33] (Moscow,
Voenizdat, 1957). Classified secret.

3 David M. Glantz, *The Initial Period of
War on the Eastern Front* (London, Frank
Cass, 1993).

4 David M. Glantz, *Forgotten Battles of the
Soviet-German War (1941–1945), volume 1: The
Summer–Fall Campaign (22 June–4 December
1941)* (Carlisle, PA, self-published, 1999),
19–44; and David M. Glantz, *The Battle
for Leningrad, 1941–1944* (Lawrence, KS,
University Press of Kansas, 2002), 37–
50. The German 8th Panzer Division
suffered grievous losses in this fighting.

5 Glantz, *Forgotten Battles, volume 1*, 47–51;
Glantz, *The Initial Period of War*, and
David M. Glantz, *The Battle for Smolensk*
(Carlisle, PA, self-published, 2001), 11–
23.

6 Glantz, *Forgotten Battles, volume 1*, 44–7.

7 *Ibid.*, 51–71, and Glantz, *The Battle for
Leningrad*, 54–9.

8 Glantz, *The Initial Period of War*, and
Glantz, *The Battle for Smolensk*, 43–56.

9 Glantz, *Forgotten Battles, volume 1*, 71–4.

10 During this disaster, the Red Army's
reserve front managed to record a signal
victory at El'nia. See Glantz, *The Battle
for Smolensk*, 56–92, and David M.
Glantz, *Barbarossa: Hitler's Invasion of
Russia 1941* (Stroud, Tempus Publishing,
2001), 75–115. The latter also covers

other 'forgotten battles' in the 1941
campaign.

11　Glantz, *Barbarossa*, 154, and 'Boevye
deistviia Sovetskikh voisk na
Kalininskom napravlenii v 1941 gody (s
oktiabria 1941 po 7 ianvaria 1942 g)'
[Combat operations of the Soviet Army
on the Kalinin axis (from October 1941
through January 1942)], in *Sbornik voenno-
istoricheskikh materialov Velikoi
Otechestvennoi voiny, vypusk 7* [Collection of
military-historical materials of the Great
Patriotic War, issue 7] (Moscow,
Voenizdat, 1952). Classified secret.

12　For further details, see David M. Glantz,
*Forgotten Battles of the Soviet-German War
(1941–1945), volume 2: The Winter Campaign
(5 December 1941–27 April 1942)* (Carlisle,
PA, self-published, 1999), 11–7.

13　*Ibid.*, 63–118, and Glantz, *The Battle for
Leningrad*, 149–183.

14　This offensive was forgotten, in part,
because it was an embarrassing failure
and, in part, because the 2nd Shock Army
was commanded by Lieutenant General
A. A. Vlasov, who surrendered to the
Germans and later formed the Russian
Liberation Army (ROA) that sought to
fight alongside German forces until the
war's end.

15　For further details on both operations,
see Glantz, *Forgotten Battles, volume 2*, 67–
72 and 118–155.

16　The Russian have described the
Leningrad and Volkhov Fronts'
Siniavino offensive in August and
September 1942 against Army Group
North and the Western and Kalinin
Front's Rzhev-Sychevka offensive against
Army Group Centre's defences in the
Rzhev salient during July and August
1942, but only partially.

17　David M. Glantz, *Forgotten Battles of the
Soviet-German War (1941–1945), volume III:
The Summer Campaign (12 May–18 November
1942)* (Carlisle, PA, self-published, 1999),
86–101.

18　*Ibid.*, 6–86.

19　*Ibid.*, 101–29.

20　For details see Glantz, *The Battle for
Leningrad*, 213–31.

21　Under Stalin's direction, in mid-
November 1942, the Red Army struck
back at the Germans along virtually every

major strategic axis along the Soviet–
German front. In addition to conducting
Operation Uranus in the Stalingrad
region, the Red Army's Kalinin and
Western Fronts, operating under
Zhukov's personal direction in Operation
Mars, struck hard at the defences of
Army Group Centre's Ninth Army,
which was lodged firmly in the Rzhev-
Viaz'ma salient astride the equally vital
western axis. On 24 November the
Kalinin Front's 3rd Shock Army attacked
the defences of Army Group Centre's
Third Panzer Army at Velikie Luki, and,
the next day, five more of Zhukov's
armies (the 41st, 22nd, 39th, 31st, 20th,
and 29th) attacked Ninth Army's
defences around the entire periphery of
Rzhev salient, which Germans and
Soviets still recognised as 'a dagger aimed
at Moscow'. Finally, on 28 November
the North-western Front's forces
assaulted the defences of Army Group
North's Sixteenth Army around the
infamous Demiansk salient. All of these
offensives also sought to tie down
German forces and prevent
reinforcement of Axis forces in the
Stalingrad region.

22　For details on Operation Mars, see David
M. Glantz, *Zhukov's Greatest Defeat: The
Red Army' Epic Defeat in Operation Mars,
1942* (Lawrence, KS, University Press of
Kansas, 1999), and David M. Glantz,
*Forgotten Battles of the Soviet-German War
(1941–1945), volume IV: The Winter Campaign
(19 November 1942–21 March 1943)* (Carlisle,
PA, self-published, 1999), 17–67.

23　Prior to Stalin's death in 1953, Soviet
historians avoided writing about any of
the Red Army failures other than the
most obvious. Thereafter, during
Khrushchev's de-Stalinisation
programme (1958–64), when Zhukov
and Khrushchev were at odds, most
histories credited Vasilevsky and
Eremenko for the Stalingrad victory, but
still avoided any mention of Operation
Mars. After Khrushchev' s removal as
Party First Secretary and Soviet leader in
1964, in part with the military's
acquiescence if not full support, histories
began according Zhukov virtually full
credit for orchestrating the Stalingrad

victory, while continuing to maintain utter silence about Operation Mars.

24 In mid-December 1942, after Zhukov's offensive along the western axis had failed, the Stavka shifted its attention to the south, where it exploited the success the Red Army had achieved at Stalingrad. Encouraged by the offensive progress its forces recorded in late December and January south of the Don river and east of Rostov, in late January and early February 1943, the Stavka ordered the Red Army to conduct additional simultaneous offensive operations along the north-western, western, and central axes. In reality, by ordering these offensives, the Stavka sought nothing short of the complete defeat of all three German army groups and a broad-front advance by the Red Army to the eastern borders of the Baltic region and Belorussia and the Dnepr river line to the Black Sea. Collectively, these operations formed the Orel–Briansk–Smolensk strategic offensive and Operation Polar Star. Taken together with its planned operations into the Donbas and Khar'kov regions, the Stavka's four strategic offensives involved the forces of virtually every Red Army front operating across the entire expanse of the Soviet–German front from the Baltic Sea to the Black Sea.

The Central Front was formed in early February 1943 from the Don front's 65th and 21st Armies, which had just completed liquidating German forces encircled at Stalingrad, and the 2nd Tank and 70th Armies from the Stavka reserve. Its commander was Army General K. K. Rokossovsky, the former commander of the Don front. For details on the Orel–Briansk–Smolensk offensive see Glantz, *Forgotten Battles, vol. IV*, 213–311; David M. Glantz, 'Prelude to Kursk: Soviet Strategic Operations, February–March 1943', *The Journal of Slavic Military Studies*, Vol. 8, no. 1 (March 1995), 1–35; and V. A. Zolotarev, ed., 'Preludiia Kurskoi bitvy' [Prelude to the Battle of Kursk] in *Russkii arkhiv: Velikaia Otechestvennaia*, 15 (4:3) [The Russian archives: The Great Patriotic (War), 15 (4–3)] (Moscow, Terra, 1997).

25 The failure of this massive offensive was largely due to the hasty but tardy regrouping of requisite forces northward to the region west of Kursk, inadequate logistical support, poor co-ordination, deteriorating weather conditions, and the success of Manstein' s Donbas and Khar'kov counter-strokes, which forced the Stavka to divert critical strategic reserves to contain Manstein's assaults. In fact, the impact of Manstein's counter-strokes was so severe that they were equivalent in effect to a fully-fledged counter-offensive.

26 Zhukov chose the indirect approach by launching his main attack with the north-western front from the Staraia Russa region to avoid further costly operations in the immediate vicinity of Leningrad. For details see, Glantz, *Forgotten Battles, vol. IV*, 381–430, and Glantz, *The Battle for Leningrad*, 286–98.

27 Operation Polar Star failed largely because the Germans abandoned the Demiansk salient on the eve of the offensive and, more importantly, because the Stavka deprived Zhukov of the 1st Tank Army, which it dispatched south to counter Manstein's threatening counter-strokes.

28 For details on the southern front's role in the Donbas (Mariupol') offensive, see Glantz, *Forgotten Battles, vol. IV*, 83–183.

29 Soviet military histories claim that heavy fighting occurred throughout the planned German withdrawal, when, in fact, the heavy fighting occurred when Red Army forces attempted to penetrate new defences German forces erected after their withdrawal. See Glantz, *Forgotten Battles, vol. IV*, 311–81.

30 As had been the case in earlier wartime campaigns, after the Red Army's operating fronts had achieved their initial strategic objectives in the summer and fall of 1943, the Stavka assigned them new offensive missions in the hopes of producing utter German collapse. In retrospect, it is now quite clear that these missions were overly ambitious and beyond the capability of the fronts to carry out. Nevertheless, in fairness to the Stavka, the excessive optimism it displayed when formulating these

missions also indicated that it was pursuing the entirely valid if not obligatory practice of attempting to exploit every Red Army strategic success to the maximum extent possible.

31 For example, during each stage of the summer–fall campaign, the Red Army launched major offensives along the western, south-western, and southern axes and operations of lesser significance along the north-western and Caucasus axes.

32 For details see David M Glantz, *Forgotten Battles of the Soviet–German War (1941–1945), volume V, The Summer–Fall Campaign (1 July–31 December 1943)* (Carlisle, PA, self-published, 2000), Part One, 107–159.

33 *Ibid.*, 19–61. Russian historians have studiously avoided the July operation, preferring instead to cover in detail their offensive in the region in August 1943.

34 *Ibid.*, 159–170. Although the Red Army's forces seized Siniavino Heights, as has been the case in most of its six previous unsuccessful attempts to seize the heights, Russian historians have studiously ignored this costly battle.

35 *Ibid.*, 171–407 and David M. Glantz, *Forgotten Battles of the Soviet-German War (1941–1945), volume V, The Summer–Fall Campaign (1 July–31 December 1943)* (Carlisle, PA, self-published, 2000), Part Two, 408–563. See also, I. Glebov, 'Manevr voisk v Chernigovsko-Pripiatskoi i Gomel'sko-Rechitskoi nastupatel'nykh operatsiakh' [Manoeuvre of forces in the Chernigov–Pripiat and Gomel'–Rechitsa offensive operations], *Voenno-istoricheskii zhurnal*, no. 1 (January 1976), 13–18, (hereafter cited as *VIZh* with appropriate article and date); K. N. Galitsky, *Gody surovykh ispytanii 1941–1944* [Years of rigorous education 1941–1944], (Moscow, Nauka, 1973), 347–8; and M. Absaliamov, 'Iz opyta vzaimodeistviia vozdushnykh dsantov s partisanami v Velikoi Otechestvennoi voine' [From the experience of the co-operation of airborne forces with partisans in the Great Patriotic War], *VIZh*, no. 11 (November 1964), 104–108.

36 In particular, historians have totally ignored the Western Front's many costly and futile offensives against German Fourth Army's defences in eastern Belorussia, primarily to protect the reputation of the front commander, V. D. Sokolovsky, who rose to prominence in the post-war years.

37 Glantz, *Forgotten Battles of the Soviet-German War, vol. 5*, Part Two, 564–673.

38 *Ibid.*, 674–818. Although the three Red Army fronts repeatedly tried to revive their offensives and, in the process, seriously dented German defences in several sectors, the defences held, and both Krivoi Rog and Nikopol' remained in German hands until early 1944. Since war's end, the Nikopol' defence has been an integral part of the instruction at the German Fuhrungsakademie.

39 Although it was relatively easy to overlook these follow-on and continuation offensives because most of them failed, the Stavka's rationale for conducting them was quite clear. Based on its previous wartime experiences, by 1944 the Stavka routinely expanded its strategic horizons while the Red Army was conducting major offensive operations by assigning its operating fronts new and more ambitious missions. The Stavka justified this practice on the grounds that total German collapse was imminent, and, unless offensives were developed relentlessly, opportunities would be lost. When the Stavka ordered its overextended forces to perform these new missions, it consciously accepted the risk that its attacking forces could fall victim to the sort of counter-strokes that Manstein had sprung on Red Army forces in the Donbas in early 1943. This, in fact, occurred on numerous occasions, albeit on a smaller scale, during the spring of 1944. In fairness, however, the dramatic successes the Red Army achieved in 1944 and 1945 make it far more difficult to assess accurately whether additional military operations at the end of any major offensive thrust were simply attempts to exploit success or were simply designed to posture forces more advantageously for subsequent offensive action or to deceive the enemy regarding the Stavka's future offensive intentions.

40 This heavy and bloody fighting was indicative of how difficult it would be for the Red Army to smash its way through the Panther Line and invade the Baltic region later in 1944. The only account of the action at Narva, Pskov, and Ostrov is found in Glantz, *The Battle for Leningrad 1941–1944*.

41 The only Soviet accounts of the struggle around Kalinkovichi are M. Panov, 'V boiakh za Kalinkovichi' [In combat for Kalinkovichi], *VIZh*, no. 5 (May 1978), 46–51, and D. Malkov, 'Vnezapnaia ataka' [Surprise attack], *VIZh*, no. 3 (March) 1964, 55–60. Both minimise the effects of Rokossovsky's offensive. The full offensive's full effects are apparent from the German Second Army's records, which show a sizeable Red Army penetration into southern Belorussia. Try as the Stavka did, however, Red Army forces were unable to make further significant advances into Belorussia. During the waning stages of the offensive, an angry Stavka relieved Sokolovsky from command of the western front. At least in part, the entire Belorussian offensive has languished in obscurity to protect the reputation of Sokolovsky, who, during the period from 1952–1960, survived the wartime embarrassment and rose to become the chief of the Soviet army general staff and one of the Soviet Union's leading strategic theorists. See, for example, M. A. Gareev, 'Prichiny i uroki neudachnykh nastupatel'nykh operatsii Zapadnogo fronta zimoi 1943/44 goda' [The causes and lessons of unsuccessful western front operations in winter 1943/44], *Voennaia mysl'* [Military thought], no. 2 (February 1994), 50–58, and M. A. Gareev, 'O neudachnykh nastupatel'nykh operatsiakh sovetskikh voisk v Velikoi Otechestvennoi voine: Po neopublikovannym dokumentam GKO' [About unsuccessful offensive operations of Soviet forces in the Great Patriotic War: According to unpublished GKO documents], *Novaia i noveishaia istoriia* [New and newer history], no. 1 (January 1994), 3–29. The two superb studies by Gareev exemplify what must be done to fill in the historical gaps in the history of the war. For a German account, see the operational and intelligence records of Third Panzer Army and Fourth Army. The Ninth Army's records, which were captured by the Soviets and do not exist in the West, also should provide details on these failed Soviet operations. See also such excellent German unit histories as A. D. von Plato, *Die Geschichte der 5 Panzerdivision 1938 bis 1945* [A History of 5th Panzer Division 1938–1945] (Regensburg, Walhalla u. Praetoria Verlag, 1978).

42 The attacking Red Army forces reportedly lost 350 tanks, including several new IS-2 heavy tanks. The heavy fighting in the Iassy sector did not end until early June. For the German perspective on the Targul-Frumos operation, see H. von Manteuffel, *The Battle of Targul-Frumos* (unpublished manuscript and briefing, 1948); F. von Senger und Etterlin, *Der Gegenshlag* [The encounter battle]; and the operational records of the German Eighth Army. On the Soviet side, see F. I. Vysotsky, M. E. Makukhin, F. M. Sarychev, M. K. Shaposhnikov, *Gvardeiskaia tankovaia* [Guards tank] (Moscow, Voenizdat, 1963), 101–106; V. A. Zolotarev, ed., *Velikaia Otechestvennaia voina 1941–1945 v chetyrekh knigakh* [The Great Patriotic War 1941–1945 in four volumes] (Moscow, Nauka, 1999); V. A. Zolotarev, ed., 'General'nyi shtab v gody Velikoi Otechestvennoi voiny: Dokumenty i materially 1944–1945 gg.' [The General Staff in the Great Patriotic War: Documents and materials 1944–1945], Russkie arkhiv: Velikaia Otechestvennaia, 23 (12–4) [The Russian archives: The Great Patriotic (War), 23 (12–4)] (Moscow, Terra, 2001); V. A. Zolotatev, 'Stavka VGK: Dokumenty i materially 1944–1945' [The Stavka VGK: Documents and materials 1944–1945], Russkie arkhiv: Velikaia Otechestvennaia, 16 (5–4) [The Russian archives: The Great Patriotic (War), 16 (5–4)] (Moscow: Terra, 1999); and 'Umanskaia nastupatel'naia operatsiia voisk 2-go Ukrainskovo fronta vo Vtorom udare' [The 2nd Ukrainian Front's Uman' offensive operation during

the second blow], Sbornik voenno-istoricheskikh materialov Velikoi Otechestvennoi voiny, vypusk 15 [A collection of military-historical materials of the Great Patriotic War, issue 15] (Moscow, Voenizdat, 1955). Classified secret.

43 When the offensive ended on 27 October, Red Army forces had penetrated up to forty miles into East Prussia. This failed offensive indicated that more extensive preparations were required if the Red Army was to conquer Germany's East Prussian bastion. See a particularly detailed account of this operation in the Third Panzer Army's records. See also, M. Alekseev, 'Nachalo boev v Vostochnoi Prussii' [The beginning of combat in Belorussia], VIZh, No. 10 (October 1964), 11–22. G. F. Krivosheev, ed., Grif sekretnosti sniat: Poteri vooruzhennykh sil SSSR v voinakh, boevykh deistviiakh i voennykh konfliktakh [The secret classification is removed: The losses of the USSR's armed forces in wars, combat operations and military conflicts] (Moscow, Voenizdat, 1993), 227, provides casualty figures for what he calls the Goldap operation.

44 At the same time, the 1st Ukrainian Front was to capitalize on and support a popular insurrection against German authorities in Slovakia.

45 The 2nd Ukrainian Front's 6th Tank Army captured Debrecen, but, thereafter, strong German and Hungarian counterstrokes savaged the front's exploiting cavalry-mechanised groups near Nyregyhaza in northern Hungary, far short of its ultimate objective. Soviet historians have examined the 38th Army's Dukla Pass offensive, the 4th Ukrainian Front's operations in the Carpathians, and the 2nd Ukrainian Front's Debrecen offensive, but have neglected tying all three together.

46 All Russian accounts claim that Stalin halted the offensive on 2 February for a variety of reasons, including threats to the two fronts' flanks, stubborn resistance on the part of by-passed German forces, and logistical difficulties.

47 At Yalta, Roosevelt and Churchill agreed that the Red Army would capture Berlin.

While the agreement also delineated spheres of influence in eastern and central Europe, it said nothing about the future disposition of Austria. The recently released unexpurgated memoirs of Rokossovsky and other senior Soviet commanders disagreed vehemently with Stalin's decision to abort the Red Army's February Berlin offensive.

48 The resistance by the First Panzer Army hindered communications between the 1st and 2nd Ukrainian Fronts operating in Poland and Hungary.

49 On 1 April 1945, the Stavka redesignated the 2nd Baltic Front's forces that were conducting the siege as the Courland Group of Forces and subordinated them to the Leningrad Front.

## Chapter 15   ORDINARY COLLABORATORS

1 Omer Bartov, Hitler's Army: Soldiers, Nazis, and War in the Third Reich, New York, Oxford University Press, 1992; Vernichtungskrieg. Verbrechen der Wehrmacht 1941 bis 1944, eds. Hannes Heer and Klaus Naumann (Hamburg: HIS Verlagsges., 1995).

2 Edward B. Westermann, '"Ordinary Men" or "Ideological Soldiers"? Police Battalion 310 in Russia, 1942', in German Studies Review, vol. XXI, N 1, February 1998, pp. 41–68.

3 Christopher R. Browning, Ordinary men. Reserve Police Battalion 101 and the Final Solution in Poland (New York, Harper Collins, 1992).

4 I am also very much in debt to Peter Black, chief historian at the US Holocaust Memorial Museum, who kindly shared his vast knowledge of the problem with the author.

5 In Polish and German it is spelled 'Trawniki'.

6 SS-Ausbildungslager.

7 Nowadays it is the Federal Security Service of the Russian Federation (FSB).

8 Tom Teicholz, The Trial of Ivan the Terrible: State of Israel vs. John Demjanjuk (New York, St. Martin's Press, 1990), p. 206–207.

9 Yoram Sheftel, Defending 'Ivan the Terrible' (Washington, Regnery Publishing, Inc., 1996), pp. 339–79.

10 Not all documents are declassified. Major German wartime Travniki documents are kept in the FSB collection (fond) 16, inventory (opis) 312 'e'. Trial proceedings against each particular person are kept under consecutive numbers. Many files of the Travniki are kept in the former KGB (now SBU) archives in the Ukraine. Especially in the cities of Ivano-Frankovsk, Kiev, Lvov and Donetsk. Photocopies of few files are available at the archives of the United States Holocaust Memorial Museum (USHMM). See RG 06.025.

11 Circular of the Reichsführer SS, 25 July 1941. National Archives, T-454, Roll 100, Frame 700.

12 Statement of Ivan Bogdanov. Central FSB Archive, file N-20827, pp. 230–31.

13 This figure might be exaggerated. Many Travniki guards mentioned a number between one and two thousand Jewish prisoners.

14 *Enzyklopädie des Holocaust. 2. Auflage* (München, Piper Verlag, 1998), band 3. S. 1425–7.

15 Sometimes Germans had too many volunteers, other times too few. Even in desperate situations some POWs realised that it was a betrayal to join the German police.

16 Author's archive. A copy of interrogation of Stepan Kopytyuk. Original file is in SBU Archive in Lvov, Ukraine, file 29805, pp. 60–61, 66–8.

17 Central FSB Archive. Collection 16. Inventory 312 'e', files 409, 410, 411.

18 Author's archive. A copy of interrogation of Nikolai Skorokhod. Original file is in SBU Archive in Lvov, Ukraine, file 11042, pp. 59–62.

19 Statement of Stepan Moskalenko. Central FSB Archive, file 20827, p. 247.

20 Statement of Ivan Bogdanov. Central FSB Archive, op. cit., p. 236.

21 Author's archive. A copy of interrogation of Ivan Shvidkiy. Original file at SBU Archive in Donetsk, Ukraine, file 56433, pp. 40–43.

22 Central FSB Archive, file N–21052, pp. 89–90, 298–9; USHMM, RG 06.025, file 22.

23 During trial proceedings several Travniki guards mentioned that they had rejected participation in the 'actions' but no evidence was provided either by the other members of the killing team or from German wartime documents.

24 Statement of Stepan Moskalenko. Central FSB Archive, file 20827, p. 247.

25 Statement of Fedor Monin, op. cit., p. 260.

26 As an illustration see: V. D. Poremski, *Strategiya antibolshevistskoy emigratsii* (Strategy of the antibolshevik emigration) (Moscow, Posev, 1998); *Estonian Freedomfighters in World War Two* ([published in the USA, no place given] The Vôitleja Relief Foundation Book Committee, [1998]).

27 Yoram Sheftel, op. cit., pp. ix–xi, 380–95.

## Chapter 16   THE SS-20 MISSILE – WHY WERE YOU POINTING AT ME?

1 Those wishing a detailed account of the tortuous progression towards the elimination of Theatre Nuclear Forces from Europe through the eventual resolution of the INF Treaty should see Haslam, J., 1989, *The Soviet Union and the Politics of Nuclear Weapons in Europe 1969–87: The Problem of the SS-20* (London, Macmillan); Nitze, P. H., 1989, *From Hiroshima to Glasnost: At the Centre of Decision* (New York, Grove Weidenfeld); Savel'yev, A. G. and Detinov, N. N., 1995, *The Big Five: Arms Control Decisionmaking in the Soviet Union* (Westport, Ct., Praeger).

2 Evidence recently uncovered from the former East German archive indicates that the level of concern engendered within the Soviet leadership was such that some went so far as to consider the possibility of a pre-emptive strike against the West. Hellen, N, the *Sunday Times*, London, 1997, 'Kremlin Was Poised to Launch Nuclear Strike', 30 November, p. 5.

3 Azrael, J. R., 1987, *The Soviet Civilian Leadership and the Military High Command, 1976–1986* (Santa Monica, Ca., RAND Corporation), pp. 5–12, and Cooper, J., 'The Defence Industry and Civil-Military Relations', in Colton, T. J. and Gustafson

T. (eds.), 1990, *Soldiers and the Soviet State: Civil-Military Relations from Brezhnev to Gorbachev* (Princeton N.J., Princeton University Press), pp. 166–170.

4 University of Edinburgh, Department of Defence Studies Archive.

5 *Ibid.*, file 1.

6 *Ibid.*

7 Danilevich served as an Assistant for Doctrine and Strategy under two chiefs of the general staff and was director of the general staff authors' collective that composed and refined between 1977 and 1986 the top-secret, three-volume *Strategy of Deep Operations*.

8 University of Edinburgh, Department of Defence Studies Archive, file 1.

9 *Ibid.*, file 1. Although Chelomei's SS-11 had originally entered service in 1965, an uprated version, the UR-100K, was tested in July 1969 and entered service in March 1971. It seems likely that it was to this system that Danilevich was referring.

10 It is however interesting to note that a nuclear strike against Soviet territory may well have elicited a strategic strike of similar magnitude upon a specific target on US territory itself rather than a response confined within the European theatre.

11 University of Edinburgh, Department of Defence Studies Archive, file 1.

12 *Ibid.*

13 This was a reaction against Khrushchev's intended reliance upon ballistic missile forces, with its attendant threats to the other service branches.

14 University of Edinburgh, Department of Defence Studies Archive, files 5 and 7.

## Chapter 17   COLD WARS NEW AND OLD

Some of the material from this contribution also appears in Paul Dukes, *The USA in the Making of the USSR: The Washington Conference, 1921–1922, and 'Uninvited Russia'* (Routledge Curzon, 2004).

1 Fred Halliday, *The Making of the Second Cold War* (London 1983), p. 5.

2 Ernest R. May, 'The Cold War', in C. Vann Woodward, ed., *A Comparative Approach to American History* (Washington, DC, 1968), p. 373.

3 W. T. R. Fox, 'The Super-Powers Then and Now', *International Journal*, vol. 35, 1979–80, pp. 417–30. 'Super-power' makes an appearance in *Encyclopaedia Britannica*, Thirteenth Edition (London and New York, 1926), vol. 3, p. 681, 'as the systematic grouping and interconnection of existing power systems to the end that greater economy will be effected'. But the power systems are electrical, not political. During the First World War, there was much discussion of a 'Super-State' (see, for example, J. A. Hobson, *Towards International Government*, (London, 1915), pp. 86–7). And we shall soon encounter President Harding's use of the term 'supergovernment' in his inaugural address. Perhaps, therefore, the term 'Super-Power' as used by Fox was already at an embryonic stage of development twenty years and more previously.

4 Valentin Kudrov, *Soviet Economic Performance in Retrospect: A Critical Re-examination* (Moscow, 1998), pp. 52, 71–2, 92, 123–4.

5 Walter LaFeber, *The Clash: US–Japanese Relations throughout History* (New York, 1998), p. xix.

6 *Congressional Record*, 4 March 1921, pp. 4–6. Norman Angell's *America and the New World-State: A Plea for American Leadership in International Organization* (New York, 1915) was among the works arguing for the USA's leadership before the entry into war.

7 Geddes to Curzon, 15 April 1921, enclosed in Curzon to Lloyd George, 20 April 1921, Lloyd George Papers, F/13/2/19, as cited in Lloyd C. Gardner, *Safe for Democracy: The Anglo-American Response to Revolution* (New York, 1987), p. 307. Earlier, Geddes had already written to Lloyd George's secretary of a group in Harding's entourage aiming 'to transfer the centre of English speaking power to North America ... They regard England as crippled and this as their opportunity and they propose to grasp it – not in hatred but in fulfilment of their country's destiny.' Geddes to Kerr, 3 January 1921, Lloyd George Papers, F/60/4/11 as cited by Erik Goldstein, 'The Evolution of British Diplomatic

Strategy for the Washington Conference',
in Erik Goldstein and John Maurer, eds.,
*The Washington Conference 1921–22: Naval
Rivalry, East Asian Stability and the Road to
Pearl Harbor* (Ilford, 1994), p. 13.

8 Minutes of the Imperial Conference,
CAB 32/2, First and Second Meetings,
as cited by Erik Goldstein, 'The
Evolution', pp. 6, 11, 15.

9 John St Loe Strachey, 'English-speaking
Peoples, Relations of', *Encyclopaedia
Britannica*, Thirteenth Edition, vol. 1,
pp. 1011–12; Denna Frank Fleming, *The
United States and World Organization, 1920–
1933* (New York, 1938), p. 79.

10 John Chalmers Vinson, *The Parchment
Peace: The United States Senate and the
Washington Conference, 1921–1922* (Athens,
Georgia, 1955), pp. 57, 90, 95–6; Thomas
H. Buckley, *The United States and the
Washington Conference, 1921–1922*
(Knoxville, 1970), pp. 17–18, 32–3.

11 See Paul Dukes and Cathryn Brennan,
'"The Uninvited Guest": Soviet Russia,
the Far Eastern Republic and the
Washington Conference, November
1921 to February 1922', *Sibirica*, vol. 2,
no. 2, 2002.

12 Harold J. Goldberg, ed., *Documents of
Soviet-American Relations*, vol. 1, *Intervention,
Famine Relief, International Affairs, 1917–1933*
(Gulf Breeze, Florida, 1993), pp. 262–3.

13 J. M. Thomson, *Russia, Bolshevism and the
Versailles Peace*, Princeton, New Jersey,
1966; A. J. Mayer, *Politics and Diplomacy of
Peacemaking: Containment and Counter-
Revolution at Versailles 1918–1919* (New
York, 1967).

14 Raymond Leslie Buell, *The Washington
Conference* (New York, 1922), and Yamato
Ichihashi, *The Washington Conference and
After: A Historical Survey* (Stanford,
California, 1928). Two more recent
scholarly works with a narrower focus
are Thomas H. Buckley, *The United States
and the Washington Conference, 1921–1922*
(Knoxville, Tennessee, 1970), and John
Chalmers Vinson, *The Parchment Peace, the
United States Senate and the Washington
Conference, 1921–1922* (Athens, Georgia,
1955).

15 Ernest R. May, 'Foreword', in Erik
Goldstein and John Maurer, *The
Washington Conference, 1921–22: Naval Rivalry,*

*East Asian Stability and the Road to Pearl
Harbor* (London, 1994), pp. iv–viii. May
refers to Hedley Bull, 'Strategic Arms
Limitation: The Precedent of the
Washington and London Naval Treaties',
in Morton Kaplan, ed., *SALT: Problems and
Prospects* (Morristown, NJ, 1973).

16 A. Iu. Sidorov, *Vneshniaia politika sovetskoi
Rossii na Dal'nem Vostoke, 1917–1922*
(Moscow, 1997).

17 *Ibid.*, pp. 127–33. Two perceptive post-
Soviet articles by Marina Fuchs also merit
attention, the first analysing the role of
the regions in the foreign policy of Soviet
Russia in the Far East in the first half of
the 1920s, the second scrutinising
characteristics of the development of
US–Soviet relations in the context of the
strengthening of US–Japanese military-
political rivalry, 1917–1923. Like Sidorov,
Fuchs underlines the importance of the
Far Eastern Republic as a 'buffer',
pointing out the significance of networks
of communication developed across vast
distances by Chicherin, Trotsky and other
individuals at a time when Soviet Russia
as a whole was far from constituting a
unitarian state. She looks at not only the
official diplomatic links between the
powers concerned with the Far East in
the years following the Russian
Revolution but also the activities of
secret agents – a corrective to any
unreserved acceptance of the higher
motives of the powers involved. See M.
B. Fuks, 'Rol' regional'nykh vlastnykh
struktur vo vneshnei politike Sovetskoi
Rossii na Dal'nem Vostoke v pervoi
polovine 1920-kh godov', *Russkii
istoricheskii zhurnal*, tom 1, no. 2, 1998;
'Osobennosti razvitiia sovetsko-
amerikanskikh otnoshenii v kontekste
usileniia voenno-politicheskogo
sopernichestva na Dal'nem Vostoke
mezhdu SSHA i Iaponiei, 1917–1923',
*Russkii istoricheskii zhurnal*, tom 1, no. 3,
1998.

18 E. I. Popova, 'Vashingtonskaia
konferentsiia 1921–1922gg. v otsenke
sovetskikh istorikov', G. N. Sevost'ianov
and others, eds., *Amerikanskii ezhegodnik
1971* (Moscow, 1971), pp. 166–190.

19 E. I. Popova, 'Vashingtonskaia
konferentsiia', pp. 167–74.

20 Alexander Hamilton, 'The Value of Union to Commerce and the Advantages of a Navy', and the similar views of James Madison in Benjamin F. Wright, intro. and ed., *The Federalist*, (Cambridge MA, 1966), pp. 141–2, 296–7.

21 For successive attempts to set out aspects of this comparison, with some reiteration but also a certain amount of refinement, see the following books by Paul Dukes: *The Emergence of the Superpowers: A Short Comparative History of the USA and the USSR* (London, 1970); *The Last Great Game: USA versus USSR: Events, Conjunctures, Structures* (London, 1989); *World Order in History: Russia and the West* (London, 1996); *The Superpowers: A Short History* (London, 2000).

22 For the most complete overview, see Norman E. Saul's three-volume work, *The United States and Russia: Distant Friends ... 1763–1867; Concord and Conflict ... 1867–1914; and War and Revolution ... 1914–1921,* all published by University Press of Kansas in 1991, 1996 and 2001 respectively.

23 Samuel P. Huntington, *The Clash of Civilizations and the Remaking of World Order* (New York, 1996), pp. 20–1, 31–2, 164, 301–21.

24 Zbigniew Brzezinski, *The Grand Chessboard: American Primacy and Its Geostrategic Imperatives* (New York, 1997), pp. 25, 44, 118. Zbigniew Brzezinski and Samuel P. Huntington, *Political Power: USA–USSR* (New York, 1964), was one of the more perspicacious works produced during the Cold War era.

25 Dmitri Trenin, *The End of Eurasia: Russia on the Border between Gepolitics and Globalization* (Moscow, 2001), pp. 208, 211, 220, 248, 261, 336, with Trenin's own italics.

## Chapter 18   THE NEW CENTRAL ASIA

1 John Erickson, 'Eurasian Manoeuvres', in Sally N. Cummings (ed.) *Oil, Transition and Security in Central Asia* (London, Routledge, 2003).

2 Martha Brill Olcott, 'Taking Stock of Central Asia', *Journal of International Affairs*, vol. 56, no. 2, Spring 2003, pp. 3–17.

3 'Central Asia: A Last Chance for Change', Central Asia Briefing, International Crisis Group, Osh/Burssels, 29 April 2003, at: www.crisisweb.org/.

4 Martha Brill Olcott, 'Revisiting the Twelve Myths of Central Asia', Carnegie Endowment for International Peace, Working Papers, number 23, September 2001.

5 International Institute for Strategic Studies, *Strategic Survey* (London, Oxford University Press, 1998).

6 John Roberts, 'Caspian Oil and Gas: how far have we come and where are we going?', in *Oil, Transition and Security in Central Asia.,* op. cit.

7 Rosemary Forsythe notes that 'Oil reserve estimates for the region vary greatly and range from 30bn to 200bn barrels. These estimates include proven and possible reserves. Industry and analysts often use a middle-range figure of 90bn, similar to China or Mexico.' See her *The Politics of Oil in the Caucasus and Central Asia* (London, IISS/Oxford University Press, 1996), p. 62.

8 J. Nanay, 'The US in the Caspian: The Divergence of Political and Commercial Interests', *Middle East Policy*, 6 October 1998, pp. 150–57.

9 Gawdat Bahgat, 'Pipeline Diplomacy: The Geopolitics of the Caspian Sea Region', *International Studies Perspectives*, vol. 3, 2002, p. 313.

10 For an excellent analysis of Caspian pipelines, see John Roberts, *Caspian Pipelines* (London, Royal Institute of International Affairs and Brookings Institution, 1996).

11 John Roberts, 'Caspian Oil and Gas: how far have we come and where are we going?' in *Oil, Transition and Security in Central Asia*, op. cit., p. 157.

12 Lena Jonson, *Russia and Central Asia: A New Web of Relations, Central Asian and Caucasian Prospects* (London, The Royal Institute of International Affairs and Brookings Institution, 1998).

13 For a useful summary of Russia's 'near abroad policy', see M. A. Smith, *Russian Foreign Policy 2000: The Near Abroad,* Conflict Studies Research Centre, December 2000.

14 Mark Webber, *CIS Integration Trends:*

*Russia and the Former Soviet South* (London, The Royal Institute of International Affairs and Brookings Institution, 1997).

15 For an excellent analysis, see Carol R. Saivetz, 'Putin's Caspian Policy', *Caspian Studies Program Policy Brief*, no. 1, October 2000, Harvard University, John F. Kennedy School of Government, Caspian Studies Program.

16 Gareth Winrow, *Turkey in Post-Soviet Central Asia* (London, The Royal Institute of International Affairs and Brookings Institution, 1995). See also his 'Turkey and Central Asia', in Roy Allison and Lena Jonson (eds.), *Central Asian Security: The New International Context* (London, Royal Institute of International Affairs and Brookings Institution, 2001), pp. 199–218.

17 Edmund Herzig, *Iran and the Former Soviet South* (London, The Royal Institute of International Affairs and Brookings Institution, 1995).

18 Edmund Herzig, 'Iran and Central Asia', in Roy Allison and Lena Jonson, *Central Asian Security*, p. 193.

19 John Erickson, 'Eurasian Manoeuvres', op. cit.

20 Pauline Jones Luong and Erika Weinthal, 'New Friends, New Fears in Central Asia', *Foreign Affairs*, March/April 2002, pp. 61–70.

21 'Russia Tops US in Central Asia', Office of Research, Opinion Analysis, Department of State, Washington, 31 May 2002, prepared by Steven A. Grant, p. 9.

22 'Russia Tops US in Central Asia', p. 6.

23 'The IMU and the Hizb-ut-Tahrir: Implications of the Afghanistan Campaign', Central Asia Briefing, International Crisis Group, 30 June 2002, p. 2, at: www.crisisweb.org/.

24 Martha Brill Olcott and Bakhtiyar Babajanov, 'The Terrorist Notebooks', *Foreign Policy*, March/April 2003, pp. 30–40.

25 'The IMU and the Hizb-ut-Tahrir', p. 8.

26 Olcott and Babajanov, 'The Terrorist', p. 40.

27 Martha Brill Olcott, 'Drugs, Terrorism, and Regional Security: the Risks from Afghanistan', Carnegie Endowment for International Peace, at: www.ceip.org/...

/OlcottTestimony031302.asp?pr=2& from=pubdat, p. 5.

28 'Central Asia: Drugs and Conflict', International Crisis Group, *ICG Asia Report*, no. 25, 26 November 2001, at: www.crisisweb.org/.

29 Olcott, 'Drugs, Terrorism', p. 5.

30 For useful discussions of water resources in Central Asia, see P. Micklin, *Managing Water in Central Asia* (London, Royal Institute of International Affairs, 2000); D. R. Smith, 'Environmental Security and Shared Water Resources in Post-Soviet Central Asia', *Post-Soviet Geography*, vol. 36, no. 6 (1995), pp. 387–98, and Stuart Horsman, 'Water in Central Asia', in Jonson and Allison, Central Asian Security, pp. 60–94. See also Eric Sievers, *The Post-Soviet Decline of Central Asia: Sustainable Development and Comprehensive Capital* (London and New York, RoutledgeCurzon, 2003).

31 'Central Asia: Water and Conflict', International Crisis Group, ICG Asia Report no. 34, 30 May 2002, p. i , at: www.crisisweb.org/.

32 'Central Asia: Border Disputes and Conflict Potential', International Crisis Group, ICG Asia Report, no. 33, 4 April 2002, at: www.crisisweb.org/.

33 Roy Allison, 'Structures and frameworks for security policy cooperation in Central Asia', in Roy Allison and Lena Jonson, *Central Asian Security*, p. 260.

34 The Shanghai Forum adopted that name when Uzbekistan attended the Shanghai Five Summit of China, Russia, Kazakhstan, Kyrgyzstan and Tajikistan in Dushanbe in July 2000. The chief result of the Dushanbe summit was a joint declaration, signed by the five leaders and the creation of a regional anti-terrorist centre, with headquarters in Bishkek. Marat Mamadshoyev, 'The Shanghai G-5 Becomes the Shanghai Forum', 7 July 2000, at: www.eurasianet.org.

35 Roy Allison, 'Structures and Frameworks for security policy cooperation in Central Asia', in Roy Allison and Lena Jonson (eds.), *Central Asian Security*, p. 236 and p. 222.

36 Alexei Malashenko and Martha Brill Olcott, *Islam Na Postsovetskom Prostranstve: Vzgliad Iznutri* (Moscow, Art Business

Centre, Moscow Carnegie Centre, 2001), especially pp. 100–204.

37  Shirin Akiner, *Central Asia: Conflict or Stability and Development?* (Minority Rights Group International Report, 1997), p. 14.

38  Ahmed Rashid, *Jihad: The Rise of Militant Islam in Central Asia*, p. 228.

39  Yaacov Ro'i, *Islam in the CIS: A Threat to Stability?* (The Royal Institute of International Affairs, 2001), p. 84.

40  Later Sergei Duvanov, a journalist, was, like Mukhtar Ablyazov and Galimzhan Zhakiyanov of the oppositional movement Democratic Choice of Kazakhstan, arrested and jailed – but on a trumped-up rape charge.

41  Freedom House Index, 2002, at http://www.freedomhouse.org/index.htm.

42  Rafis Abazov, 'Kyrgyzstan and Issues of Political Succession', *Jamestown Russia and Eurasia Review*, vol. 2, issue 11, 27 May 2003.

43  Transparency International Corruption Perceptions Index, at www.transparency.org.

44  United Nations Human Development Report 2002, at http://hdr.undp.org/reports/global/2002/en/.

**Chapter 19   RUMOURS AS EVIDENCE**

1  Frances Stonor Saunders, *Who Paid the Piper? The CIA and the Cultural Cold War* (London and New York, 1999). For a more balanced picture by a British historian, Hugh Wilford, an expert on both the American and British literary scenes in the post-war era and before, and who unlike Ms Saunders, understands the Cold War as something that engaged British and American cultural values as well as those preached by their Soviet and Sovietophile opponents, see *The CIA, the British Left and the Cold War. Calling the Tune?* (London, 2003).

2  In the 1950s I was active as a contemporary historian of international relations, both in my capacity as a member of the staff of the LSE and as a freelance writer working in and around the field of contemporary international affairs at the Royal Institute of International Affairs and similar quasi-academic institutions and publications in London. The existence of the IRD, the names of some of its staff and their various fields of interest were by no means secret. As has been the practice of the Foreign Office research department, the Cabinet Office Intelligence analysts and other similar organisations, their staff were encouraged to take part in academic conferences and seminars, publish articles and even books. They had, after all, passed through much common ground in the armed services and the universities, and were only following the lead given them by the generation that had manned the British intelligence services, PWE, SOE, Bletchley Park and similar organisations during the war years. The Study Group on British Interests in the Mediterranean and the Middle East, for which I acted as junior rapporteur in the years 1956–8, included two MPs, both with wartime and post-war connections with the Intelligence services, a banker who had served in SOE in Greece, three retired senior commanders in the Middle East, all with political experience, two journalists, both of whom had worked for PWE during the war, two ex-diplomats, both of senior ambassadorial rank and experience of working with and as consumers of the products of the intelligence services; in fact the majority of the group had known each other and of each other for two decades of war and peace. The then Director of the RIIA, Monty Woodhouse, had been a central figure during the war in SOE operations in Greece, had then joined MI6 and played a central part in the joint Anglo-American organised putsch against M. Mossadegh, the Iranian premier who had organised the expropriation of the Anglo-Iranian Oil Company's holdings in Iran and the driving into exile of the shah. It is the interconnections of British political society that the younger school of historians – who think in broad categories such as British Intelligence, with which as British society expanded in the last three decades of the last century, they may have had little or no contact – find so difficult to digest or fit into the

private morality plays that they introduce into their own historical research.

3  M. R. Doherty, *Nazi Wireless Propaganda. Lord Haw-Haw and British Public Opinion in the Second World War* (Edinburgh, 2003). It should be noted, in view of the strictures listed above on the scope of university media and communications studies, that this work is published under the sponsorship of the University of Leeds Department of Communications Studies.

4  See the three volumes of his memoirs collected together under the title *I Claud. The Autobiography of Claud Cockburn* (Harmondsworth, 1967) and John Henry Cockburn, *The Years of 'The Week'* (Harmondsworth, 1971). For an examination of the reportage of *The Week* in the first six months of 1939 against the evidence provided by the historical documentation available in the 1950s and 1960s see D. C. Watt, 'That was "The Week" that was', *Encounter*, May 1972.

5  London, 1987.

6  London, 1989.

7  Franklin Reed Gannon, *The British Press and Germany, 1936–1939* (Oxford, 1971); Benno Morris, *The Roots of Appeasement. The British Weekly Press and Nazi Germany during the 1930s* (London, 1991).

8  Information on the security service's interest in the *Whitehall Letter* from the late Rt Hon. Kenneth Younger, PC, to the author, in the 1960s when he was Director of Chatham House. Younger worked for MI5 from 1938–1943. Information on the relations between the editors of the *Whitehall Letter* and Vansittart and Leeper from correspondence with Gordon Lennox and an interview with Toby O'Brien, deputy editor of the *Whitehall Letter*.

9  The history of this war scare can be traced in D. Cameron Watt, *How War Came. The Immediate Origins of the Second World War* (London and New York, 1989). It was based on the conjunction of a press war between the German and Belgian press arising out of incidents at an international football match in Brussels, the hopes of the French general staff that their Belgian opposite numbers might be frightened by the British into agreeing to joint staff talks, the independent action of an anonymous German social democratic organisation and a series of direct plants on the British by members of the conservative-bureaucratic opposition to Hitler in Germany, using Sir Robert Vansittart's own private intelligence service to encourage the British to take a stronger line vis-à-vis Hitler.

10  Doherty, op. cit. p. 111.

11  On which see Gordon Brook-Shepherd, *The Iron Maze. The Western Secret Service and the Bolsheviks* (London, 1998).

12  One is reminded that the Soviet success in *recruiting* potential agents in Cambridge in the 1930s, while resulting in the recruitment of Donald Maclean and John Cairncross, both of whom held positions at various times close to the higher military command of the war in Britain, did not result in the recruitment of a single military man with knowledge of how modern war was made or the limitations of logistics on military action. Both men, in truth, belonged to the generation for whom senior military men were synonymous with stupidity, inhumanity and a general misunderstanding of the modern world to whose overthrow both men were psychologically committed.

13  Gabriel Gorodetzki, *Grand Delusion. Stalin and the German Invasion of Russia* (Yale, 1989), pp. 103–04. For the Italian version see Mario Toscano, *L'Italia e 10 Patto Tedesco-Sovietico*, reprinted in Toscano, *Designs in Diplomacy*.

14  There is a very considerable literature on this, beginning with John Erickson's *The Soviet High Command* (London, 1962), a book which so won the approval of the Soviet military for its objectivity when it appeared that they pirated it. A recent summary of the now voluminous works on the subject, including the memoirs of Soviet generals and studies by Russian military historians is William J. Spahr, *Stalin's Lieutenants: A Study of Command under Stress* (Novato, California, 1997).

15  D. C. Watt, 'Who Plotted against Whom? Stalin's Purge of the Soviet High Command Revisited', *Journal of Soviet Military Studies*, vol. 3/1, March 1990.

16 David Garnett, *The Secret History of the Political Warfare Executive* (London, 2001).

17 Garnett, p. 214.

## Chapter 20   THE EDINBURGH CONVERSATIONS

1 Anatoli Dobrynin, *In Confidence* (New York, Random House, 1995), pp. 522–3.

2 The author is deeply indebted to Mr Michael Wescott, who worked in the office of the Principal of the University of Edinburgh for an extended period in the 1980s and who functioned as the main organising force for the UK side in the Edinburgh Conversations. A great deal of what is related here is based on a monograph (*Random Ramblings*) he wrote that details his experiences.

3 Lieutenant Colonel Carl Reddel, who was serving as a US Air Force Research Assistant at the time; he later became head of the History Department at the USAF Academy in Colorado.

4 NATO doctrine at the time was based on *flexible response*, which did indeed allow the possibility, not the likelihood, of using nuclear weapons first to ward off an onslaught of a superior conventional force invasion from the East.

5 Much later, in December 1995, it was disclosed by Andrei Parastaev, when he came to Edinburgh to give a talk for the Edinburgh Lothian Lectures series, that the Politburo took great interest in the Edinburgh Conversations and paid considerable attention to their proceedings.

6 Yanayev later became Vice President of the Soviet Union under Mikhail Gorbachev and supposedly led the abortive coup attempt.

7 The comuniqué read:

> From the 28th to the 30th September 1987, a further meeting was held in Moscow between the Soviet, British and American participants who exchanged opinions on the European situation and on the world at large. Their attention focused on the most important problems – reduction of nuclear weapons, the burden of conventional armaments and the

enhancement of European and global security as well as development of mutual understanding and international co-operation.

> 1 The danger of nuclear war is nothing less than a threat to the existence of civilisation. It is therefore essential that both East and West understand the need for co-operation and a common search to resolve key questions which face humanity. Under these conditions, new thinking is required which should facilitate a change in attitudes on both sides, and gives a special opportunity to reconfirm the shared interests of East and West in human survival. An escape from stereotypes in the images of states, which dominate East–West attitudes, has always been a leading purpose of the Edinburgh Conversations.

> 2 Diversity of political systems and the need for a spirit of interdependence in facing global problems underline the importance of efforts to achieve security – which is both universal and comprehensive, since it is clear that nothing can be solved merely by building up military potential. In these circumstances, participants noted that due to the nature of modern weapons no one nation can consider its security in isolation from general security. In other words, it is impossible at present to separate national from global security in all its dimensions – political, military, economic, human and ecological.

> 3 Participants felt that the meetings of the leaders of the USSR and the USA in Reykjavik appeared to have opened up a real possibility for implementing practical steps towards nuclear disarmament and arms control. The achievement in principle of a treaty on the elimination of medium and short range missiles has created the possibility for more effective progress towards strengthening peace, security and the creation of a

world without war or the threat of war. The hope was expressed that further steps would be taken, namely, a 50% reduction in strategic offensive weapons to be agreed in the course of further negotiations. In this context, the participants emphasised the importance of the Anti-Ballistic Missile Treaty. Great hopes have also been placed on the forthcoming Soviet/American full-scale phased negotiations aimed ultimately at the total cessation of nuclear tests.

4 Participants also discussed prospects for the conclusion of an international convention on the banning and destruction of existing chemical weapon stockpiles and their production facilities. They emphasised the importance they attached to making further progress in these negotiations.

5 Participants agreed that a reduction in the level of nuclear confrontation in Europe must be matched by measures capable of lowering and finally excluding, the possibility of not only nuclear but also conventional war on the continent. In this connection they favoured working out at an early date, a mandate to start negotiations on armed forces and armaments on an all-European scale. Appropriate cuts would level out existing asymmetries on both sides. In the process of reduction, priority should be given to cuts in those types of weapons which facilitate surprise attack. All this must proceed under strict verification, in conformity with the disarmament measures.

6 It was noted that a new approach to international security could be based only on a foundation of confidence created through experience of co-operation and by developing direct dialogue between East and West. The aim would be to ensure that strategic doctrines and military concepts of the alliances should be based on defensive principles.

7 Participants noted the importance of further development and enhancement of the process of the Conference on Security and Co-operation in Europe and emphasised the clear relationship between the CSCE and disarmament. A successful conclusion of the Vienna meeting of the CSCE participants and significant and balanced agreement adopted by them could form an important practical step in the development of co-operation in the political, economic and humanitarian spheres in Europe.

8 In the ecological perspective, the military and political confrontation between East and West appears as a dangerous distraction from the fundamental long-term issues of the environment and economic development of mankind as a whole on a small and vulnerable planet. The participants welcomed new multi-disciplinary research programmes relevant to environmental protection and wiser use of the earth's resources. They reasserted the shared interest of East and West in these civilian issues, solutions for which require a combination of traditional and humanitarian values and an intellectual partnership at the very frontiers of knowledge, to tackle technical and social problems of unprecedented complexity and magnitude.

9 Participants emphasised the importance of a constructive dialogue within the international community for creating the foundation of a world secure for all. They expressed their determination to continue the Edinburgh Conversations which have contributed to the course of greater mutual understanding and confidence in the search for more effective ways of achieving reductions in nuclear and conventional armaments and greater security at a lower level of forces.

8 The full, much shorter than usual, communiqué read:

    1 From the 5th to the 8th of December 1988, a further round of the Edinburgh Conversations was held in Edinburgh under the auspices of the University of Edinburgh to continue the theme of *Common Security: Perspectives and Possibilities for the Future.*

    2 The Soviet concept of *Perestroika* (reconstruction) and Western perceptions of it were extensively discussed with special attention to the appraisal of aims, objectives, dilemmas and possible implications for international relations.

    3 The participants considered various ways of promoting conventional stability in Europe, including confidence-building measures, the reduction of conventional forces and the means to prevent surprise attack.

    4 The relationship between NATO and the Warsaw Pact was discussed as well as the concepts of 'defensive' and 'reasonable' sufficiency.

    5 Extensive discussions took place with regard to the economic, political and military implications of 1992 for the future of Europe and common European interests.

    6 The participants heartily welcomed Mr Gorbachev's statement at the United Nations as a significant and important step in promoting a more constructive approach both to arms control and international relations.

    7 The Conversations have, once again, underscored the importance of continuing frank and sustained discussion of issues as a means of promoting mutual understanding.

# NOTES ON CONTRIBUTORS

## Bartov, Omer

Omer Bartov is the John P. Birkelund Distinguished Professor of European History at Brown University. His books include *The Eastern Front 1941–45* (1985, 2nd edn 2001), *Hitler's Army* (1991), *Murder in Our Midst: The Holocaust, Industrial Killing, and Representation* (1996), *Mirrors of Destruction: War, Genocide, and Modern Identity* (2000), and *Germany's War and the Holocaust* (2003). He has edited the volumes *The Holocaust* (2000), *In God's Name: Genocide and Religion in the Twentieth Century* (2001, with Phyllis Mack), and *The Crimes of War: Guilt and Denial in the Twentieth Century* (2002, with Atina Grossmann and Mary Nolan). His new book, *The 'Jew' in Cinema: From the Golem to Don't Touch My Holocaust* has just been published.

## Beaumont, Roger

Roger Beaumont recently retired after teaching history at Texas A&M University since 1974. Co-founder and North American editor of *Defense Analysis*, 1983–9, he is author of a dozen books and monographs, including *Sword of the Raj: The British Army in India 1757–1947* (1975), and, most recently, *Right Backed by Might: A History of The International Air Force Concept* (2001), and over eighty book chapters and articles. Beaumont served in the US Army in the late 1950s and early 60s as a military police officer, has lectured at higher military schools in Europe and the United States, and was Secretary of the Navy Fellow at the US Naval Academy (1989–90).

## Beevor, Antony

Antony Beevor, a former professional soldier, is the author of ten books, including *The Spanish Civil War*, *Inside the British Army*, *Crete – The Battle and the Resistance*, which won a Runciman Award, *Paris After the Liberation: 1944–1949*, *Stalingrad*, which won the Samuel Johnson Prize, the Wolfson Prize for History and the Hawthornden Prize, and *Berlin – The Downfall, 1945*. He is currently working on an edition of the wartime notebooks and correspondence of Vassili Grossman. He is also the Chairman of the Society of Authors.

## Bellamy, Christopher

Christopher Bellamy is Professor of Military Science and Doctrine and Director of the Security Studies Institute, Cranfield University, based at the Defence Academy of the UK. Before joining Cranfield in 1997 he was for seven years Defence Correspondent of the *Independent*. A military historian and Russian linguist by training, he completed his PhD at Edinburgh in 1987–91 under John Erickson's supervision. He is author of five major books including *Red God of War: Soviet Artillery and Rocket Forces* (Brassey's, 1987) and *Knights in White Armour: the New Art of War and Peace* (Hutchinson, 1996, and Pimlico, 1997). He was also consultant editor (Eastern Front) for *The Times Atlas of the Second World War* (1989), and, most recently, associate editor of, and a principal contributor to, *The Oxford Companion to Military*

*History* (2001). He is currently completing *Absolute War: Soviet Russia versus Germany and Japan, 1941–45, a New History*, forthcoming.

## Buckley, Mary

Mary Buckley taught for seventeen years at the University of Edinburgh and briefly in London. In the Easter term of 2004 she was Visiting Fellow at the Centre for Research in the Arts, Social Sciences and Humanities (CRASSH), University of Cambridge, and a Visiting Fellow at Hughes Hall, working on debates in the Russian Federation on trafficking in persons. Her recent work on the Soviet 1930s and on contemporary Russian domestic and foreign policy has been published in *The Journal of Communist Studies and Transition Politics, Social History* and *European Security*. She is co-editor of *Global Responses to Terrorism* (Routledge, 2003).

## Cant, James Farquhar

University of Glasgow: 1987–91, MA (Hons.) in Scottish and Modern History. University of Glasgow: 1994–8 PhD in Politics. Has also worked as a history teacher in a number of schools in Scotland and Australia. Now employed by the Ministry of Defence, though presently on secondment to the Scottish Executive.

## Chapman, John

John W. M. Chapman studied Russian history with John Erickson at the University of St Andrews and subsequently shared a mutual interest in military and communications intelligence with a focus on Japan and its relations with European states as a research student at Oxford and Chicago, subsequently lecturing at Sussex and as Professor of International Relations at Ritsumeikan University in Kyoto. Founding editor of the OUP journal *Japan Forum* until 1996 and currently Hon. SRF at the Scottish Centre for War Studies in the University of Glasgow, in conjunction with reconstructing a hill farm in Galloway, owned from 1767 to 1809 by the family of a Scots-born director of Russian Army medical services.

## Cummings, Sally

Sally N. Cummings is Lecturer in International Relations at the University of St Andrews, UK. She is the author of *The Dynamics of Centre-Periphery Relations in Kazakhstan* (Brookings and Institution and Royal Institute of International Affairs, 2000), editor of *Oil, Transition and Security in Central Asia* (Routledge, 2003), *Power and Change in Central Asia* (Routledge, 2002) and co-editor of *Kosovo: Perceptions of War and Its Aftermath* (Continuum, 2002).

## Dukes, Paul

Emeritus Professor at the University of Aberdeen, with which he has been associated since 1964. He has published widely on Russian, European and comparative history. He is author of *The Superpowers: A Short History* (Routledge, 2000), *Paths to a New Europe: From Premodern to Postmodern Times* (Palgrave, 2004), *The USA in the Making of the USSR: The Washington Conference, 1921–1922 and 'Uninvited Russia'* (RoutledgeCurzon, 2004).

## Fedosov, Dmitry

Dr Dmitry G. Fedosov. Senior Research Fellow, Institute of General History, Russian Academy of Sciences, Honorary Research Fellow, University of Aberdeen. Field of study: early modern history of Scotland and Russo-Scottish links from the Middle Ages to the early twentieth century.

## Förster, Jürgen

Jürgen Förster is an independent scholar who lives in Freiburg i. Br. and was affiliated with the Militärgeschichtliches Forschungsamt, now in Potsdam, for over thirty years. He has taught at various national and international universities – recently at the University of Glasgow, and in 2004, at the University of Melbourne. He has written numerous articles and published four books as author/co-author dealing both with the inter-war period and with the national socialist era.

## Glantz, David

Colonel Glantz founded and currently edits the *Journal of Slavic Military Studies* and is a member of the Academy of Natural Sciences of the Russian Federation. In 2000 he received the Society for Military History's Samuel Eliot Morison Prize for his work in the field of Soviet military history. Among the numerous books he has authored on Soviet and Russian military affairs are *August Storm: The Soviet 1945 Strategic Offensive in Manchuria*, 2 vols. (1983), *A History of Soviet Airborne Forces* (1984 and 1994), *Soviet Military Deception in the Second World War* (1989), *Soviet Military Intelligence in War* (1990), *The Role of Intelligence in Soviet Military Strategy in the Second World War* (1990), *Soviet Military Operational Art: In Pursuit of Deep Battle* (1990), *From the Don to the Dnepr: A Study of Soviet Offensive Operations, December 1942–August 1943* (1990), *The Soviet Conduct of Tactical Maneuver* (1991), *The Military Strategy of the Soviet Union* (1992), *When Titans Clashed: How the Red Army Stopped Hitler* (1996), *Stumbling Colossus: The Red Army on the Eve of World War* (1998), *Kharkov 1942: The Anatomy of a Military Disaster* (1998), *Operation Mars: Marshal Zhukov's Greatest Defeat* (1999), *Kursk 1943: The End of the Blitzkrieg* (1999), *Leningrad: 900 Days of Fire* (2001), *Barbarossa: Hitler's Invasion of Russia* (2001), *The Battle for Leningrad, 1941–1944* (2002), *The Soviet Strategic Offensive in Manchuria, 1945* (2003), and *Soviet Operational and Tactical Combat in Manchuria, 1945* (January 2003). He has edited *The Initial Period of War on the Eastern Front: 22 June to August 1941* (1993), the two-volume study, *The Evolution of Soviet Operational Art 1927–1991: The Documentary Basis* (1995), and *Hitler and His Generals: Military Conferences 1942–1945* (2002).

## Hansen, Lynn

Lynn M. Hansen was a serving officer in the US Air Force when he spent a year with Professor Erickson in Defence Studies at the University of Edinburgh during the late 1970s. After retiring from the military Hansen spent a short stint at Texas A&M University before being named as Deputy Head of the US Delegation to the Stockholm Conference on Confidence and Security-building Measures with the personal rank of ambassador. Under President Reagan he served as Assistant Director of the US Arms Control and Disarmament Agency in Washington. Under President Bush senior he was ambassador and head of the US delegation to the Negotiations on Conventional Armed Forces in Europe. Prior to this last assignment Hansen was the John M. Olin Distinguished Professor of National Defense and Security Studies at the USAF Academy. He is now retired and on assignment for his church in Hamburg, Germany. He and his wife Faith have been married forty-four years and have seven children and twenty-two grandchildren.

## Kudryashov, Sergei

Dr Sergei Kudryashov is an editor-in-chief of the Russian journal *Istochnik* and lives in Moscow. He has lectured in various universities of the UK: Nottingham, Leeds, Aberdeen and Cambridge. As a Leverhume Trust Fellow he was attached to the School of History at the University of East Anglia in 1996–7. He has published substantially on various aspects of the Second World War with major emphasis on German occupation of the Soviet Union, collaboration and debates in modern historiography.

## Mertsalov, Andrei

Andrei Nikolaevich Mertsalov, professor, doctor of history (PhD History), Guards Colonel (retired), veteran of Moscow, Stalingrad, Kursk battles, liberation of Belorussia and Poland and capture of Berlin. Professor at Voronezh and Kaluga State Universities. Since 1980 leading researcher at the Institute of Russian History of the Russian Academy of Sciences. His latest most important books are *Stalinism and the War*, and *Zhomini*.

## Pennington, Reina

Reina Pennington, PhD, is Director of the Studies in War and Peace programme at Norwich University, where she teaches military, Russian, and European history. Pennington is a former air force intelligence officer; she served as a Soviet analyst with the Aggressor Squadrons. Her books include *Wings, Women and War: Soviet Airwomen in World War II Combat* (2001) and *Amazons to Fighter Pilots: A Biographical Dictionary of Military Women* (2003). She was recently appointed to the Department of the Army Historical Advisory Committee (DAHAC).

## Service, Robert

Robert Service is Professor of Russian History at Oxford University and a Fellow of St Antony's College. He has published several books, including *Lenin: A Biography* (2000) and *A History of Modern Russia. From Nicholas II to Vladimir Putin* (2003) and *Stalin: A Biography* (2004). He is a Fellow of the British Academy.

## Stone, Norman

Professor of International Relations, Bilkent University, since 1997, Director of the Russian Centre, earlier Professor Modern History, University of Oxford (1984–1997) and Lecturer in Russian and German History, University of Cambridge (Fellow of Trinity College) 1965–84. Born Glasgow 1941. Principal publications: *The Eastern Front 1914–1917*, *Hitler*, *Europe Transformed 1878–1919*, *The Other Russia*. Frequent contributions since 1984 to the British and other media, including *The Times*, *Wall Street Journal* and *Frankfurter Allegemeine* on matters relating to Russia, Germany and Turkey; board member of the Margaret Thatcher Foundation.

## Strachan, Hew

Hew Strachan has been Professor of the History of War and Fellow of All Souls College, Oxford, since 2002. Before that he was Professor of Modern History and Director of the Scottish Centre for War Studies, University of Glasgow. His books include *European Armies and the Conduct of War*, *The Politics of the British Army*, and the first volume of his history of the First World War, *To Arms*.

## Watt, Donald Cameron

B. 17 May 1928. Educ. Rugby School (scholar), 1940–46, Oriel College, Oxford (Scholar), 1948–51. Military service 1946–8, Sgt in FSS, Intelligence Corps, British Troops Austria; historian at Foreign Office Research Dept, 1951–4; Asst. Lecturer, (1954–6), Lecturer (1957–63), Snr Lecturer, (1963–5) in International History, London School of Economics and Political Science; Reader (1966–71), Titular Professor (1972–81), Stevenson Professor of International History, in University of London, (1982–93) at LSE. Emeritus Professor 1994; Rockefeller Fellow in the Social Sciences, Washington Center for Foreign Policy Studies, 1960–61; editor *Survey of International Affairs*, Royal Institute of International Affairs, 1962–71; Official Historian att. Cabinet Office Historical Section 1976–present. Books: *Britain and the Suez Canal* (1956), *Britain Looks to Germany* (1965), *Personalities and Policies* (1965), *A History of the World in the Twentieth Century, Pt I, 1900–1918* (1967); editor, Hitler's *Mein Kampf* (1969, 1990), *Too Serious a Business* (1974), *Succeeding John Bull: America in Britain's Place, 1900–1975* (1984), *How War Came: the Immediate Origins of the Second World War* (1989); editor (with James Mayall), *Current British Foreign Policy, Documents, Statements, Speeches*, vols. 1970–72; editor (with K. Bourne, FBA), *British Documents on Foreign Affairs, Selected from the Foreign Office Confidential Print, 1860–1939*; Hon. Fellow Oriel College, Oxford; Corresponding Fellow, Polish Academy of Arts and Sciences, Cracow.

# INDEX